AMIENS
TO THE
ARMISTICE

Also from Brassey's

Brassey's Companion to the British Army
Antony Makepeace-Warne

Brassey's History of Uniforms Series
World War One: British Army
Dr Stephen Bull
World War One: German Army
Dr Stephen Bull

AMIENS
TO THE
ARMISTICE

The B E F in the Hundred Days' Campaign,
8 August-11 November 1918

J P Harris
with Niall Barr

BRASSEY'S
LONDON • WASHINGTON

First English Edition 1998

UK editorial offices: Brassey's, 583 Fulham Road. London SW6 5BY
UK orders: Bailey Distribution Ltd, Unit 1, Learoyd Road,
New Romney, Kent TN28 8XU

North American orders: Brassey's Inc., PO Box 960,
Herndon, VA 20172

J P Harris has asserted his moral right to be identified as
the author of this work.

Library of Congress Cataloging in Publication Data
available

British Library Cataloguing in Publication Data
A catalogue record for this book is available from the British Library

ISBN 1 85753 149 3

Typeset by M Rules
Printed in Great Britain by
Creative Print & Design (Wales), Ebbw Vale

CONTENTS

LIST OF ILLUSTRATIONS

MAPS

TABLES

ACKNOWLEDGEMENTS

Thanks are due to the staff of the Public Record Office, the Imperial War Museum, the Liddell Hart Centre for Military Archives at King's College London, the National Army Museum, the Royal Artillery Institution and the library of the Tank Museum, Bovington. A particularly heavy debt is owing to Diane Hillier, Sarah Oliver and their colleagues at the library of the RMA Sandhurst. The present Earl Haig has given kind permission for quotations to be made from his father's diary. I am grateful to my old friend Mr David Fletcher of the Tank Museum for finding and supplying the cover photograph.

The following scholars and friends read parts (in some cases a high proportion) of the book in draft and made valuable comments: Dr Stephen Badsey, Dr John Bourne, Mr Lloyd Clark, Mr John Lee, Mr Chris McCarthy, Mr Sanders Marble, Dr Gary Sheffield, Mr Peter Simkins and Professor Hew Strachan. Thanks are owing to all these kind people for their expertise and encouragement. Numerous conversations with my old friend and former colleague Dr Paddy Griffith, and a battlefield tour in his always entertaining company, helped shape my understanding of the subject. My colleague Mr Keith Chaffer has drawn all the maps. Thanks have been given to Diane Hillier as librarian at the RMA but they are also due for her encouragement and forbearance as a friend. For all the faults in the book the responsibility is, of course, the author's alone.

INTRODUCTION

The campaign of the 'Hundred Days', 8 August to 11 November 1918,[1] was, in terms of sheer scale, the greatest in British military history. It was also, arguably, the campaign in which ground forces under British command exercised the most influence on the history of the world in the twentieth century. Yet, while the Battle of the Somme of 1916, the Third Battle of Ypres in 1917 and the March retreat of 1918 have all made a major impact on British national consciousness, the Hundred Days' campaign is relatively little known. Who has heard of the Battle of the Scarpe, the Battle of the Selle or the Battle of the Sambre? The problem appears to be not so much that these battles were forgotten, but that they never sank into national consciousness in the first place. On 17 October 1918 Sir Douglas Haig complained to Geoffrey Dawson, the editor of *The Times*, that the victories his Armies were winning were being given relatively little coverage in the national press.[2] The last year of the war was crowded with events and the public was war-weary and saddened by heavy losses. Newspapermen probably believed that the public would rather read about almost anything than major battles fought by British troops. Many books appearing in the inter-war period made some reference to the Hundred Days' fighting but, as far as the present writer knows, no complete volume was devoted to the British Expeditionary Force (BEF) as a whole in this campaign. By the time the two volumes of the British official history covering this period appeared, another great war had gripped the public's attention. Though they are indispensable works of reference these volumes are, in any case, all but unreadable. Monographs have been published on particular formations in the

Hundred Days and there are several books attempting to cover all the Western Front fighting of 1918. But the present work is (again, as far as the author knows) the first attempt at a one-volume account of the BEF as a whole in this particular campaign.

The inspiration to start work on the present book came from a variety of sources. The author has been aware of the campaign for a long time, having been taught during the 1960s by a superannuated, and distinctly choleric, schoolmaster who had taken part in it. In the early 1970s the vivid account of the 1918 fighting by Essame, another veteran, made a profound impression on him.[3] The renaissance of First World War studies in Britain, Canada and Australia in the 1980s and 1990s has been an important influence and the celebrated study of Rawlinson's command by Robin Prior and Trevor Wilson particularly so.[4] In addition to offering some important insights into the conduct of war on the Western Front 1914–18, Prior and Wilson have helped re-establish the history of military operations as a fit subject for serious scholarship, a position it should never have lost. Historical interpretation does not stand still and some of Prior's and Wilson's interpretations of the Hundred Days are challenged in this book. These challenges, however, are made respectfully.

Though the author hopes that he has assessed reasonably objectively the military performance of the BEF as compared with the German Army, no pretence of neutrality can be made as between the relative liberalism and democracy of Britain, France and America on the one hand, and German authoritarianism and militarism on the other. One of the ingredients of the motivation of British and Dominion troops appears to have been a continuing belief in the cause for which they were fighting – the prevention of German militarism dominating Europe by force.[5] The BEF in the Hundred Days was an army of liberation, a fact of which its troops became acutely aware from early October as they moved into areas which still had substantial civilian populations. The locals received them with an enthusiasm which was sometimes ecstatic. Though, for want of space, such scenes of rapture in liberated towns and villages will seldom be referred to in this work, they are vividly and movingly described in contemporary accounts[6] and undoubtedly contributed to the liberators' sense of purpose.

This is a fairly short book on a very big campaign and it has obvious limitations. It focuses on the BEF, with only sidelong glances at allied armies. It views the Germans mainly through British eyes, though as British intelligence was evidently very good most of time, that is, perhaps, not too serious a problem. The focus is on the 'operational level' of war, that is to say the conduct of military operations at the Army Group, Army and Corps levels of command. Only rarely has it been possible to examine the handling of individual divisions and smaller formations and units. The ordinary soldier's physical and psychological experience of combat – what an earlier Sandhurst historian termed 'the face of battle' – is but little examined here, though it is an important subject. Critical determinants of combat effectiveness such as administration, officer–man relations and the enforcement of discipline are also omitted, though in the knowledge that other scholars are working in these areas.[7]

Historians are inevitably concerned with time and timings and a few technical points in this regard must briefly be addressed. Readers more conversant with the Second World War and later conflicts will be familiar with the use of 'D-Day' to designate the first day of a major operation and 'H-Hour' for the start time. In the British Army in the First World War the equivalents were 'Z day' or just 'Z' and 'Zero hour' or simply 'Zero'. This book sticks with the contemporary usage. The BEF officially changed over from the 12-hour to the 24-hour clock on 1 October 1918.[8] Encountering timings in both 'clocks' in the primary sources, the author decided at an early stage to use 24-hour clock timings throughout. As the 24-hour clock is now familiar from railway and airline timetables etc., it is not anticipated that this will create problems for most readers.

J.P. Harris
Sandhurst, April 1998

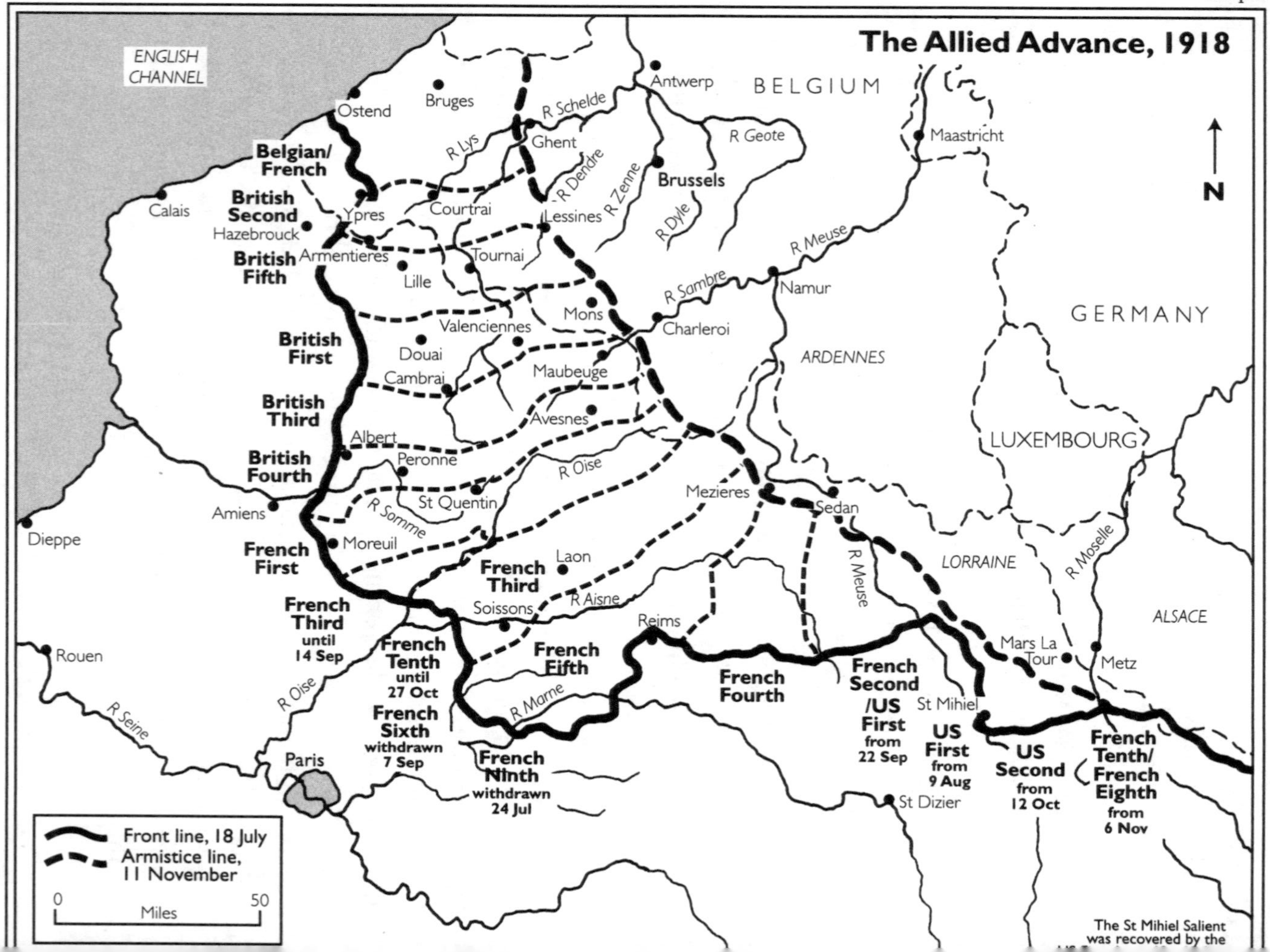

Map 1

The Allied Advance, 1918

N ←

ENGLISH
CHANNEL

Calais
Ostend
Bruges
Antwerp
Maastricht
BELGIUM
R Geote
R Zenne
Brussels
R Dyle
GERMANY
R Dendre
R Schelde
Ghent
R Lys
Courtrai
Lessines
Tournai
Namur
R Sambre
R Meuse
Hazebrouck
Ypres
Armentieres
Lille
Mons
Charleroi
LUXEMBOURG
Belgian/
French
British
Second
British
Fifth
British
First
Douai
Valenciennes
Maubeuge
Avesnes
ARDENNES
R Moselle
British
Third
Cambrai
Peronne
R Oise
Mezieres
Sedan
R Meuse
Maastricht
British
Fourth
Albert
St Quentin
R Somme
Laon
Soissons
R Aisne
LORRAINE
Amiens
French
First
Moreuil
R Somme
French
Third
French
Fifth
Reims
R Marne
Mars La
Tour
Metz
ALSACE
French
Third
until
14 Sep
French
Tenth
until
27 Oct
French
Sixth
withdrawn
7 Sep
Soissons
French
Ninth
withdrawn
24 Jul
French
Fourth
French
Second
/US
First
from
22 Sep
St Mihiel
US
First
from
9 Aug
US
Second
from
12 Oct
French
Tenth/
French
Eighth
from
6 Nov
Dieppe
Rouen
R Seine
Paris
R Oise
St Dizier

The St Mihiel Salient
was recovered by the

| | Front line, 18 July |
| | Armistice line, 11 November |

0   Miles   50

1

THE STRATEGIC BACKGROUND

FOUR BLOODY YEARS

At the start of what became known as the campaign of the Hundred Days, on 8 August 1918, Great Britain had been at war for just over four years. So far, it had been the bloodiest, costliest and most depressing war in British history. Except in a handful of peripheral campaigns there had been few clear-cut victories. Even on the periphery, defeat, or at least frustration, had been the norm for much of the conflict. On the vital Western Front, most offensives by the Allies (the French and the British) had gained little ground. Some had been terribly costly. The Germans, on the other hand, had conquered a great deal of territory – nearly all of Belgium and a large part of north-east France. They seemed to have come dangerously close to conclusive victory on two occasions: August–September 1914 and March–June 1918. Even without decisive victory, the ground they had conquered gave them potentially useful bargaining counters for a possible future peace conference. Admittedly, by midsummer 1918, the situation, from the point of view of Great Britain and her Allies, offered some hope. But even at the beginning of August few dared to suppose that within 15 weeks the fighting would be over and the Allies victorious.

1914–15

At the beginning of August 1914 Germany and Austria-Hungary, on the one hand (joined by Turkey in November), found themselves ranged against Serbia, Russia and France on the other. After a complex crisis in July 1914, the Austrian government, with German support, used the assassination of the heir to the Austrian throne by a Bosnian Serb nationalist in the Austrian-ruled province of Bosnia-Herzegovina, on 28 June 1914, as justification for an attack on Serbia. It was an attack which the Austrian government had long contemplated and which the Austrian General Staff had long planned.[1] During the July Crisis the Germans tended to encourage rather than to moderate the belligerence of their Austrian allies.[2] Precisely why they did this is still debated amongst historians. But there can be no doubt that some influential member of the policy-making elite had concluded that if Germany were to escape encirclement by powers hostile to her ambitions, a great European war was inevitable in the long run. Austria, Germany's sole reliable ally, was, however, showing tendencies to disintegration. France's ally, Russia, on the other hand, seemed to be gaining strength by industrialisation and economic growth. These worrying trends seem to have brought some Germans to a second dangerous conclusion: Germany's chances of winning the inevitable war would be optimised if it came sooner rather than later.[3]

The German General Staff regarded a long war on two fronts as a nightmare. France and Russia had the greater combined population and, therefore, a greater reservoir of military manpower than Germany and Austria, and would find it easier to feed their peoples in a protracted struggle. Apparently for these reasons, the German General Staff believed it vital for Germany to win quickly. It planned to defeat France before the Russian Army completed its mobilisation.[4] But the German attempt to crush the French Army in six weeks, by a massive turning movement through neutral Belgium not only failed, it brought Great Britain into the war.[5]

The British government was, for very good reasons, keen to prevent German domination of Continental Europe. The British General Staff had made provisional arrangements in peacetime for the despatch of an Expeditionary Force to fight against the German Army in defence of France.[6] The German violation of Belgian neutrality on 3 August 1914 made the declaration of war by the British government on 4 August much more popular on the home front than it might otherwise have been. The little British Expeditionary Force (BEF), consisting mainly of regular and former regular soldiers, played a small but arguably vital role in the defeat of the initial German campaigns in the west. Most of the honours for the decisive Battle of the Marne, in September, must be awarded to the French. But the British played a more prominent role at the First Battle of Ypres in October–November – another Allied defensive victory which prevented the Germans gaining a decisive advantage in 1914.[7]

Particularly dangerous for the Germans in the long term was British sea-power. The Royal Navy was the most powerful in the world. The Germans, despite the most strenuous efforts in the earlier years of the century, had failed to match it. By remote blockade the British largely cut Germany off from extra-European sources of food and raw materials.[8] Of almost equal importance in the ultimate defeat of Germany was British industry, which, though falling behind that of Germany in certain areas by 1914, still had formidable productive capacity and impressive skill. Great Britain's financial strength (in the early part of the war at any rate) coupled with a vast mercantile marine, which was in turn backed by the Royal Navy, allowed its industry almost unrestricted access to overseas sources of supply for raw materials. When British productive potential was added to that of France, and to the infant but fast-growing capacity of Russia, the Allies could, eventually, out-produce the Germans and the Austrians (the Central Powers) in most types of munition. When the war began, the bulk of British and Dominion manpower was totally untrained for war, but the not inconsiderable combined populations of the British Empire also helped to stack the odds against Germany in a long war.[9]

It may appear surprising, given the heavy demographic, naval and industrial odds against the Germans, that they had not only remained undefeated until the summer of 1918, but looked as though they might win. Germany derived important advantages from her central strategic position. But much of the explanation must lie with the excellence of the

German Army and the relative inferiority of most of the opposing armies for a large part of the war. The roots of German military excellence lay deep in German society. Germany combined the greatest wealth, the finest education and the most advanced technology in Continental Europe, with an authoritarian political system and a tradition of militarism.[10] The army was large and well-equipped even in peacetime. The officer corps had unique social privilege and prestige and, through the famous General Staff, its leaders had a very substantial influence on state policy. The British pre-war officer corps was tiny by Continental standards and only a weak magnet for the more enterprising and ambitious in British society. In the 'smarter' regiments junior officers' pay often failed to cover their expenses and even senior officers had little influence on the running of the British state in peacetime. Though France and Russia had large armies, the career of an army officer in those countries was poorly remunerated and lacking in social prestige. In Germany, on the other hand, middle-class officers could gain prestige, power and influence (as well as comparatively generous salaries) by entering into partnership with those from the generally earnest and hard-working Prussian aristocracy, the traditional mainstay of the Hohenzollern dynasty.[11]

Before the war, the Germans had been worried both by the impressive size of the Russian Army and by its seemingly rapid rate of modernisation. But at the outbreak of war the Russians were still a long way behind the Germans in the professionalism of the officer corps, the education and initiative of the other ranks and the technical training of the army generally. The Russian industrial base was under-developed and could not keep the army adequately supplied. Despite its millions of hardy, long-suffering peasant soldiers and a few good generals, the Russian Army's performance against the Germans was, on the whole, woefully inadequate. A Russian drive into East Prussia failed miserably in August 1914, one Russian Army being practically destroyed in the Battle of Tannenberg. The Russians then spent much of the war on the receiving end of German offensives. Even so, they made an enormous contribution to the Allied war effort. On 1 May

1917 there were 99 German divisions on the Eastern Front compared with 141 in the West. The Russians at that period were tying down a total of 153 divisions belonging to Germany, Austria and Turkey.[12]

The Russians could, moreover, inflict severe defeats on the Austrians from time to time. The Austrian Army had many of the same weaknesses as the Russian and an even more serious problem of combat motivation. Many of the nationalities of this multinational army were very little motivated to fight for the Habsburg ruling dynasty.[13] The Austrians needed German stiffening and Bulgarian assistance even to crush the small Balkan power of Serbia. But such was the power and skill of the German Army that it could, at the same time, hold off French and British offensives on the Western Front and take the offensive, usually in conjunction with the Austrians, on other fronts. The Germans were on the offensive against the Russians for most of 1915, driving them out of Poland and inflicting casualties from which they never fully recovered. In the same year, the Germans played an important role in overrunning Serbia.[14]

1916

The German Army, having defeated French offensives relatively easily in 1915, and having inflicted terrible losses on the French Army in the process, mounted their own offensive towards the emotionally significant French fortress city of Verdun, the bombardment commencing on 21 February 1916. The original idea seems to have been not so much to take Verdun as to bleed the French Army white. France had a much smaller population than Germany and the Verdun gambit was designed to cause the French such casualties that they would be forced to sue for peace. With France out of the war, Great Britain and Russia would also be forced to accept Germany's terms. But the Germans around Verdun found themselves bleeding almost as profusely as the French.[15] While fighting there was still going on, they found themselves hit by a predominantly British offensive on the Somme – the infantry attacks commencing on 1 July. The

French Army had carried the burden of the Allied war effort on the Western Front up to this point and was becoming depleted and exhausted. The British Expeditionary Force, now consisting mainly of wartime volunteers, was beginning to take over the leading role.[16]

Unlike most Continental states Great Britain had no conscription in peacetime. The British did not introduce it until January 1916. In 1914 almost the only reserves behind the small Regular Army had been retired regulars and the amateur soldiers of the Territorial Force, the latter having no obligation to serve overseas. The part of British industry specialising in making the weapons of land warfare had been correspondingly small. Yet, within the first two years of the war, the British had put an expeditionary force of more than 60 divisions (largely composed of wartime volunteers) into northern France and the small part of Belgium not occupied by the Germans. By July 1916 they were supplying it plentifully with most types of munitions, although, in the vitally important case of the artillery shell, the quality left a lot to be desired. Before 1 July 1916 a substantial proportion of the BEF troops had not yet seen action. Their morale was high. They had a type of fighting spirit which sometimes began as naïve idealism but which, in most cases, converted quite readily to grim determination and stoical persistence.[17]

The British, as the first use of tanks on 15 September 1916 indicated, were adaptable and technically innovative. But during the Somme fighting of that year, lasting into November, they were not, as a general rule, particularly skilful operationally. They took casualties which were heavier than necessary and substantially higher than those of the Germans. But the raw power of the BEF and the martial qualities of the British soldier severely shook German confidence. Far from winning the war on the Western Front in 1916, the Germans realised that they were in serious trouble.[18]

The Germans also had crises on the Eastern Front in 1916. A Russian offensive in June, organised and commanded by Brusilov, the ablest of the Russian generals, did colossal damage to the Austrian Army and might have precipitated an Austrian collapse had the Germans not reinforced the Austrians with their own troops.[19] The entry of Rumania into the war on the side of the Allies in late August turned out, however, to be a positive benefit to the Germans. German, Austrian, Bulgarian and Turkish forces attacked Rumania, overrunning much of the country and giving the Germans access to its oil and grain.[20] Yet, by the end of 1916, with heavy commitments east and west, the German Army felt itself stretched almost to breaking point. The policy of bleeding the French had apparently failed.

1917

From 29 August 1916 the German war effort was directed largely by General Erich Ludendorff, who in partnership with Field Marshal Paul von Hindenburg had made a formidable reputation on the Eastern Front. Under their guidance the German Army, while attacking in the East, remained on the defensive in the West during 1917. In the spring of that year, on a crucial section of the Western Front, the Germans made a scorched earth retreat to well-prepared defensive positions which the Allies christened the Hindenburg Line.[21] This was a clever move which shortened the German line, saved manpower and greatly dislocated Allied plans for a spring offensive. The failure of the French offensive mounted under the direction of General Nivelle in the Chemin des Dames area on 16 April 1917 precipitated very serious mutinies involving much of the French Army.[22]

Much less clever than the retreat to the Hindenburg Line was the German initiation of unrestricted submarine warfare in February 1917. The decision to do this was indicative of a feeling of desperation amongst the German policy-makers – the product of ever-mounting casualty figures, long-term fears about the manpower situation and increasing manifestations of discontent on the home front. A major factor in the discontent was the British naval blockade, which was producing food shortages and considerable malnutrition. Inefficient rationing, which ensured that the wealthy often continued to eat well while the working classes went hungry, considerably exacerbated class antagonism and social unrest. Submarine (U-boat) warfare against Great Britain was a natural German response to the blockade. But goods bound to and from Great Britain were carried in the ships of several nations, including the United States. Some American civilians were in the habit of visiting Great Britain, sometimes conveyed on British ships. The German government had already been in trouble with the Americans over civilian deaths at sea. Unrestricted submarine warfare, a policy of sinking without warning any ship that moved on certain areas of sea regardless of flag flown, was almost bound to lead to all-out war with the United States.[23]

American bankers, sympathetic to democracies fighting German militarism and having an eye to a lucrative business, were already financing the British war effort. But the Germans were ill-advised to provoke the United States into further involvement. That country, in addition to its financial strength, had awesome industrial capacity and a vast reservoir of fresh manpower. Unrestricted submarine warfare was thus a tremendous gamble. It made sense only on the assumption that the U-boats would cripple Great Britain and force the British to sue for peace before American military power could be fully developed. In the first few months after the policy came into effect the U-boats sank so many ships that Great Britain's ability to continue the war was indeed placed in doubt. But the introduction of a highly organised convoy system had reduced losses to manageable proportions by the summer. Meanwhile the U-boat campaign, coupled with the exposure by British signals intelligence of German efforts to encourage the Mexicans to attack the United States, had precipitated President Woodrow Wilson to ask Congress, on 2 April, for a declaration of war. The declaration was duly made on 6 April 1917.[24]

But it would be many months before American divisions were committed to battle. General Pétain, Nivelle's replacement as French commander-in-chief, had, in the meantime, to overcome the state of mutiny into which the French Army had fallen after the Nivelle offensive. This he achieved by appeasing the moderate majority with concessions – generous leaves, improved conditions and the general avoidance of battle. Those regarded as 'ring leaders', thus isolated, were imprisoned. Only 55 were shot. Most senior French soldiers and statesmen seem to have believed it vital, from spring 1917, that the French Army remain largely on the defensive in the West until the Americans were ready to take an equal share of the fighting.[25] Some of the British War Cabinet, most notably David Lloyd George who had become Prime Minister in December 1916, took a similar view. But not so Field Marshal Sir Douglas Haig, Commander-in-Chief of the BEF since December 1915.

Haig had long intended that a British offensive be launched in Flanders. But, at the beginning of 1917, he had been overruled by his own government and ordered to co-operate with General Nivelle. In accordance with these instructions, the BEF had mounted an offensive in front of Arras, on 9 April, to distract German attention from Nivelle's supposedly resounding French blow. After the failure and dismissal of Nivelle, Haig returned his attention to Flanders. His intentions were grandiose. He intended his forces not only to break out of the awkward Ypres salient but to liberate a substantial part of the Belgian coast. The Royal Navy was very keen on the latter objective and to some extent lobbied for it – the Germans having many of their submarine pens on that shore.[26] The British had a success early in June when General Sir Herbert Plumer's Second Army took the Messines ridge. But most of the Third Battle of Ypres (31 July–6 November 1917), while intensely bloody and miserable for both sides, seemed remarkably barren of results.[27]

By summer 1917 the BEF had learned much about operations and tactics and was well equipped and supplied. Had Haig made his main effort of that year on more favourable ground, his forces could, perhaps, have done considerably more damage to the Germans than they did to themselves. The British did have some success on 31 July, the first day of infantry attacks for the Third Ypres campaign. They did reasonably well again, after an interval of dry weather, in late September and early October. But their hard-learned skills were at a massive discount in the morass which characterised much of the battlefield for much of the campaign. Haig tried to restore his fortunes by a relatively small-scale offensive towards Cambrai, employing innovative artillery tactics and a large number of tanks, commencing on 20 November 1917. This had some success at first but ended as a drawn battle, having no strategic impact.[28]

In the course of 1917 Russia underwent progressive internal collapse. There was relatively little fighting on the Eastern Front that year,[29] allowing the Germans and Austrians to husband their resources. The Russian monarchy fell in March, Tsar Nicholas II abdicating when his generals showed reluctance to help him crush agitation and disorder on the home front. Russia, led by parliamentary politicians whom the tsarist system had deprived of all experience of government, tried simultaneously to continue the war and, in appalling circumstances of military defeat and domestic chaos and deprivation, to make a transition to democracy. Predictably this did not work. In November an armed coup by the Marxist Bolshevik party effectively took Russia out of the war.[30]

German troops released by the virtual collapse of the Russian war effort in 1917 were put to effective use. The Germans were able to assist the Austrians with a major offensive on the Italian front (the 'Battle of Caporetto') starting on 25 October 1917. The Italians had entered the war against the Central Powers in May 1915. Since then, the Italian Army had been tying down a substantial part of the Austrian Army. At Caporetto the Italians suffered a sensational débâcle. Their front in the Julian Alps and on the River Isonzo collapsed and was only stabilised on the River Piave after a retreat of about 70 miles. British divisions were sent from the Western Front to help save Italy from collapse.[31]

By early December 1917 the Allies were aware that, for the time being, they had lost the strategic initiative.[32] With the fighting having stopped on the Eastern Front and with a formal peace treaty between the Germans and the Bolsheviks in the offing, the Germans were free to transfer large forces from the Eastern to the Western Front. The Italians obviously needed time to recover from the Caporetto disaster and the Germans also considered it safe, in the short term, to withdraw their forces from Italy. Transfers of forces from the Eastern and Italian fronts made it possible for the Germans to mount a great offensive in the West in the first half of 1918. But the ever expanding numbers and gradually increasing competence of the American Expeditionary Force meant that if the Germans had not won a decisive victory by the end of the summer they would not be able to do so in this war.[33]

JANUARY–AUGUST 1918

The British had reasonably good intelligence on German operational and tactical methods and correctly regarded the techniques used at the Battle of Riga on the Eastern Front on 1 September 1917 as a model for larger German offensives in the West in spring 1918. The Germans would commence their operations with extremely intense but relatively short artillery bombardments. They would then mount their infantry attacks in successive waves.[34] Though the British did not spell this out in the intelligence analysis referred to above, the first wave would comprise elite storm troops practising infiltration tactics. Attacking in small groups rather than continuous lines, the storm troops would try to find soft spots in the Allied lines, by-passing centres of strong resistance and penetrating into the rear as rapidly as possible, ultimately trying to reach the Allied gun line and to silence the guns. Waves of less skilled infantry behind them would mop up and help continue the advance. The British were certainly aware of German storm troops, who had been employed against them at Cambrai. British military intelligence also predicted fairly accurately the location of the first strike and gave adequate temporal warning. Army commanders were informed at a conference at Doullens on Saturday, 2 March 1918, that a German attack in Picardy, on the fronts of the Third and First Armies, was 'imminent'.[35]

The Fifth Army, under General Sir Hubert Gough, at the southern end of the British front, had been left very weak in relation to the stretch of front it was holding. It had only 12 divisions to hold 42 miles. (General Byng's Third Army on Gough's left had, by contrast, 14 divisions on a 28-mile front.) The BEF at this period was suffering an acute, general manpower shortage. Casualties had of course been heavy, and industry made large and important demands for men to be kept on the home front. But the degree of manpower shortage actually experienced by the BEF early in 1918 was owing, at least in part, to the mistrust which existed between Lloyd George and Haig. Horrified at the fruitless squandering of British lives which, in his view, had characterised Third Ypres, Lloyd George seems deliberately to have restricted the flow of manpower to the Western Front, apparently trying to ration Haig to the amount which would suffice for defence while denying him the opportunity to take the offensive. There were more British divisions in subsidiary theatres than was reasonable in view of the great German effort expected in the decisive theatre and an excessive number of troops were kept at home.[36]

The Prime Minister seems to have seriously underestimated the potency of the coming German offensives, although this also appears true, to a lesser extent, of the Commander-in-Chief.[37] Whatever the stength of the coming German effort, Haig felt better able to take risks in the Somme area than further north, and eased any anxiety he may have had for the Fifth Army by a somewhat half-baked arrangement with Pétain whereby the French would reinforce Gough if his front was attacked heavily. Haig's real nightmare appears to have been a major defeat in the northern part of the front which would cut his communications with the Channel ports and thus with his sources of supply. This concern was natural and appropriate. In leaving the Fifth Army as weak as he did, Haig miscalculated, but not fatally.[38]

On 21 March the Germans launched an offensive, code-named 'Michael', on the Somme. The German Seventeenth, Second and Eighteenth Armies with some 71 divisions struck the 26 divisions of the British Third and Fifth Armies. The German artillery outgunned the British in this sector by more than two to one. The German infantry who attacked that morning had the cover of fog which was especially dense in the southern part of the attack frontage and it was von Hutier's Eighteenth Army which had the greatest success, against the British Fifth. By 24 March the situation was looking desperate. Though there was little panic, the British Fifth Army and the southern wing of the Third Army were in full retreat.

Pétain had sent some French divisions to take over the southern sector of Gough's front. But he seemed to Haig to be primarily concerned with the security of Paris rather than with keeping in touch with the BEF in the north. Pétain was keen to keep forces in hand to resist attacks which he expected later. He was worried about Haig's forces falling back towards their base of supply – the Channel ports. It was in these circumstances that, at an Allied conference held at Doullens on 26 March, the British and French governments, with Haig's support, appointed General Foch 'to ensure the co-ordination of the Allied Armies on the Western front'. Foch's terms of reference were slightly increased on 3 April when a conference at Beauvais entrusted him with the 'strategic direction of military operations', a formula which the Americans endorsed. On 14 April Foch was formally given the title 'Général-en-Chef des Armées Alliées en France'.[39]

Meanwhile, the British Third Army had foiled a German attempt to widen northward the bulge that they had created in the BEF's front. In an offensive code-named 'Mars', mounted on 28 March, nine German divisions hit four British divisions in the area north of the Scarpe. Had they been successful in taking Vimy Ridge and capturing Arras, the Germans apparently intended to exploit as far as Boulogne, some 72 miles away on the Channel coast. But 'Mars' was stopped dead by the evening of the first day, the Germans having suffered very heavy casualties for virtually no gain of ground. Meanwhile, south of the Somme, where the Germans had made the greatest progress, they were fast losing momentum. Their own casualties had been very heavy and they were suffering from a degree of physical exhaustion at least as great as that of the Allied troops they were pursuing.

They had the exhilaration of victory to sustain them, but were trying to press the advance in the face of their own exhaustion and Allied air superiority. By 5 April the Germans had virtually ceased their effort south of the Somme and the vital hub of Allied communications at Amiens seemed safe for the time being.[40]

The Germans launched their next stroke, code-named 'Georgette', on 9 April, on a 12-mile front between Armentières and La Bassée Canal on the front of the British First Army. It was a scaled-down version of the 'George', the offensive that Ludendorff had originally intended for this sector. Ludendorff had committed and expended more forces than originally intended in the Somme region. He nevertheless hoped to capture the important rail junction of Hazebrouck and was prepared to exploit to the Channel coast if a favourable opportunity arose. On the first day of 'Georgette' the Germans penetrated to a maximum depth of three and a half miles. On 10 April they extended the offensive further to the north into the area of the British Second Army. It was at this stage, knowing that he had practically no reserves left, and fearing for the loss of the crucial rail centre of Hazebrouck, that Haig's anxiety peaked. On 11 April he issued a famous, but totally uncharacteristic, order of the day. Declaring that his forces were now fighting with their 'backs to the wall', he exhorted them to a make a supreme effort 'for the safety of our homes and the freedom of mankind'. Such messages are more likely to relieve the feelings of the sender than to influence the course of events. The German drive towards Hazebrouck had lost momentum before British troops received Haig's order.[41]

The Germans went on attacking in various parts of Flanders until the end of April. The British were compelled to abandon the ground they had gained in the Third Ypres campaign. But the Germans never really came close to taking the Channel ports on which the BEF depended. They met especially stout resistance from the well-rested Belgian Army at the northern end of the front and their efforts in that sector were shattered. On 24 April they renewed their effort in the Somme region, towards Amiens, but this also failed. From the end of April a lull descended on those parts of the front for which the British Commander-in-Chief was responsible. The Germans had battered the BEF terribly, leaving many of its divisions depleted and very tired. But they seem to have suffered at least equal casualties themselves and were as far away as ever from a decisive victory. Realising that he was not getting the results he wanted, Ludendorff had decided to shift his main effort (at least for the time being) further south.

Ludendorff ultimately intended to renew the offensive in the north. But in order to get decisive results there he decided it was necessary first to divert the attention of the Allies, and commit their reserves, in Pétain's sector. The first of his offensives in this area, code-named 'Goerz', was mounted on the Chemin des Dames sector on the Aisne early on the morning of 27 May. The Germans achieved the highest degree of surprise of any of their offensives that year. Haig and Foch were still focusing on the north and the French Army commander on the spot ignored warnings from his own intelligence. The French had left their forces in this sector exposed on a forward slope. They were pulverised by the German artillery and shattered by the infantry attack. Three very tired British divisions, which had been sent south as a token British gesture of solidarity with the French (who had given the British quite a lot of help in Flanders), found themselves directly in the path of this hurricane and suffered terrible losses. The German troops of General von Boehn's Seventh Army were able to advance ten miles in one day, crossing the Aisne and reaching the Vesle near the town of Fismes. Though the Germans were stopped outside Rheims on 1 June, further to the west other troops had reached the Marne near Chateau-Thierry, only 56 miles from Paris, by 3 June.[42]

Though his Chemin des Dames offensive had made far greater progress than he had expected, or even intended, Ludendorff was not altogether happy with the situation at the beginning of June. His forces had arguably penetrated too far towards the Marne on too narrow a front. In an effort to widen northwards the salient that they had created, and to force Foch to commit more of his reserves before resuming the offensive in Flanders, the

German mounted a fresh effort astride the Matz, a tributary of the Oise, on 9 June. This was initially quite successful, penetrating six miles on the first day. But on 11 June a French five-division counter-attack into the German right flank (two of the divisions employed being American) effectively terminated it.

Ludendorff once again delayed what he now intended to be his culminating offensive (code-named 'Hagen') in Flanders. He launched a massive effort around the city of Reims on 15 July in order to widen the bulge he had created in the French front, and to help keep it supplied by securing Reims as a rail centre. East of Reims the offensive was stopped dead. West of the city it made good progress initially and the German troops crossed the Marne. But Ludendorff had not achieved surprise. A major French counter-offensive had been prepared and on 18 July the Germans were dealt a tremendous blow in the right flank. Within three days they had suffered a major defeat, usually known as the Second Battle of the Marne, American divisions on loan to the French having played a significant part. The Germans withdrew under pressure as their salient was attacked from both sides. Georges Clemenceau, France's fiercely determined but somewhat anti-military premier, was sufficiently impressed to make Foch a Marshal of France – the highest military honour that can be given to a French general.[43]

THE STRATEGIC SITUATION IN LATE JULY–EARLY AUGUST 1918

The Second Battle of the Marne was the turning point of 1918. The German 'Hagen' offensive in Flanders was postponed indefinitely. Though neither side was certain of it at the time, there would be no more German offensives in this war. From 18 July 1918 the German Empire was in desperate trouble. An objective look at the facts of the situation pointed to ultimate German defeat, even if this were to take another year or so. It is indicative of Ludendorff's fundamental weakness of judgement that these realities appear not fully to have registered in his mind until the shock of 8 August.[44]

The most obvious problem for the Germans was the shift in the numerical balance against them. The set of comparative figures printed below in Table 1.1 indicates the approximate rifle strength of the two sides on the Western Front at the start of each month:

Table 1.1   *Approximate rifle strengths on the Western Front at the beginning of months in 1918*

	ALLIES	GERMANS
March	1,492,000	1,370,000
April	1,245,000	1,569,000
May	1,343,000	1,600,000
June	1,496,000	1,639,000
July	1,556,000	1,412,000
August	1,672,000	1,395,000[45]

The increase in German rifle strength between March and June may appear strange. The Germans were, of course, taking very heavy casualties from 21 March onwards. But at that time they had not finished transferring divisions from the East. According to British intelligence sources, 13 German divisions arrived in the West between 21 March and 9 May. German strength on the Western Front then peaked at 208 divisions. Of the 33 German divisions left in the East, only six were of good fighting quality. The one remaining German division (out of a total of 242 identified by British intelligence) was in the Balkans. The British knew in June that the arrival of any more German divisions on the Western Front was unlikely. The Germans needed to keep a minimum of forces in the East to enforce the terms of the Treaty of Brest-Litovsk, a grossly humiliating peace settlement which the Germans had imposed on Russia. Signed in March, the treaty gave the Germans, amongst other things, *de facto* control of the Ukraine. The lands conquered in the East were thought vital to Germany's chances of feeding itself through another winter.[46]

The statistics on Allied rifle strength printed above must be treated with caution. A high proportion of the increase from April onwards represents American troops arriving in France. In many cases these troops were not trained to anything like an adequate standard and would be of little use to the Allied cause in the short term. The French Army was maintaining its strength only by the use of increasing numbers of colonial, Czech and Polish troops, as well as by ruthlessly combing men out from industry. In some British divisions about half the men were now very young conscripts, many of them of inferior physical standard compared with the average volunteer soldier of 1916. Nevertheless, the situation was favourable to the Allies and likely to get much more so as the year went on.[47]

At the beginning of August the Germans seem to have had a total of 201 divisions on the Western Front, but 106 of these were so depleted or exhausted as to be unfit for immediate employment. The Allies had a total of about 186 divisions at the same date, of which some 29 were American divisions with roughly double the manpower of a British or French division, having establishments of over 28,000 men. A much smaller proportion of Allied than of German divisions was considered unfit for combat. The average American division might be under-trained and inexperienced but would improve. The Americans intended to have 80 divisions in France by the end of the year whereas the Germans, now fast running out of manpower, were likely to have to break more divisions up.[48]

Manpower, of course, was not the only factor. Firepower was critical. On the Western Front 1914–18 firepower meant, above all, artillery. In that arm the Germans seem to have suffered from numerical inferiority throughout 1918. Even in March, the German Army on the Western Front had, according to one estimate, only 14,000 barrels of all calibres against 18,500 on the Allied side. Both sides lost guns heavily in the fighting of March to July. A captured order signed by Ludendorff on 1 August indicated that in 'round numbers' 13 per cent of German artillery taking part in active operations on the Western Front had been completely destroyed by fire in a single month – the month referred to apparently being July. But the Allies appear to have replaced their losses more rapidly. Crucial to the accuracy of artillery fire at this period was air power. In that area, the Allies had in 1918, as for most of the war, a clear advantage. In August 1918 it was estimated that the French had some 2,820 military aircraft of all types, the Germans 2,592, the British 1,644, the Americans 270 and the Belgians 160. While the latest German fighter, the Fokker DVII, which started to arrive at the front at the end of April, was somewhat in advance of the best the Allies could put into the air, especially in its rate of climb, this slight qualitative edge did not offset the large Allied numerical advantage.[49]

Morale, though not quantifiable, can be a crucial aspect of a strategic situation. The British and the French armies certainly had morale problems that summer. Confidence had been severely shaken by the extent of their losses and the depth of their retreats. In the course of the war so far, France had sustained a higher proportion of deaths per head of population than any other major power. A profound sense of national exhaustion was the inevitable result. The British had also suffered terribly. They had considerable doubts about the steadiness of the very young conscripts who now made up such a large part of the BEF. But morale in the German Army was also distinctly precarious. War-weariness had been growing for years and troops brought over from the Eastern Front had, in many cases, been influenced by socialist and anti-war ideological sentiment as a result of fraternisation with the Russians. In 1918 the morale problem was quite manageable for as long as victory appeared imminent:

'Decisive victory promised a quick peace. The enthusiasm and determination manifested in the 1918 offensives were in this sense, no more than the positive expression of war weariness'.[50]

The failure of the offensives brought, crushing disappointment and left the Germans with fresh problems. While the length of their front had increased from 390 kilometres to 510 between 21 March and 25 June, they had, according to the estimate of one eminent German historian, suffered about a million casualties.[51] A high proportion of these were incurred by 'exactly the groups which had sustained the Army's morale so far. Company officers suffered particularly heavily.' German organisational, operational and tactical methods, quite effective in the short run, had exacerbated the long-term problem. The best troops were concentrated into 'mobile' divisions, leaving poorer stuff in 'position' divisions. An infantry and pioneer elite was further distilled into storm troops units. Especially 'reckless drive and initiative' were demanded of these better troops. Inevitably they suffered the greatest loss. After the March-July holocaust, therefore, the German Army was reduced not just in size but, very markedly, in quality. It only made matters worse that while the front from which the Germans had started their offensives was heavily fortified, the one on which they ended was not. Suffering from poor rations, as well as manpower shortage and physical and moral tiredness the Germans did not adequately strengthen their new positions.[52]

A factor of crucial importance, both physically and psychologically, was food. The combined effects of the blockade, the manpower crisis and maladministration meant that Germany was very inadequately supplied. The German soldier was given priority over the civilian, at least in theory, and the 'mobile' divisions were given priority over the 'position' divisions. But even the best infantry had become so used to poor rations that captured British bully beef was highly prized. Malnutrition was certainly a factor in the German Army's particular vulnerability to the influenza epidemic sweeping through Europe at this period and this had a serious impact in June and July. Though the Germans had conquered vast tracts of agricultural land in eastern Europe and had gained political control of the Ukraine, they lacked the manpower to exploit these gains adequately, and there was no prospect of a substantial improvement in the food situation for the foreseeable future.[53]

Recent studies of this war have emphasised the very close links which existed between the battle front and the home front and the importance of lines of communication between the two. In the case of Germany it has always been difficult to say whether the home front demoralised the battle front or vice-versa, but morale was going down fast on both and British intelligence was well aware of this. There had been a huge strike in Berlin in January, broken only by conscripting the ring leaders and threatening the application of military discipline to all workers involved. Intelligence summaries available to Haig noted in April that, 'Labour agitation in Germany continues in spite of measures taken by the authorities. It is said to be partly due to the despatch of a considerable number of unskilled labourers to the front, and also to the large number of wounded returning.'[54]

In June it was reported that all industries in Germany other than munitions were desperately short of raw materials and that the transport system was beginning to suffer acutely. We now know that a major part of the German munitions industry was able to keep going until the outbreak of revolution on the home front in late autumn. But, while the German Army lost no major battle for want of ammunition, some items of equipment, notably guns, could not be replaced at an adequate rate. British industry, on the other hand, had achieved extraordinary levels of war production and was being supported by fast-expanding American manufacture. A long report originating in Berne, containing the opinions of 'various public men in Germany', was made available to Haig's headquarters at the beginning of July. This suggested that the Germans 'could not possibly go on with the war during the winter, that an important military success like the capture of Paris was essential to them, that they were counting on the Allies being unable to hold together for six months'.[55] By the middle of July it was pretty clear that these conditions would not be met.

The Germans could expect no help from their allies. The collapse of the Habsburg empire, already on the cards before 1914, was now in progress. British intelligence reports for early August mentioned the 'complete collapse of the food supply in Austria'. Information derived 'from deserters, prisoners, captured documents etc.', indicated that 'disorders have been rampant in Austria-Hungary since April 1918. There is a considerable accumulation of evidence proving the prevalence of mutiny and desertion in the Army, of food riots and strikes in various localities from Bohemia in the north to Dalmatia in the south.'[56] Morale in much of the Austrian Army on the Italian front was rock bottom, with many troops only awaiting an opportunity to surrender.[57] On that front, the Italians now lacked the strengthening presence of German troops. The Germans now had the equivalent of only one division in the Balkans to help their Bulgarian allies. They had none with the Turks. On the other hand, both the British and the French still had forces in Italy and the Balkans, where the Austrians and Bulgarians respectively only needed a good hard push to make them sue for peace. In the Middle East the British Empire's forces were rapidly defeating the Turkish Army.[58] When Germany's allies collapsed, yet more Allied troops would be available for use against Germany.

But bad as Germany's strategic position was, its leaders were not yet suing for peace. Ludendorff and some others in the German high command still cherished the hope that they could renew their offensives on the Western Front and obtain a favourable peace which would make Germany's sacrifices worthwhile.[59] If such arrogance were to be overcome, Germany's defeat would have to be conclusively demonstrated on the battlefield. Given French weariness and American inexperience, if the war were to be ended in 1918 much of the demonstrating would have to be done by the BEF.

2

THE BRITISH EXPEDITIONARY
FORCE AND THE ART OF WAR

A SOPHISTICATED ARMY

The BEF of August 1914 had consisted of five infantry divisions and a large cavalry division of five brigades.[1] It comprised mainly regular and former regular soldiers. Over the next four years it underwent radical changes in organisation, social composition and ethos. It became a mass army, a 'nation in arms', which drew both officers and other ranks (and both men and women) from a wide variety of social backgrounds.[2] The same four-year period witnessed the most rapid evolution in the art of war yet known. In technical, tactical, operational and administrative terms the BEF developed into an army of great sophistication,[3] more advanced in some respects than any of its contemporaries.[4] Several scholarly works have tried to trace one or more aspect of the BEF's evolution through the whole course of the war. It is intended here to examine its characteristics as a fighting machine at one particular period – late summer 1918, immediately before the Battle of Amiens.

STRUCTURE

In the Hundred Days' Campaign the BEF contained five Armies and some 18 army corps, not counting the Cavalry Corps. For most of the period it comprised some 61 divisions, not counting the three rather weak cavalry divisions. Of the 61 divisions, five were Australian, four Canadian, one New Zealand, and two American. (At the beginning of August 1918 there were still two Portuguese divisions with the BEF and three further

American divisions, but the former were badly battered and the latter were soon to be removed from British control.) The remaining divisions were recruited wholly or largely in the United Kingdom. No figure is readily available for BEF personnel at the start of the Hundred Days but at the Armistice there were to be 1,794,000 excluding 'coloured labour'.[5]

Battalion and regimental spirit could be important in giving the soldier a sense of identity. For our purposes, however, the division, commanded by a Major-General, may be regarded as the basic building block of the BEF. During the Hundred Days a British infantry division had about 13,000 men at full strength.[6] The infantry component of the division consisted, in most cases, of three infantry brigades, each of three battalions.[7] Battalions were divided into four companies and a headquarters, each company having four platoons. Platoons in turn comprised a small headquarters and four sections. In the Hundred Days it was normal for rifle sections to have about seven men. Lewis gun sections, of which there were two in many platoons, often had only four men each.[8]

The infantry component of the division was supported by two brigades of divisional artillery, each of three six-gun batteries of 18-pdr field guns and one battery of six 4.5-inch field howitzers, giving the division some 48 artillery tubes at full strength. In a big attack a division would, however, normally have more field artillery support than this. Extra artillery brigades from divisions not engaged were routinely attached and Army Field Brigades could be allocated by Army headquarters.[9] In addition to their field guns and howitzers, divisions had two medium trench mortar batteries of six 6-inch Newton mortars which were also manned by artillery personnel.[10] A battalion of the Machine Gun Corps, comprising four companies, each with 16 Vickers guns, giving 64 Vickers guns in total, was a standard part of the infantry division's structure.[11] There were three field companies of engineers, a signals company and a pioneer battalion per division. Finally there were three field ambulance units and the logistical troops.[12]

British (as opposed to Dominion) divisions were regarded, with a few exceptions[13] as belonging to one of three basic categories: Regular, Territorial Force and New Army. Regular divisions were those which were once composed mainly of regular (professional) soldiers and former regular soldiers still liable to be called up in wartime. Territorial divisions were originally composed mainly of men from the Territorial Force, a force of part-time, amateur troops, raised for home defence. New Army divisions at first consisted predominantly of wartime volunteers.[14] The three types were each considered to have their own generic ethos. Some individual divisions from all three types had very specific individual identities and such divisions could serve as a strong focus of loyalty. In the case of Territorial and New Army divisions, the identity was often based, at least in part, on the region from which they were principally recruited, and this was often reflected in the divisional title. The 9th (Scottish) and the 36th (Ulster) were two notable New Army divisions.[15] The 46th (North Midland) Division, a Territorial Force division, did outstandingly well in the Hundred Days.[16] Certain divisions gained a reputation as 'good' divisions and were frequently used for major assaults. Some, especially the 9th (Scottish) and the 18th (Eastern), developed the reputation for being tactically and technically innovative as well as 'good'.[17]

Even in 1918, divisions were still thought to be influenced by their Regular, Territorial or New Army origins and in some cases retained a strong individual identity. There were, however, powerful forces at work which were tending to make the British divisions of the BEF more homogeneous. Conscription had been introduced in the United Kingdom in January 1916 but no new conscript divisions were formed. Instead conscripts were used to replace casualties in all the existing types of British division. Because casualties were so high in the latter part of 1917, and again in spring 1918, the great majority of British divisions in the BEF in August 1918 contained a high proportion of young conscripts.[18] During the acute emergency of spring 1918 returning wounded were, in many cases, not going back to the units which they had left but being sent to wherever the need for manpower was most pressing. The reduction in divisional size, early in 1918, from twelve battalions to nine resulted in the breaking up of battalions which had long been integral parts of particular divisions and this, too, contributed to a sense that divisional identity was being eroded.[19]

Immediately above division in the hierarchy of formations came corps. Normally commanded by a Lieutenant-General, a corps did not have a fixed structure ('order of battle' in military parlance) but was essentially a headquarters, with some aircraft, artillery, administrative and logistical troops attached, which controlled a variable number of divisions. Except in the case of the Australians and Canadians, corps was rarely a focus of loyalty for the ordinary soldier of the BEF. British divisions seldom stayed in the same corps long enough to allow a corps identity to develop.[20] As a command level, however, corps was important. In the Hundred Days some major operations were planned principally at this level[21] and some were also conceived by corps headquarters.[22] The fact that Army commanders and their immediate staffs could generally rely on a high degree of experience and competence in corps headquarters at this period also enabled them to couch the plans made at Army headquarters in fairly broad terms, allowing a lot of the detail to be filled in by the corps staffs.

Crucial to the ability of a corps headquarters to influence the battle were the corps artillery and corps aircraft. In the Hundred Days, corps artillery (sometimes referred to as 'the corps heavies') normally comprised some 30 long-range guns (generally 60-pdrs) for counter-battery work, some 60 medium (normally 6-inch) howitzers, and about 24 heavy howitzers of either 8-inch or 9.2-inch calibre.[23] Significantly corps commanders were also the lowliest Army officers to have aircraft under their control. Quite a large part of the Royal Air Force consisted of so-called corps squadrons (of which each corps normally had one), specialising in photographic reconnaissance, artillery spotting and 'contact patrols' which were intended to report the progress of advancing troops. By means of wireless fitted in these aircraft, corps commanders were often better informed about the progress of an attack than subordinate divisional commanders who were physically closer to the action.[24] Even in the Hundred Days most corps still had some 'corps cavalry' for reconnaissance and screening purposes.[25] For much of the war such cavalry had been rarely useful for its intended purpose and was more often employed on rather menial tasks. The increased mobility of the Hundred Days was to give it slightly better opportunities.

Two or more corps were grouped as an Army under the command of a General. Like corps, Armies were essentially headquarters organisations with some of their own artillery, air power and logistics troops. Corps could rotate in and out of armies, although, during the Hundred Days, there seems to have been somewhat more stability in this regard than hitherto. The amount of artillery held at Army level varied considerably but was very substantial. On 27 September 1918, for example, First Army had 594 heavy and siege guns and howitzers, 48 anti-aircraft guns and 18 brigades of field artillery. This was, of course, in addition to all the artillery held by subordinate formations.[26] The guns and howitzers held at Army level came directly under the command of the Army's Major-General Royal Artillery (head gunner) who could also issue artillery instructions for all the guns held in the Army including those held by corps and divisions.[27] An RAF Brigade, normally of three 'Wings', was attached to each Army, the RAF Brigadier commanding being directly subordinate to the Army commander. The 'Army Wing' of an RAF Brigade comprised fighter and bomber squadrons, the 'Corps Wing', the reconnaissance, spotting and contact patrol aircraft of the Corps squadrons. The 'Balloon Wing', of course, controlled balloons, still sometimes important in the direction of artillery fire.[28]

As a command level Army was crucial. Success or failure in a major battle would depend vitally on the decisions made and the staff work done in Army headquarters, a fact appreciated by all ranks. An Army commanders' principal staff officers were his Major-General General Staff (effectively his chief of staff and second in command), his Major-General Royal Artillery and his Chief Engineer.[29] If they and the Army commander worked smoothly and efficiently together they could create the atmosphere of a well-run family to which others would want to belong. It was an ethos which General Sir Herbert 'Daddy' Plumer and his Second Army staff had become proverbially good at establishing. By contrast subordinate formations often experienced severely dysfunctional relations with the Fifth Army staff of General Sir Hubert Gough, a fact which may have made it easier for the government to scapegoat Gough for the disaster to Fifth Army in March 1918.[30] General Sir Henry Rawlinson's Fourth Army headquarters, without inspiring quite the same affection as Plumer's Second Army, established a reputation for efficiency and became, in operational terms, the most conspicuously successful team during the Hundred Days.[31]

GHQ AND SIR DOUGLAS HAIG

Above the whole hierarchy of formations came General Headquarters (GHQ). GHQ was based at Montreuil on the River La Canche, near France's west coast, about 20 miles south of Boulogne. It had been there since 31 March 1916. Most of those employed at GHQ worked in buildings which belonged to the Ecole Militaire. The Commander-in-Chief was based in a château outside the town. Amongst GHQ's functions were to serve as the connecting link between the forces in the field and the government in London, to organise co-operation between the British and Dominion forces and other Allied armies on the Western Front, and to co-ordinate the actions of the forces under its own command. In order to keep its own armies fighting effectively GHQ had to train them and supply them with food, fodder and all forms of munitions. To accomplish these tasks it had to organise the transport system in the BEF's rear and to build new railways, roads and canals where these were required. Finally GHQ was responsible for administering medical, veterinary and chaplain services.[32]

The most important military posts at GHQ, apart from that of the Commander-in-Chief himself, were those of the heads of Branches: the

Military Secretary, the Chief of the General Staff, the Adjutant-General and the Quartermaster-General. The Military Secretary ran a small branch dealing with honours and promotions. The General Staff was divided into the Operations Section, which co-ordinated the actions of the British Armies, the Intelligence Section, which gathered and assessed information on the enemy, and the co-ordinating Staff Duties Section. The Adjutant-General's Branch was concerned with discipline and other personnel matters. The Quartermaster-General's Branch, by far the biggest, dealt with supply and transport. Altogether GHQ had about 5,000 military personnel including a few guards. Fewer than 600 of these were officers, of which about half served at Montreuil, and half at outlying directorates. Most worked for the logistical branches, under the Quartermaster-General.[33]

Dominating GHQ was Field Marshal Sir Douglas Haig, Commander-in-Chief since December 1915. Given that Haig commanded the BEF throughout the period covered in this book, it is here necessary to give some account of his background and character. He was from a lowland Scottish family, his branch of which had made its money distilling whisky. While still in his twenties he had decided not merely to make soldiering his career but to devote most of his life's energy to it. Commissioned from Sandhurst into the cavalry, he managed to forge connections, partly through his wife, with the royal family. This greatly aided his career. Yet he was also dedicated and hard-working, acquiring a professional knowledge above the average for an officer of his generation as well as creditable war service in the Sudan and South Africa.[34]

In many respects Haig was remarkably open minded. He was, for example, by no means reactionary in his political and social attitudes. In 1911 he suggested, in private correspondence, that India be gradually prepared for something equivalent to Dominion status.[35] He was not a racist or an anti-Semite. He advocated giving Indians commissions in Indian regiments and was one of the main sponsors of the military career of Sir John Monash, an Australian of German-Jewish origin who was to command the Australian Corps during the Hundred Days.[36] He was not a snob. On a number occasions during the war he declared himself impressed by trade unionists and other people of working-class origins whom he entertained at GHQ.[37] He did not, on the whole, like politicians, but was on terms of the greatest mutual respect with the Liberal, reforming and very intellectual pre-war Secretary of State for War, Richard Haldane.[38] Interested in new military technologies, Haig was an early advocate of military aviation,[39] though never a believer of 'strategic' bombing. His support was crucial to the development of tank forces within the British Army.[40] Another virtue was that he was mentally and morally robust. Many would have broken down under the strain to which he was subjected.

Haig's strengths were, however, offset for much of the war by some serious weaknesses. Though highly literate, he was not good at expressing himself face-to-face. By no means cold-hearted, he struck most people as a remote figure. Most other senior officers were in awe of him. He was by nature excessively optimistic, a dangerous tendency. For much of the war he seemed to surround himself with people prepared to tell him what he wanted to hear, or at least disinclined to shatter his illusions. Like most generals in all the armies involved, Haig never really came to terms with the aberrant Western Front conditions of 1915–17 which seemed to contradict much of what he had been taught during his formal military education, favouring defence rather than attack, caution rather than boldness. A cavalry officer by origin, Haig perpetually hankered for a war of rapid movement which Western Front conditions did not permit. In theory he believed in a devolved style of command. In practice he often interfered unwisely in the plans of his Army commanders, pressing for greater audacity than situations warranted and wasting British and Dominion lives as a result.[41]

In early 1918 things did not look good for Haig. Mainly as a result of the very heavy losses in the Third Ypres campaign the government at home had, to a very large extent, lost confidence in him. Haig's survival as Commander-in-Chief was probably owing to a combination of royal favour and the lack of a credible alternative. In the short term, things were only to get worse, Fifth Army's defeat in March further endangering his position.

But once he had ridden out the storms of the spring, things began to look much better for him. The military conditions of the second half of 1918 were more suited to Haig's temperament. Developments in military technology and tactics, some of which he had actively fostered, as well as a changed strategic environment, now began to favour a more audacious approach.[42]

Haig also seems to have benefited at this period from a more competent, less sycophantic team, at GHQ. Lieutenant-General Sir Herbert Lawrence had replaced Lieutenant-General Sir Launcelot Kiggell, a close friend of Haig's, as Chief of the General Staff. Major-General Richard Butler, Kiggell's deputy, had also been removed from GHQ and sent to command the III Corps. The perpetually over-sanguine Brigadier-General Charteris, to whom many attributed blame for the disasters of 1916 and 1917, had been replaced as BGGS Intelligence.[43] For most of the summer this post was held by Brigadier-General E.W. Cox, but Brigadier-General G.S. Clive replaced him when he drowned bathing in the sea on 26 August.[44] Both Cox and Clive appear to have provided Haig with balanced and reasonably accurate intelligence pictures. Though the removals of Kiggell and Charteris were forced on Haig, he seems to have had few problems working with their replacements. It is very difficult to ascertain the influence of the new appointees on particular decisions, but it was widely believed in the BEF at the time that GHQ was better for the changes.[45]

Leaving the bulk of GHQ's administrators at Montreuil, for much of his final campaign Haig lived and worked somewhat closer to the action, as part of an Advanced GHQ. Consisting of a relatively small team of staff officers and aides this was normally based in a railway train, parked in a convenient siding. From the train Haig would frequently tour the front. Moving partly by car and partly on horseback he would call at Army, corps and divisional headquarters.[46] In the period covered by this book, therefore, Haig was not as remote a commander as he has sometimes been portrayed. He could, and did, express displeasure when he thought commanders were displaying insufficient aggression.[47] When he believed it merited, however, he liked to give praise. During the Hundred Days he gave it frequently.[48]

THE IMPORTANCE OF THE DOMINION FORCES

We have already noted that ten of the infantry divisions in the BEF were recruited in the Dominions. In addition there was a fine South African infantry brigade. These bare figures, however, only begin to suggest the great importance of the Dominion troops to the British war effort in the latter part of 1918. Even in purely quantitative terms they understate it. Whereas the British had reduced their infantry divisions to nine battalions, the Dominions had chosen to maintain four battalions per brigade, twelve battalions per division, though the Australians, who maintained a purely voluntary system of recruitment, were not able to sustain this throughout the Hundred Days. Canadian divisions, in addition to being larger, were more lavishly equipped than their British counterparts, having a good deal more firepower and more engineering support.[49]

In August 1918 there can be little doubt that, as well as being larger, the Dominion divisions were, on average, qualitatively superior to divisions from the home islands, though the degree of this has sometimes been exaggerated and though some home islands divisions performed as well as any from the Dominions. There were several reasons for the high quality of Dominion troops. All commentators seem to have agreed that they were, on average, better physical specimens than their British counterparts.[50] This was probably because working people in the Dominions ate better and had a healthier, more outdoor life-style than those who remained in the home islands. Ordinary soldiers from the Dominions also had, some observers considered, a greater degree of initiative than the average amongst British troops – a quality sometimes attributed to the less rigidly hierarchical, less deferential nature of Dominion societies and to the promotion of Dominion officers on grounds which had nothing to do with social status.[51] There can be no doubting that Dominion troops were tactically and technically innovative and audacious though they had no monopoly on these qualities and it is important to remember that a very substantial proportion of them were British born.[52]

Another factor making for the special importance of the Australian and Canadian Corps was that they had distinct and continuous identities as corps. Their component divisions spent more time working together under the same corps staffs and this facilitated training and optimised performance. British corps were by contrast rather random and transient groupings of divisions. According to a recent study only 16 British divisions remained in the same corps throughout the Hundred Days, 22 served in two different corps and 12 served in three different corps.[53] Another important point is that neither of the Dominion corps was directly in the path of any of Ludendorff's hammer blows of the first half of 1918, though Australian forces played a major role bringing the German push towards Amiens to a halt after it had spent its initial fury. Many of the best British divisions, on the other hand, had sustained very heavy losses by the middle of the year, including a high proportion of their experienced officers and NCOs. Nine British divisions were so smashed up that they had to be altogether reconstituted.[54] That summer they were trying to absorb and train the young conscripts sent as casualty replacements. In early August 1918, therefore, a very high proportion of the effective combat power of the BEF was vested in the Dominion corps.

INFANTRY

Infantry was the most numerous arm on the Western Front and had a practically irrefutable claim to be considered the most important. No other arm except dismounted cavalry, which was in effect a sort of temporary infantry, could hold ground. Artillery did most of the killing but it would have been quickly wiped off the battlefield without friendly infantry to screen and protect it. As Haig insisted, the importance of all other arms had to be measured in terms of the assistance they could give to the infantry.[55] But the infantry itself underwent dramatic change during the war.

When the war started nearly all British infantry soldiers had been riflemen, equipped with bayonets as side-arms. Officers had swords and revolvers. (The sword turned out to be totally useless as an infantry weapon on the Western Front. Revolvers were more useful and seem to have been quite widely employed by officers and NCOs, though generally as side-arms rather than principal weapons.)[56] The only other infantry weapon was the Vickers machine gun of which there were two per battalion. Before the war Great Britain spent relatively little on its Army compared to the great Continental powers. Yet in the Short Model Lee-Enfield rifle and the Vickers machine gun, both of .303 calibre, the nation had equipped its infantry with weapons which were as good as or better than those in service with any European army. In slightly improved versions, each was still in use until the 1950s. Both weapons, however, while excellent for defence, were of limited use for attacking an entrenched enemy.[57]

For harassing troops in trenches, mortars – smooth-bore tubes with a simple firing mechanism and a high trajectory – proved useful and became standard infantry weapons for the first time in history. Numerous types were introduced. The most commonly used with British infantry was the 3-inch Stokes which had a range of about 400 yards and could fire six 11-lb bombs in a minute. To move the weapon and a modest ammunition supply forward in an assault, an eight-man team was required, but this was some-times done. There were two batteries of 3-inch Stokes per infantry brigade. The 6-inch Newton mortars, held at divisional level, and the 9.45-inch mortar, of which there was an establishment of one battery per corps in 1918 and which fired the devastating 'flying pig' projectile, were consid-ered artillery weapons and manned accordingly. The 4-inch Stokes was mostly used by the Special Brigade (chemical warfare) troops of the Royal Engineers for projecting smoke or gas. All the mortars available to the BEF in 1918 were really too heavy to be good weapons of mobile warfare. During the Hundred Days, attempts were sometimes made to overcome this limitation by mounting them on trucks but it is not clear how suc-cessful this was.[58]

In the assault, infantry relied heavily on artillery fire-support. But such support had to be pre-programmed. Inevitably synchronisation between it and the advancing infantry would sometimes be lost. The infantry had no rapid or reliable means of asking the artillery to adjust its fire once an attack had begun. There was not yet a wireless (radio) light enough to be carried into battle on a man's back. Field artillery, moreover, the type of artillery which offered infantry the most intimate support, had limited range. Infantry might have the opportunity to advance beyond that range – something which was to occur frequently in the Hundred Days. If infantry wanted to resist an utterly slavish reliance on artillery support in favourable as well as in adverse circumstances, and the best infantry generally did, they needed effective weaponry that they could carry with them.[59]

One type of man-portable weapon useful for attacking an entrenched enemy was the grenade. In previous conflicts it had been regarded as a specialist item but in this war it became a standard infantry weapon. The type most widely available in the BEF in the second half of the war was the Mills, a simple blast bomb. But the British also used various types of incendiary grenade, including one containing white phosphorus. British grenades were generally powerful which was good for clearing trenches and dugouts but were rather heavy and could not be thrown as far as standard German grenades. To achieve a greater range the standard Mills bomb could be fired from a cup fitted to a rifle muzzle. Grenades specially designed to be launched from rifles could go further still.[60] Rifle grenades were crucial to BEF infantry tactics in the Hundred Days and were expended in large numbers.[61]

The most important man-portable weapon gained by the BEF's infantry in the course of the war was an automatic rifle – the Lewis gun, discussed below. The belt-fed, water-cooled, tripod-mounted Vickers machine gun, however, remained an excellent weapon for defence. Techniques were also developed for using it in the indirect fire role, using the curved trajectory to rain bullets onto an enemy who was out of sight of the firing position. Partly because indirect fire techniques were thought to demand specialist skills, the Vickers was taken away from the infantry battalion during 1915. Its use was taken over by a new organisation – the Machine Gun Corps.

When massed, Vickers guns could fire barrages in support of infantry assaults, supplementing the field artillery. Pioneered by the Canadian Corps in 1917, the use of this technique had become a matter of routine in most BEF formations by the Hundred Days. By that time, however, the Vickers had long since ceased to be an infantry weapon as such.[62]

The infantry received the Lewis gun instead. Air-cooled and fed with ammunition from a rotary magazine or drum on top of the breech, the Lewis was initially considered an automatic rifle rather than a machine gun. It did not have the range, accuracy or rate of fire of the Vickers. Though less so than the Vickers, it was still bulky and heavy, as were its ammunition drums. It was rather prone to stoppages and it needed a four-man team to serve it. It was, therefore, not particularly popular with the infantry when first introduced. Yet it could be carried forward in the assault very much more easily than the Vickers. It proved very useful in helping to suppress enemy machine-gun posts during an attack and for beating off early counter-attacks. By 1918 it had become, as one historian has put it, 'the true centre of the platoon's firepower and the pivot of its manoeuvres'.[63]

Table 2.1   *Some Characteristics of British small arms, machine guns and mortars*

WEAPON	DESCRIPTION	APPROX. COMBAT RANGE IN YARDS	NORMAL NUMBER OF ROUNDS PER MINUTE
.455 Webley	Revolver	10	6
.303 Lee Enfield	Rifle	300	5
.303 Vickers	Machine Gun	2,000	250
.303 Lewis	Automatic Rifle	400	100
Mills Bomb	HE Grenade	30	2
Rifle Grenade	HE Projectile	200	1
3-inch Stokes	Light Mortar	400	12
9.45-inch Mortar	Heavy Mortar	1,000	1[64]

By the end of the 1916 battle of the Somme the British infantry platoon had developed, in the wake of its French counterpart, into a sort of miniature combat team, employing a variety of weapons. During 1917 and the first half of 1918 it was often the case that one of the four seven- or eight-man sections in the platoon would consist of specialist rifle grenadiers, another of specialist hand grenadiers and a third of Lewis gunners, leaving only one section expecting to use rifle (traditionally employed) and bayonet as their primary weapons.[65] By the Hundred Days, however, specialist rifle and hand grenade sections had, in theory at any rate, been abolished. By that stage every infantryman was expected to be proficient in the use of the hand grenade and might carry one or two. Specialist rifle grenadiers were integrated into the ordinary rifle sections of which there were at least two in the platoon. Specialist Lewis gun sections, however, of which there could also be two in the platoon, were retained.[66]

Almost as important as the weapons available to the infantry were the assault formations it adopted. Over the course of the war there were debates about whether to attack in a series of extended lines or 'waves' on the one hand or in small flexible columns, sometimes called 'worms', on the other. The creeping barrage artillery tactic was best adapted for use with linear formations. In the Hundred Days the most forward troops would generally arrange themselves in lines or waves while those to the rear would employ artillery formation of sections and platoons in single file. Once beyond the range of the field artillery firing the creeping barrage, and especially once the enemy field fortifications had been penetrated, the infantry would fight forward in any way it could. The best British and Dominion infantry was prepared to be no less flexible than German storm troops in this regard and would use fairly similar tactics.[67]

In terms of keeping casualties down, the shape of attack formations seem to have mattered a good deal less than their density. At least one highly intelligent officer argued, in late 1917, that the BEF was still tending to use excessively dense formations and that this was responsible for unnecessary casualties.[68] Highly dispersed infantry attack but with the support of powerful concentrations of artillery represented efficiency in his view. By the Hundred Days, under the stimulus of manpower shortage and encouraged by the less solid German field fortification normally encountered, British and Dominion forces appear generally to have adopted this philosophy.[69]

In the Hundred Days it was usually not considered necessary to carry bulky and heavy materials to refortify a position as soon as it had been captured. Powerful, determined German counter-attacks were somewhat less likely than they had been earlier in the war. As stubborn trench fighting was less common, it was also reasonable for infantry to carry fewer grenades. Taken together these things meant that attacking British and Dominion troops were not such pack animals as they had been earlier in the war.[70] This, of course, left them with more energy for fighting.

ARTILLERY

The artillery available to the BEF can be divided into four broad categories: horse, field, heavy and anti-aircraft. The Royal Horse Artillery (RHA) was equipped with a light 13-pdr gun. The RHA was of only marginal significance on the Western Front after 1914 and we can virtually ignore it. Anti-aircraft artillery was a new development of considerable importance but mattered somewhat less to the British than to the Germans in the latter part of 1918, as the Allies had a high degree of air superiority and the German Air Service tended to operate over the British side of the lines mainly at a high altitude or at night. The British had 364 anti-aircraft guns on the Western Front at the Armistice, certainly not a large figure for such a big army. Field and heavy artillery are the categories to which we must give most attention. The Royal Field Artillery (RFA) operated the 18-pdr guns and 4.5-inch howitzers which gave the most intimate support to the infantry. Until late 1916 these were all held at divisional level. Additional Army Field Artillery Brigades were then established which could reinforce the firepower available to attacking divisions without robbing others. The heavy artillery held at corps and Army level was operated by the Royal Garrison Artillery (RGA).[71]

The main offensive roles of the field artillery as they emerged in the period of positional warfare 1915–17 were cutting the barbed wire in front of German positions on the one hand and firing 'barrages' on the other. In 1915 and 1916 wire cutting was normally done with shrapnel shell, the type most commonly available at that time. Shrapnel shell was fired so as to burst in the air over the target, propelling downwards a shot-gun scatter of 400 spherical bullets. Though not terribly efficient, wire cutting using shrapnel could work. High explosive (HE) shells fitted with the 106 'graze' fuse, first used on a substantial scale in spring 1917, were, however, more effective. This 106 fuse would explode the shell on very light contact either with the wire itself or with the ground immediately beneath it, stopping the shell from burying itself and thereby wasting much of its explosive force. Given this technology, and provided that the German wire could be observed, the British artillery could quite efficiently cut it to shreds.[72]

The concept of the 'barrage' was not widespread with gunners before 1914. The term derived from the French for barrier and both term and tactical concept were picked up by the RFA from the French Army. Artillery barrages were walls of exploding shells erected between friendly and enemy forces. They could be entirely defensive in character but they also played a vital role in the tactics of the attack. For a trench raid a 'box barrage' could be used to seal off an area of the enemy's defences. In bigger attacks barrages could be programmed to lift from one line of enemy trenches to the next, doing so at the same sort of rate as the infantry were expected to advance. Sometimes known as a 'lifting' or 'jumping' barrage this was the type the British generally used up to the start of the Somme offensive on 1 July 1916.[73]

During the Somme fighting the BEF adopted an improved technique, the 'creeping' barrage. German machine gunners had learned that when a big attack was expected, they were safer in shell holes in front of or between the trenches, rather than in the trenches themselves. Thus they could often survive and remain active, checking the hostile advance. The creeping barrage helped overcome this problem. To an observer at a distance the barrage would appear to creep along the ground – hence its name. In fact it moved forward in a series of short steps or jumps of 50 or 100 yards. The idea was that the whole of the ground over which the infantry was advancing would be swept by fire immediately before they arrived on it. Barrages in general belonged to the category of 'suppressive' or 'neutralising' as opposed to 'destructive' fire. The purpose of a creeping barrage was not so much to kill enemy infantry and machine gunners as to drive them to the bottom of their trenches and shell holes. Allied infantry arriving on their positions immediately after the barrage had passed would then deal with them with grenade, rifle or bayonet. If there had been a considerable interval of time between the barrage passing over a position and the attacking infantry arriving on it, the defenders might have recovered their nerve, resumed their firing positions and recommenced firing. It was thus vital for attacking infantry to stay very close to their barrage – 'hugging' the barrage as it was generally known. Experienced infantry regarded it as necessary to accept some casualties from their own barrage in order to reduce the number inflicted by the Germans.[74]

When first introduced, 'creepers' normally consisted of shrapnel. By summer 1918 a mixture of shrapnel, HE and smoke was normal. Smoke shell, first used by the BEF at the Battle of Arras in April 1917, was a very important innovation in itself and its extensive use became a characteristic of British tactics. A considerable depth (or thickness) was considered an important feature in a barrage and by 1917 there could be as many as seven lines of exploding shells. Infantry had to be taught to hug barrages, in order to derive the maximum benefit from them, but it was also crucial for the barrage to be paced realistically. What was realistic for any particular attack depended on the nature and condition of the ground that the infantry had to traverse and the strength and determination of resistance expected. In the Hundred Days, 100-yard lift every three minutes was considered fairly normal in the early stages of an attack, dropping to 100 yards every four minutes in the later stages, when the infantry might be more tired and the opposition more organised.[75]

Heavy artillery had two main roles: 'counter-battery' fire (shooting at the enemy's artillery) and the bombardment of enemy positions too distant or too well protected to be dealt with by the field artillery. These roles were vital and there was consequently an enormous expansion in the British heavy artillery in the course of the war. The effective fulfilment of its roles was found to require the development of new techniques, some of them unknown before 1914. From an early stage in the war it became very clear that the closest relationship existed between artillery and air power. For the acquisition of distant targets and especially for counter-battery work, artillery spotting by aircraft and aerial photography and photographic interpretation became vitally important techniques. All had become fine arts by summer 1918.[76]

British gunners had realised before the war that indirect fire – firing at targets which could not be seen from the gun position – would be the normal operating method for both heavy and field artillery. But they seem to have expected that most fire would be observed – the fall of shell being reported back to the battery by telephone from an observation post on the ground, from a balloon, or – at the furthest edge of technological possibility – by wireless from an aeroplane. All these methods were in fact used. As things turned out, however, a high proportion of fire, especially at long ranges, could not be observed at all. Possession of convenient high ground could not be guaranteed, nor would fighting always cease when visibility was poor or when the wind was too strong for the aircraft of the period. In major battles telephone lines, unless buried extremely deep, were often cut. Accurate shooting, when fall of shell could not be observed and corrected, was always problematical. But a range of techniques and technologies, developed and refined during the course of the war, made it, within limits, possible.[77]

The first step was to have really accurate maps. None were available for France and Belgium at the start of the war but the BEF made them for its part of the Western Front. Then every time a battery took up a new position careful survey had to be done to ensure that it was accurately plotted on the map – a procedure which applied to both field and heavy artillery. By the Somme offensive of 1916 batteries were normally issued with a 'battery board' – a sheet of gridded paper on a flat zinc or plywood surface on which was indicated the battery's own position, those of important targets and other localities in the vicinity, and bearings from the battery to each of these. But until late 1917 it was not possible for gunners to rely on survey alone to achieve accuracy. Bearings had to be checked and some adjustment made for barrel wear. This was normally done by firing at an observed target and adjusting according to reports received of the fall of shot – a practice known as 'registration'. Once a battery had registered in this way much of its subsequent firing might be unobserved. Several further developments were necessary, however, before accuracy could be achieved without this sort of 'noisy' registration by fire.[78]

Shells of the same calibre varied somewhat in weight and thus behaved differently in flight. Barrel wear reduced muzzle velocity and resulted in shells dropping short. Different guns in the same battery would, owing to different levels of wear, have different muzzle velocities. When fired on the same bearing and elevation they could send their shells to widely differing places. Weather conditions including temperature, atmospheric pressure and humidity, as well as wind speed and direction, could have a marked effect on the flight of a shell, especially at long ranges. Developments in artillery technique during the course of the war helped overcome all these problems. It became standard practice to weigh shells minutely as they left the factory and again in the field and to sort them into batches of practically identical weight. A method was developed of measuring the muzzle velocity of each gun, a process known as 'calibration', and making allowance for this before the gun was fired. By 1918, except in periods of rapid movement, batteries could normally expect to receive several meteorological reports a day and possessed tables to enable them to judge their aim accordingly.[79]

These improvements in accuracy were accompanied by developments in target acquisition. Artillery spotting from aircraft, aerial photography and photographic interpretation – the most important methods for long-range gunnery – were carried out with improved equipment and increasing skill. For counter-battery work two other significant methods, flash-spotting and sound-ranging, were introduced in the course of the war. Flash-spotting was first employed in 1916. Mainly useful at night, the technique involved observers in several precisely plotted positions watching for muzzle flashes from enemy guns and recording the precise time of the sighting, using a device known as a buzzer-board, and also recording its bearing. The position of the enemy battery could then be identified by finding the point at which the bearings intersected. Though still used in 1918, the method's effectiveness had diminished with the German adoption of low-flash propellants the previous year.[80]

Sound-ranging was more complex and used some very sophisticated technology. The basic conception was to pick up, on a number of separate microphones, the report of a gun being fired and to record with great precision the slightly different time it was received at each. The exact position of the microphones and the speed of sound being known, it was possible to locate the battery using trigonometry. In certain conditions very good results could be achieved. The system depended on the wind blowing in the right direction, that is, from the enemy's guns towards the microphones and the prevailing wind on the Western Front – west to east – was unfavourable. It was a technique most effective in relatively quiet times. In major bombardments the sheer volume of data could swamp it. Despite these drawbacks the BEF had established, by August 1918, some 40 sound-ranging sections, each with the manpower of an infantry platoon. The pioneers boasted, perhaps with some exaggeration, that their sections could set up their equipment as rapidly as a battery could establish itself in a new position.[81]

By the autumn of 1917 the British artillery had made gigantic technical strides. Its progress in gunnery, together with developments in other arms, actually gave it the capacity to overcome the entrenched military stalemate on the Western Front. This, however, was far from evident in the closing stages of the Third Battle of Ypres. For much of that battle almost all refinements in gunnery and in the tactics of other arms had been invalidated by the weather and the ground. With atmospheric murk above, a swamp beneath and driving rain in between, nothing worked properly. But, at the opening of the Battle of Cambrai on 20 November 1917 the BEF and especially its artillery put into practice most of what it had learned about the art of war in the previous three years. The artillery demonstrated on a large scale for the first time the important method of 'silent registration'.[82]

Ever since the British had first assumed the offensive under the conditions of entrenched stalemate, at Neuve Chapelle in March 1915, their generals had been concerned to achieve some degree of surprise.[83] As German field fortifications became stronger, especially as the belts of barbed wire grew thicker, this became increasingly difficult. Even using HE and the 106 fuse thick belts of wire could not be gapped adequately without fairly lengthy preliminary bombardments. The possibility of using tanks *en masse* largely solved this problem. Provided they were used on suitable ground they could be relied upon to crush gaps through the wire. This would not, however, obviate the need for a great deal of suppressive artillery fire – both barrage and counter-battery – when the tank/infantry attack started. The additional artillery needed to support the offensive could, of course, be moved in at night and camouflaged before daybreak. But all batteries taking up new positions would have to register. If a large number were registered in the usual way, by firing at observed targets and making necessary adjustments, no matter how carefully this were concealed in the normal pattern of shelling, the element of surprise might be lost. The art of gunnery had, however, developed so far by late autumn 1917 that both barrage and counter-battery fire might be delivered with reasonable accuracy without registration by fire. Persuaded of this, General

Sir Julian Byng absolutely forbade any such shooting by batteries taking up new positions in the Third Army area prior to the Cambrai offensive. All new batteries were ordered to be registered silently, using maps and mathematics. This worked remarkably well, contributing to the fairly high degree of surprise attained on 20 November 1917. It made possible the advance of about four miles achieved in the course of that day.[84]

By November 1917 the BEF's artillery had proved itself capable of generating awe-inspiring 'storms of steel'[85] with reasonable accuracy and no warning. In these respects British gunnery seems to have been the most sophisticated in any army. Just as it was perfecting its art of attack, however, the BEF lost the initiative on the Western Front owing to Russia's virtual collapse and the transfer of large German forces from the East. (Some such forces, arriving fortuitously, helped stop the British offensive in front of Cambrai in November 1917.)[86] Yet, when the British were able to resume the offensive in late summer 1918, their artillery methods proved devastatingly effective. In addition to the refinements of technique discussed above, the BEF's gunners, on the basis of their war experience so far, could normally estimate with reasonable accuracy how many field guns per mile of front would be required to fire a barrage in support of attacking infantry and how many heavy pieces were needed to suppress enemy artillery and troops in fortifications. These things depended on a host of variables, these including the density of German troops on the ground, the extent and sophistication of German field fortifications, the state of German morale, the quality of British intelligence (it being much easier to suppress an enemy if you could precisely locate all his batteries and other key positions) and the weather, which could have an enormous impact on artillery accuracy. Simplistic calculations helped little and rigid rules were not applied. Some highly successful attacks employed fewer guns per yard of front than some notable failures.[87]

British artillery in 1918 also had the luxuries of seemingly limitless quantities of ammunition and of an abundance of guns. Great Britain produced 10,680 guns and howitzers in 1918 alone and there were 6,437 guns and howitzers in battery service on the Western Front at the end of the war. In the final campaign about 30 or 40 per cent of the BEF's fighting personnel were gunners.[88]

Table 2.2 *Some standard British artillery weapons*

WEAPON	TYPE	LEVEL HELD	SHELL WEIGHT IN POUNDS	MAX. RANGE (YARDS)
13-pdr	RHA gun	Cav. Div.	12.5	5,900
18-pdr	Field gun	Inf. Div./Army	18.5	6,525
4.5-inch	Field howitzer	Inf. Div./Army	35	7,300
60-pdr	Long-range gun	Corps/Army	60	12,300
6-inch how.	Howitzer	Corps/Army	100	9,500
8-inch how.	Howitzer	Corps/Army	200	12,300
9.2-inch	Howitzer	Corps/Army	290	13,935
12-inch	Howitzer	Army	750	11,340[89]

ARMOUR

The development of armour in the British armed forces was pioneered by the Royal Naval Air Service in 1914–15. The celebrated Rolls-Royce armoured car, developed from the Silver Ghost touring car, was available by spring 1915. From autumn 1914 until summer 1918, however, armoured cars were of little use on the Western Front. They could not negotiate the shell holes and trenches which scarred the battlefields. In February 1915 the Admiralty, under the direction of Winston Churchill, the First Lord, began the development of the tank as an extension of its work with armoured cars. The culmination of this process – the rhomboidal British heavy tank, first employed in action on 15 September 1916, was produced in several marks. Marks IV and V, in service during the Hundred Days, were capable of about 4 and nearly 5mph respectively.

Heavy tanks were designed to be able to flatten paths through barbed wire, to cross most types of trench and to destroy machine-gun nests either by fire or by crushing. Heavy tanks were produced in 'male' and 'female' versions, males mounting 6-pdr guns as well as machine guns, females machine guns only. They were largely bullet proof but could be destroyed by a direct hit from any form of artillery piece. Ergonomically they were appalling. The tracks were not sprung and crews often had a bone-shaking ride. Interior temperatures could easily rise to 100°F on a summer's day. The atmosphere within was normally thick with petrol fumes and carbon monoxide.[90]

Most of the vehicles the Tank Corps had in early August 1918 were heavy fighting tanks, but there were other types. Some of the older heavy tanks had their guns removed and were converted into Supply tanks, useful for carrying stores forward under fire for other tanks or, indeed, for the infantry. Gun Carrier tanks, originally designed to provide armoured motor transport for field guns, were, in practice, normally used as additional Supply tanks. A few vehicles were modified as Wireless Tanks to carry the heavy radio sets of the period. The Medium A or Whippet was a lighter type introduced in late 1917. Capable of up to 8mph, but only lightly armed, they were designed for pursuit and exploitation. The armoured car made something of a comeback on the Western Front in 1918 as an additional instrument for the same purposes and in August 1918 the Tank Corps had one battalion, the 17th, equipped with them. They were a good deal faster than the Whippets but largely road-bound.[91]

The Tank Corps in August 1918 was organised into five brigades. Brigades had varying numbers of battalions, often three. Battalions consisted of three companies, each of twelve tanks at full strength, divided into three sections of four tanks or four sections of three. The Tank Corps' headquarters administered tanks and tried to develop ideas for their use. In battle, however, tanks came under the command of the infantry formations and units to which they were attached. Effective British tank strength at any time is very difficult to assess. In battle, tanks became casualties at a very high rate. Even when not in battle they frequently developed mechanical problems and spent a good deal of time being repaired or awaiting repair. The maximum number of armoured fighting vehicles that the British ever deployed for action on a single day during this war was the 552 assembled for the Battle of Amiens. The maximum number seeing action on a single day was the 430 engaged on 8 August 1918, the first day of that battle.[92]

In pioneering an entirely new arm the British had shown remarkable ingenuity and considerable faith. The French were, perhaps, no less visionary, but were several months behind the British in getting tanks to the battlefield. They never managed to produce a good heavy breakthrough tank in this war, though, in 1918, their Renault FT light tank proved itself a good machine for relatively open warfare. The Germans did not use tanks at all until spring 1918 and then only in small numbers. Their one production model – the A7V – had very poor cross-country mobility and the Germans tended to achieve better results with captured British models. Captured British tanks in German service outnumbered the A7Vs right through to the Armistice.[93]

The armour the BEF had in August 1918 was a useful addition to its combat power. Together with developments in military airpower, in artillery techniques and in infantry weapons and tactics it made offensive operations somewhat easier than they had been in 1915 or 1916. But it was not capable of operating at a high tempo. Years of further technical and organisational development would be necessary before armoured forces could help bring about a dramatic transformation in the conduct of land warfare.[94]

AIR POWER

Of far greater importance to the BEF than its armour was air power. Haig had been something of an enthusiast for military aviation long before the war and during the war aircraft were always near the top of his list of munitions production priorities. Bombing was vigorously practised by both sides on the Western Front, by day and by night, but it rarely had more than a marginal impact on the conduct of ground operations. Other sorts of air activity were, however, absolutely vital. Aerial reconnaissance was one of the most important means of intelligence gathering – the arts of aerial photography and photographic interpretation being developed almost from scratch in this war. Aerial photography was, as we have noted, crucial to the acquisition of targets for the heavy guns, and aircraft fitted with radio could 'spot' for the artillery – communicating directly with the guns and helping them to bring fire onto the target. Contact patrols by aircraft were vital for reporting the movements of infantry and tanks to the corps and army headquarters trying to command them during major attacks.[95]

Because use of airspace was so valuable, it had to be fought for. Both sides started developing specialist fighters, which in British service were confusingly known as 'scouts', in 1915. For most of the war the Allies, owing to sheer weight of numbers, had air superiority. At two periods of the war, autumn 1915–spring 1916 and autumn 1916–spring 1917, the Allies lost air superiority because the Germans produced fighters which were qualitatively far superior to their own. Especially in the second of these periods, British airmen had suffered heavy casualties.[96] The British seem to have taken these experiences to heart and to have redoubled their efforts in the struggle for air superiority. In 1918 they had the highest proportion of fighters to other aircraft of any belligerent.[97] The standard British fighters of August 1918, the SE5a, the Sopwith Camel and the Sopwith Dolphin were not quite as good as the latest German type, the Fokker DVII.[98] When the Germans flew, moreover, they generally flew in substantial numbers and RAF losses in August and September were to be heavy. In general, however, British numerical superiority more than offset the German qualitative advantage and the British Armies would reap the benefits of air superiority during the Hundred Days.[99]

In the last year of the war both sides made increasing use of fighters for low-flying ground attack. The Germans developed some aircraft especially for this role, some of which were all metal. At the end of the war the British were just introducing a specialist armour-plated ground-attack aircraft – the Sopwith Salamander – but this saw little war service. The principal aircraft that the British used in this role in the Hundred Days, as throughout 1918, was the Sopwith Camel. Generally the role was not popular with Camel squadrons. Exposing aircraft to massed rifle and machine-gun fire from the ground was, of course, extremely dangerous and the danger was thought to be of a more random nature, less influenced by the level of skill of those taking part, than that encountered in air-to-air combat. Experienced fighter pilots who had become flight and squadron leaders were, it was reckoned, almost as likely to be killed as novices. The loss of a few such men could destroy in a day the fighting power of a squadron which may have taken months or years to develop. Yet the moral effect of low-flying attack on enemy ground troops could be substantial enough to make it well worth the effort and the losses in some circumstances.[100]

The establishment of the Royal Air Force as a service quite separate from Army and the Royal Navy, on 1 April 1918, generally made little difference to the way air forces co-operated with the Army on the Western Front. This co-operation was generally of the most loyal and devoted nature. The philosophy of Sir Hugh Trenchard, who commanded the Royal Flying Corps (the principal antecedent of the RAF) on the Western Front was that: 'No call from the Army must ever find the RFC wanting.'[101]

The approach of Major-General Sir John Salmond, who replaced Trenchard on 20 January 1918 and was to command the RAF on the Western Front throughout the Hundred Days, was not essentially different. Like the RFC before it, the RAF's general policy was one of continuous aggressive action, pressed almost regardless of casualties. This was especially evident during the great crisis of the spring when the RFC/RAF committed maximum effort to ground attacks and appears significantly to have slowed the German advance. In terms of reconnaissance, aerial photography, artillery spotting, contact patrols and fighter ground attack the BEF was generally to have, during the Hundred Days, the very best service that atmospheric conditions would allow. These activities were, of course, made possible by the continuous struggle for air superiority in which the fighters were engaged.[102]

On 8 August 1918 the RAF had 1,782 aeroplanes on the Western Front organised in 92 squadrons. Most of these belonged either to one of the five RAF Brigades (normally of between 200 and 300 aircraft) each of which formed an integral part of a BEF Army, or to the IX Brigade, a powerful air power reserve, at the disposal of the RAF's Western Front headquarters, which could be deployed to the most critical areas of the front. There was also the Independent Air Force, a mere 86 aircraft on 8 August, supposed to be for the strategic bombing of Germany but which had in fact been devoting a significant proportion of its effort to hitting German air bases and railway targets in France. The RAF Brigades attached to each of the Armies were, as we have already seen, divided into 'Wings'. Wings consisted of a variable number of squadrons. The numbers of aircraft per squadron also varied considerably, but for fighter squadrons the norm was about 20 aircraft each.[103] There were to be just over 54,000 RAF personnel on the Western Front at the height of the Hundred Days' campaign.[104] But the RAF ended the war with 291,175 personnel worldwide[105] a fact which lends some credence to the view occasionally expressed by Haig that the RAF used manpower rather inefficiently.

CAVALRY

Since late 1914, cavalry on the Western Front had done most of its fighting dismounted. Since pre-war days British cavalry had been well-trained in the use of the rifle, and even the machine gun,[106] as well as the sword. This was fortunate as the continuous front, the high force densities, the firepower of the weapons deployed, and the battlefields scarred by trenches and barbed wire, all combined to diminish the opportunities for mounted action. Yet, owing very largely to Haig's insistence, a Cavalry Corps of three cavalry divisions was still in existence on the Western Front in August 1918. These divisions were of some use as mobile reserves in the fighting of the first half of 1918. In August GHQ hoped they would find a breakthrough to exploit. They were organised into three brigades, each of three regiments, each of three squadrons. Each cavalry division had one brigade of the RHA, with three batteries of six 13-pdr guns, a total of eighteen 13-pdr guns per division. During the period of acute manpower shortage, from the second half of 1917, cavalry had a very low priority for replacements and by the end of the war the whole corps numbered only 14,000 men, barely the strength of the cavalry division in 1914.[107]

In addition to the cavalry of the Cavalry Corps, most infantry corps still retained a cavalry regiment or a squadron or two as 'corps cavalry' to help with screening, reconnaissance, pursuit and exploitation in mobile warfare. There had been so little mobility up to the beginning of 1918 that, in view of the manpower crisis, the War Office had decided to abolish corps cavalry but the decision had not been fully implemented when the German spring offensives began and things became more fluid again.[108]

CHEMICAL WARFARE

After the Germans had used chlorine on 22 April 1915 the British began organising themselves to retaliate and the use of poison gases became a routine part of warfare on the Western Front. The most important method which the Germans used to deliver gas in the last year of the war was the artillery shell. Gas shell accounted for a large part of their total shell expenditure in 1918. Their most effective gas was 'mustard gas', a persistent chemical which, in addition to being potentially lethal when inhaled, could burn any exposed part of the anatomy. Gas shell could be especially effective in the counter-battery role, a fact clearly demonstrated on 21 March 1918. Just having to wear respirators greatly slowed a gun crew's rate of fire even if no member of the crew became a casualty.

The British, in August 1918, did not yet have shell filled with 'mustard', although they had it filled with other gases, notably phosgene. The first major consignment of mustard gas shell reached British forces in the field in late September 1918.[109]

As an agency for the delivery of gas, the British had, in addition to their artillery, the Special Brigade of the Royal Engineers. The Special Brigade's most important weapon in the latter half of the war was the Livens Projector, a sort of crude mortar which could pitch a drum containing about 30lb of gas for about 1300 yards. These weapons, fired *en masse*, could contaminate a large area. They could also be used to fire oil drums which burst into flames on impact. Though the Livens was a weapon best suited to static warfare, it was still useful on occasion up to November 1918.[110]

The fact that they did not have mustard gas shell for most of the Hundred Days put the British somewhat behind the Germans in the offensive aspect of chemical warfare. The British, on the other hand, had a somewhat superior respirator on general issue to their troops and standards of protection against gas thus appear to have been better for British than for German infantry.[111] In the final analysis, while gas added another dimension of fear and unpleasantness to warfare, its casualty-producing power has been much exaggerated and its influence on the course of operations during the Hundred Days was generally small.[112]

INTELLIGENCE

Intelligence was a branch of the art of war in which the British, by 1918, were markedly superior to the Germans. The principal methods of gathering intelligence seem to have been aerial reconnaissance (especially photographic reconnaissance), infantry patrols and raids, prisoner interrogations, and signals intelligence. Signals intelligence included the monitoring of enemy communications, the analysis of traffic patterns, and the breaking of codes and ciphers.[113] Though there was at least one significant intelligence failure in the BEF during the Hundred Days – in the run-up to the Battle of the Selle which opened on 17 October – such occurrences were rare. The British generally had a pretty good idea of what German forces they faced, their strength and their state of morale. For the Germans, on the other hand, the fog of war on the Western Front during the Hundred Days seems to have been a veritable 'pea-souper'. The British valued surprise and went to great lengths to achieve it, employing both tight security measures and quite elaborate deception plans. A fair degree of surprise was, as we shall see, frequently gained, though how far this was due to British skill and how far to German incompetence is difficult to judge. By 1918 the British certainly seem to have been putting better people into intelligence and, perhaps, taking more notice of them, than were the Germans. The British ascendancy over the Germans in intelligence matters, especially in signals intelligence, was, of course, reasserted in the Second World War.[114]

ADMINISTRATION, LOGISTICS AND MILITARY ENGINEERING

Works of military history intended for the general reader seldom devote much space to these essential but unglamorous aspects of the art of war and this can be no exception. But it is necessary, at least, to point out how important these things were. British rear-area services were not, perhaps, in the strict sense 'efficient'. Some commentators thought they used up too much manpower to be given that accolade. In the last two years of the war, however, they were 'amazingly thorough'. The remarks of an eyewitness who was one of the war's ablest historians are worth quoting:

Was there required some new-fangled Lewis gun mounting . . . a message. . . to some workshop . . . brought a hundred in a week. Copies innumerable of an enlarged aeroplane photograph wanted in a hurry for a raid could be printed off . . . in twenty-four hours. The little [corps] press seemed to pour forth up-to-date maps. If there was the slightest hitch about rations it was the topic of conversation for a week. The post-office was an unceasing marvel . . . letters for men in the saps [most forward positions] reached them in two or three days.[115]

The transport system in the BEF's rear was run efficiently enough to permit remarkable concentrations of force to be carried out with speed and secrecy. This was proved in November 1917, at the time of Cambrai, and would be again in preparation for the Amiens battle of August 1918. But for the logisticians and military engineers (or 'sappers', as they were generally called) the biggest challenge of the war was still to come. Could they supply the entire BEF while it was in motion, still consuming massive quantities of rations and munitions, but traversing areas in which the Germans had systematically wrecked the railways and the roads and which they had liberally sown with mines? Could the sappers bridge the numerous rivers and canals in the BEF's path, sometimes in the very van of the attack and under intense fire? Had the answer to either of these questions proved negative there would not have been much of a campaign.[116]

DOCTRINE

Any discussion of the BEF's art of war in 1918 must make some reference to the issue of the formulation and dissemination of military ideas. It has been suggested that whereas the Germans had 'doctrine', continuously revised and updated by assiduous analysis of actual operations, the bumbling British merely had 'dogma' to which their high command adhered in the face of all practical experience. This is a travesty.

The British, like the Germans, analysed all their major operations (and most minor ones) with a view to learning their lessons. At the beginning of the war they had a much smaller number of trained staff officers than the Germans because they had a much smaller army. Yet the wartime Armies improvised by Great Britain and the Dominions were, if anything, even more open to experiment and innovation. All arms made technical and tactical innovations and great effort was put into the dissemination of ideas and methods, especially from the beginning of 1916. Dissemination was conducted by the wide distribution of official pamphlets and by lectures and training courses at a vast number of schools. It has already been indicated that in armour the British were the principal pioneers and that, by the last year of the war, they had the most sophisticated artillery tactics. The tactics and performance of the German storm troops were indeed impressive but the storm battalions were a relatively small elite. In 1918 the majority of German infantry relied on rather crude methods. During the Hundred Days a reasonable level of sophistication in infantry tactics appears to have been more widespread in the British than in the German Army.[117]

HAMEL

The little Battle of Hamel, fought on 4 July, was a virtuoso display of all that the BEF had learned about the art of attack up to the midsummer of 1918. The operation, intended to eliminate a small German salient in the Fourth Army area on the Somme, was carried out by three brigades of the Australian 4th Division (incorporating four companies of the 33rd American Division) attacking on a front of 7,000 yards with the support of 600 guns and about 60 tanks of V Tank Brigade. Tanks and infantry trained together in preparation for the attack. The training helped overcome a prejudice against tanks which the Australians had held since the Battle of Bullecourt (part of the Arras offensive) in April 1917 when tanks tasked to co-operate with them failed to turn up. At Hamel, as at Cambrai, the attackers achieved a very high degree of surprise by dispensing with a preliminary bombardment and by silently registering extra batteries brought in to support the attack. Two-thirds of the 302 heavy guns employed were given counter-battery tasks. The operation began at 03.10. The infantry advanced behind a heavy barrage put down by the field artillery. The tanks, starting immediately behind the infantry, moved up to help them deal with any German infantry or machine gunners still resisting once the barrage had gone over them. Aircraft were used to drop extra ammunition to Australian machine gunners once they had reached their objectives. Though a limited operation, it was a complete success. Some 40 German officers and 1,467 other ranks, 113 machine guns, 23 mortars and one 7.7cm field gun were captured and a lot of other casualties inflicted, for about 1,000 total casualties to the Australians and Americans.[118]

The action at Hamel, though on a small scale, was of great importance. General Sir Henry Rawlinson and his Fourth Army headquarters saw it as a model for a future operation on a much bigger scale and it is to preparations for that operation that we must now turn.

3

PREPARING TO STRIKE

RAWLINSON TAKES COMMAND

At 16.30 on 28 March 1918 General Sir Henry Rawlinson formally took over command of the Fifth Army from General Sir Hubert Gough who had been relieved of his post as a result of the disaster which had befallen his forces in the German 'Michael' offensive. Rawlinson was fortunate in the timing of his appointment which immediately preceded the loss in momentum of the German offensive in this part of the front. On 2 April, Fifth Army was renamed Fourth Army. Somewhat confusingly, a new Fifth Army, commanded by General Sir William Birdwood, was established later in May, and at the beginning of July it took over a section of front straddling the River Lys between Second Army to the north and First Army to the south.[1] Birdwood's Army would play a very minor role in subsequent events. Rawlinson's formation, on the other hand, would be near centre stage for much of the rest of the drama. Its role for the rest of the spring was to defend the vital rail centre of Amiens.[2] For this it was substantially reinforced. In particular Rawlinson gained four of the five Australian divisions and the highly efficient Australian Corps headquarters. On 31 May Lieutenant-General Sir John Monash took command of the Australian Corps. Like Rawlinson, Monash was to play an important role in the campaign of the Hundred Days. By profession he was an engineer, but had been a keen amateur soldier in peacetime. Rather unusually for a senior officer of this period, he was of Jewish descent.[3]

Rawlinson is a central figure in the story of the BEF in 1918. He was from an established and fairly wealthy family; his father, a baronet, was a brilliant linguist and sometime member of the Council of India. Educated at Eton and Sandhurst, Rawlinson had seen much active service before 1914, having fought in the Sudan and in the Second Boer War.[4] He had also excelled in pre-war exercises and was regarded by his peers as distinctly crafty – 'a fox'.[5] In this war, however, he had not yet lived up to the promise of his earlier career. Indeed, he and his Fourth Army headquarters had presided over what, in terms of loss of human life, is still the worst disaster in British military history – some 19,000 fatal casualties being sustained for very little gain of ground at the opening of the great Somme offensive, on 1 July 1916.

One of Rawlinson's salient characteristics appears to have been a high degree of personal ambition, and for much of his First World War career this seems to have been allied to a certain lack of moral courage. In 1916 he had allowed a sensible plan for the opening of the Somme offensive, conceived in his own headquarters, to be overruled by Haig in favour of a much more ambitious and dangerous scheme. Rawlinson's inability to stand up to the misguided interventions of his Commander-in-Chief caused him continuing difficulties throughout the 1916 Somme campaign. Though not disgraced or dismissed when the campaign ended, Rawlinson found himself, probably more by accident than design, on the sidelines for most of the following year. In February 1918 he took over from General Sir Henry Wilson as British Military Representative on the Supreme War Council at Versailles and it was from that appointment that he went on to the defence of Amiens.[6]

Gough's misfortune was Rawlinson's opportunity. He was again in command of an Army and was reunited with the group of senior staff officers which had served him since 1916. These included Major-General A.A. 'Archie' Montgomery, his chief of staff, Major-General C.E.D. 'Buddy' Budworth, his head gunner, Major-General R.U.H. Buckland, his Chief Engineer and Major-General H.C. Holman, his Deputy Adjutant and Quarter-Master General. Undoubtedly Rawlinson drew comfort and support from these long-serving colleagues, some of whom he seems to have regarded as personal friends.[7] They had become a very effective team.

Essentially the same group which had presided over the disaster of 1 July 1916 was about to initiate the greatest series of victories in British military history. Generally the team functioned discreetly – excessively so from the historian's point of view. It would be very interesting to know, for example, how important was the part played by Montgomery in the formulation of Rawlinson's plans, but the documents give few clues.

THE TOP-LEVEL PLANNING

Having secured the defence of Amiens in the spring, after a brief renewal of German offensive efforts in this sector on 24 April, by midsummer Rawlinson was burning with ambition to mount an offensive blow. His Fourth Army consisted, by that time, of two corps: III Corps under Lieutenant-General Sir Richard Butler, with three divisions between the Ancre and the Somme, and Monash's Australian Corps, with four divisions, straddling the Somme.[8]

The immediate stimulus for Rawlinson's scheme for a major BEF offensive in front of Amiens was the high morale and exceptional aggressiveness of his Australian divisions. Australian troops had demonstrated, in a series of relatively minor operations, the extreme weakness of the Germans in this sector. They had played a crucial role in driving the Germans out of the village of Villers-Bretonneux on 25 April and, with the aid of a brigade of tanks, had won a small but convincing victory at Hamel on 4 July. They had also adopted a practice of constantly raiding German positions and gradually eating away portions of the German line, a process they referred to as 'peaceful penetration'. That these small-scale, piecemeal attacks and raids worked so well was perceived by Fourth Army to be proof not only of Australian prowess (which, by this stage in the war, no-one doubted) but also of the inadequacy of German field fortifications and of a serious decline of German morale and fighting efficiency.[9]

On 5 July, immediately after Hamel, Rawlinson made an informal suggestion to Haig for a major offensive in the Fourth Army sector. He was encouraged to develop the idea and on 13 July was instructed by Lieutenant-General Sir Herbert Lawrence, Chief of the General Staff at GHQ, to submit a formal proposal.[10] This he did on 17 July. Rawlinson proposed an operation by 11 BEF divisions, including both the Australian and Canadian corps, the two most cohesive and formidable corps the BEF possessed. The operation was to be mounted on a 19,000 yards front from Morlancourt in the north to Demuin in the south, the attack straddling both the River Somme and the smaller River Luce to its south. (See Map 2.) In Rawlinson's words:

The conditions which obtain on this front at the present time are extremely favourable to the carrying out of a successful offensive. These are:-

(a) *The weakness of the enemy's defences opposed to us. There are no well organized systems of defence. The trenches captured on the 4th July were bad and there was little wire.*

(b) *The poor morale of the enemy's divisions on this front.*

(c) *The moral superiority of the Australian Corps over the enemy during the last three months.*

(d) *The absence at present of any considerable reserves behind the hostile divisions holding the front.*

(e) *The open nature of the country, which renders it particularly favourable for an operation with tanks. This is accentuated by the absence of shell craters and the dry weather of the last few months.*

(f) *The excellence of the observation obtainable from our positions and the good artillery positions that are available (including those now in French hands).*

The advantages of an attack on this front will be:-

(a) Assuring the safety of AMIENS and driving the enemy out of shell range of the town.

(b) The improvement of our position as regards its junction with the French.

(c) The gain of further valuable observation and the improvement of our positions defensively.

(d) The shortening of the Allied front.

(e) The possibility of inflicting a serious blow on the enemy at a time when his morale will be low owing to the failure of the CHAMPAGNE offensive.[11]

The operational method which Rawlinson suggested was quite explicitly based on that used at Hamel. Fundamental to the whole operation was the achievement of a very high degree of surprise. As at Hamel, he intended, from the earliest stages of the planning, to forgo any preliminary artillery bombardment and to rely on a creeping barrage and on counter-battery fire which would open only at Zero hour for the infantry assault.

'As in the case of the attack on July 4th, it is proposed to employ as many fighting tanks as possible, so as to save casualties to the infantry, and also to make full use of any supply tanks that may be available, so as to reduce infantry carrying parties. Whippets will be required for exploiting success'.[12]

Rawlinson proposed that the advance should occur in three stages. The first objective was the so-called Inner Defence Line of the city of Amiens which had been constructed by the French in 1916 and which lay some 1,000–2,500 yards beyond the German front line. This would be the objective of one British division north of the Somme and two Australian divisions and one Canadian division to its south. Having reached their initial objective these troops would stop and consolidate. A further four divisions of the same national composition would then pass through the first four in a 'passage of lines' or 'leap-frog' manoeuvre and go some 3,000 yards further. After a brief pause at this intermediate position, which did not correspond to any particular German defensive line, the same troops would push on to the third objective, the Amiens Outer Defence Line, about 1,000 yards further on. Some tank and infantry exploitation beyond this point was allowed for if circumstances were favourable. And if the operations in the Canadian sector went especially well, Rawlinson considered that 'an opportunity may present itself for the Cavalry Corps to follow them up, cross the LUCE between CAYEUX and DEMUIN and exploit the success in a southerly direction, thus threatening the rear of the enemy facing the French between MOREUIL and MONTDIDIER and capturing their guns'.[13]

GHQ's reaction to Rawlinson's proposals was favourable, although he did not receive a written reply for nearly a week. On 23 July, however, Rawlinson received a note marked *PERSONAL* and *VERY SECRET*:

> *Your plans are approved generally and you should proceed with your preparations as rapidly as possible and submit your requirements in artillery . . .*
>
> *You should, however, not communicate with the G.O.C. French First Army on the subject for the moment until the general lines of co-operation with the French have been finally arranged between The F.M.C.-in-C. and General Foch.[14]*

But Rawlinson's initial plan did in fact undergo a number of revisions. The first major change forced upon him was an increase in French participation, involving a lateral extension of the scope of the attack.

At his headquarters at Bombon Château near Melun, 25 miles southeast of Paris, Foch held conferences with Haig, Pétain and Pershing on 24 and 28 July to plan future offensive action. At these conferences he gave formal sanction to the Amiens operation. But he conceived it merely as one part of a series of counter-offensives intended to clear three important lateral railways running north–south along the Allied front from actual German disruption or the threat of it. The Paris–Avricourt railway in the Marne area, then cut at Château Thierry was to be cleared by the continuance of the French counter-offensive already in progress (now generally known as the Second Battle of the Marne). The Paris–Amiens railway was to be removed from danger by a joint British Fourth and French First Army offensive. Finally the Paris–Avricourt line in the Verdun area would be rendered secure by an American operation against the St Mihiel salient.[15]

Rawlinson had intended the Amiens operation to be mounted by the BEF alone. He had been quite emphatic on that point:

> ... I am strongly averse to the operation being a closely combined Franco-British undertaking. It is almost impossible to keep such an operation secret. Too many persons know about it. Moreover, the decision as regards the time of zero, the actual date of attack, the methods employed, the co-ordination of the barrages, etc., add greatly to the normal difficulties of such an operation and should be eliminated if it [sic] possible to do so.
>
> If the French desire to take part in this offensive, an attack launched from the direction of MONTDIDIER will lead to far greater strategical results. This would not entail close co-ordination of times, dates, barrages, etc., as would be the case if the two Armies were operating side by side, and should, therefore, offer no serious difficulties.[16]

While Foch consented to Rawlinson's request that Fourth Army's front be extended some 7,000 yards into what had been the trenches of General Debeney's French First Army, to its south (thus placing Fourth Army on both sides of the River Luce) he also insisted that the part of Debeney's Army north of the River Avre co-operate directly with Fourth Army, attacking alongside it, as opposed merely to protecting its flank or mounting a diversionary effort. In order to minimise any difficulties in co-ordination that this might occasion, Foch decided to place Debeney under Haig's command during the planning and execution of the Amiens attack.[17]

Foch also forced one further change. The operation was now to be mounted on 8 August, two days earlier than originally intended. Foch wanted to maintain the pressure on the Germans who were then in retreat in the Champagne region. Rawlinson heard about this change only at 18.45 on 28 July. The logistical and administrative difficulties of mounting an operation on this scale were enormous. The curtailing of carefully worked out timetables at this point necessitated Herculean labour, especially in the transport and dumping of ammunition. Rawlinson's consent to the change appears to have been obtained only by the direct insistence of GHQ.[18]

A final alteration in the concept of operations was insisted upon by Haig on 5 August, a mere 72 hours before the operation was due to begin. In a visit to Fourth Army headquarters, Haig insisted that if the operation went well, reserves should be pushed as far as the line Chaulnes–Roye, five miles beyond the Amiens Outer Defence Line which was Rawlinson's ultimate objective. The general line of advance should be in the direction of Ham, a further 15 miles away.[19] This belated attempt to convert a limited, opportunistic attack into a dramatic breakthrough operation was rather typical of Haig's generalship up to this point in the war. But unlike some of his earlier efforts to expand the scope of operations it had no adverse practical result. Fourth Army could (and did) treat it merely as an injunction to be prepared for a deeper exploitation if the initial attack went better than expected. It necessitated no fundamental change in the basic plan.

EFFORTS TO ACHIEVE SURPRISE

The success of the operation was heavily dependent on gaining a very high degree of surprise. Fourth Army's intelligence believed it confronted seven German divisions, most of them depleted and of low quality, all belonging to the German Second Army under General von der Marwitz, between the Luce and Albert. As Fourth Army would not be attacking on the whole of its front on 8 August it would initially expect to engage six German divisions. As the Canadians pushed south of the Luce they could expect to encounter a seventh. The Germans still had substantial reserves available and even if complete surprise were achieved on 8 August, it was estimated that they would be able to throw another eight divisions into the battle by the evening of 11 August. (This turned out to be an underestimate.)[20] The planners believed that if the Germans got wind of the offensive a day or two in advance, its prospects would be utterly wrecked. Even a few hours' notice might allow them to shift guns, drastically reducing the effect of British counter-battery work.

One aspect of the effort to achieve surprise was sheer secrecy. Formal operations orders were issued relatively late. What would today be called the 'need-to-know principle' was scrupulously observed:

At the first conference held by Sir Henry Rawlinson on July 21st at Fourth Army Headquarters at Flixecourt only the Chief Staff Officer and Artillery Commander of the Fourth Army and the Commanders and Chief Staff Officers of the Canadian and Australian Corps, together with a representative of the Tank Corps were present. Subsequent conferences were held every few days, but in different places, so that the constant gathering of commanders would be less likely to attract attention. The numbers attending the conferences gradually increased as the date of the attack approached and it became necessary for more officers to be consulted. The principle followed was for staffs and formations to be informed as late as possible, but in sufficient time to ensure that complete preparations could be made.

The GHQ operations order was issued only on 29 July and the Fourth Army orders in instalments between 31 July and 5 August. The infantry divisions to take part in the attack were told nothing until 31 July. The troops in the firing line were not briefed until about 36 hours before Zero.[21]

The obsession with secrecy was made explicit in the first part of the Fourth Army operations order, issued on 31 July:

(a) *It is of the first importance that secrecy should be observed and the operation carried out as a surprise.*

   Commanders will take all possible steps to prevent the scope or date of the operation becoming known except to those taking part. Any officer NCO or man discussing the operation in public or communicating details regarding it to any person, either soldier or civilian, not immediately involved will be severely dealt with.

(b) *All movements of troops and transport in an easterly direction will take place by night, whether in the forward or the back areas of the Fourth Army, on or after 1 August, except when absolutely necessary to move by day.*

(c) *G.O.C., 5th Brigade R.A.F. will arrange with corps for aeroplanes to fly over Fourth Army area during days when flying is possible and to report to Corps H.Q. any abnormal movement of troops or transport within our lines.*

(d) *Work on back lines will be continued as at present so that there may be no apparent change in our attitude.*

(e) *The Canadian Corps and divisions in reserve to III Corps will not open any wireless stations until after Zero.*

(f) *Commanders will ensure that the number of officers reconnoitring the enemy's positions is limited to those for whom such reconnaissance is essential.*

   Nothing attracts attention to an offensive more than a large number of officers with maps looking over the parapet and visiting OPs.

   Commanding officers of units holding the front line should report at once to higher authority any disregard of these orders.[22]

In order to drum in the basic message a small notice, headed with the clear imperative 'KEEP YOUR MOUTH SHUT', and inveighing against careless talk, excessive inquisitiveness and giving out more than name, rank and serial number if captured, was issued to all ranks.

Very tight control was also exercised over the movement of civilians. This was made easier by the fact that the city of Amiens had been evacuated in March at the height of the German offensive and a 'Forbidden Zone' established in Fourth Army's rear. Access to this area was tightly controlled by French military police and the few civilians who were allowed to remain had to carry passes. Their movements were tightly controlled by British military police.[23]

An intense preliminary artillery bombardment was, as at Cambrai and Hamel, to be forgone. Right up to Zero hour the pattern of artillery activity was intended to appear absolutely normal to the enemy:

Active counter-battery work and harassing fire will be maintained.

Such registration as is necessary should be carried out under cover of this fire. The necessity for concealing the increase in the number of guns on the Army front must be borne in mind, and on no account should a large number of guns be employed at any one time . . . Normal fire should, so far as possible be carried out from positions other than the permanent position of batteries.[24]

In contrast with Third Army's preparations for the attack towards Cambrai on 20 November 1917, it was neither necessary nor desirable for Fourth Army to register silently all the new batteries moving into its area in early August 1918. Up to November 1917 the Cambrai sector had been exceptionally quiet. The Amiens sector was not like that and as Archibald Montgomery, Rawlinson's chief of staff, explained in his account of the campaign:

In order to support the advance of the infantry with a creeping barrage accurate registration of the supporting artillery is essential, and, however carefully guns may be calibrated and their position resected, it is always advisable to check calculation with a few rounds in order to ensure that there shall be no error. In consequence programmes were carefully worked out giving the times at which guns should fire and the numbers of rounds to be fired, so that even though the amount of artillery in the line had been doubled, the enemy should not appreciate it.[25]

But while the artillery of III Corps and the Australian Corps was able to employ the 'disguised registration' method which Montgomery describes above, owing to the special secrecy attached to the movement of the Canadian Corps into the Fourth Army area and to the late positioning of its guns, Canadian artillery was obliged to register silently.[26]

One way in which the Germans could have been alerted to the imminence of an Allied offensive in this sector was by aerial reconnaissance. Fortunately for Fourth Army the RAF had established a marked air superiority in the Amiens area for several weeks before the opening of the battle. The RAF's task seems to have been made easier in this respect by the involvement of a high proportion of German air power in the fighting in the Champagne area further south. Few German reconnaissance machines were active in the Amiens area and even fewer managed to cross British lines. When they did, they were prevented by the activity of the Fourth Army anti-aircraft defence and by RAF air patrols from taking many useful photographs. Yet Rawlinson took no chances and continued to insist on the most thorough camouflage and on confining virtually all forward movement to the hours of darkness.[27]

Secrecy, camouflage, the maintenance of air superiority and the continuation of an apparently normal pattern of activity were not, however, the only methods employed to achieve surprise. Much effort was also devoted to deception. This was of particular importance in relation to the redeployment of the Canadian Corps, the trickiest single problem in the maintenance of the security of the operation. The Canadians were perhaps the most powerful, cohesive corps in the BEF as well as the most tactically and technically innovative.[28] They had a formidable, totally justified, reputation as shock troops. The fact that they had hardly been engaged during the German offensives earlier in the year, and were thus exceptionally well rested and battle-fit, gave them an even greater importance in the general scheme of things.[29]

In late July the Canadian Corps was part of First Army. It had two divisions resting and two in the line. The divisions in the line had only recently entered it. Their quick withdrawal would be likely to ring alarm bells with German intelligence. In order to confuse the enemy as to its intentions for the Canadian Corps, GHQ sent two Canadian battalions, two Canadian casualty clearing stations and both Canadian and Tank Corps wireless sections to the Second Army front. They were positioned in the vicinity of Kemmel Hill, an important tactical feature, captured by the Germans in their 'Georgette' offensive, which the Germans would undoubtedly expect the BEF to try to retake. These two Canadian battalions were to be ordered 'to prepare the front for attack pending the arrival of the remainder of the Canadian Corps'. Clearly GHQ was quite prepared to deceive its own troops in order to make its deception of the enemy the more convincing – the Canadian battalions concerned were supposed actually to believe that they were preparing an assault on Kemmel Hill.[30] But GHQ did not place all its deception eggs in the basket of a Kemmel Hill attack. Its policy seems to have been to mystify and mislead the enemy by suggesting a number of threatening scenarios, including an attack in the First Army area in front of Arras:

> *The First Army will arrange to locate and operate one Cavalry Wireless Set behind the ARRAS front.*
>
> *The First Army will also arrange for training to be carried out with one Tank Battalion behind the ARRAS front in daylight. No particular care should be taken to camouflage the Tanks of this Battalion when not in use.*
>
> *Wireless sets of Reserve Divisions in the Third and First Armies will be set up and operated behind the ARRAS front. Wireless sets*

of Reserve Divisions in the Second Army will be set up and oper-
ated behind the KEMMEL front. The wireless activity of all other
reserve formations will cease forthwith.

First and Second Armies will make no attempt to conceal move-
ments of M.T. columns and troops in an easterly direction.

All movements out of the areas of these Armies will, as far as
possible be carried out at night.[31]

The apparent threat to Kemmel Hill and the apparent build-up in the Arras area might be relied upon to confuse the Germans in the short run. But the Canadians would be arriving in rear areas of Fourth Army from the end of July. Fourth Army HQ was not certain that this fact could be kept secret. It would, as Archibald Montgomery, Fourth Army's historian, indicates, inevitably 'become known to a large number of junior officers and other ranks of the administrative services and railways who must necessarily assist in the move'.

It is indicative of the subtlety of thought and the awareness of human nature which commanders and senior staff officers of the BEF had achieved by this stage in the war that Fourth Army did not rely on its own 'KEEP YOUR MOUTH SHUT' instructions, clear, explicit and menacing as these were. There was, indeed, an assumption that they would be violated. As Montgomery puts it, it was taken for granted that, amongst administrative and transport officers concerned with the move of the Canadian Corps, there was 'bound to be a great deal of discussion as to the object of the movement, and rumours of it might reach the enemy through his secret service in time to give him warning'. This made a further 'cover story' necessary. General Foch had asked that a British corps be held in reserve west of Amiens behind the junction of the British Fourth and the French First Armies. XXII Corps, which had been carrying out this role until recently, had now been sent south to assist the French. The story fostered by Fourth Army was that the Canadian Corps, together with a brigade of tanks, an RAF squadron and some additional heavy artillery, was being moved in to replace XXII Corps as part of a powerful Allied reserve for this critical sector of the front. But complete reliance was not placed on that story either. As Fourth Army's historian puts it:

> At the same time, in order to cause confusion of thought, a rumour, previously in circulation, that the Canadian Corps would relieve the Australian Corps was not denied. The result of all these conflicting reports was that opinion in England and at the bases was about equally divided between Ypres, Arras and Champagne as the destination of the various reinforcing formations but whether they were for offensive or defensive purposes was not known.[32]

THE CONCENTRATION OF FORCE

Between 27 July and 10 August numbers of men and horses in the Fourth Army nearly doubled, rising from 257,567 of the former and 54,323 of the latter to 441,588 and 98,716 respectively.[33] On the eve of the offensive, Fourth Army consisted of:

Canadian Corps: Commanded by Lieutenant-General Sir Arthur Currie
1st, 2nd, 3rd and 4th Canadian Divisions

Australian Corps: Commanded by Lieutenant-General Sir John Monash
1st, 2nd, 3rd, 4th and 5th Australian Divisions

III Corps: Commanded by Lieutenant-General Sir Richard Butler. 12th, 18th, 47th and 58th Divisions with 33rd American Division attached

Cavalry Corps: Commanded by Lieutenant-General Sir Charles Kavanagh. 1st, 2nd and 3rd Cavalry Divisions

V Brigade RAF 15th (Corps) Wing, six corps squadrons
22nd (Army) Wing, eight fighter squadrons, two bombing squadrons
1 fighter reconnaissance squadron

	1 day bomber squadron
	1 night bomber squadron
3rd, 4th and 5th Brigades, Tank Corps	Eight battalions of Mark V tanks, two of Mark V*, two of Medium As (Whippets) and one of armoured cars.

Of these forces the whole of the Canadian Corps, the 1st Australian Division, two of the three divisions of the Cavalry Corps, 3rd and 4th Tank Brigades and six additional RAF squadrons had all been brought into the Fourth Army during this period. In addition to the formations mentioned above, the 63rd (Royal Naval) Division, the 17th (Northern) Division and the 32nd Divisions were assembled close behind the battle front as a general reserve. By 8 August the 63rd Division was behind the III Corps, the 17th Division behind the Australian Corps and the 32nd Division behind the Canadian Corps.[34]

Fourth Army's artillery had been roughly doubled from about 1,000 to just over 2,000 barrels. According to Budworth, Fourth Army's chief gunner, on 8 August there were some 1,292 field guns and field howitzers in the Army, 672 heavy guns of various types, and 40 AA guns. His detailed breakdown of the Army's artillery assets was as follows:

18-pdrs	–	954
13-pdrs, RHA	–	56
4.5-inch hows	–	282
60-pdrs	–	144
6-inch hows	–	336
8-inch hows	–	90
9.2-inch hows	–	54
6-inch guns	–	40
12-inch howz	–	6
12-inch gun	–	1
340-mm French gun	–	1
A.A. guns	–	40[35]

There was a field gun or field howitzer every 29 yards of the front on which the Fourth Army attacked, and a heavy gun or howitzer every 59 yards. The Germans were thought to have about 680 guns which would be in position to engage Fourth Army forces taking part in the attack, though only some 530 of these were directly to Fourth Army's front.[36]

The concentration of Allied air power for this offensive was also impressive. The RAF's V Brigade, under Brigadier L.E.O. Charlton, was an integral part of Fourth Army. For this operation it was to have a strength of 332 aircraft. It was to be mainly responsible for close support of Fourth Army's advance and monitoring its progress by means of contact patrols. Attacks on more distant targets, enemy airfields and the railway system behind the stretch of front attacked, were to be mainly the responsibility of IX Brigade, the RAF's headquarters brigade, which for this offensive had 294 machines. The III Brigade and some squadrons of other brigades were also made available. A total of 800 RAF aircraft were thus ready to be employed in the offensive, including 376 fighters, 73 fighter reconnaissance machines, 147 day bombers and 110 Corps aeroplanes. To these can be added 1,104 aircraft placed at the disposal of General Debeney commanding French First Army. The Germans had only some 365 aircraft immediately available to oppose them on this sector of the front, the greatest concentration of German air power being in the Champagne area where they had 850 aircraft, of which 430 were single-seater fighters.[37]

Also playing a significant part in tipping the balance against the Germans on the first day of the offensive was the Tank Corps which assembled for the attack ten battalions of heavy tanks (Mark Vs and Mark V*s) with 342 machines between them, plus two battalions of Medium A Whippets with 72 machines between them and 120 supply tanks: 534 tanks altogether, to which must be added the battalion of armoured cars. If the Germans had any armour at all on the front of the attack it does not appear to have participated in the battle.[38]

CORPS REDEPLOYMENT

Getting the corps properly deployed for the attack was no easy matter. Rawlinson had always intended that Fourth Army should take over a 7,000-yard stretch of front from French First Army, this ground being taken over by the Australian Corps in the first instance. To compensate the Australians for this southward extension of the Corps boundary, III Corps would also extend its boundary southward, relieving the Australians as far south as the Somme. In order to achieve complete surprise it was vital that the Canadian Corps should not move into the front line before Z, yet the Canadians still had to be properly deployed for the attack and to be able to pass through the existing Fourth Army front without difficulty.

On the night of 31 July, III Corps relieved the Australians as far south as the Somme. On that night and the following night, the Australians took over from the French the stretch from Monument Wood, just south of Villers-Bretonneux, to the Amiens–Roye road. The Canadian Corps was moved into position behind the 4th Australian Division, on Fourth Army's extreme right, between 4 and 7 August, but the front line continued to be held by 13th Australian Brigade, spread very thinly across this sector. This brigade was not relieved by the Canadians until 02.10 on 8 August, a little more than two hours before zero. It then went to join 1st Australian Division which had only just arrived in Fourth Army's area on 7 August and which was to form the Australian Corps' reserve.[39]

THE GROUND IN DETAIL

Rawlinson had mentioned in his original proposal to GHQ on 17 July that the ground for the offensive was generally open and good going for tanks. But the scope of the operation had been considerably expanded since then, the attack front having been widened from 19,000 yards to 30,000 yards. The ground to be traversed was now more variable. The frontage now extended from the River Ancre in the north to near Moreuil in the south, Fourth Army's attack sector being from the Ancre to the Amiens–Roye road inclusive, with the French First Army operating to the south of the road. The ground in the centre of the attack sector, the wide plateau between the Somme and the Luce, presented few difficulties. It was generally flat and open, the only possible physical obstacles being villages and woods scattered at wide intervals. Even the nature of the buildings in the villages was reasonably favourable to an attacker, as many were flimsily constructed and did not lend themselves naturally to defence. It was over this favourable ground that the attack of the Australian Corps and that of the 1st and 2nd Canadian Divisions was to be mounted.

To the south lay the valley of the Luce. This was a small stream but, owing to extensive marshes on both sides, it was potentially a considerable obstacle. There was only one intact bridge within German lines, that being in the village of Demuin. The attack of the Canadian 3rd Division, the most southerly division of the Canadian Corps, would straddle the Luce and would also include the relatively high ground to the south of that stream, between it and the Avre. This last was vital ground which it was most important to capture quickly.

But in general the most difficult ground was that in the III Corps' sector to the north of the Somme. The plateau between the Ancre and the Somme was fairly smooth and without natural obstacles between the British front line and the woods of Tailles and Gressaire. But from then on the southern slopes of the plateau going down to the Somme are steep and the ground broken by pronounced gullies. This ground was recognised as being very poor going for tanks. Much of it could also be commanded by the Germans from the high ground of the Chipilly Spur in a bend of the River Somme immediately to the east.[40]

THE FINAL PLAN FOR THE INFANTRY ATTACK

For the attack of 8 August the Amiens Outer Defence Line, the ultimate objective for the Australian and Canadian Corps, was marked on operations maps as the Blue Line in the Australian sector and as the Dotted Blue Line in the Canadian sector. It was between 10,500 and 14,000 yards from the start line. Even if German resistance turned out to be weak any body of troops was bound to become tired if they tried to cover all of this distance in a single day's attack. Fourth Army had thus always intended to do the operation in a series of three bounds, with pauses for consolidation after each.

In the final version of the plan the first bound varied from 3,500 to 4,000 yards. This was about the limit to which the field artillery could deliver an effective creeping barrage and if a rapid advance could be made to this depth, much of the field artillery that the Germans had in the attack sector would be overrun. The limit of the first bound was marked on operations maps as the Green Line. At this point there was to be a two-hour pause. A protective barrage would be put down in front of the Green Line while forces which had hitherto been in reserve would catch up. These reserves would then 'leap-frog' to make the next bound of between 2,000 and 5,000 yards. The limit of the second bound was chosen with the needs of defence in mind. Known as the Red Line, it would be a 'favourable line for consolidation should further advance on the first day prove impossible'. If German resistance were not too intense at this point, however, it was intended that the same troops should push on quickly to the final objective.

While the basic plan was made at Army level, the corps commanders were allowed some latitude in how they performed the leap-frog manoeuvre and in arranging the detail of the artillery fire-plan in their sectors. With regard to the leap-frog, the Australians and Canadians intended to do things slightly differently. The Australian approach was, in general terms, the simpler. Two divisions, 2nd and 3rd Australian, would conduct the initial assault. The 5th and 4th Australian Divisions would leapfrog 2nd and 3rd respectively at the Green Line.

To their south the approach of the Canadians was a little more complex. In the northern half of the Canadian sector the initial attack was to be carried out by two divisions: 2nd Division in the north and 1st in the centre, both to attack on narrow fronts. The leap-frog at the Green Line would be performed by brigades within these divisions. For the initial attack astride the Luce, however, and in the difficult ground between the village of Demuin and Rifle Wood, the Canadian Corps Commander, Lieutenant-General Currie, felt that a single divisional commander needed to take control. This job was given to Major-General L.J. Lipsett of 3rd Canadian Division, elements of this division being assigned to perform the first two bounds, involving the capture of both the Green and the Red Lines. The 4th Canadian Division would then take over and push on to the Blue Line.

One of the refinements of the Canadian Corps plan was to be the employment of an 'Independent Force' under Brigadier-General Brutinel, the commander of the intensely innovative Canadian Machine Gun Corps. 'Brutinel's Force', as it was also referred to, consisted largely of machine guns mounted in light trucks and a section of medium trench mortars mounted in lorries. Its role was to pass through the 3rd Canadian Division and secure the Canadian Corps' flank along the Amiens–Roye road between the second and third objectives. If circumstances were favourable it was then to assist the cavalry in exploitation beyond the third (Blue Line) objective.

The III Corps' role in the offensive was very much more limited than that of the other two corps. In reality, its attack seems to have been designed to do little more than offer flank protection for the main thrust south of the Somme. Owing to the difficulty of the ground in this sector only one tank battalion was provided. It was not intended that the III Corps should attempt to get to the Amiens Outer Defence Line on the first day as the other corps were to do. The III Corps was to carry out a two-phase attack. In the first phase the leading brigades of the 18th Division and the 58th Division, the latter on the right, with the Somme between it and the Australians, were to take the first (Green Line) objective which included the village of Sailly Laurette and Malard Wood. During a pause on the Green Line it was intended that a brigade 'leap-frog' take place. Two brigades, one from each division, would then push on to take the second and final (Red Line) objective for the day which was to include the commanding ground of the Chipilly Spur, Gressaire Wood and the southern portion of Tailles Wood. To the north there would be a subsidiary attack by the 12th Division which would envelop the village of Morlancourt from the north while elements of 18th Division enveloped it from the south.[41]

THE FIRE-PLAN

In view of the need for a very high degree of surprise, and in keeping with the Hamel model, there was to be no preliminary bombardment, the pattern of artillery fire before Zero hour remaining absolutely normal. The Fourth Army artillery instruction stipulated that, from Zero, a minimum of two-thirds of the available heavy artillery (672 barrels) should be employed firing a counter-battery programme. Of the remainder, part was to be used to bombard identified strong points (though there were few enough of those) and part to fire a sort of longer-range barrage to intercept German troops fleeing from the field artillery's 'creeper'. The exposure of III Corps' northern flank was a source of some anxiety, as there was to be no offensive north of the Aisne. Fourth Army's staff decided to use 60-pdr guns to put down a protective barrage on that flank.

The timing of the creeping barrages fired by the field artillery's 18-pdrs was to be arranged by III Corps north of the Somme, between the Somme and the Luce by the Fourth Army centrally, and south of the Luce by the Canadian Corps. For the Australian Corps the procedure was as follows:

All Field Artillery lifts will be 100 yards.
The Field Artillery barrage will come down at Zero 200 yards beyond the infantry tape line [i.e. the start line for the infantry attack].

The first two lifts will be at Zero + 3 and Zero + 5.
The next eight lifts will be at 3-minutes interval.
From the eleventh lift until the green line [the first objective] *is reached, lifts will be at 4-minute intervals.*
A protective barrage will be maintained in front of the green line until Zero + 4 hours, after which all barrages will cease.[42]

The variations in the frequency of lifts were owing to careful calculations of the speed at which it was believed the infantry would be able to cover particular stretches of ground which would in turn partly depend on the resistance they were likely to meet and partly on how tired they were. In order that the attacking infantry should receive adequate artillery support during their advance beyond the Green Line 'minute arrangements were made for pushing forward artillery units after Zero. Roads and tracks were allotted and preparations made for bridging trenches rapidly.' A few field artillery units were not to be employed in the barrage at all so that they could be limbered up and ready to dash forward. Others were to limber up as soon as their part in the barrage was complete.

The natures of ammunition to be used were left to the corps. In their creeping barrages the III Corps and the Canadian Corps were to employ mainly shrapnel, the Australians a mixture of shrapnel and HE. Some smoke shell was also to be used both as part of the creeping barrages and to create smoke screens in particular localities. For the counter-battery programme HE shell with the 106 'graze' fuse was the type employed.[43]

THE AIR PLAN

On 1 August, Major-General Sir John Salmond, commanding the RAF in France, submitted a general plan to Haig for the use of the substantial amount of air power concentrated for this offensive. As with the Army's so with the RAF's planning, much emphasis was placed on concealment and deception. To attract German attention to Flanders additional aerodromes were to be occupied in the Second Army area and air activity in that vicinity was to be stepped up. Aircraft flights on the night of 7/8 August were to be used to drown the noise of assembling tanks. At dawn on 8 August RAF bomber squadrons supported by fighters would attack nearby German aerodromes. Fighter squadrons would afterwards stand-by to operate on the Fourth Army front if German air activity became important. It was considered that German reinforcements were unlikely to reach the area before evening. Railway stations at Chaulnes and Péronne would then be bombed in order to disrupt them.

The section dealing with the RAF in Fourth Army's 'General Instructions' specified that each corps, including the Tank Corps and the Cavalry Corps, would have a squadron allocated to contact patrol work. The Tank Corps had the 8th Squadron which had been specially trained for co-operation with tanks. The eight fighter squadrons of the V Brigade's 22nd Wing would be 'exclusively employed in engaging ground targets by bombing and machine gunning on the whole Army front'. The fighters of the IX Brigade RAF were to 'maintain constant patrols at height over the front of attack' and were to be assisted in this by those of the III Brigade if necessary.[44]

ALLOCATION OF HEAVY TANKS

Of the ten battalions of heavy tanks available, four were allotted to the Canadian Corps, four to the Australian Corps, one to the III Corps and one kept in Army reserve. Each of the four divisions taking part in the Australian Corps' attack was supplied with 20–30 Mark V tanks. Each of the two second echelon divisions, the 5th Australian Division on the left and the 4th Australian Division on the right was also supplied with half a battalion of Mark V* tanks. The Australian Corps was also allotted, for exploitation, the one battalion of armoured cars available. The Canadians allotted a battalion of Mark Vs to each of their leading divisions, from north to south: the 2nd, 1st and 3rd Canadian Divisions. A battalion of

Mark V*s was allotted to the 4th Canadian Division which was in echelon behind the 3rd. The Mark V*s were a lengthened and roomier version of the Mark V. They were not very manoeuvrable and therefore not a very good fighting machine. Their role in the coming operation was to carry machine-gun teams forward under armour to help consolidate the ground won.[45]

THE CAVALRY AND THE WHIPPETS

The cavalry role was to pass, as soon as seemed possible, through the leading elements of the Canadian and Australian Corps and to secure the Amiens Outer Defence Line ahead of the infantry. If all went well up to that point, there was to be further exploitation in a south-easterly direction towards Roye and Chaulnes in an effort to cut the communications of German forces facing the French First Army. Lessons had clearly been learned from Cambrai, when the cavalry was held so far back that the almost inevitable failures of communication made the seizure of fleeting opportunities practically impossible. To avoid such waste of opportunity in the Amiens operation the 3rd Cavalry Division was placed temporarily under the command of the Canadian Corps and one brigade of the 1st Cavalry Division was put under the Australian Corps. Once these bodies of cavalry had passed through the infantry they were again to come under the command of the Cavalry Corps. The two battalions of Whippet tanks were put under Cavalry Corps command, but from each battalion one company of 16 tanks was to accompany the leading troops of the 1st and 3rd Cavalry Divisions, thus coming under the Australian and Canadian Corps commanders respectively at the start of the battle.[46]

CO-OPERATION WITH THE FRENCH

As Rawlinson had foreseen, co-operation with the French proved difficult. The opening of the offensive was to be synchronised along the entire Fourth Army front. General Debeney, however, did not believe it possible for First French Army to fit in with this precisely. The French were unwilling to attack on their front without a preliminary artillery bombardment, albeit a relatively short one. One of the reasons for this seems to have been that they had few tanks available to assist them though there may have been more to it than that. Had French artillery opened fire ahead of Fourth Army's Zero this would obviously have alerted the Germans in the whole area east of Amiens and largely wrecked Fourth Army's chances of surprise. The French, therefore, were to launch their infantry attack 40 minutes after Fourth Army's Zero. This was finally set for 04.20 – an hour before sunrise – in order to allow the attacking troops to break the crust of the German defence in darkness.[47]

ALARMS AND EXCURSIONS

On 3 August a German raid overran an Australian post near Hourges on the Amiens–Roye road at Fourth Army's junction with French First Army. A sergeant and four men were captured. Fourth Army HQ was worried that the Germans would be warned of the impending onslaught. Careful inquiries as to the extent of the knowledge these men were likely to possess, indicated, however, that they knew nothing. They had recently been overheard discussing the long spell which they expected to spend on their present stretch of front which, indeed, they had taken over from First French Army only about three days previously.[48]

Much more serious was an attack on 6 August by the high quality 27th Württemberg Division, a formation which had been sent to the German Second Army from the Lille area to stop the rot caused by Australian 'peaceful penetration'. The attack was made south of Morlancourt, shortly after dawn, against positions which the Australians had captured on 29 July. At the time of the attack this sector was in the hands of the 18th (Eastern) Division of the III Corps which had taken it over from the Australians on the night of 31 July. The 18th Division was in the process of carrying out an inter-brigade relief, always an awkward moment to be hit. Delivered on a 4,000 yard front, the attack penetrated in places to a depth of 700 yards and captured around 200 prisoners. It was not possible for the planners at Fourth Army HQ to say precisely what the sum total of the knowledge about the impending offensive of all these people actually was, still less to assess what they might give away under interrogation. It was a big worry. No operation on this scale could be mounted without accepting some risks, however, and preparations continued. But quite apart from its implications for secrecy, the German attack of 6 August significantly dislocated III Corps' preparations for the offensive. An 18th Division counter-attack the following morning regained much of the lost ground and captured 70 Germans. But these actions forced late changes to the plans for the offensive in this sector – the infantry start-line and the barrage had to be rearranged. Just as seriously, the 18th Division's 54th Brigade, which had been intended to lead the 18th Division's attack on 8 August, was so exhausted by the fighting on 6 and 7 August, that it could not be used, and 18th Division had to borrow the 36th Brigade from the 12th Division as a last-minute substitute.[49]

FORMING UP

Getting into position for the big attack was a particular problem for the tanks. The forward move of the tanks from the 'tankodromes' where they were based on first arrival in the Fourth Army area to their assembly positions for the attack was conducted in two stages. On the night of 6 August they were deployed to their 'preparatory positions' about three miles behind the front line. This was a move the tanks had to make across country, under their own power and at night. It was thus vital that their routes were very carefully reconnoitred beforehand. In some cases white tape was laid to guide their drivers. The same applied to the tanks' moves to their assembly positions, about 1,000 yards behind the front line, carried out on the night of 7 August just a few hours before Zero. So thoroughly were these moves organised by the Tank Corps that virtually all the tanks arrived in their correct positions on time. It was thought inevitable that the noise of the movement of so many tanks would be detected by the Germans unless special efforts were made to conceal it. The RAF had promised to fly low over the area for this purpose but on the night of 7 August flying conditions were particularly bad. Only one pilot, Lieutenant G.A. Flavelle of No. 207 (Handley Page) Squadron, actually went up to perform this task, though he was active for about three hours.

The infantry divisions and brigades also had to be marshalled in their allotted assembly areas on the night of 7 August. This was an especially complicated task for the Canadians, who did not even occupy the front line in the sector from which they were to mount their attack until about two hours before Zero. During the night the infantry was then formed up, many of them well out into No Man's Land, in the formations in which they were to make the attack. These positions had to be reconnoitred very carefully, guides and markers provided and white tapes laid down to indicate the start lines for the successive waves.[50]

All these arrangements proceeded without serious interference by the Germans. Though some divisions were shelled in their forming-up position, it was not the sort of very high intensity counter-preparation bombardment which would indicate that the advantage of surprise had been lost. Casualties were not heavy. The omens were generally good. Confidence was high. Fourth Army was a coiled spring. Some 2,000 guns were about to signal its release.[51]

4

THE BATTLE OF AMIENS

ZERO

For Fourth Army's waiting infantry, much of it already out in No Man's Land, the minutes before Zero were tense. In his memoirs, the Australian Corps' commander, Lieutenant-General Sir John Monash, evoked the atmosphere:

In black darkness 100,000 infantry . . . are standing grimly, silently, expectantly . . .; all feel to make sure that their bayonets are tightly locked, or to set their steel helmets firmly on their heads; company and platoon commanders, their whistles ready to hand, are nervously glancing at their luminous watches, waiting for minute after minute to go by and – giving a last look over their commands – ensuring that their runners are by their sides . . . and that the officers detailed to control direction have their compasses set and ready . . . Overhead drone the aeroplanes and from the rear, in swelling chorus, the clamour of the tanks grows every minute louder . . . In hundreds of pits, the guns are already run up, loaded and laid on their opening lines of fire; the sergeant is checking the range for the last time; the layer stands silently with his lanyard in hand. The section officer, watch on wrist, counts the last seconds: 'A minute to go' – 'Thirty seconds' – 'Ten seconds' – 'Fire!'[1]

At 04.20 on 8 August 1918 some 2,000 guns of the British Fourth Army roared at the German Second Army. To senior officers observing

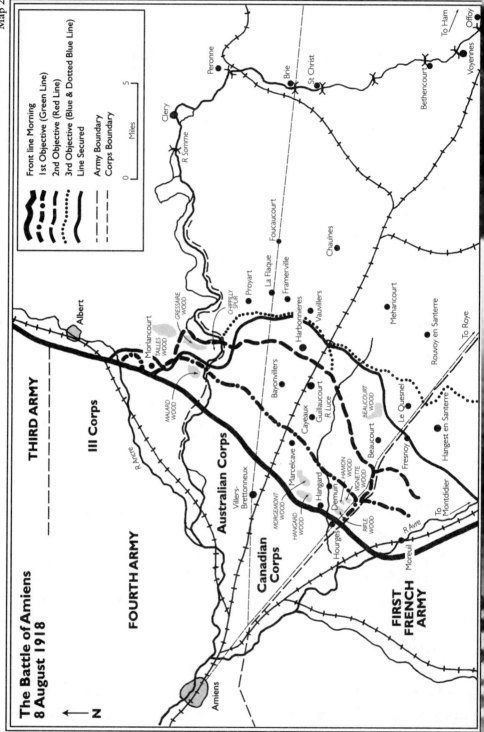

Map 2

**The Battle of Amiens
8 August 1918**

N

THIRD ARMY

III Corps

FOURTH ARMY

Australian Corps

Canadian
Corps

FIRST
FRENCH
ARMY

Front line Morning
1st Objective (Green Line)
2nd Objective (Red Line)
3rd Objective (Blue & Dotted Blue Line)
Line Secured

Army Boundary
Corps Boundary

0   Miles   5

Amiens

Villers-
Brettonneux

Albert

R Ancre

MORGEMONT
WOOD

HANGARD
WOOD

Marcelcave

Hourges

Demuin

Hangard

RIFLE
WOOD

HAMON
WOOD

VIGNETTE
WOOD

Moreuil

R Avre

To Montdidier

Fresnoy

Beaucourt

BEAUCOURT
WOOD

Le Quesnel

Hangest en Santerre

To Roye

Cayeaux

Guillaucourt

R Luce

Bayonvillers

MALARD
WOOD

Morlancourt

TAILLES
WOOD

GRESSAIRE
WOOD

CHIPILLY
SPUR

Proyart

La Flaque

Framerville

Foucaucourt

Harbonnieres

Vauvillers

Meharicourt

Rouvoy en Santerre

Chaulnes

R Somme

Clery

Peronne

Brie

St Christ

Bethencourt

Voyennes

Offoy

To Ham

from the rear the eastern horizon appeared to light up. A high proportion of the shells detonated in a barrage which started just 200 yards in front of the infantry's leading wave. This was the signal to advance. The infantry of the first wave moved forward purposefully, but without unseemly haste, to close up to the barrage. All they had to do now was to follow the barrage, itself timed to move at a fairly stately pace, all the way to the Green Line. Germans who were an immediate obstacle to progress would have to be disposed of, but there was no need to get them all, waves further back would mop up. For the leading brigades as a whole, their job for the day would be practically done once the Green Line was reached, an advance of 3,000–4,000 yards. With luck they would do it in two hours. With that line consolidated, other brigades would pass through.[2]

Over much of the front, and especially near the river banks, there was a thick mist. In some places smoke shell added to the general opacity at this dark hour. The low visibility increased German bewilderment and fright and tended to reduce the volume and accuracy of German fire. But it was also a source of anxiety to the attacking infantry who feared that they would get lost. The noise of the friendly barrage immediately to their front helped them to keep a sense of direction. But the bursting shells could not be seen until they were dangerously close.[3]

THE AUSTRALIAN SECTOR

Of the three corps of Fourth Army corps attacking on 8 August, the Australians had the most straightforward task, essentially one big thrust, in a single direction, over good going, with plenty of artillery and tank support. They had thus formulated what was, in broad terms, the simplest plan – an attack in two echelons of two divisions each. The divisions attacking in the first echelon were the 3rd Australian Division, under Major-General J. Gellibrand to the north, and on its right flank, slightly further to the south, the 2nd Australian Division, under Major-General C. Rosenthal, each attacking with two brigades up. Each of the leading brigades had a company of 12 Mark V tanks, a section of four tanks generally being allocated to each battalion. Each brigade also had a supply tank to bring up ammunition and engineering stores.[4]

The Australian divisions in the first echelon suffered virtually no German artillery fire and, in general, resistance to their advance was weak. A very high degree of surprise had been achieved. Overwhelmed by the intensity of the barrage, the Germans were driven down into their dug-outs from which they emerged, in most cases, only to surrender. In some places, owing to the very low visibility, the infantry lost the barrage and in such circumstances even isolated pockets of resistance might have slowed things down significantly and caused serious casualties. The initiative and daring of the Australian infantry, sometimes valuably assisted by the tanks, prevented this. By about 07.15, the Australians had gained their first (Green Line) objective in its entirety.[5]

During the two-hour pause at the first (Green Line) objective the 4th Australian Division, commanded by Major-General E.G. Sinclair-Maclagan, passed through the 3rd Australian Division, and the 5th, under Major-General Sir J.T. Hobbs, passed through the 2nd. The advance resumed at 08.20 sharp. The four brigades which led the advance now each had a field artillery brigade and a section of an engineer field company attached, forming a brigade group under the infantry brigadier. The artillery brigades had earlier been involved in firing the barrage, but had kept their horses near at hand, and, when the infantry had reached the first objective, had limbered up and dashed forward to join their groups. The 4th and 5th Australian Divisions were each allocated 30 Mark V tanks which had not yet been engaged, as well as a company and a half of Mark V* machines, carrying machine gun and Lewis gun detachments. The 1st Cavalry Brigade, with 16 Whippet tanks, moved immediately in the rear of the attacking infantry divisions. The armoured cars of the 17th Battalion of the Tank Corps were also in the wake of the advance, looking for an opportunity to strike deep into the enemy rear.[6]

Even though the supporting barrage of Fourth Army's field artillery had now ceased, remarkably little resistance was encountered. By 10.30 the Australians had reached their second (Red Line) objective along its entire length, overrunning a lot of German artillery and taking large numbers of prisoners in the process. Most of the opposition in front of the Australians came from machine-gun nests, but these do not appear to have been numerous enough to have caused serious delay. They were dealt with either by tanks or by the Australians themselves, some of whom beat down their fire with Lewis guns and rifles while others worked around their rear. The 5th Australian Division, on the right, had the easier time of it, meeting so little opposition that its leading battalions actually arrived on the objective at 09.00, well ahead of schedule. The 4th Australian Division also appears to have met little resistance from German troops immediately to its front. But owing to the relative failure of III Corps' attack north of the Somme, the division took a good deal of artillery and machine-gun fire from the Chipilly Spur on its left flank. While this increased casualties and compelled a slower advance than that of the 5th Australian Division, the 4th Australian Division still reached the Red Line on time. At about 09.15, even before the Red Line had been consolidated, advance guards of 1st Cavalry Division had begun to push through the Australian infantry, probing towards the Amiens Outer Defences – the final objective.[7]

Shortly before they arrived at the Red Line, a group of 12 armoured cars of the Tank Corps' 17th Battalion passed through the leading infantry of the 5th Australian Division, and made a dash down the Amiens–Brie road. Upon reaching La Flaque the cars found that they commanded an excellent view along the road in an easterly direction almost as far as Foucaucourt. They fired at Germans retreating down the road and caused panic amongst drivers of transport vehicles, who lost control of their horses. Resulting collisions partially blocked the road. Moving off the Amiens–Brie road itself, some cars then turned north in the direction of Proyart and others south towards Framerville. The armoured cars wreaked havoc amongst German transport and rear echelon personnel at both villages and caused considerable losses. At Framerville many documents were captured from surprised staff officers of the German 51st Corps and some of these later turned out to have crucial details of the Hindenburg Line defences. The cars continued to patrol till dusk. In Fourth Army's assessment they contributed significantly to the demoralisation of the Germans in this sector.[8]

The 5th Australian Division which had attained the Red Line (second objective) so easily had pushed on with little delay and reached its final (Blue Line) objectives between 10.30 and 11.00, a good deal earlier than expected. Because of the continuing flanking fire encountered from the north of the Somme, however, 4th Division did not commence its advance from the Red Line until 11.00. On the extreme left of the Australian sector, on the south bank of the Somme, the Blue Line was not in fact reached that day. The Australian Corps' performance had, however, been outstanding. Of the three Fourth Army corps it had taken the largest number of prisoners and guns.[9]

THE CANADIAN SECTOR

The Canadians had a significantly more complex and difficult task than the Australians. The Australians had been in the sector for months, knew the ground and had been able to take their time siting and registering their artillery. The Canadians, recently arrived in the sector, had been given very limited opportunities for reconnaissance. Their artillery, put into position largely within the last 24 hours, had been compelled to register 'silently', by photographs, maps and mathematics, without firing ranging shots. The ground on the Canadian Corps' right was, moreover, by far the most difficult that Fourth Army's troops had to negotiate south of the Somme. On their right flank the Canadians would not be supported by an infantry assault at Zero. For the first 40 minutes the First French Army would be offering artillery support only.[10]

Despite the difficulties which had confronted their artillery in preparing for the attack, when they attacked at 04.20 the Canadian infantry found their supporting barrage excellent. The German artillery was, however, not quite so thoroughly suppressed as it was in the Australian Corps' area. The Germans managed a counter-barrage, albeit a rather feeble one, in at least the southern part of the Canadian sector. On the left, adjacent to the Australians, the attack was conducted by 2nd Canadian Division, commanded by Major-General Sir H.E. Burstall. The 4th Canadian Brigade accompanied by 28 Mark V tanks of the 14th Battalion of the Tank Corps was assigned to take the first (Green Line) objective. In the Corps' centre was the 1st Canadian Division under Major-General A.C. Macdonell, also attacking with one brigade up. Its leading brigade, the 3rd Canadian Brigade, had 42 Mark V tanks to help it reach the Green Line. Each of these leading brigades attacked on a frontage of about 2,500 yards. The Canadians, like the Australians, enjoyed the cover of a fairly thick mist up to about 06.30.[11]

The 4th Canadian Brigade met considerable initial resistance from a trench about 1,000 yards east of their start line but this was overcome with the aid of the tanks. The numerous German machine-gun nests along the Amiens–Chaulnes railway, the boundary between the Australian and Canadian Corps, were also successfully dealt with, partly thanks to the excellent co-operation between the Canadians and the 7th Australian Brigade operating on the Australian Corps' far right. Considerable opposition had been expected from German positions in the village of Marcelcave and up until 06.00 heavy artillery bombarded the village. When the artillery lifted, the Canadian infantry attacked both frontally and from the north, some Canadians having worked round the left flank of the position. Though the fighting in the southern part of the village was intense, the location was entirely cleared within three-quarters of an hour, tanks playing a substantial part.

By 06.45, however, the mist in this sector was clearing. As the tanks pushed on east of Marcelcave they were engaged over open sights by a large concentration of German field artillery and sustained heavy losses. The casualties to the tanks did not stop the advance, however, and by 07.45, a little behind schedule, the Green Line had been secured along the whole front of the 2nd Canadian Division. The 1st Canadian Division met less resistance than its northern neighbour, though some very gallant actions were fought against enemy posts holding out in Morgemont and Hangard Woods, and it had secured its Green Line objectives by 06.20. After a brigade leap-frog had been carried out, the advance was renewed at 08.20. Once again, the resistance was stiffer in the 2nd Canadian Division's sector, but the Red Line was reached, along the front of both the 1st and the 2nd Canadian Divisions, by shortly after 12.30 in the afternoon.[12]

Of the Canadian divisions, the 3rd Division under Major-General L.J. Lipsett had the most difficult task. Its attack, in the southernmost portion of the Fourth Army sector, straddled the River Luce. This stream could not be forded and marshes on both its banks formed an area of swamp 200 yards wide in some places. At Zero, moreover, there would be only very limited support from the French on the right flank, to the south of the Amiens–Roye road. The division's main task was to secure a plateau on the south bank of the Luce. Until Zero, Fourth Army held only one relatively small bridgehead south of the stream – at Hourges – and that was dominated by German trenches on the forward slope of the plateau. The slopes were, however, slightly convex and an advance of 1,000 yards from the bridgehead would secure dead ground. Lipsett therefore concentrated 9th Canadian Brigade, together with one company of supporting tanks, in the bridgehead in darkness before Zero. One part of the brigade (comprising mainly 43rd Battalion) was intended to advance to seize the edge of the plateau at Zero. This would afford room for the rest of the brigade to deploy in dead ground, after which it would push eastward along the Luce in the directions of Demuin, Hamon Wood and Vignette Wood.

The 43rd Canadian Battalion, the extreme right-hand battalion of the whole of Fourth Army, had the particularly tricky task of taking Rifle Wood. Only 500 yards south of the bridgehead, this location was thought to be heavily defended. A frontal attack up the forward slope of the plateau was judged likely to prove costly, and it had thus been decided to take the wood by an enveloping manoeuvre. While the 9th Canadian Brigade was carrying out these tasks, the 8th Canadian Brigade would be attacking north of the Luce, through the village of Hangard. Despite the complexity of its tasks, the 3rd Canadian Division made excellent progress. The division had reached the Green Line all along its sector by about 08.30. Between the first and second objectives there was little resistance and by shortly after midday the Red Line was also reached.[13]

Between the Green and Red Lines the 3rd Cavalry Division passed through the 3rd Canadian Division with, appropriately enough, the Canadian Cavalry Brigade leading. This brigade got as far as the village of Beaucourt but was then held up by fire from Beaucourt Wood. The cavalry tried to take the wood at the gallop but the intensity of the fire was too much for them. Their advance appears to have lost impetus at this point. But the other brigades of the 3rd Cavalry Division, to their left, were able to press on to their final objectives. The 4th Canadian Division, the second echelon infantry division in the south of the Canadian Corps' sector, moved off from its start line at 05.20 and started passing through the 3rd Division on the Red Line at 12.40. German resistance in this most southerly sector of the Fourth Army front was fairly stout and, though most of the final objective was taken by 18.10, an area around Le Quesnel remained in enemy hands at the end of the day.

Meanwhile, elements of the 1st Cavalry Division had passed through the 2nd Canadian Division around the village of Guillaucourt at about 11.15, and had pushed on towards the Amiens Outer Defence Line. The 2nd Canadian Division had some communications problems: the 6th Canadian Brigade of that division receiving orders to advance to the final objective only at 14.30. Nevertheless the 1st and 2nd Canadian Divisions had reached all of their final (Blue Line) objectives by 17.35.[14]

THE III CORPS SECTOR

By the evening of 8 August, the Australian and Canadian Corps had each made dramatic advances, achieving almost all that Fourth

Army headquarters had dared hope for them. But results were less favourable on the flanks, markedly so in the III Corps' sector north of the Somme.

The major part of the III Corps' operation was mounted immediately north of the Somme by the 18th Division under Major-General R.P. Lee and the 58th Division under Major-General F.W. Ramsay. The right of the 58th Division rested on the north bank of the Somme and it intended to maintain liaison with the Australians south of the river. The III Corps' creeping barrage was laid on by 350 field pieces while 200 heavy howitzers and long-range guns engaged enemy artillery and strong-points. The same thick mist which had offered protection to the Australians and Canadians cloaked the first few hours of the III Corps' attack. German artillery fire was not heavy but resistance from German infantry and machine-gunners was generally much more serious than south of the Somme. This was particularly the case in Malard Wood, which was one of the 58th Division's objectives in the first bound of the offensive. The 174th Brigade, the first echelon brigade of that division, had an exceptionally hard fight for the wood, and elements of the 53rd Brigade, the second echelon brigade of the 18th Division, became sucked into this fighting. The wood could not be regarded as essentially in British hands until 09.00 and some parties of Germans held out for several hours longer. This put the III Corps' operations badly behind schedule. On emerging from Malard Wood, shortly after 09.00, and attempting to push on towards the Chipilly Spur, the 173rd Brigade, the second echelon brigade of the 58th Division, ran into intense fire from the Spur and could make little progress. At about the same time the 53rd Brigade was counter-attacked heavily by German troops emerging from Gressaire Wood.[15]

A relatively minor operation by Major-General H.W. Higginson's 12th Division (less the 36th Brigade) to secure ground north of the village of Morlancourt was completely successful. But when night fell on 8 August, the III Corps held little territory beyond the Green Line, a line which they were supposed to have consolidated by about 08.00. The failure to take the

Chipilly Spur had, as we have already seen, caused a shortfall in the advance on the far left of the Australian sector.[16]

The relative failure of the one British corps when compared with the striking successes of the two Dominion corps involved in this attack has occasioned much comment – and a good deal of chauvinistic pride on the part of the two emerging nations.[17] But Rawlinson appears never to have intended the III Corps to do much more than offer a degree of flank protection for the main thrust south of the Somme. The main part of the III Corps punch, immediately north of that river, was delivered by just two relatively weak divisions in contrast with the eight larger Dominion divisions to its south. Inevitably the III Corps' divisions, battered in the spring fighting, and now made up, in large part, of recent conscripts, were nothing like so well trained as the Dominion formations, which had escaped the initial fury of the German spring offensives, and were manned largely by experienced troops. The III Corps was attacking over much more difficult ground than that between the Somme and the Luce, and was doing so with much less tank support than that allocated to the Dominion troops. The action of the 27th Württemberg Division on 6 August had seriously dislocated the preparations for the attack of 8 August and the recent heavy fighting in this area meant that the degree of surprise achievable north of the Somme was very much reduced. Indeed, instead of surprising German formations which were, in general, already depleted and demoralised, III Corps met an alert enemy including the high quality Württemberg division. Given these facts the III Corps' capture of more than 2,000 prisoners on 8 August seems a fair achievement.[18]

Some recent historians have blamed Rawlinson for failing to replace the III Corps' divisions with fresher British troops before 8 August.[19] This scarcely seems reasonable. Surprise was basic to the whole Fourth Army plan. The staff work involved in concealing the movement of the Canadian Corps and putting it into the line immediately before the attack was Herculean and its successful achievement something of an administrative miracle. It is hardly surprising that the Fourth Army staff did not undertake a simultaneous exercise of the same nature on the northern wing.

CAVALRY AND WHIPPETS

This was the British cavalry's most successful day of the whole war on the Western Front. The 2nd Cavalry Division, which was Lieutenant-General Kavanagh's Corps reserve at the start of the battle, saw little action. But the other two – the 1st Cavalry Division north of the Luce and the 3rd Cavalry Division south of it – saw plenty, successfully passing through the attacking infantry in the latter part of the morning. They played a significant role in maintaining the momentum of the Fourth Army attack and carrying it rapidly forward to the Amiens Outer Defence Line. The cavalry certainly took well over 1,000 prisoners on 8 August, probably as many as 3,000, as well as numerous guns. One regiment, the 5th Dragoon Guards, of the 1st Cavalry Brigade, in 1st Cavalry Division, took about 600 prisoners in a single incident, intercepting a trainload of reinforcements between Vauvillers and Framerville.[20]

One reason for the relative neglect of the cavalry achievement in some accounts of the battle may be an administrative factor. Counts of prisoners were officially recorded at corps 'cages'. The cavalry at Amiens, however, did not employ cages of its own but handed all prisoners over to the nearest infantry division. Cavalry were supposed to obtain receipts for prisoners handed over to infantry formations but under the pressures of battle this was not always done. It seems that all prisoners taken by the cavalry on 8 August 1918 were thus officially counted as prisoners of the Dominion corps.[21] Not wishing to be encumbered with captured guns, the cavalry seems to have left these too to be secured by the Dominion infantry.[22]

Cavalry–Whippet co-operation idea was not a great success. The mobility characteristics and vulnerabilities of these instruments were too dissimilar. When the going was good the Whippets had difficulty keeping up with the cavalry and in general they made little impact in this battle. One Whippet, Lieutenant Arnold's 'Musical Box', did perform remarkable feats of arms but its story became known only after the Armistice, when its commander was released from German captivity. Arnold was part of a tank company attached to leading troops of the 1st Cavalry Division. But, after doing some good work with them, Musical Box became detached and fought a lone action between Bayonvillers and Harbonnières, doing great execution amongst the German motor and horse transport columns. It was finally knocked out, probably by a field gun, some time after 14.00.[23] Musical Box's achievements were much vaunted by British tank enthusiasts between the wars. But its fate could equally well have served as a warning that tanks are very vulnerable when not intimately supported by other arms.

THE FRENCH SECTOR

The French First Army had opened an intense preliminary bombardment of German positions at 04.20 – Zero hour for Fourth Army. But infantry attacks by the French XXXI Corps did not begin until 45 minutes later. Two divisions were tasked to clear commanding ground in the angle between the Luce and the Avre, while a third division seized the town of Moreuil. At 08.00 the French offensive was extended to the south by the French IX Corps, on the Avre front to the right of the XXXI Corps. Though the French fell somewhat short of their final objectives, not taking the village of Fresnoy, their attack performed a useful function. They had advanced up to five miles, inflicted heavy losses on the Germans and made the right flank of the Canadian Corps much more secure than it otherwise would have been. Along the boundary between French First Army and the Canadian Corps on the Amiens–Roye road the French received a great deal of co-operation from Brigadier Brutinel's 'Independent Force' with its mobile machine guns and mortars. The boundary between the Canadians and the French at nightfall on 8 August was just west of Le Quesnel.[24]

AIR ACTION

The first day of the Battle of Amiens involved some of the most intense air fighting of the First World War. The air action on 8 August should have been one-sided. At the beginning of the battle the Allies had, as we have seen, 1,904 aircraft available for use on the 25-mile front between Courcelles and Albert. The Germans had only some 369 machines immediately available for action in the same area, their main strength being in Champagne. But the Allies were not to use their air power to the best advantage and the Germans were to show much greater operational flexibility in the use of theirs than the British had anticipated.[25]

For the first four to five hours of the offensive there was very limited close air support to ground forces. The dense mist, which so aided Fourth Army in most respects, rendered its air power almost impotent. RAF sources indicate that this was no mere ground mist – a fog bank extended from the ground up to 500 feet. This drastically reduced the effectiveness of the IX Brigade's attacks on the enemy airfield at St Christ as well as that of the V Brigade's close support. The RAF was able to have little impact on the ground battle until the fog began to clear, at around 09.00, by which time the Green Line had been reached practically everywhere, some cavalry had been passed through and, in most places, the advance to the Red Line was well under way.

For the next three or four hours, however, the air above Fourth Army's attacking troops was alive with friendly aircraft. Between 09.00 and about noon both German machine-gun posts holding up Fourth Army's infantry and German artillery resisting the advance of its tanks and armoured cars were bombed and strafed. German lorries were blown off the roads, horse-drawn transport wrecked or stampeded and staff cars shot up and their occupants killed. Less sensational but also important in aiding the infantry advance were smoke-screens formed from phosphorus bombs. Because there was an acute shortage of smoke shell for 60-pdr guns, the ground troops relied on the RAF to generate smoke screens in several parts of the battlefield which were beyond the range of the field artillery.[26]

In the early afternoon, however, the RAF made a dramatic change of plan and radically shifted the focus of air activity. About midday, aircraft reports indicated that the roads leading to the bridges over the River Somme at Péronne, Brie, St Christ, Bethencourt, Voyennes and Offay were swarming with German troops in full retreat. The destruction of the bridges, not hitherto designated as an RAF task, would have served two purposes. It would have sealed off the retreat of those Germans who were attempting to flee the onslaught and, more importantly, it would have greatly delayed the arrival of reinforcements to check it. The types of bomb available to the RAF were not really heavy enough to destroy the bridges entirely. But even the substantial disruption of German movement across the Somme would have been a major achievement and Sir John Salmond considered it worth striving for. He cancelled all other bombing missions given to the RAF and all other missions given to the fighters of the IX Brigade. For the afternoon of 8 August attack on the Somme bridges was to have absolute priority. Missions were to be flown against them not only by the bombers but also by Camels and SE5as carrying 25-lb bombs. Such missions were to be flown 'as long as weather and light permit'.

A total of 205 sorties were flown against the Somme bridges during the daylight hours of 8 August by DH9 and DH4 bombers and by fighters carrying bombs. Some pilots flew three sorties against these targets that day. By the time the attacks on the bridges had started, however, German fighter reinforcements were arriving in the area and ferocious aerial combat took place. The attacks on the bridges had to be at low level not only because they were relatively small targets but also because there was thick cloud above 2,000 feet. The fact that the British were now concentrating their air effort on low-level attack on a small number of fixed points made interception easy for the Germans who had the further advantage that their main fighter formations were based at aerodromes at Ennemain and St Christ which were very close to the bridges. During the afternoon the RAF appears to have left these aerodromes quite unmolested. German fighters were thus able to fly sorties at a much higher rate in defence of the bridges than the RAF could manage attacking them. The German fighters committed included large numbers of the Fokker DVII biplane. When fitted, as many now were, with the 185 horse-power BMW engine, the DVIIs were the highest performance fighter available to either side. The RAF had placed itself at a further disadvantage in dealing with these formidable adversaries by double tasking its own fighters. The Camels and SE5as, which should have been protecting the DH4s and DH9s, were too busy aiming and dropping their own bombs.[27]

The excessive concentration on the Somme bridges and the faulty tactics used in those attacks were not the only RAF errors that day. Though some squadrons had been assigned to the maintenance of fighter cover over the battlefield that morning, they appear to have been flying relatively high, above the clouds.[28] Formations of between five and eight Fokker DVIIs, apparently flying in under the cloud base, began to appear over the battlefield in the late morning and swooped on RAF corps aircraft and on machines engaged in ground attack.[29]

Even without intervention from enemy aircraft, low-flying ground attack was, of course, a highly dangerous activity. The aircraft of the period were relatively fragile and very vulnerable to all kinds of ground fire. Any loss of concentration by the pilot was, moreover, more dangerous at low altitude. There appear to be no statistics indicating what proportion of RAF losses on 8 August were sustained from ground fire and what proportion from encounters with enemy aircraft. But so heavy were these losses that one historian has termed Thursday 8 August 1918 a 'black day for the RAF'[30] as well as for the German Army. Forty-five aircraft failed to return from sorties flown in the daylight hours on 8 August. A further 52 were totally wrecked or damaged badly enough to be written off squadron strengths. Thus some 96 aircraft altogether were destroyed out of a total strength committed of about 700: a wastage rate of more than 13 per cent. Casualties to personnel totalled 80 of which 57 were missing, 4 were known to be killed and 9 were wounded.[31]

BLACK DAY FOR THE GERMAN ARMY: ANALYSIS

The verdict of Ludendorff's memoirs that 8 August 1918 was 'a black day for the German Army in the history of this war'[32] is well known. The scale and nature of the German defeat, however, require some analysis here.

The importance of this day's battle cannot really be measured in geographical terms. It is true that the advance made by Fourth Army was as much as eight miles. But no great city had been liberated and no location of strategic importance seized. Pushing the enemy back to the Amiens Outer Defence Line may have made Amiens more secure. But the real danger of that city falling to the Germans had passed back in April. Certainly communications behind the Allied front were made easier by the victory – one of Foch's declared intentions. But, as with most actions on the Western Front between the end of 1914 and the Armistice, the significance of 8 August must be measured mainly in terms of attrition – attrition to personnel, war material and, a factor of the greatest importance, morale.

German losses were prodigious. Perhaps as many as 18,000 prisoners were taken, around 15,000 of them by Fourth Army, over 3,000 by the French. One set of statistics[33] details captures of German personnel as follows:

Table 4.1   *Captures of German prisoners 8 August 1918*

OFFICERS	OTHER	RANKS	TOTAL
Canadian Corps	114	4,919	5,033
Australian Corps	183	7,742	7,925
III Corps	75	2,388	2,463
Fourth Army	372	15,049	15,421
French First Army	150	3,000	3,150 (all French figures approx.)
Grand Total	500	18,000	18,500 (all bottom line figures approx.)

Other German casualties can only be estimated. A monograph by the German official historians, however, put German Second Army losses for 8 August at 650 to 700 officers and 26,000 to 27,000 other ranks. The Germans did not normally count as losses lightly wounded men, likely to return to duty quickly. The Germans were thus prepared to admit to 9,000 killed or seriously wounded, in addition to those lost as prisoners. Fourth Army's total casualties for 8 August seem to have been under 9,000.[34] Their losses in matériel also alarmed the Germans. General von der Marwitz, commanding the German Second Army, is said to have admitted the loss of 400 guns on 8 August alone. Captures claimed by Fourth Army amounted to:

Table 4.2   *Captures of German guns by Fourth Army*

Canadian Corps	161
Australian Corps	173
III Corps	40(approx.)
Total	374(approx.)[35]

If we take into account captures by the French (and there certainly were some) the figure of 400 seems about right. The same total is given in the official German monograph on the battle.[36] But what was even more shocking to the German leadership than the scale of these losses was the way they were incurred. It was clear that many troops had been captured unwounded and some seem to have been only too eager to give themselves up. Ludendorff was informed of groups of German soldiers surrendering to single British horsemen. In some units the officers had lost all control and had fled with their men.[37]

BEF SUCCESS: ANALYSIS

The magnitude of the victory of 8 August was owing to the BEF's pitting its maximum available strength, including the two formidable

Dominion Corps, against an accurately identified area of acute German weakness. The identification of German vulnerability in the Amiens sector – a combination of inadequate physical defences and depressed fighting spirit – was mainly due to the enterprise and aggression of the Australians. Fourth Army headquarters recognised the opportunity and proposed an intelligent scheme to exploit it, though how far this was conceived by Rawlinson personally and how far by others in Fourth Army is impossible to say. Haig deserves credit for approving the scheme and for giving Rawlinson the reinforcements needed to make it work. Foch's insistence on involving French First Army provided some assistance to the Canadian advance on the right flank and increased the scale of the victory. His bringing forward of the start date for the operation by two days, however, threatened to dislocate timetables and, with less efficient staff work than that of the BEF at this stage in the war, could have caused chaos.

In the final analysis, however, this was a victory for which no single leader deserves tumultuous acclaim. It was a victory of Allied, but mainly BEF, teamwork. Rawlinson's plan (assuming that he was in fact its main author) was eminently sensible but scarcely required genius to conceive. Its successful implementation, on the other hand, was a mammoth task which depended on a vast number of his subordinates at all levels (and some of their colleagues in other Armies) doing their jobs extremely well. In particular, the concentration of overwhelming force with such extraordinary speed and stealth required painstaking, meticulous staff work. The red-tabbed staff officers of the BEF, often derided by contemporaries, and, as individuals, largely unknown to history, are the unsung heroes of 8 August 1918.

Much of the success was owing to the very high degree of surprise which was undoubtedly achieved. Had the Germans got wind of Fourth Army's plans, even an hour or so before Zero, they could have severely disrupted Fourth Army's deployment by firing a counter-preparation programme with their artillery. If they had known a few hours earlier than that, they could also have greatly degraded Fourth Army's counter-battery programme by relocating their guns. Had they become aware of British intentions in time to bring up some reserve divisions, they could probably have stopped the Fourth Army attack somewhere between the Green and Red Lines. Fourth Army's creeping barrage carried the Australians and Canadians only as far as the first objective. After that they were dependent on themselves and whatever help that tanks and cavalry could offer. German reinforcements of reasonable quality posted, in a high state of readiness, beyond the Green Line could have forced Fourth Army to accept, at best, a very limited kind of victory. The disruption of the III Corps' preparations by the 27th Württemberg Division indicates that the Germans still had troops of reasonably high quality available.

That Fourth Army's artillery superiority played a vital role is obvious. The success of the counter-battery effort seems particularly remarkable. The positions of about 95 per cent of the German guns (504 out of 530) facing Fourth Army had been accurately identified before the attack started and two-thirds of Fourth Army's 672 heavy guns had been used in an effort to suppress them. More than 70 per cent of Fourth Army's casualties were thought to have been from small arms (presumably including machine-gun) fire, only 27 per cent from artillery. Casualties amongst Fourth Army's gunners were apparently nil. Relatively few German guns were destroyed by Fourth Army's fire. In some cases, dead gunners were found at their posts. In others, there were dead horses: the gunners had limbered up (or attempted to do so) to shift the battery position, or perhaps to flee without the extra ignominy of abandoning their guns. Many German guns, however, were captured with camouflage netting still around them and breech and muzzle covers still on, indicating that they were not manned at all on 8 August, and that perhaps no serious attempt had been made to do so. The effectiveness of artillery in the suppressive role must always depend to some extent on the degree of determination of its victims to resist suppression and it would indeed be surprising if the generally low morale in the German Second Army had not affected its gunners.

Demoralisation was not universal, however. In some parts of the battle-field, German guns were served with determination and caused considerable loss especially to British tanks.[38]

Fourth Army had enjoyed an initial advantage in numbers of men as well as weight of metal. In the main effort, ten BEF divisions were attacking seven German divisions – seemingly not a vast superiority. But the average BEF division was considerably stronger than the average German by this time. Some of the divisions facing the Fourth Army, moreover, were very weak, even by German standards: Fourth Army's estimate immediately before the battle was that none of the divisions facing it was more than 3,000 strong. The Canadian divisions, on the other hand, were exceptionally strong by BEF standards. Even including the four divisions that the Germans had in reserve in this sector, a BEF superiority of 75,000 to 37,000 has been estimated.[39]

Infantry skills also played a crucial part in the BEF victory. They seem to have been as important as the tanks in allowing the Dominion infantry to fight forward beyond the Green Line, where the creeping barrage ceased. Because of the mist and stubborn local resistance or a combination of the two, some infantry lost the barrage even before they got that far. And, while the general performance of the German Second Army on 8 August was not impressive, stubborn resistance was encountered in some places, much of it from machine-gunners. German machine-gunners were picked men, normally of extreme tenacity. Even on this 'black day' a minority lived up to their reputation. Tanks, when and where available, were an effective answer to German machine-guns, except in the denser woods. If no tank were within sight when difficulties arose, however, there was no easy way of summoning one. Yet, even without tanks, machine-gun posts and isolated strong-points did not prove enduring obstacles to Australian and Canadian infantry. Lewis guns, light mortars, rifles, rifle grenades, hand grenades and bayonets were all employed, often with potent synergy. In the final analysis, however, the overcoming of local opposition depended on the sheer heroism of individual officers and men.[40]

PLANS FOR Z + 1

Haig paid a visit to Rawlinson's headquarters at Flixecourt around midday on Thursday 8 August 1918. He was thrilled with the news he heard there. He thought the situation south of the Somme had developed 'more favourably for us than I, optimist though I am, had dared hope'.[41] Later that afternoon orders were issued from his Advanced GHQ that, having secured the old Amiens Outer Defence Line, Fourth Army should push forward on 9 August to establish itself 'on the general line ROYE–CHAULNES–BRAY-SUR-SOMME–DERNANCOURT'. This would involve a further advance of seven miles. Outposts were to be 'thrown forward' even further east and 'touch maintained with the enemy'.[42] Haig clearly had visions of such a high degree of mobility having been restored that maintaining contact with a fast-fleeing enemy might prove difficult. Though he had better grounds for optimism at this juncture than at any time since he took over as Commander-in-Chief, his imagination was still running ahead of events.

Rawlinson, however, did not argue and Haig's instructions, with a bit more detail added, were passed on to Fourth Army's corps. An unfortunate feature of the Fourth Army operations order was that it obliged the Australian Corps, probably the least exhausted of the three, to conform, on 9 August, to the movements of III Corps in the north and the Canadians in the south, while leaving Currie of the Canadian Corps to set the time for the general advance that morning.[43] In the event, neither of the flanking corps was to start early. The III Corps' troops were extremely tired after the heavy fighting of the previous day and were still facing stiff opposition. The Canadians who were also tired were, in addition, the victims of a confusion of orders.

Haig had indicated a south-easterly direction for Fourth Army's thrust on 9 August in order to assist the continuing efforts of the French First Army and the Canadians would have the leading role in this. Thus, having arranged for the forward movement of his three reserve divisions, one behind each attacking corps, Rawlinson motored forward from his headquarters at Flixecourt, to that of the Canadian Corps at Gentelles, arriving between 16.00 and 16.30. On hearing of the tiredness of the Canadian troops Rawlinson promised to release the fresh British 32nd Division from his reserve to the Canadian Corps to help with the following day's operations. The Canadians made their initial plans for operations on the morrow on the basis that they would have this formation. Rawlinson's promise of it was, however, countermanded in a rather peremptory manner later that evening (apparently after consultation with Rawlinson) by the Fourth Army chief of staff, Archibald Montgomery. From the Canadian point of view it was a clear case, as Napoleon used to say, of 'order, counter-order, disorder'. It dislocated Canadian planning that night and appears to have contributed substantially to a loss of momentum in Fourth Army as a whole the following day.[44]

It is likely that Montgomery's intervention on the evening of 8 August had deep roots. In 1916 he had been a proponent of a fairly cautious 'step by step' approach to operations. A sensible plan which he had drafted for the first day of the Somme offensive had been approved by Rawlinson, but overturned by Haig in favour of a more ambitious scheme which over-stretched Fourth Army's resources and resulted in the disaster of 1 July.[45] Fourth Army headquarters had originally conceived the attack of 8 August 1918 as a short, sharp, opportunistic blow. Such a blow had been success-fully delivered. Montgomery was probably very wary of interventions by Haig designed to convert the battle into an open-ended, unlimited offen-sive – something the Commander-in-Chief had done with adverse results to Third Army's Cambrai attack of November 1917. Given the well-known German propensity for rapidly bringing up reserves and mounting violent counter-attacks, he was probably also concerned that Fourth Army keep its own reserves in hand. The fact that Montgomery was able to make such an intervention, against the spirit of orders emanating from the Commander-in-Chief, without adverse consequences for his career, sheds an interesting light on his relationship with Rawlinson and on the centrality of his posi-tion at Fourth Army headquarters.

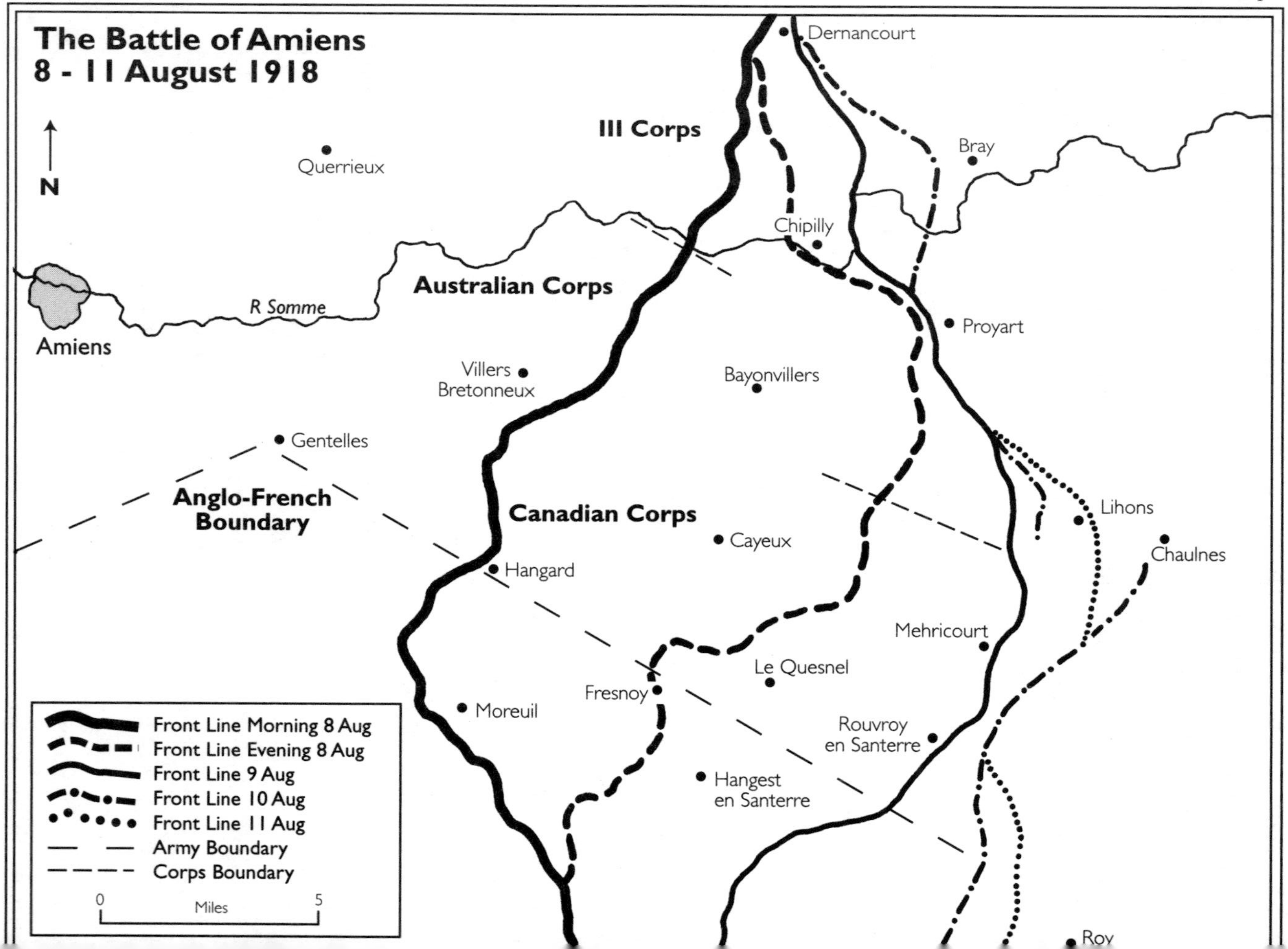

Map 3

The Battle of Amiens
8 - 11 August 1918

N →

Amiens

R Somme

Querrieux

III Corps

Dernancourt

Bray

Proyart

Chipilly

Australian Corps

Villers
Bretonneux

Bayonvillers

Gentelles

Anglo-French
Boundary

Canadian Corps

Hangard

Cayeux

Moreuil

Fresnoy

Le Quesnel

Mehricourt

Rouvroy
en Santerre

Hangest
en Santerre

Lihons

Chaulnes

Roy

	Front Line Morning 8 Aug
	Front Line Evening 8 Aug
	Front Line 9 Aug
	Front Line 10 Aug
	Front Line 11 Aug
	Army Boundary
	Corps Boundary

0   Miles   5

Z+1

There was always a tendency for entropy to overtake the attacking side after the first day of a Western Front offensive. Troops who had fought the previous day would be physically and mentally tired, often verging on exhaustion. If the infantry had achieved any significant advance this would carry them beyond the range of their field artillery and the latter would have to be moved forward. Until new battery positions were properly surveyed (which inevitably took a considerable time), the accuracy of indirect fire from batteries pushed forward to support the infantry would inevitably be much reduced. Communications, largely dependent on a telephone system left behind when the attackers moved into No Man's Land, would tend to break down. Without telephone links to the infantry and without the benefits of field survey, field artillery would often be reduced to assisting the infantry in the crudest way – moving right to the front and engaging the enemy by direct fire. This was worth doing sometimes, and was done in this battle, but was inefficient. All these problems beset Fourth Army on the morning of 9 August. In addition, a combination of battle damage, mechanical breakdown and crew exhaustion meant that fewer than half the tanks available on 8 August were still running. Only some 155 actually participated in attacks.[46]

German reinforcements, on the other hand, were arriving more rapidly than expected. Six divisions, or elements thereof, arrived during the night, another three in the course of the day. Granted, they were, in many cases, depleted formations, worn out in previous battles and, in some instances, arriving with little artillery. They could still plug gaps. German performance was very mixed. Some of the German Second Army troops who had experienced the disaster of 8 August were intensely demoralised. There were instances of panic flights and of formations offering continued resistance being derided as 'war prolongers'. But in some places, at some times, resistance was stiff and on the battlefield as a whole it tended to consolidate in the course of the day.[47]

Air support to Fourth Army on Friday 9 August was disappointing. The RAF had, as we have seen, taken heavy losses the previous day and the Germans had been strongly reinforced. The fatal attraction of the Somme bridges continued to exercise its grip on the RAF command, and other tasks, including the provision of fighter cover below cloud level, were correspondingly neglected. German fighters arrived over the battlefield in large numbers and inflicted losses on British aircraft and ground forces. The RAF lost another 45 aircraft, three-quarters of them over the Somme bridges.[48]

While acknowledging the existence of many problems beyond its control, both the Canadian and the British official histories indicate that the principal cause of Fourth Army's loss of momentum on Friday, 9 August was the confusion caused by Montgomery's countermanding of the orders to the Canadian Corps the previous evening – a self-inflicted wound.[49] At 05.30 the village of Le Quesnel was captured by elements of the 4th Canadian Division in what was meant to be a preliminary operation. After this overture, however, there was an inordinate delay before the opera commenced. What was meant to be the Canadian Corps' main attack began in a ragged fashion between 11.00 and 13.00. A lack of cohesion was pretty general in Fourth Army that day. Altogether, 16 of the Army's brigades attacked on 9 August but they commenced at 13 different times. Some received plentiful artillery support, others none at all. Only one fresh BEF division was committed on 9 August – the 1st Australian, which had been in corps reserve and it did some of the most effective fighting. One regiment of the 33rd American Division, a formation which Fourth Army had not been intended to commit at any stage of this battle, was thrown in to assist III Corps during the afternoon and it too performed well.[50]

Despite all its difficulties Fourth Army made an average advance of three miles on 9 August – extraordinary progress for the second day of a Western Front offensive. By nightfall in the III Corps' sector the Chipilly Spur, Gressaire Wood and Tailles Wood had all been taken. Further south

Framerville was in Australian hands and Méharicourt and Rouvroy-en-Santerre had been liberated by the Canadians. Five hundred prisoners had been taken by the Australians alone, lesser numbers by the other corps.[51]

Z + 2

By Saturday 10 August, the sting had gone out of the Fourth Army offensive. Neither Haig nor Rawlinson gave much positive direction for this day's action – the corps were merely told to push on towards the objectives set for the previous day – though the Australian Corps was to relieve III Corps north of the Somme as far north as the Corbie–Bray road. Little fresh impetus was imparted – only one additional BEF division, the 32nd Division, finally released to the Canadian Corps the previous afternoon, was committed to the fighting. Though more artillery had moved up, tank casualties had been high, and according to the Tank Corps' own records, only 85 tanks were engaged on 9 August.[52] (The British official history gives the still lower figure of 57.) The same lack of co-ordination which had been a hallmark of offensive action the previous day was equally in evidence on 10 August. Yet, by the standards of previous offensives in this war and this theatre of operations, Fourth Army continued to do well, achieving a maximum advance, in the Canadian sector, of about two miles. On the right flank, where the German Eighteenth Army was making a planned withdrawal, the French gained about three and a half miles.[53]

Rawlinson thought that his Army badly needed a rest. The main Allied effort, he considered, should be shifted to his flanks. The French to his south should do more, he thought, and General Sir Julian Byng's Third Army, in front of Albert on Fourth Army's northern flank, should be thrown in.[54] Haig agreed that more effort was needed in other sectors. That morning he sent instructions to General Horne, commanding British First Army, to complete his plans for the capture of La Bassée and the Aubers Ridge, an operation to be mounted in conjunction with an assault on Kemmel Hill by Second Army and a Third Army push in the direction of Bapaume.[55]

The same afternoon Haig visited the Canadian Corps headquarters and later some of the divisional headquarters. Both Sir Arthur Currie and Major-General Lambert, who commanded the 32nd Division, impressed upon Haig that resistance in front of Fourth Army was stiffening markedly and that the terrain it now confronted was equally unfavourable. Fourth Army had now reached the old 1916 Somme battlefield. Ahead was an obstacle course of old trenches, dug-outs and shell craters. The Germans would be able to exact a high price for further advances.[56] But Haig did not yet halt the Fourth Army offensive. GHQ's orders for 11 August were that: 'The offensive operations of the French First Army and the British Fourth Army will be continued with a view to securing the general line GUISCARD–HAM–PERONNE and gaining the crossings of the river SOMME.'[57]

But the offensive was at least to be widened. The French Third Army was to join in on the right of the French First Army, and to attempt to clear the Germans out of the Noyon area. The British Third Army was ordered 'to carry out raids and minor operations in order to ascertain the enemy's intentions on the ALBERT–ARRAS front' and to push advanced guards forward in the direction of Bapaume if the opportunity arose.[58] Whatever Rawlinson's misgivings about pitching his troops into another day's battle he made no protest. His HQ relayed Haig's instructions, with a bit of detail added, to the corps. For the third day running Currie was to fix the start date for the general advance.[59]

THE LAST DAY

The fighting of Sunday 11 August needs little narration. Practically all the Fourth Army troops committed were nearing exhaustion and only 38 tanks were in action.[60] The balance of numerical advantage was shifting in favour of the Germans. South of the Somme, nine Fourth Army divisions faced twelve German divisions (three of them rested and fairly fresh) which had arrived as reinforcements, in addition to the wreckage of the original German Second Army. On the positive side, Fourth Army had now brought up most of its artillery and the Germans were probably still out-gunned. But artillery was not at its most effective under these fluid conditions. Fourth Army's gunners generally had only the vaguest notion of the location of German defensive positions and even less idea of the positions of German guns. Indeed for much of the time since 8 August they had been having difficulty working out where their own infantry were. In these circumstances laying on a true creeping barrage was an impossibility and the infantry had, at best, to be content with the less intimate support offered by rolling and standing barrages.[61]

Though on the right, against an opposition consisting only of rearguards, the French First and Third Armies effected an advance of about a mile and a half along almost their entire front, Fourth Army gained relatively little ground that day. The Australians secured Lihons but there were several German counter-attacks against both them and the Canadians. In the face of one of these the extreme left of the Canadian Corps, which had advanced slightly further than the Australian right, was compelled to relinquish some ground.[62] By midday corps commanders seem to have decided not to press the advance very hard.

By 11 August, Haig was well aware that German resistance on the Fourth Army front was stiffening and seems to have been thinking in terms of shifting the main effort further north. He saw General Byng, the Third Army commander, that morning and instructed him to be ready to attack in the direction of Bapaume as soon as he had received necessary reinforcements.[63] Rawlinson, speaking to Haig that afternoon, argued that there should be a pause in Fourth Army's operations while another big set-piece attack was organised.[64] Haig does not appear to have taken any definite decision on this and his diary does not even mention a conversation with Rawlinson.[65] Rawlinson, however, told a corps commanders' conference that afternoon that he had decided on a pause in major offensive operations until 14 or 15 August, though the corps were free to mount minor attacks to improve their positions in the meantime.[66] An order indicating that the next big attack would be on 15 August was issued by Fourth Army the following day.[67] Though this was not clear at the time, the Battle of Amiens was over.

RESULTS

Most of the damage which the Battle of Amiens inflicted on the German Army occurred on the first day. The results of the next two days' fighting were still favourable to the Allied cause but to a diminishing extent. There are some difficulties in quantifying the physical damage precisely. It seems safe to say that the Germans lost between 400 and 500 guns altogether and that Fourth Army took between 18,000 and 19,000 prisoners. The British official historians, while not impressed by the vigour of French efforts in this battle, were prepared to credit the French with taking over 11,000 prisoners, putting the total at just under 30,000. Even if the French figure is treated with some scepticism, a total somewhere between 25,000 and 30,000 seems a reasonable estimate. The same British official historians, using a formula for relating prisoners to other casualties which is of dubious relevance to this particular battle, estimated total German casualties at 75,000 which is probably too high. Fourth Army's total casualties were around 22,000 and those of the French about the same. But Fourth Army's fatal casualties were relatively low – only about 4,000. In terms of numbers of men permanently lost to the war machines of the two sides there can, therefore, be no doubt that this battle massively favoured the Allies.[68]

In terms of its effect on morale the Battle of Amiens was even more beneficial to the Allied cause. The German Army's defeat struck hardest at the highest level. Ludendorff had manifested neurotic symptoms for years. From the accounts of those who had frequent dealings with him it seems that these became harder to control after 8 August 1918. Methodical work became very difficult for him, his irritability more extreme, the weighing of evidence and the formulation of rational judgements largely beyond him. Fear of triggering a general collapse of morale in the German Army made him hesitate to sanction an immediate withdrawal to the powerful defensive position which the Allies referred to as the Hindenburg Line, though this was probably the best course of action in the circumstances and was strongly recommended by some of his most respected military colleagues. Amiens, however, did drive a simple message into Ludendorff's brain. He had lost the initiative and could no longer win a decisive military victory. The best he could now do was to fight defensive battles while seeking a compromise peace which might leave Germany in possession of some of its wartime gains.[69]

5

WIDENING THE OFFENSIVE

FOURTH ARMY: 12–15 AUGUST

On 11 August Haig had tacitly consented to Rawlinson's decision to halt Fourth Army's attack for the time being. But in Haig's mind this was merely a pause to regroup. The very next day, on 12 August, he ordered a renewal of Fourth Army's effort, in an essentially south-easterly direction, to commence on 15 August. Third Army, on Fourth Army's left, was supposed to join the offensive on or about 20 August.[1] Whatever misgivings Rawlinson may have had, he did not express them at this stage and Fourth Army's headquarters drafted orders for its corps which were in line with GHQ's instructions.[2] But the big Fourth Army attack scheduled for 15 August did not happen.

Because of the direction of the proposed thrust, it was obvious that the Canadian Corps, on Fourth Army's southern wing, would have to play the leading role. The Germans on the Canadian front had been massively reinforced since 8 August. (Indeed the famous German Alpine Corps had appeared opposite them on 11 August.)[3] The Germans were fully alert and, on the old 1916 Somme battlefield, were holding ground which accorded every advantage to the defender. At a meeting with Rawlinson on 13 August Lieutenant-General Sir Arthur Currie, commanding the Canadian Corps, produced aerial photographs of the German positions facing the Canadians and indicated that he regarded the proposed attack as 'rather a desperate enterprise'. He anticipated heavy casualties for little useful result.[4] Currie, in peacetime an estate agent and amateur soldier, was now an experienced corps commander. His views deserved to be taken seriously on those grounds alone. As the head of a national contingent, moreover, he had a degree of power and influence vastly greater than that of any corps commander from the mother country. It was an influence he had already demonstrated his preparedness to use.[5]

On the morning of 14 August Rawlinson showed Haig the same photographs, together with a letter in which Currie forcefully expressed his opposition to the intended attack. Rawlinson lent his own support to the Canadian case and Haig apparently accepted it without demur.[6] At 15.00 the same day Haig spoke to Foch on this issue. There was then something of a confrontation – Foch trying to insist on adherence to the original plan. Haig, always jealous of his prerogatives, insisted that he alone was answerable to the British government and people for the fate of British and Dominion troops.[7] Foch backed down for the time being, though he and his staff continued to urge a renewed Fourth Army over the next few days.[8]

THIRD AND FIRST ARMIES: 13–14 AUGUST

By the time Haig cancelled the Fourth Army attack his headquarters had issued more definite orders for offensive action to Third and First Armies. On 13 August General Sir Julian Byng, the Third Army commander, was told to prepare an attack on a four mile front between Moyenneville in the north and Ablainzeville in the south, Moyenneville being about seven miles to the south of Arras. The attack was to be delivered at the earliest possible date subsequent to the renewed Fourth Army attack then scheduled for 15 August. Third Army's mission was to rupture the German defences and 'if circumstances permit' to exploit in the direction of Bapaume. Byng was promised the 3rd Division, the 5th Division, the 63rd (Royal Naval) Division and the 17th (Northern) Division as reinforcements to help him effect the planned breakthrough, as well as an unspecified number of tanks and artillery pieces. Two cavalry divisions were to be placed at Byng's disposal for exploitation.[9] On 14 August

General Sir Henry Horne, commanding First Army, was informed that Third Army was expected to attack in about six days' time and that he was to prepare a supporting offensive on its left flank.[10]

At 11.45 on 14 August Third Army reported to GHQ that the German Seventeenth Army to its front was withdrawing from the six-mile broad salient south of Bucquoy.[11] Third Army had half expected some sort of German withdrawal and was now harassing the retreating Germans with artillery and offensive patrols. The British at the time could only guess at how far the Germans were intending to pull back. We now know that Ludendorff had sanctioned a withdrawal of a mile or two on the Seventeenth Army's front for the purpose of straightening out the line and economising on manpower. The withdrawal affected the German outpost zone only, not the main defensive position.[12]

By the morning of 15 August Third Army troops had entered the villages of Serre and Beaumont Hamel and were probing the outskirts of Bucquoy and Beaucourt.[13] But it was a cautious pursuit – Byng was taking no chances. Haig was keen to impart greater vigour and later the same day GHQ ordered Byng to press the enemy back 'energetically' in the direction of Bapaume and to make every effort to prevent rail and road communications being destroyed. Byng was told to expect to receive five tank battalions, with 156 tanks between them, in addition to the other reinforcements which he had already been promised.[14]

BYNG AND THE PLANNING FOR THE THIRD ARMY OFFENSIVE OF 21 AUGUST (See Map 4)

From a distinguished military family, educated at Eton and commissioned into the 10th Royal Hussars, General Sir Julian Byng had served creditably in the Sudan in the 1880s, in the South African War of 1899–1902 and at Gallipoli in 1915. On the Western Front he had one of the best records of all the senior British officers. As commander of the Canadian Corps he had been largely responsible for planning the successful assault on

Vimy Ridge on 9 April 1917. Later the same year, as commander of Third Army, he had approved, developed and implemented a highly innovative scheme for an attack towards Cambrai on 20 November 1917. Though the success of the German counter-attack, ten days later, blemished his reputation somewhat, Byng appears to have learnt from the experience. Third Army stood up reasonably well to the German offensive of spring 1918. Byng's Western Front career had been characterised by a commendable concern not to waste the lives of his men, and experience had made him very respectful of the military capacity of the German Army.[15] By August 1918 he seems to have become war-weary. His conduct for most of the Hundred Days would be characterised by great caution.

Byng's Army in mid-August 1918 consisted of three corps: from north to south the VI, the IV and the V Corps. Again from north to south, the VI Corps consisted of the 59th, the Guards and the 2nd Divisions, the IV Corps of the 37th, the New Zealand and the 42nd Divisions and the V Corps of the 21st and the 38th Divisions. Of the reinforcements Haig was now sending him Byng allocated the 3rd Division to the VI Corps , the 5th and the 63rd to the IV Corps, and the 17th to the V Corps. He kept the 62nd Division and the 1st and 2nd Cavalry Divisions in Army reserve.

By 21 August Third Army thus had 13 infantry divisions. It faced eight German divisions in the line and another two in reserve. British divisions at this period were, on average, substantially stronger than their German counterparts and there is no doubt that Third Army had a fairly major numerical supremacy, though this is difficult to quantify precisely. In qualitative terms, however, Byng's superiority was certainly not as great as that accorded to Rawlinson for the attack of 8 August. Only one of the German divisions, the 4th Bavarian Division, was of top quality, but Byng regarded about 50 per cent of his own infantry as mere 'boys' – recent conscripts of 18 or 19 years of age, who were likely to do well only if their baptism of fire was successful and not too traumatic. This assessment of the forces under his command appears to have reinforced Byng's tendency to caution.[16]

The ground over which Third Army was now to attack incorporated the southern edge of the 1917 Arras battlefield in the north and the northern end of the 1916 Somme battlefield in the south. It was a rolling chalk country, dotted with villages, though many of these had either been smashed up in earlier fighting or systematically wrecked by the Germans as part of their scorched earth retreat to the Hindenburg Line in February 1917. In the southern section of the Third Army area much of the V Corps front was on the west bank of the Ancre. This stream had been canalised at a higher level than the surrounding country. The banks having been broken by shelling, the country on either side had become a marsh covered with a tangle of fallen trees, branches and reeds. In some places the Germans had, almost superfluously, added wire to this obstacle course.[17]

In planning their attack across this terrain the British, as with the Fourth Army operation of 8 August, placed heavy emphasis on the attainment of surprise.[18] On 18 August GHQ issued the following instruction:

In order to prevent our troop movements being followed by means of our wireless activities, following precautions will be observed:-

1. *The Third Army will ensure that no additional wireless activity becomes apparent on their front.*
2. *The Fourth Army will maintain their present wireless activity, particularly in the case of the Cavalry Corps, Tank Corps and resting divisions.*
3. *All Armies will ensure that the wireless activity on their front remains, as far as possible, as at present, in spite of any moves of Corps, Divisions, Artillery, R.A.F. and Tanks, which may take place.*[19]

Third Army took elaborate precautions to preserve secrecy and the date and time of the attack (Zero was 04.55 on 21 August) was not disclosed until 19 August.[20] As with the Fourth Army attack of 8 August there was to be no preliminary bombardment. Prior to 21 August no alterations were to be made in the expenditure of artillery ammunition, aeroplane and anti-aircraft activity or road and railway repair and construction. All movements of troops into and within the Army area, were to take place at night.[21]

Third Army's artillery instructions were particularly strong in their emphasis on secrecy. Guns moved into Third Army in preparation for the offensive were to be carefully camouflaged and wheel tracks dug over or concealed. There were to be no gunners anywhere near them in daylight. Normal firing as carried out during the weeks before preparations for the offensive began, was to continue up to Zero hour. If a battery position in frequent use was to be moved within the Third Army area for the purposes of this operation, a single gun was ordered to be left in the old position and was to continue to fire from it. Not a single round was to be fired in registration. Artillery new to the area was to be registered silently with the aid of the Field Survey Sections of the Royal Engineers. On the night before the attack normal artillery fire was to be kept up from old positions in order to help drown the noise of the assembly of tanks.[22]

There were, according to GHQ's records, 828 field artillery pieces in Third Army on 21 August and 466 heavier weapons, giving a total of 1,294 barrels. According to these figures, Third Army had a field gun or field howitzer for every 43 yards of front and a heavier piece for every 76 yards. Third Army's own statement of its artillery strength at this time was, however, significantly higher than this (996 field and 482 heavy pieces) and Third Army did not mount a major offensive effort on its whole front. Thus gun density on the attack frontages was probably somewhat higher than the GHQ figures reproduced in the British official history suggest. Yet it was certainly significantly lower than had been available to Fourth Army on 8 August (a field gun for every 29 yards and a heavier piece for every 59 yards) and Third Army's artillery was, of course, assisting an attack by generally less experienced infantry. As the Third Army attack had been in preparation for a much shorter period, moreover, the standard of artillery intelligence was not so high. By no means had all German gun positions been identified for counter-battery purposes.[23]

Details of the fire-plans were left to the corps to devise but the Army artillery instruction laid down the broad principles. The field artillery was to commence barrage fire at Zero, while the heavier guns opened up simultaneously on German artillery positions and more distant strong-points. At least 70 per cent of the medium and heavy pieces were to be employed in the counter-battery role. To help ensure accuracy, a meteorological update was to be provided at Zero minus four hours. The proportion of smoke shell to be employed in the barrage would depend on the weather but was not to exceed one shell in six.[24]

The main offensive missions were allotted to Lieutenant-General Sir Aylmer Haldane's VI Corps on Third Army's left and Lieutenant-General Sir Montague Harper's IV Corps in its centre. Lieutenant-General C.D. Shute's V Corps facing the marshy Ancre on the Army's southern wing, was given only a subsidiary role. Two objectives were set for the VI and the IV Corps. The preliminary objective – the capture of the remainder of Ablainzeville and Bucquoy, together with the Moyenneville–Ablainzeville Spur – involved an advance of a mile or two only (the actual distance varying in different parts of the front). The main objective, only to be tackled if the preliminary operation were a success, was the line of the Arras–Amiens railway in the northern part of the attack frontage and the higher ground east of the railway along the line Gomiecourt–Bihucourt–Irles further south. Attaining it would involve an advance of more than four miles further in some parts of the IV Corps sector. Some exploitation beyond that line was allowed for if circumstances were favourable. But Third Army's orders were given in a spirit of very great caution. Corps commanders were told that attacks were not to be pressed in the face of very stiff resistance and heavy casualties.[25]

The 1st and 2nd Tank Brigades were allotted to the IV Corps and the VI Corps respectively and some training in tank/infantry co-operation was organised. Mark IV, Mark V, Mark V* and Whippet tanks and armoured cars were all being used in the offensive – the more mobile the vehicle the more distant the objective allocated. It was not anticipated that tanks would be used for deep exploitation and the experiment of Whippet/cavalry co-operation made by Fourth Army on 8 August was not to be repeated.[26]

Byng apparently saw very little chance of deep exploitation by anyone. He assigned a role to only one of the two cavalry divisions which GHQ had provided and the instructions given to the commander of that formation – Major-General R.L. Mullens of the 1st Cavalry Division – were extremely vague.[27] As Third Army's summary of operations put it: 'As the country was not very favourable for mounted action and opportunities would probably be fleeting the GOC Cavalry Division was left a free hand in carrying out his general task of exploitation . . .'.[28]

On 19 August Haig went to see Byng at Third Army HQ at Villers L'Hôpital. The cautious spirit in which Byng was planning the operation became obvious to Haig. Predictably he did not approve. He told Byng that Third Army's object ought to be to rupture the enemy's front completely, prevent the Germans destroying roads and bridges and push on rapidly in the direction of Bapaume. He insisted that Byng give greater opportunity to the cavalry and that he allocate a cavalry regiment to each of the attacking corps in order that corps commanders could rapidly exploit any success attained. While outwardly complying with the Commander-in-Chief's instructions Byng appears not to have changed his fundamental concept of operations.[29]

THE AIR PLAN FOR 21 AUGUST

As with the Fourth Army attack earlier in the month, a great deal of air power was made available to support the offensive. By 20 August the III Brigade RAF, an integral part of Third Army, included ten squadrons of single-seater fighters (largely Camels and SE5as). It also had squadrons of day bombers, night bombers and corps aircraft. The cavalry and the Tank

Corps each had one corps squadron attached for contact patrol work. One Camel squadron was tasked to deal with German anti-tank guns and a map was prepared for it showing the probable location of such weapons. Three further fighter squadrons were given ground attack missions, one in support of each of Third Army's infantry corps. But for this offensive a smaller proportion of fighter strength was to be committed to ground attack than had been the case on 8 August, and a correspondingly larger amount to the maintenance of air superiority. Four fighter squadrons of I Brigade (which normally co-operated with First Army) were ordered to carry out offensive patrols in the upper air (above 10,000ft) over and around Third Army's battlefield, while four of III Brigade's own squadrons would mount patrols below that altitude. A further two fighter squadrons belonging to IX Brigade were placed at III Brigade's disposal. Night bombers were to hit railway targets on the night of 21/22 August. Plans were made for the bombing of German airfields, headquarters and lines of communication from first light.

In the RAF, as in the Army, the greatest pains were taken to ensure that secrecy was maintained. Detailed plans including the date of Z day and the time of Zero hour were communicated to the wings only on 19 August. The squadrons were not informed until after the last patrol on Z – 1. No alterations in the normal pattern of air activity were allowed to take place before Zero. Some aircraft were detailed to fly over the front to drown the noise of the tanks on the night of 20/21 August. Similar night patrols were to be mounted by other RAF Brigades over fronts of First and Fourth Armies, where of course no tank actions were intended, so as to confuse the enemy and not draw particular attention to Third Army.[30]

ACTION ON 21 AUGUST

Just as with Fourth Army's attack on 8 August, the elements invalidated the RAF's plans to support the initial phase of Third Army's attack operation on 21 August. On the night of 20/21 there was heavy ground mist and

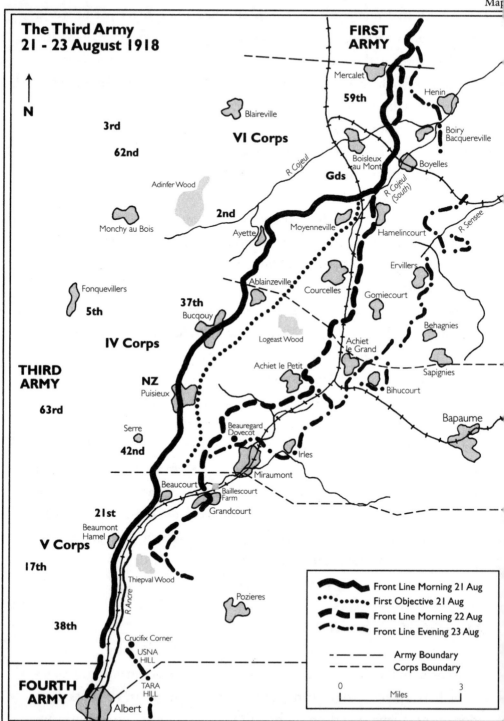

**The Third Army
21 - 23 August 1918**

N

FIRST
ARMY

Mercalet

59th

Henin

Boiry
Bacquereville

Blaireville

VI Corps

3rd

62nd

Boisleux
au Mont

Boyelles

Gds

R Cojeul

R Cojeul
(South)

Adinfer Wood

2nd

Moyenneville

Hamelincourt

R Sensee

Monchy au Bois

Ayette

Ervillers

Ablainzeville

Courcelles

Gomiecourt

Fonquevillers

5th

37th
Bucqouy

Logeast Wood

Achiet
le Grand

Behagnies

Sapignies

IV Corps

THIRD
ARMY

63rd

NZ
Puisieux

Achiet le Petit

Bihucourt

Bapaume

Serre

42nd

Beauregard
Dovecot

Irles

Miraumont

Beaucourt

21st

Beaumont
Hamel

Baillescourt
Farm

Grandcourt

V Corps

17th

Thiepval Wood

Pozieres

R Ancre

38th

Crucifix Corner

USNA
HILL

FOURTH
ARMY

TARA
HILL

Albert

～～～	Front Line Morning 21 Aug
••••••••	First Objective 21 Aug
▬ ▬ ▬	Front Line Morning 22 Aug
‑•‑•‑•	Front Line Evening 23 Aug
— — —	Army Boundary
– – –	Corps Boundary

0   3
Miles

drizzle which made the planned night bombing operations impossible. Thick fog for several hours after dawn rendered ground attack missions and the bombing of German aerodromes impracticable until about 10.00. After that the RAF undertook a good deal of useful ground attack work but, as on 8 August, proved unable to prevent some intervention by German aircraft. RAF offensive patrols met little opposition in the upper air. But some German fighters were able to get in at lower altitudes, intercepting RAF machines engaged in low-flying attack and, in a number of cases, causing disruption to advancing British troops. In contrast to 8 August, however, RAF losses were light with only two officers confirmed as killed and another three brought down on the German side of the lines. The RAF claimed four Fokker DVIIs destroyed.[31]

But the main action was, of course, on the ground. The VI Corps used no tanks in the first phase of the operation reserving its allocation for the second phase. Attacking with elements of the Guards Division and the 2nd Division, VI Corps took the Moyenneville–Ablainzeville Spur, its first objective, by 05.40. A few German machine-gun nests appear to have offered the only opposition and their fields of fire were drastically restricted by the fog, so losses amongst the attacking troops were light. The IV Corps, attacking with, from left to right, the 37th, the New Zealand and the 42nd Divisions, had taken its first objective by about 06.00. Opposition in this part of the front seems to have been slightly more serious, especially in front of the 37th Division, but was overcome with the aid of tanks. Twenty-two Mark IVs of the 7th Tank Battalion led the 37th Division's advance, the tanks moving immediately behind the creeping barrage and the infantry 50 yards behind them.[32]

The fortunes of these two corps when it came to the advance on the second objective were more varied. The VI Corps which had an easier mission as it was much closer to the objective, was fairly successful. After carrying out a leap-frog on the first objective, fresh elements of the Guards Division and the 3rd Division reached the Amiens–Arras railway, along the whole attack frontage, except for half a mile on the extreme right, by about 11.30. They did this with little tank support. Tanks were meant to join the infantry at the first objective and lead the advance to the second, but most became lost in the fog. The railway turned out to be the German main line of resistance. Having reached it the VI Corps' troops sustained fairly heavy shelling and machine-gun fire and, in accordance with Byng's instructions, they halted.[33]

The IV Corps had a harder time. At Zero plus 90 minutes, having leapfrogged the 37th Division on the first objective, the 63rd (Royal Naval) Division and the 5th Division were meant to push on to the railway. The New Zealand Division was to protect 5th Division's right flank while the 42nd (East Lancashire) Division took the high ground around Beauregard Dovecot and maintained touch with the V Corps to the south. Over most of the IV Corps' sector the railway was beyond the range of the field artillery from its initial positions. Though two artillery brigades were rushed forward as planned, their support proved inadequate to overcome German resistance. Between 10.00 and 11.00 the mist began to clear and tanks approaching the railway were knocked out by German guns. Attempts to reinforce IV Corps' artillery proved costly. Advancing batteries became good targets for German guns and some were strafed by German aircraft. The 63rd Division met fierce resistance from Achiet le Grand and its cemetery, opposition which the weak artillery support now available to the division was unable to overcome. The Hood Battalion of that division was actually counter-attacked by elements of the 4th Bavarian Division and driven back a few hundred yards. The 42nd Division was not able to take the Beauregard Dovecot that day. By dusk, though the IV Corps had managed to advance about three miles on a three-mile front, it did not hold the line of the railway at any point.[34]

Shute's V Corps made some progress north of the Ancre. Following an intensive bombardment by artillery and mortars, the 21st Division had taken the village of Beaucourt by 06.38 and three hours later it had gained the line of the sunken road west and north-west of Baillescourt Farm where it was in touch with the 42nd Division. Further south the 38th (Welsh)

Division pushed patrols across the Ancre but these met fairly serious resistance. A crossing in force did not seem possible. During the afternoon, therefore, Byng ordered the V Corps to halt the 38th Division until Albert had fallen to the Fourth Army – an event expected the following day. Once Albert had fallen the right flank of the stretch of German front resting on the Ancre would be turned.[35]

For the cavalry and the armoured cars there was nothing useful to be done on any part of the Third Army front on 21 August. With the German main line of resistance unbroken, no opportunity for exploitation existed. This became clear to everyone by the second half of the afternoon and at some time between 16.15 and 16.30, Third Army ordered the 2nd Cavalry Brigade, attached to VI Corps, to withdraw from the battlefield.[36]

THE GERMAN RESPONSE

German prisoners told their interrogators that they had been uneasy about the possibility of a British attack throughout the previous week but had no definite idea of when it might occur. The fresh 4th Bavarian Division had been moved into the line three days previously and some redeployment of troops already in the area had taken place. In the face of a major attack like this the Germans had planned to evacuate a forward zone 3,000–4,000 yards deep. Elements of the 4th Bavarian Division had apparently not been adequately briefed, and counter-attacked around Achiet le Petit when they should have retreated to the main defensive positions along the railway.[37]

Despite heavy losses in some units, on the evening of 21 August, General von Below, the commander of the German Seventeenth Army, seems to have been congratulating himself. The British, he believed, had shot their bolt, expending their effort on overrunning the forward zone and suffering heavy casualties in the process. Having brought up a reserve division, he seems to have been very confident that his Army could more than hold its own. He was, indeed, planning a major counter-attack.[38]

BYNG'S DECISION TO PAUSE

Von Below had seriously misread the battle. The Third Army had not strained itself to the utmost on 21 August but had carried out a cautious, limited kind of assault. It had crumpled the German forward defence zone, broken into the main defensive position in some places, and brought the whole of the main German defensive position within artillery range. It had taken around 2,000 prisoners, in addition to the other casualties inflicted, at a modest cost to itself. After a foggy start 21 August had become a very hot day and Third Army's troops were naturally fatigued, but they still had a great deal of fight left in them.[39]

Byng, nevertheless, ordered that the attack was to halt on 22 August while the infantry rested and regrouped and the artillery moved up. In itself this was reasonable. But he did not commit himself to a substantial attack at any point in the immediate future. He merely ordered that on 23 August the VI Corps should advance its front north of Moyenneville to gain a good departure position for 'a further possible advance' against the spur running north-east from Hamelincourt at a date unspecified. It is easy to appreciate Byng's concern not to overtask inexperienced troops. But these instructions were super-cautious in spirit and extraordinarily vague as to future intentions.[40]

Byng's decision to pause was reported to Haig at about 22.30 that night. The Field Marshal was not pleased. The scent of final victory was now strong in his nostrils and, like a bloodhound, he was in hot pursuit. On 20 August the French Tenth Army under General Mangin, one of the most resourceful and aggressive of the French generals, had mounted a twelve-division attack in a northerly direction on the Aisne between Compiègne and Soissons. An average of 3,000 yards was gained and fairly heavy losses inflicted. Mangin pressed ahead on 21 August and by that evening had advanced five miles in two days. Also on 21 August the French Third Army, under General Humbert, resumed the offensive on Mangin's left flank and had some success. Haig had already arranged for an attack immediately north of the Somme by the III Corps, the northernmost corps of Fourth Army, the following morning – 22 August. He had expected Third Army to continue the pressure on Fourth Army's left flank. Against the background of general success Byng's inaction was frustrating.[41]

The recollection of his own remarks to Winston Churchill, the Minister for Munitions, a few hours earlier, may have exacerbated Haig's irritation with Byng. Churchill had been talking about a grandiose munitions production programme for completion in June 1919. Haig had been irritated and had told Churchill that every effort should be made to win the war by autumn 1918. The Germans ought to be kept under continuous pressure, Haig had argued, and given no chance to recover from their current acute difficulties. The decision of Byng, one of his own subordinates, to take a break from offensive action at this critical time, must have seemed quite contrary to the spirit he had been trying to convey to Churchill. Haig expressed to Third Army that same night, as he put it in his diary, 'the *wish* that the attack should be resumed at the earliest possible moment'.[42]

ACTION ON 22 AUGUST

There was no major offensive action by Third Army on 22 August. That morning, on Third Army's front, it was the Germans who attacked. General von Below's orders, however, appear to have been received at divisional level rather late on the night of 21/22 August and the attacks put in that morning and during the early afternoon were ill-prepared, disjointed and easily defeated.[43] By weakening and tiring German units, these ill-organised counter-attacks made them more likely to succumb to the renewal of the Third Army offensive which, unknown to von Below, was being planned for the following day.

Fourth Army was the only BEF formation to launch a substantial attack on 22 August and even that was basically a one-corps affair. Since its last big offensive ended, on 11 August, Fourth Army had been drastically reduced. The Cavalry Corps had been withdrawn into reserve on 12

August and the Canadian Corps formally transferred to General Horne's First Army nine days later.[44]

On 22 August Fourth Army consisted only of III Corps and the Australian Corps, though the latter had swollen to the prodigious size of eight divisions, including the 32nd (British) Division and two Canadian divisions not yet transferred to the First Army. The III Corps, temporarily commanded by Lieutenant-General Alexander Godley (Sir Richard Butler being ill) held the front between the Third Army boundary, about a mile north of Albert, and the area in front of Bray-sur-Somme. It consisted, from left to right, of the 18th, the 12th and the 47th Divisions, with the 58th Division in corps reserve. The 3rd Australian Division, on the III Corps' right, held the stretch of front from Tailles Wood to the Somme Canal. Godley's mission was to make an advance of two miles, clearing the four German divisions to his front out of a recently established but well organised system of trenches facing the old Amiens Outer Defence Line, taking the town of Albert (or the ruins thereof) and securing a ridge of high ground between the Somme and the Ancre. The 3rd Australian Division was to secure the southern flank of the III Corps by advancing its left about 2,000 yards to some high ground immediately to the north of Bray-sur-Somme. Zero was to be 04.45 on 22 August.[45]

As was becoming normal with British offensive operations at this period, the intention was to achieve a high degree of surprise, forgoing a preliminary bombardment, though continuing with the normal amount of harassing fire. In fact, as a major battle had been in progress immediately to the north on the previous day, the Germans in this sector were alert. During the hours of darkness prior to the attack the German artillery was very active, putting down a great deal of high explosive and gas shell. But, while the shelling caused considerable casualties it did not prevent the troops deploying for the assault.[46]

On the left the 18th (Eastern) Division secured Albert between 04.45 and 09.45, in a methodical step-by-step operation with powerful artillery support. German resistance in Albert does not appear to have been intense and British casualties were light. At 04.49, four minutes after the start of the 18th Division's attack, 250 field artillery pieces laid a barrage 300 yards in front of the start line of the 47th and 12th Divisions. The infantry and a few tanks attached to them closed up to the barrage, which included a proportion of smoke shell, and hugged it as it moved forward at the rate of 100 yards every four minutes. Except in one small area these divisions had achieved their objectives by the end of the morning, as had the 3rd Australian Division, attacking on their right flank.[47]

But the III Corps' victory that day was slightly marred by an evening reverse. The 47th Division had been heavily shelled all afternoon and at about 17.50 it was counter-attacked. Its 142nd Brigade was pushed out of the area known as Happy Valley, which it had taken earlier in the day. Coping with the counter-attack left the 47th Division and much of the 12th Division too exhausted to continue the offensive the following day.[48]

THE ARMIES' PLANS FOR 23 AUGUST

During the morning of Thursday 22 August while his troops were defeating the German counter-attacks ordered by von Below, Byng was substantially revising his plans for 23 August. Having noted Haig's irritation at his decision to pause, Byng realised that the very limited operation he had intended for 23 August would not be acceptable to the Commander-in-Chief. Apparently wishing to avoid Haig's wrath, Byng worked closely with Haldane, the VI Corps' commander, to plan a more vigorous attack. Byng then proceeded to Advanced GHQ where he discussed his revised plan with Herbert Lawrence, Haig's chief of staff, who gave it his approval.[49]

Since the operations of 21 August, Haldane's VI Corps had been substantially reinforced by the 52nd Division, the 56th Division and the 57th Divisions and by the 63 tanks of the III Tank Brigade. According to the formal orders issued by Third Army on the morning of 22 August, the VI Corps was to capture Gomiecourt on the night of 22/23 August and then to push on in the direction of Ervillers and Sapignies. As soon as Gomiecourt had been taken by the VI Corps, the IV Corps was to attack the main German defensive position between Achiet le Grand and Irles. The V Corps was ordered to link up with the III Corps, on the left of Fourth Army, and to turn the German position at Thiepval from the south. All of Third Army's corps were thus to be involved in the 23 August operation, not just VI Corps as Byng had originally intended. The aim was now to break the front of the German Seventeenth Army that day and to inflict a major defeat.[50]

The fairly aggressive tone of the formal orders which Third Army issued on the morning of 22 August was strengthened by a handwritten note it sent to its corps about midday, perhaps after Byng's return from Advanced GHQ:

'Zero hour for the combined operation of the 4th and 6th Corps will be 11 a.m. August 23rd. The operation will be carried out whether Gomiecourt is taken tonight or not. If Gomiecourt is not taken 6th Corps will renew its attack on that place at 11 a.m. tomorrow August 23rd.'[51]

Third Army's plan for the operations of 23 August was thus drawn up in considerable haste and was inevitably couched in general terms. Much detailed work had been left to corps and divisional commanders and their staffs and they were left little time for planning and preparation.

While Third Army's operations of 23 August were to have a much greater scope than Byng had originally intended, Fourth Army's were to be significantly more modest than Rawlinson had hoped. Owing to the exhaustion of the 12th and 47th Divisions, as a result of the German counter-attack on the evening of 21 August, Rawlinson reluctantly accepted that, in III Corps, only the 18th Division could attack on 23 August. Fourth Army's main effort on 23 August would be mounted by the Australian Corps south of the Somme. Monash intended to mount a three-stage attack with two divisions: the 1st Australian Division and the 32nd Division in order to secure the general line Square Wood–Chuignes–Herleville.[52]

THE AIR PLAN FOR 23 AUGUST

As usual the RAF made quite elaborate plans to assist ground operations. The III and V Brigades organised close support for Third and Fourth Armies respectively while the IX Brigade had a more independent role and operated to a greater depth behind the front.

A heavy night bombing programme directed at German rail communications was organised by V Brigade for 22/23 August. During the daylight hours seven fighter squadrons were to use some of their aircraft in ground attack roles, five in support of Third Army and two in support of Fourth. As in previous operations, both III and V Brigades gave strong emphasis to protecting the tanks. But, after the shock of 8 August, the RAF was now well aware of the speed with which Germans could concentrate their air power and, as on 21 August, arranged for a good deal of fighter cover over the battlefield.

One of the lessons of the fighting of 8–11 August for the RAF was the need for improved communications, both to speed up the engagement of targets of opportunity on the ground and to give warning about enemy aircraft. To this end, a Wireless Central Information Bureau (CIB) was established at Villers-Bretonneux on 14 August. The CIB was designed to receive messages from aircraft fitted with wireless – mainly from corps aircraft – and to transmit them as rapidly as possible to the headquarters of fighter and bomber squadrons. In the case of enemy air activity it would also use a 24-ft arrow on the ground to point RAF fighters already airborne in the right direction, fighters not normally being fitted with radio at this period. The CIB was to conduct a major operation for the first time in the operations of 23 August and was to fulfil its intended functions to some effect.[53]

ACTION ON 23 AUGUST

The BEF's operations on Friday 23 August have a somewhat ragged appearance. A series of attacks was mounted by different formations at different times, with only limited co-ordination between them. As Haig had forced upon Byng a scale of activity for that day much greater than the latter had originally intended, the planning at corps level was inevitably somewhat hurried and unco-ordinated.

In Third Army both the VI Corps and the IV Corps mounted preliminary operations before their main attacks. Supported by their divisional artillery plus one extra brigade loaned by the 5th Division, elements of the 42nd Division and the New Zealand Division (IV Corps) seized the Beauregard Dovecot and the ridge north-east of it against light opposition in an attack commencing at 02.30. There were few casualties and some prisoners were taken. The IV Corps had thus gained commanding ground overlooking the Albert–Arras railway – the forward edge of the main German defensive position.[54]

The next move came at 04.00 as the 3rd Division of VI Corps advanced to seize the village of Gomiecourt. The 3rd Division had the support of seven brigades of field and two of heavy artillery and was assisted by a total of twelve tanks drawn from the 7th and 12th Battalions of the Tank Corps. The infantry of the two attacking brigades hugged their creeping barrage all the way to the objective. The tanks had some difficulty crossing the railway but eventually caught up with the infantry and performed useful work dealing with machine-gun posts. Gomiecourt was securely in British hands by 05.00. Casualties had been light and more than 300 prisoners had been taken.[55]

The main attack of the VI Corps began at 04.55. The objective was a ridge, about 1,200 yards from the start line, east of the line Boiry Becquerelle–Boyelles–Hamelincourt. This sector had seen no serious fighting on 21 August and there was some prospect that this northward extension of operations would take the Germans by surprise. The attack involved, from north to south, the 52nd, the 56th and the Guards Divisions, each supported by a battalion of tanks. The three attacking divisions followed a creeping barrage, consisting of 84 per cent shrapnel and 16 per cent smoke, fired by 17 brigades of field artillery. Seven brigades of heavy artillery fired on German battery positions and bombarded likely centres of resistance. Again, resistance was light and came mainly from machine-gunners. In some cases tanks helped overcome it while in others the machine-gunners retreated once British infantry had worked round their flanks. The VI Corps had taken all its objectives by 08.00.

Hearing that the attack had been everywhere successful, Haldane gave orders at 09.25 that the Guards Division push across the Sensée to the St Leger Ridge and that the 56th and 52nd Divisions should conform to the movements of the Guards. The Guards seized the St Leger Ridge and all three divisions gained a good deal of ground as the day progressed. But they did so rather unevenly. At nightfall they did not hold a very coherent defensive position though fortunately this did not matter as the Germans were in no position to counter-attack.[56]

Meanwhile, the 2nd Division had passed through the 3rd Division and at 11.00 had attacked towards the villages of Ervilliers, Behagnies and Sapignies. Co-ordination between the arms was mishandled in this attack. The artillery support was on exactly the same scale as had been available to the 3rd Division, but because 15 Whippet tanks were to lead the advance, the pace of the barrage was speeded up to 150 yards per minute rather than 100. This proved rather too slow for the Whippets but too fast for the infantry who tended to lose the barrage. In some sectors where the Whippets ran into difficulties, infantry were left with neither artillery nor tank support. Ervilliers had nevertheless been taken by 13.00, but infantry approaching Behagnies and Sapignies were met by intense artillery and machine-gun fire and those places remained in German hands. In the course of the day the VI Corps had managed an average advance of 2,000–3,000 yards on a front of 12,000 yards.[57]

The main attack of the IV Corps began at 11.00. The 37th Division, which had relieved the 63rd Division during the night, advanced on the defended villages of Achiet le Grand and Bihucourt, while the 5th Division moved on to Irles. The attack of these two divisions was supported by eleven brigades of field and four of heavy artillery as well as thirteen tanks. By nightfall all three villages were in British hands, although Irles, where very intense machine-gun fire was encountered, was not taken until 19.00. On 23 August, therefore, IV Corps had successfully broken into the main German defensive position from which it had been repulsed on 21 August and made an average advance of over 2,000 yards.[58]

On the left and centre of V Corps there was little change on 23 August. On the corps' right, however, a brigade of the 38th (Welsh) Division advanced at 04.45 with the support of its divisional artillery and a small number of tanks to seize the small hill known to the BEF as Usna, part of the so-called Tara–Usna position. Tara was simultaneously attacked by a brigade of the 18th Division with roughly the same level of artillery and armour support. Complete success had been attained by about 06.00. The 38th Division followed this by taking the position known as Crucifix Corner and by pushing patrols into Thiepval Wood.[59]

South of the Somme the Australian Corps mounted an operation of considerably greater tactical complexity than any carried out by a Third Army corps that day. Space permits little more than a mention here. Supported by a limited operation by the 32nd Division on its right, the 1st Australian Division captured the Froissy plateau and the village of Chuignes, shattering three German divisions and capturing 2,596 prisoners, 23 guns and 167 machine guns in the process. It was one of the most remarkable performances by any BEF division in the whole war, achieved against an enemy who (though demoralised) was fairly alert from the outset and whose artillery remained active all day. The Australians suffered about 1,000 casualties in the process.[60]

Air power had played some part in the events of 23 August, though its role was minor compared with those of the artillery and infantry. The night of 22/23 August was fine and moonlit and the bombing carried out by IX Brigade on railway targets in the German rear achieved greater success than was normal for that kind of activity. Somain, Cambrai junction and Valenciennes stations were all attacked. At Somain twelve direct hits were claimed, including four on an ammunition train which was set on fire, causing numerous explosions. Two further trains were hit, one in the station. Further bombing attacks were carried out behind the lines in daylight hours and there was a good deal of fighter ground attack – some of it conspicuously successful, the Camels of No. 73 Squadron effectively neutralising German batteries firing on tanks at Hamelincourt and Boyelles. Aircraft of corps squadrons also engaged ground targets on occasion, an RE8 of Third Brigade giving useful assistance to New Zealand troops. German airmen seem to have had little opportunity to intervene in the ground battle on 23 August and the RAF appears to have taken few casualties.[61]

About 98 tanks were employed on 23 August – about 60 with Third Army and 38 with the Australian Corps. Over much of the front they played a significant role in the victory, though successful attacks were also carried out without their help, especially by 3rd Australian Brigade which had to negotiate the slopes in front of Froissy Beacon – too steep for tanks. The intense heat of this day ensured that virtually all crews who saw action were suffering from acute exhaustion by its end which, together with petrol fumes and carbon monoxide poisoning, made some crews very ill indeed.[62]

On 23 August, Third Army had taken about 5,000 prisoners and Fourth Army upwards of 3,000.[63] In the period 21–23 August, therefore, the Germans had lost well over 10,000 men to the British Third and Fourth Armies in prisoners alone. They had suffered two serious defeats at the hands of the BEF in little more than a fortnight.

ANALYSIS

The victory of 21–23 August was won mainly by an Army commanded by a general who lacked confidence in his own troops and was reluctant to attack vigorously. Unlike Rawlinson in July and early August, Byng saw no great opportunity beckoning on his front. Without direct orders from Haig it is very unlikely that he would have mounted a major attack. The balance of forces between Third Army and the Germans in front of it on 21 August was not so favourable as it had been for Fourth Army on 8 August, thus the circumspect approach Byng adopted for operations on 21 August was quite reasonable. His decision to pause on 22 August, permitting his infantry some opportunity for rest and reorganisation and allowing artillery to be brought up, was arguably the correct one. But he carried caution too far. It is difficult to justify his very half-hearted initial plan for 23 August.

Ultimately the tension between Haig, the chronic optimist, and Byng, apparently suffering at this period of the war from excessive pessimism, seems to have proved fortuitous. It led to a more favourable result than would, perhaps, have been the case had operations been directed wholly by either. Third Army's cautious attack of 21 August crumpled the German forward defence zone and made some penetration into the main defence zone without incurring excessive losses. Encouraged by the apparent lack of vigour on the British side, von Below decided to mount a major counter-attack. This was inappropriate and seems seriously to have weakened his Army. Had Byng been left to his own devices, however, Third Army would have made only the feeblest of efforts on 23 August. Haig's insistence on a much more substantial attack took advantage of German weakness and resulted in a considerable victory.

The Fourth Army attack of 8–11 August had employed the BEF's two most formidable corps: the Australian and the Canadian. These formations had enjoyed an extraordinary degree of surprise, crushing fire superiority and the most massive armour support in the history of warfare up to that point. All but one of Third Army's divisions were from the mother country and most consisted largely of young conscripts. Yet by 18.00 on 24 August nearly 10,000 prisoners – 287 officers and 9,565 other ranks – had passed through Third Army's corps cages since the start of its offensive three days earlier.[64] This is highly significant. The first few days of the Battle of Albert proved that the BEF as a whole, not merely the exceptionally powerful Dominion corps, could inflict serious defeats on the Germans. It could do so with a lesser degree of surprise, with a much less pronounced superiority in artillery, and with much less armour than it had used on 8 August.

6

THE ADVANCE TO THE HINDENBURG LINE

HAIG'S STRATEGIC APPRECIATION: 22–23 AUGUST

Late on the night of Thursday 22 August Haig sent a telegram to the commanders of all the British Armies. Both an appreciation of the current military situation and an exhortation to redoubled effort, it came rather too late to affect the fighting of 23 August but seems to have influenced the conduct of operations on subsequent days, to which, indeed, it was more relevant. The key paragraphs are worth quoting:

I request that Army Commanders will, without delay, bring to the notice of all subordinate leaders the changed conditions under which operations are now being carried on . . .

The methods which we have followed, hitherto, in our battles with limited objectives when the enemy was strong, are no longer suited to his present condition.

The enemy has not the means to deliver counter-attacks on an extended scale, nor has he the numbers to hold a position against the very extended advance which is now being directed upon him.

To turn the present situation to account the most resolute offensive is everywhere desirable. Risks which a month ago would have been criminal to incur, ought now to be incurred as a duty.

It is no longer necessary to advance in regular lines and step by step. On the contrary, each division should be given a distant objective which must be reached independently of its neighbour, and even if one's flank is thereby exposed for the time being.

Reinforcements must be directed against the sectors where our troops are gaining ground not where they are checked . . .

The situation is most favourable; let each one of us act energetically, and without hesitation push forward to our objective.[1]

This was Haig's formal declaration that the almost static, positional warfare conditions of 1915–17, which had always seemed to him both aberrant and abhorrent, were finally a thing of the past. Normal, mobile warfare, to which he had devoted so much professional study before 1914, was now back. Just how optimistic he was at this period is indicated by an entry in his diary for 23 August. Byng, the Third Army commander, had given an order which would have resulted in the wide separation of the 1st and 2nd Cavalry Divisions. Haig, on the other hand, 'wished the cavalry kept together as a corps for strategical objectives in view of the possibility of the rapid disintegration of the enemy'.[2]

The Commander-in-Chief's imagination was again running ahead of events. There would be no opportunity for the large-scale employment of cavalry in the immediate future. On 24 August German resistance was still stubborn on many parts of the fronts of the British Third and Fourth Armies.[3] It was certainly true that the Germans had taken terrible losses and that their morale was sinking fast. A letter written by a soldier of the 217th Reserve Infantry Regiment of the 225th Division indicated, for example, that 'over the last few days our company has lost over 70 men and I am amongst those who remain, 10 NCOs and 26 men, and we still have to hold on. Our battalion is now equal to a company and a company to a platoon. Our three regiments are now only equal to one.'[4] Haig's suggestion that flank protection was no longer important, however, needed considerable qualification.[5] Though the Germans did not always withdraw in a completely orderly fashion, they normally managed to cover their retreats with rearguards composed of the most reliable and

Mark V tanks of the 10th Tank Battalion in a cornfield on 9 August 1918, second day of the Battle of Amiens.

German prisoners of war arriving at a cage on 9 August.

Artillery in open warfare: an Australian 18-pdr gun in action on 23 August, during the Battle of Albert.

A 60-pdr gun in action in the early morning of 27 September, at the start of the Battle of the Canal du Nord.

Mark V tanks fitted with cribs for the attack on the Main Hindenburg System. German prisoners are in the central foreground with Tank Corps and Australian personnel standing around them.

Canadians entering Cambrai on 9 October.

A Sopwith Camel: one of the standard British fighters of 1918.

*The BEF as an army of liberation: men of the 8th Liverpool Irish,
57th Division, Fifth Army, enter Lille, recently abandoned by the Germans,
on 18 October 1918.*

Another scene of the entry into Lille.

Haig with the Prince of Wales outside the GHQ train on 11 November 1918.

determined troops. Enfilading machine-gun fire delivered by such people was as dangerous as ever.[6] In order to bring the Germans to breaking point without crippling losses to themselves, British forces would have to apply pressure with somewhat greater caution than Haig's message of 22 August suggested.

BRITISH THIRD ARMY AND FOURTH ARMY FRONTS: 24–29 AUGUST

After the 'black day' of 8 August, Ludendorff had refused to make any major withdrawal but had sanctioned the preparation of a so-called 'Winter Position', based partly on the Canal du Nord and partly on the south–north line of the Somme. As the position's name suggests Ludendorff intended that the German Army hold it throughout the winter of 1918–19. It was, however, still incomplete when, in the Battle of Albert, the Germans suffered their second heavy defeat within a month and Ludendorff was forced to sanction a withdrawal to it. The retreat was supposed to pivot from the north, where it would be anchored on a genuinely formidable position known to the British as the Drocourt–Quéant Line and to the Germans as the Wotan Position, a northward extension of the Hindenburg Line (Siegfried Position). The German Second and Eighteenth Armies received the order to withdraw on Monday 26 August and were supposed to start moving on the night of 27/28 August.[7] By that time, however, parts of the German Seventeenth and Second Armies (facing British Third and Fourth Armies respectively) were already being bundled un-ceremoniously backward.

Obedient to the spirit of Haig's instructions, Byng's and Rawlinson's forces mounted major night attacks in the small hours of Sunday 25 August, taking advantage of a nearly full moon. These efforts met with substantial success and both Armies continued the effort in the daylight hours.[8] Rawlinson, however, was having serious doubts whether he could maintain the same kind of pressure for much longer. Fourth Army now consisted only of III Corps, the Australians and the 32nd Division, the latter operating as part of the Australian Corps. Rawlinson considered his forces tired and in need of relief. He had asked for fresh divisions but Haig had said he could spare none. Haig was shifting the main weight of the offensive further north.[9] Rawlinson therefore suggested to Monash, on the afternoon of 25 August, that the Australian Corps' effort should be eased down.[10] Monash, however, had the bit between his teeth. He felt there was plenty of fight left in his troops and that the Germans were weakening. Responding to Monash's leadership, the Australian Corps drove on relentlessly over the next week and Rawlinson made no attempt to interfere.[11] The III Corps, on Fourth Army's left, kept pace fairly well. By Thursday 29 August the Australian Corps had reached the south–north stretch of the Somme. Third Army, meanwhile, pushed forward in the face of opposition which was seldom negligible and often intense. On 29 August Bapaume, evacuated by the Germans the night before, was occupied by the New Zealand Division.[12]

The pursuit and harassment of a retreating enemy could not be controlled in detail by Army commanders and their staffs. All they could do was to set general objectives, leaving the detail to be filled in by subordinate formations and units. As a recent study of the Fourth Army commander puts it:

> From 23 August to 3 September Rawlinson enjoyed the unfamiliar experience of presiding over a battle field that moved every day. Apart from indicating the general line of advance. . . he had little call to intervene in these conditions. Actions were continuous and small in scale.[13]

In the relatively mobile warfare of this period corps commanders, too, were often little more than spectators and the actual conduct of operations tended to devolve on divisional, brigade, battalion and sub-unit commanders.[14]

As the British Third and Fourth Armies advanced, both sides adapted their tactics to conditions of semi-mobile warfare. The Germans covered their retreats with rear-guards consisting primarily of machine-gunners, assisted by some field artillery. British and Dominion forces, conversely, made increasing use of advanced guards. On 26 August all three of III Corps' divisions employed one brigade as an advanced guard, one as a support and one as a reserve.[15] The need to overcome efficiently the resistance of German machine-gun-based rearguards placed a particular premium on the co-ordination of fire and manoeuvre at company and platoon level. Pivoting, as they had long been trained to do, on the suppressive fire of their Lewis gun sections, platoons would try to use ground skilfully to approach the enemy closely enough to use other weapons. Often the fatal blow would be struck with a rifle grenade. Between 27 August and 2 September over 20,000 rifle grenades were issued to the 2nd Australian Division alone.[16]

Artillery was still vitally important to both sides but each was now using it rather differently. In the relatively fluid conditions which now existed, British and Dominion forces were tending to use creeping barrages less frequently. 'Creepers' took a good deal of time to arrange and were most effective if the infantry's start line were straight, a condition which often did not apply. Hurricane bombardments or standing barrages directed against particular centres of resistance were easier to arrange and increasingly substituted. In addition, field guns, and sometimes heavier pieces, were pushed well forward to offer more intimate support.[17] For the Germans one of the most difficult problems of the retreat was how to withdraw their guns. Their normal procedure was to preface an artillery withdrawal by an intense bombardment, for the dual purpose of intimidating would-be attackers and using up all the ammunition dumped near the gun positions. They would then accompany the withdrawal of their field guns by the more intense activity of their heavier artillery and vice-versa, and a small number of field guns or mortars would form an integral part of most rearguards.[18] When withdrawing under great pressure the gunners could not always rely on the help of their infantry, as an extract from orders to the German 2nd Guards Division for 27 August makes clear:

According to reports to Army Headquarters the infantry of other divisions ... hardly made any use of their rifles. The whole defence has been left to the machine guns and artillery. A large number of cases have also been substantiated in which companies of infantry have passed through the artillery lines and have not observed the request of the artillery to protect them ... By order of the Army, artillery officers are empowered to find out the name of every unit and commander who refused protection to the artillery and to report them.[19]

It was difficult for the British to know how best to use their tanks in these more mobile conditions. Since 8 August tanks had become almost universally popular with British and Dominion infantry and were in constant demand. But they were very few in relation to the size of the active front. With the exception of the Whippets (of which there was only a tiny number) they were not, moreover, really designed for mobile warfare. If they led the advance they would tend to blunder into the field guns usually found in German rearguards and be quickly knocked out. It was thus best to keep them some distance behind the most advanced troops and summon them when required. With their lack of wireless communication and limited mobility, however, there could then be difficulties in getting them to the right place promptly. Even when they did appear they were of little use in woods where German rearguards often took up position. The infantry found, therefore, that it was not advisable to rely on them. GHQ increasingly tended to keep tanks in hand for the really big 'deliberate' attacks rather than allowing them to be frittered away in the course of pursuits, during which they inevitably underwent a great deal of mechanical wear and tear.[20]

Air power was vastly more useful than armour in harassing the retreating Germans. Despite a good deal of low cloud and rain between 24 and 27 August, corps aircraft were still able to do some effective artillery spotting, and fighter squadrons carried out low-flying attacks on German infantry moving in the open.[21]

HAIG'S PLANS FOR FIRST ARMY: 14–26 AUGUST

There was more to Haig's direction of the campaign in late August than exhortations to Third and Fourth Armies to redouble their efforts. He planned, for the second time since 8 August, to surprise and unbalance the Germans by widening the offensive northwards. On this occasion he was to bring in the First Army, commanded by General Sir Henry Horne.

On 14 and 16 August GHQ sent warning orders to General Sir Henry Horne, commanding First Army, in the Arras sector, telling him to be prepared to mount an attack at short notice on Orange Hill and Monchy le Preux – commanding heights immediately to his front.[22] Though Horne submitted a scheme for such an operation to GHQ on 17 August,[23] only minor operations were actually mounted on the First Army front over the next few days. On 24 August, however, GHQ spelt out to Horne a complex and demanding mission. First Army was first to advance to the Drocourt–Quéant (henceforth D–Q) Line, a northward extension of the Hindenburg Line. It was then to assault and break that line and finally to 'operate in a south-easterly direction against the troops opposed to the Third Army'.[24]

Haig's hopes for the forthcoming First Army operation as expressed in his diary were even more grandiose than the orders issued to Horne suggested. Once through the D–Q Line, Haig hoped that Horne would 'press on as fast as possible against Marquion [to the east of the Canal du Nord] where the enemy's depots are which supply the whole of von Below's [Seventeenth] Army'. The Cavalry Corps, augmented by an infantry

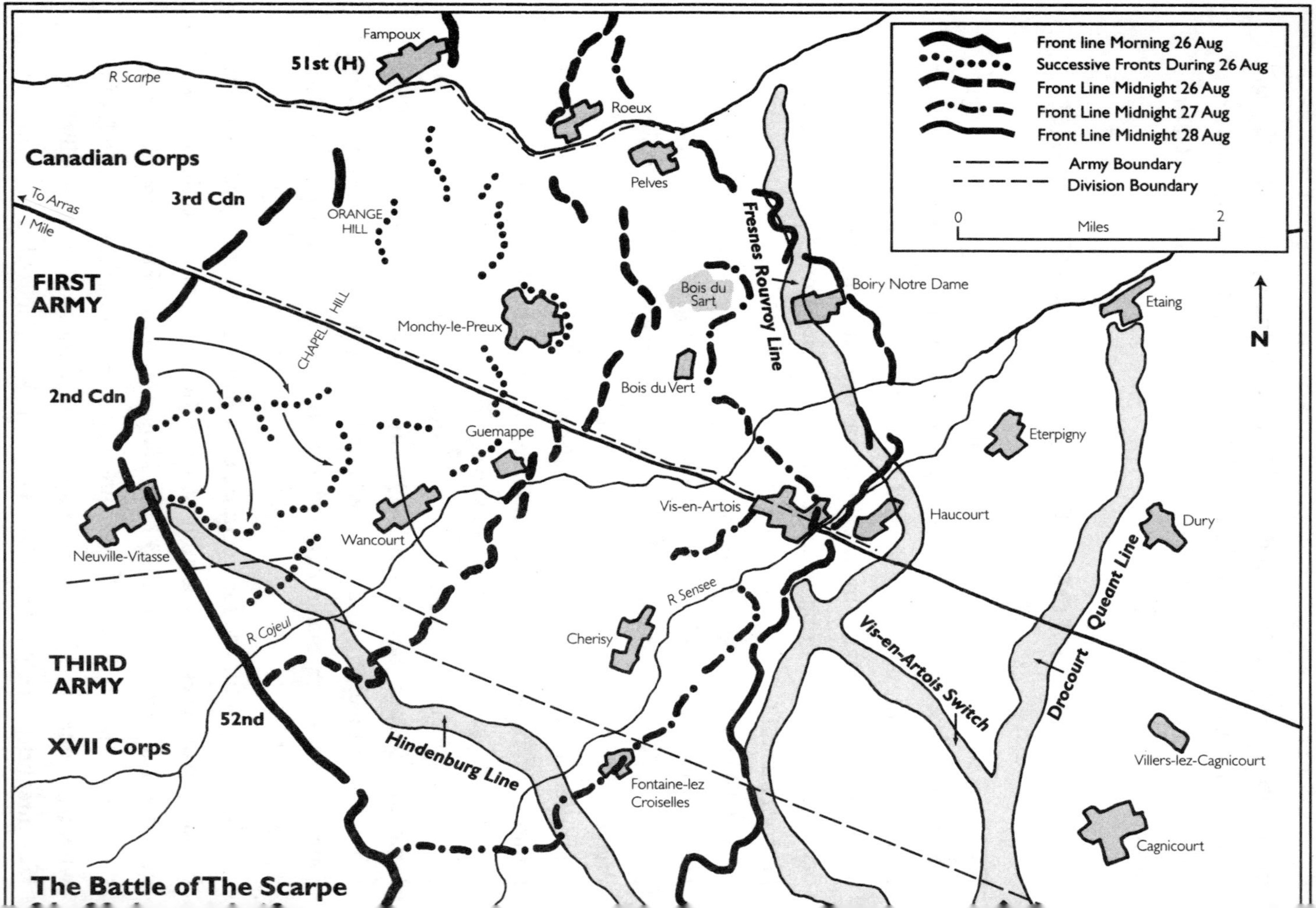

Map 5

The Battle of The Scarpe

Canadian Corps

51st (H)

3rd Cdn

FIRST ARMY

2nd Cdn

THIRD ARMY

XVII Corps

52nd

Front line Morning 26 Aug
Successive Fronts During 26 Aug
Front Line Midnight 26 Aug
Front Line Midnight 27 Aug
Front Line Midnight 28 Aug
Army Boundary
Division Boundary

Fresnes Rouvroy Line
Vis-en-Artois Switch
Quéant Line
Drocourt
Hindenburg Line

Fampoux
Roeux
Pelves
Boiry Notre Dame
Etaing
Eterpigny
Dury
Villers-lez-Cagnicourt
Cagnicourt
Haucourt
Bois du Sart
Bois du Vert
Vis-en-Artois
Cherisy
Fontaine-lez-Croiselles
Orange Hill
Monchy-le-Preux
Chapel Hill
Guemappe
Wancourt
Neuville-Vitasse
R Scarpe
R Sensée
R Cojeul
To Arras
Miles
1 Mile
N

brigade in buses and extra motorised machine-gun batteries was to be positioned so as to take advantage of the projected First Army breakthrough. Haig thought that 'after we get the Marquion–Canal du Nord Line [we] might possibly get the chance of pushing on the Cavalry Corps to the Bois du Bourlon [south-west of Cambrai] to intercept the enemy's retreat'.[25]

To be ready to exploit a favourable opportunity is good generalship. As usual, however, Haig was underestimating the difficulties which lay ahead. The Canadian Corps, Horne's chosen instrument for breaking the D–Q Line, would have to advance about six miles to the east, along the banks of the River Scarpe, just in order to reach it. During the advance the Canadians would have to tackle a number of lesser systems of fortification, some of them quite formidable in themselves. To make progress through the area still more difficult, the whole of it was scarred with a tangle of old trenches and littered with the debris of past battles. Three German divisions of reasonably good quality occupied the commanding ground immediately to the Canadian Corps' front, and there were more holding the D–Q Line itself.[26]

THE BATTLE OF THE SCARPE: 26–29 AUGUST

General Sir Henry Horne, a gunner from an Anglo-Irish background, educated at Harrow and Woolwich, has remained a rather shadowy figure for historians. He seems to have performed well as chief gunner of the cavalry division, of which Haig was chief of staff, in the South African War of 1899–1902. He had certainly been on good terms with Haig since that time. A brigadier-general in August 1914, he rose steadily in rank and authority until he took command of First Army in September 1916. As the General Officer Commanding First Army he never suffered a disaster but did not really behave like an Army commander. From the attack on Vimy Ridge on 9 April 1917 he seems to have acquired the habit of giving all substantial offensive tasks to the Canadian Corps and leaving both planning and execution very largely to that corps' commander and his staff.

That is certainly what he did with the Battle of the Scarpe (as the advance to the D–Q Line was later christened). Effective command was delegated to Sir Arthur Currie. The VIII Corps and the XXII Corps, the other corps in First Army, were used merely to secure the Canadians' left flank and First Army headquarters' only real contribution was a deception plan. The reappearance of the Canadians (universally regarded as shock troops) in this sector would have been enough to make German intelligence officers smell trouble. By the use of artillery bombardments, conspicuous tank-infantry training, dummy ammunition dumps and casualty clearing stations and false radio traffic, the First Army deception plan was intended to make them believe that the main effort would be north of the Scarpe and to draw attention away from the Arras–Cambrai road.[27]

In the advance to the D–Q Line Currie used three divisions: the 51st (Highland) Division on the left, north of the Scarpe, the 3rd Canadian Division between the Scarpe and the Cambrai road, and the 2nd Canadian Division from the Cambrai road to the Army boundary. The 1st and 4th Canadian Divisions were not involved at this stage as they only arrived from the Fourth Army area on 25 and 28 August respectively. The Canadian divisions were to try to capture Orange Hill, Chapel Hill and the hill on which stood the village of Monchy-le-Preux. Their final objective for the day was a line just east of that village. The 51st (Highland) Division was not given a specific objective. It was simply to advance along the north bank of the Scarpe keeping pace with the Canadians. Currie had 14 brigades of field and nine of heavy artillery. Casualties to tanks had been very heavy over the last couple of weeks and there were few available, the two Canadian divisions being allotted nine each. The provision of air support was a good deal more lavish. The Canadian Corps had the full support of I Brigade RAF with five fighter squadrons, one fighter reconnaissance squadron, one day bomber and one night bomber squadron and five corps squadrons. Of the corps squadrons, two were allocated for close co-operation with tanks, two with the infantry and one with the Cavalry Corps. In keeping with the increasingly nocturnal habits of all of the British forces, Currie set Zero hour for the Canadian Corps on Monday 26 August at 03.00.[28]

Owing to a combination of tight security, the deception plan and attacking at night, the Canadian Corps attack seems to have achieved a significant degree of surprise.[29] The infantry judged their artillery and machine-gun barrages excellently and these, together with the surprise and the darkness, helped keep casualties down in the first two or three hours. By 06.00, the 2nd Canadian Division had taken Chapel Hill. The 4th Canadian Mounted Rifles of the 3rd Canadian Division (attacking, of course, as dismounted infantry) took Orange Hill, first making an enveloping manoeuvre along the south bank of the Scarpe and then turning sharp right and seizing the position in a left flanking attack from the north. The 1st and 5th Canadian Mounted Rifles, respectively on the left and right, then passed through the 4th Battalion. Attacking Monchy from the north and west they had taken it by 07.40. Later in the day, the Canadians were heavily counter-attacked by the German 35th Division which had moved forward from the D–Q Line. The counter-attacks were smashed, however, and at dusk the Canadians held a line 1,000yd to the east of Monchy, having advanced about three miles in the day. It was a brilliant beginning.[30]

Over the next two days, however, German resistance consolidated and, despite the most heroic efforts, the Canadian advance gradually slowed. A particular difficulty on both 26 and 27 August was foul weather, with a low cloud-base. This greatly handicapped the RAF and made target acquisition for the artillery, especially for counter-battery work, difficult.[31] Currie hoped to break the German Fresnes–Rouvroy Line, about a mile west of the D–Q Line, in the course of 27 August, but after ferocious fighting all day, it was not possible even to reach it. The fighting on 28 August proved even bloodier. The Canadians did breach one stretch of the Fresnes–Rouvroy Line but their losses in so doing were severe.[32]

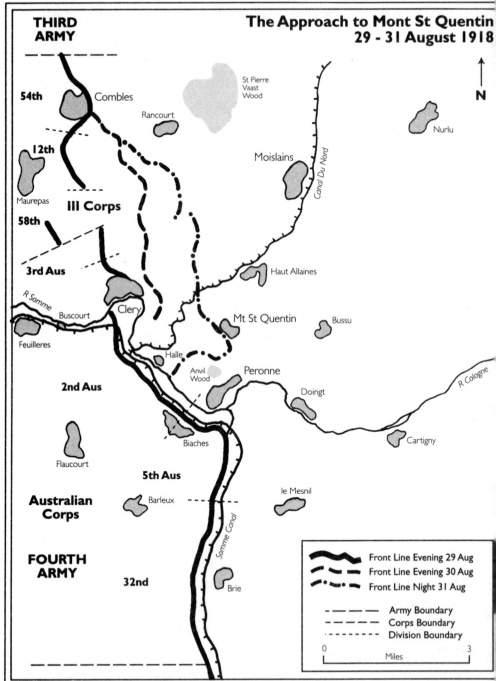

THIRD ARMY

The Approach to Mont St Quentin
29 - 31 August 1918

N

54th

Combles

Rancourt

St Pierre
Vaast
Wood

Moislains

Nurlu

Canal Du Nord

12th

Maurepas

III Corps

58th

3rd Aus

R Somme

Buscourt

Clery

Haut Allaines

Mt St Quentin

Bussu

Feuilleres

Halle

Anvil
Wood

Peronne

Doingt

R Cologne

2nd Aus

Biaches

Cartigny

Flaucourt

5th Aus

Barleux

le Mesnil

Australian
Corps

Somme Canal

FOURTH
ARMY

32nd

Brie

～～～	Front Line Evening 29 Aug
━ ━ ━	Front Line Evening 30 Aug
·—·—·	Front Line Night 31 Aug
— — —	Army Boundary
– – –	Corps Boundary
········	Division Boundary

0   3
Miles

Casualties reported by the 2nd Canadian Division and the 3rd Canadian Division for the three days' fighting from 26–28 August totalled 254 officers and 5,547 other ranks – appalling by any standard. Both divisions were exhausted and Currie decided to relieve them. He reported to Horne, on the afternoon of 28 August, that it would not be possible to attack the D–Q Line before 31 August at the earliest. On the night of 28/29 August the 2nd Canadian Division was relieved by the 1st Canadian Division and the 3rd by the 4th (British) Division. (The 4th Canadian Division had still not arrived from the Fourth Army area.) Though the Canadian attack had not so far met Haig's somewhat fanciful expectations it had been a very fine achievement. The two Canadian divisions had taken more than 3,300 prisoners, 53 guns and 519 machine guns in their three days' fighting.[33]

MONT ST QUENTIN AND PÉRONNE: 29 AUGUST–1 SEPTEMBER

By the evening of Thursday 29 August, the Australian Corps had reached the banks of the Somme from Cléry to St Christ. The Germans had at least partially destroyed all the bridges and they beat back with intense machine-gun fire all attempts to cross. The south–north stretch of the Somme, to the south of Péronne, was a formidable obstacle. There were marshes over a thousand yards wide, studded with many small islets overgrown with rushes. The river itself ran in a number of different channels. The marshes were waist-deep and the water channels could not be forded. Behind this marshy ground was the Somme Canal. North of the Somme, too, German resistance was consolidating. German artillery was becoming more concentrated and more active and it became clear that, on the Fourth Army front, the German high command intended its troops to retreat no further.[34]

In the scheme of things which GHQ outlined to the Armies on 29 August it appears to have been accepted that the Germans might successfully defend their positions along most of the Third and Fourth Army fronts for the next few days. For the restoration of mobility Haig was counting on an enveloping manoeuvre from the north:

> *The First Army will deliver an attack against the Drocourt–Quéant Line south of the river Scarpe on a date to be notified hereafter, and will exploit any success gained . . .*
>
> *The intention is then to direct the Cavalry Corps south-eastwards so as to operate against the communications of the hostile troops opposing the Third and Fourth Armies.*
>
> *The Third and Fourth Armies will co-operate by vigorous action* **with the object of holding the enemy on their respective fronts**. [Emphasis added.][35]

In reality the Canadian drive to the D–Q Line was making slow progress. Given the intensity of the resistance that the Canadians had so far encountered, it was optimistic on Haig's part to assume that they would soon break that line. It was even more so to believe that the Cavalry Corps would be able to sever or seriously threaten the communications of the Germans facing the Third and Fourth Armies. The orders which Fourth Army HQ sent to its corps commanders on 30 August were, however, in keeping with Haig's concept of operations. Rawlinson intended that his Army's main effort would be made by the III Corps, on the left.[36] That effort would pin down German troops but, in itself, was unlikely to achieve dramatic results. By the time Rawlinson's orders were issued, however, Monash, who had been the real driving force in Fourth Army since 25 August, had already set in motion a much bolder plan of operations for his own corps. So daring was it, indeed, that Rawlinson, when he was rather belatedly informed of it on the evening of 30 August, considered it foolhardy and authorised its execution with some reluctance.[37]

Monash considered the seizure of Mont St Quentin the first step to the capture of Péronne and the turning of the German position on the south–north line of the Somme. Mont St Quentin was a wide, smooth-sided hill with the ruins of a village on top, in the angle between the Somme and the Canal du Nord, a mile north of Péronne. Rising 140ft above the town, it commanded both the east–west and south–north stretches of the Somme. Its slopes were devoid of cover and protected by several belts of barbed wire. Prisoner interrogations revealed that the German high command had issued instructions that the Mont St Quentin area was to be held at all costs. Its defence was entrusted to the 2nd Guards Division, one of the best German formations remaining.[38]

At 14.30 on 29 August Monash held a conference with his divisional commanders. As it emerged from this conference his plan was that one brigade of the 2nd Australian Division would cross the Somme at Halles and take Mont St Quentin by a surprise attack. Meanwhile, a brigade of the 5th Australian Division would try to cross at the Péronne bridges and take the town directly. If that proved impossible, it would follow the 2nd Australian Division across the river and then proceed to take Péronne from the north. The 32nd Division would extend its boundary leftwards in order that the fronts of the 2nd Australian Division and the 5th Australian Division could be narrowed. Major-General Rosenthal, commanding 5th Australian Division, selected the 5th Australian Brigade for the attack on Mont St Quentin, while Major-General Hobbs, commanding the 2nd Australian Division, selected his 14th Brigade to take Péronne.

Early on the morning of 30 August three battalions of the 5th Australian Brigade were pulled out of the line, leaving just one holding what had been the brigade front. The brigade made its main crossing not at Halles, as originally intended, but at Feuillères where there was a bridge which had been adequately repaired. It then moved along the north bank of the Somme in an easterly direction towards Cléry-sur-Somme. By 21.00 German troops holding some trenches on the north-east side of Cléry had been cleared out. By 22.30 two Australian battalions, the 17th and the 20th, were established in jumping off positions for the attack on Mont St Quentin the following morning, while the 18th Battalion remained in reserve in the village. Later that night the 19th Battalion was brought across the Somme using a repaired bridge at Ommiecourt and moved into position for the following morning's attack.[39]

At 05.00 on Saturday 31 August, the 20th, 17th and 19th Battalions (5th Australian Brigade, 2nd Australian Division), comprising only 1,200 men in total, attacked towards Mont St Quentin. Their artillery support, from five brigades of field and one of heavy artillery, was rather hastily arranged and there was no creeping barrage. For infantry less well-trained and less experienced it would have been a pointless waste of life. Owing to the intense hostile fire encountered and the great dispersal of the attacking troops, control, even at the level of company officers, was well-nigh impossible. It became very much a 'soldiers' battle'. Fire and manoeuvre at platoon level were crucial, the Lewis gun and the rifle grenade being vital weapons. The benefit of surprise, highly developed infantry skills and extraordinary heroism allowed the 5th Australian Brigade to take Mont St Quentin village by 07.00. The Australians were, however, vigorously counter-attacked soon afterwards and pushed out of the village. Though not compelled to retreat a great distance, the 5th Australian Brigade suffered about 50 per cent casualties in the course of the day. At dusk only 600 unwounded Australians were holding a front of 4,000 yards. That evening the outcome of the battle still hung in the balance.[40]

The 5th Australian Division's 14th Brigade had also crossed the Somme that morning. The intensity of the fire coming from the Mont St Quentin, however, prevented it from advancing on Péronne and it was forced to take shelter in the dead ground of the Somme valley, east of Cléry sur Somme. On the night of 31 August, the exact situation of 5th Australian Brigade was not entirely clear to the commanders of the 2nd and 5th Australian Divisions, though they knew it was not in possession of Mont St Quentin village. They also realised that, having taken heavy casualties, it must now be very weak. After a conference attended by representatives of both the 2nd and the 5th Australian Divisions commencing at 21.30 on the night of

31 August, it was decided that the 3rd Australian Division's 6th Brigade (which had followed 5th Brigade across the Somme) would continue the attack on Mont St Quentin. Simultaneously, the 14th Brigade would advance on Péronne and attempt to take the town and the high ground east of it.[41]

It was nearly midnight before this conference broke up. Given that Zero had been set for 06.00 (later than was considered desirable) this left little time for passing orders down the chain of command or for working out a fire-plan. Fortunately, Brigadier-General Robertson, commanding the 6th Australian Brigade, had anticipated his orders and had already got his troops ready to move up for an attack on Mont St Quentin village. A creeping barrage could not be arranged at such notice. Instead, heavy concentrations of fire were placed on identified or suspected centres of resistance, the fire being programmed to lift from one location to the next after fixed periods of time which, it was hoped, would roughly synchronise with the infantry rate of advance. The 2nd Australian Division attack on Mont St Quentin was to be supported by five brigades of field artillery north of the river and two brigades south of it as well as by one brigade of heavy artillery. The 5th Australian Division attack along the bank of the Somme towards Péronne was supported by four brigades of field artillery and one of heavy artillery, all south of the river. The bombardments in support of both brigades began at 05.30, half an hour before Zero. German artillery became intensely active at the same time and 6th Australian Brigade was heavily shelled before it had completed its approach march.[42]

Much of the position which had been designated 6th Australian Brigade's start line turned out to be in German hands and the Brigade had intense fighting to capture it, finally succeeding with only minutes to spare before Zero. The 6th Australian Brigade attacked vigorously at 06.00 but got stuck in late morning just short of Mont St Quentin village. Brigadier-General Robertson therefore called for an intense bombardment of the village from 13.00 to 13.30 by every available gun. As soon as the bombardment ended the infantry assault was renewed and, after some close-quarter infantry fighting, Mont St Quentin was completely in Australian hands by mid-afternoon.[43]

Meanwhile at 06.00, simultaneously with the attack by 6th Brigade (Second Australian Division) towards Mont St Quentin, the 14th Brigade (5th Australian Division) had started pushing towards Péronne. It came under enfilade fire from Mont St Quentin and was opposed by German troops in Anvil Wood. By 07.30, however, it had cleared the wood in intense fighting and was continuing the advance. Péronne was surrounded by a moat and most of the causeways and bridges had been destroyed. The Australians, however, found two narrow footbridges intact to the north-west of the town and stormed across them in the face of intense fire. By 08.40 they had penetrated to the heart of Péronne and by dusk all but the north-east corner of the town was in their hands.[44]

The fighting on the Fourth Army front north of Péronne had been so intense because the Germans had concentrated some nine divisions in that sector, leaving the front south of Péronne relatively lightly held. In the three days' fighting around Mont St Quentin the Australians had taken 2,600 prisoners, these coming from the 2nd Guards, 14th Bavarian, 21st, 38th and 185th Divisions.[45] The effect of the Fourth Army (primarily Australian) victory of 30 August–1 September was that the German 'Winter Position' had been seriously penetrated. It would have been difficult for the Germans to remain on that line for long even without the Canadian action further north.

FACING THE D–Q LINE: 28 AUGUST–1 SEPTEMBER

After the heavy losses of 26–28 August, Currie had been compelled to relieve the two Canadian divisions (the 3rd and the 2nd) which he had employed so far in the drive to the D–Q Line. On the morning of 29 August, the 51st (Highland) Division remained on the Corps' left, north of the Scarpe, but the British 4th Division was now in the centre and the 1st

Map 7

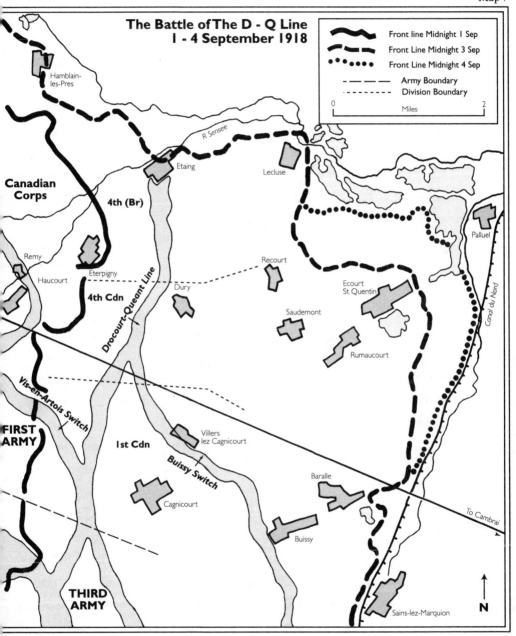

The Battle of The D - Q Line
1 - 4 September 1918

Front line Midnight 1 Sep
Front Line Midnight 3 Sep
Front Line Midnight 4 Sep
Army Boundary
Division Boundary

0   2
Miles

Hamblain-
les-Pres

R Sensee

Etaing

Lecluse

Canadian
Corps

4th (Br)

Palluel

Remy

Haucourt

Eterpigny

Recourt

Dury

4th Cdn

Drocourt-Queant Line

Ecourt
St Quentin

Saudemont

Rumaucourt

Canal du Nord

Vis-en-Artois Switch

FIRST
ARMY

1st Cdn

Villers
lez Cagnicourt

Buissy Switch

Baralle

To Cambrai

Cagnicourt

Buissy

THIRD
ARMY

Sains-lez-Marquion

N

Canadian Division on the right. Control of 51st Division passed to the XXII Corps in the course of the day, leaving the Canadian Corps with just two divisions on its front. From 29 August to 1 September the 4th Division and the 1st Canadian Division fought a series of actions designed to gain a favourable start-line from which to mount the assault on the D–Q Line. By 1 September they had completed the capture of the Fresnes–Rouvroy Line and taken most of the Vis-en-Artois Switch. While this work was in progress, much of the corps artillery was being used to soften up the D–Q Line and cut its wire.[46]

Currie was now well aware of just how difficult a task his corps faced. Some of the positions which his troops had already captured were formidable, but the D–Q Line was more so, second only to the Hindenburg Line itself. It consisted of a front system and a support line system, both well provided with concrete bunkers and machine-gun posts. In general, the front system was situated on a crest or forward slope to give the best possible field of fire. The support system was on a reverse slope for greater protection. The Buissy Switch, which connected the D–Q Line with the Hindenburg Support Line, was constructed in roughly the same way. The Buissy Switch joined the D–Q Line along the forward slope of Mont Drury between Drury and the Cambrai road. Mont Drury itself was a formidable position. Numerous machine-guns were sited on its forward slopes, there were more on the crest and reverse slopes and immediately behind those were the forward batteries of the German field artillery.[47]

Currie was not prepared 'to hustle his divisions' towards the D–Q Line for fear of exhausting and depleting them excessively before they were ready to mount the big assault. Conferences held at Canadian Corps headquarters on 29 and 30 August concluded that it was best 'not to attack it [the D–Q Line] until we are ready and then go all out', and Z-day was put off until Monday, 2 September. At the same time expectations of its results were revised downwards somewhat. First Army recognised that there was no longer much likelihood of being able to employ 'a large body of cavalry' and exploitation forces were confined to Brigadier-General Brutinel's Canadian Independent Force (motorised machine guns, and so on), one cavalry regiment and one battalion of armoured cars.[48]

Both Horne and Currie issued their orders for the attack on the D–Q Line on 31 August. Currie's plan was to break it by a narrow front attack at the most critical point, the Arras–Marquion road, and then swing outwards to roll up the German defences both north and south. Some of the dangers of a narrow-front attack would be reduced by the fact that Byng's Third Army was to join the battle on the right flank, though commencing rather later in the morning. The left flank would be secured against counter-attack by the marshes of the River Sensée and by First Army's XXII Corps. Horne's First Army plan, issued rather later in the day, called for rapid exploitation, to seize the crossings over the Canal du Nord between Palleul and Sains-lez-Marquion and the high ground immediately beyond the canal.[49]

Currie intended to attack with the British 4th Division on the left, the 4th Canadian Division in the centre and the 1st Canadian Division on the right. The 4th Canadian Division would attack on a one-brigade front, the others on two-brigade fronts. Brutinel's Canadian Independent Force and the British 1st Division would be in reserve. This scheme had to be altered, however, when Major-General T.G. Matheson, commanding the British 4th Division, told Currie, late on the afternoon of 31 August, that his losses getting to the intended start-line had been so heavy that he could now only use one brigade in the assault. The 4th Canadian Division, therefore, had to take over some of the front from the British and had itself to attack with two brigades.[50]

Twenty brigades of field artillery and eleven of heavy artillery were to support the Canadian Corps' attack. The heavy artillery was to be used to engage bridges over the Canal du Nord and the River Sensée and for counter-battery work. The field artillery was to fire a deep, dense barrage moving forward at a rate of a 100-yard lift every three minutes, until it reached the forward edge of the main belt of barbed wire in front of the D–Q Line, at which point it was to slow to a rate of a 100-yard lift every five minutes. After 152 minutes the barrage would stop moving for half an hour, offering a protective barrier behind which the infantry would consolidate its gains.[51] The air support offered to the Canadian Corps by the RAF's I Brigade was again fairly lavish and two companies of Mark V tanks from 3rd Tank Brigade were allotted to each attacking division.[52]

On 31 August General Sir Henry Wilson, the Chief of the Imperial General Staff, sent Haig a 'personal' telegram which the latter received on 1 September, the day before the attack on the D–Q Line:

> *Just a word of caution in regard to incurring heavy casualties in attacks on* [sic] *Hindenburg Line as opposed to losses when driving the enemy back to that line. I do not mean to say that you have incurred such losses, but I know the War Cabinet would become anxious if we received heavy punishment in attacking the Hindenburg Line without success.*[53]

Given the timing of his telegram it is probable that Wilson embraced the D–Q Line in his use of the term 'Hindenburg Line'. It is certainly the case that Haig was intensely irritated by Wilson's intervention at this moment:

> *It is impossible for a CIGS to send a telegram of this nature to a C-in-C in the Field as a 'personal' one. The Cabinet are ready to meddle and interfere in my plans in an underhand way, but do not dare openly say that they mean me to take the responsibility for any failure though ready to take the credit for every success! The object of this telegram is no doubt to save the Prime Minister [Lloyd George] in case of any failure . . . If my attack is successful I will remain on as C-in-C. If we fail, or our losses are excessive, I can hope for no mercy! . . . What a wretched lot of weaklings we have in high places at the present time!*[54]

One of the reasons that Haig allowed Wilson's telegram to upset him so much appears to have been that he was already in a somewhat tenser, less confident, mood than he had been a week before. On 31 August, the day before he received Wilson's telegram, he had sent his chief of staff to tell Horne and Currie that he had 'no wish to attack the Quéant–Drocourt line if they [had] any doubts about taking it'.[55] On 1 September Haig told Lawrence that he wanted to keep the Cavalry Corps strong and to commit it at the decisive moment. But he did not now think the moment would arrive until the Americans had launched a major offensive.[56] He no longer believed that a dramatic German collapse was imminent.

THE BATTLE OF THE D–Q LINE AND THE BATTLE OF BAPAUME: 2 SEPTEMBER

This account has focused on planning and preparations for the assault on the D–Q Line because it was the most formidable defensive system the British Armies were yet to tackle in 1918. On the morning of Monday 2 September, however, it was not just the Canadian Corps which mounted an attack, but all the British forces from near the River Sensée at Etaing to the River Somme at Péronne. All four corps of the Third Army and both the III Corps and the Australian Corps in Fourth Army were involved. The actions fought by Third and Fourth Armies were later designated part of the 'Battle of Bapaume'.[57]

Attacking at 05.00, by dusk the Canadian Corps had ruptured the Drocourt–Quéant Line on a frontage of 7,000 yards, captured the Buissy Switch and the villages of Villers-lez-Cagnicourt and Cagnicourt and taken over 8,000 prisoners. Success did not come easily. The Germans had seven divisions facing the Canadian Corps and the left of the Third Army. Some German units yielded quickly but the Canadians met resolute opposition from regiments of the 1st and 2nd Guards Reserve Divisions and the 3rd Reserve Division. The fighting was most intense in the village of Drury and on the slopes of Mont Drury, on the 4th Canadian Division's front.[58] The

RAF provided much support for the Canadian Corps by both artillery spotting and ground attack. Like the ground forces it paid a high price. Large formations of German fighters intervened and there were some big dog-fights. The RAF Brigades attached to First Army and Third Army lost 36 aircraft that day, while the Germans may have lost only one. There were some instances of German aircraft strafing Canadian troops and impeding their progress.[59]

Though the Canadian Corps had won a substantial victory on 2 September, at dusk the Germans were still fighting fiercely and progress was fairly slow. Nevertheless, at midday on 2 September, the German high command had ordered the German Seventeenth Army to begin to retire that night behind the Sensée and the Canal du Nord. The Second Army on its left was to retreat to the Hindenburg Line the following night and the Eighteenth and Ninth Armies further south still were also to fall back in succession. To the Canadian Corps' north the German Fourth and Sixth Armies were to withdraw between Ypres and Lens, abandoning the Lys salient. This meant that the Germans were giving up all that remained of the territory that they had conquered in March and April. The Canadian official history proudly states that the Canadian Corps' success in 'destroying the hinge of the German defence system' at the D–Q Line was thus felt 'along the whole front from Ypres to the Oise'.[60]

It is no disrespect to the Canadian achievement to suggest that it was a little more complicated than that. Once Péronne had fallen to the Australians, as it largely did on Sunday 1 September, the German Winter Position was already seriously penetrated and a further substantial German retreat was inevitable before long. The intense pressure applied on the morning of 2 September by Third Army and by the elements of the Fourth Army north of Péronne would have made it inadvisable for the German high command to delay authorising such a retreat for very long even without the Canadian effort further north. The Canadian Corps' breaking of the D–Q Line, however, made the German withdrawal more precipitate and perhaps deeper than it might otherwise have been.

THE GERMAN RETREAT: 3–10 SEPTEMBER

The Germans achieved a high degree of surprise in their withdrawal. The Canadian Corps and the Third Army went forth on the morning of 3 September to give battle, some divisions actually firing creeping barrages. In most sectors, however, the attacking troops quickly discovered that they were mounting a blow into thin air. The battlefield in front of them was eerily empty.[61]

Upon realising what had happened, GHQ ordered a pursuit, but did so in terms which were remarkably cautious, especially when compared with Haig's telegram of 22 August. The need to conserve manpower, energy and morale until a general offensive could be mounted by all the Allied armies was the dominant note:

> *The principle on which Army commanders will now operate will be to press the enemy with advanced guards with the object of driving in the enemy's rearguards and outposts, and ascertaining his dispositions.*
>
> *No deliberate operation on a large scale will be undertaken for the present. Troops will, as far as possible, be rested, our resources conserved, and our communications improved with a view to the resumption of a vigorous offensive in the near future in conjunction with an operation to be carried out on a large scale by our allies.[62]*

The duration and depth of the German retreat varied considerably. On the Canadian Corps' front it was almost complete by the night of 4 September. The bulk of the German forces in this sector were, by then, already across the Canal du Nord. Because of the generally north-west to south-east slope of the Hindenburg Line the retreat was deepest and would take longest on the Fourth Army front. There it did not really begin until the evening of 4 September. It lasted until about 11 September, by which time the German Second Army had fallen back about ten miles.[63] In a lengthy retreat of this nature the Germans were particularly vulnerable to superior air power. The RAF, however, had been operating at intense pressure since 8 August and had taken heavy casualties. Sir John Salmond decided to mirror Haig's policy of conserving resources, awaiting the commencement of the general offensive of all the Allied forces, and low-flying attacks were somewhat curtailed.[64]

By the evening of 3 September Haig was experiencing a return of the optimism he had felt on 22 August:

> *Advance is continuing to the Canal du Nord. I expect that the results of our success in yesterday's great battle should be very far reaching . . . I am inclined to think that the enemy will be unable to remain on the Hindenburg Line for any time, but will seek for rest and peace behind the Meuse and Namur defences, in order to rest his shattered divisions.*[65]

We now know that some senior German officers wanted to do much as Haig suggested here, but Ludendorff overruled them.[66] By 6 September the British had evidence from captured documents and prisoner interrogations that the Germans intended to make a determined stand on the Hindenburg Line. Indeed, the German retreat on the southern part of the British front had virtually ceased by about 10 September, well short of the Hindenburg Line proper.[67]

BRITISH PLANNING: 7 SEPTEMBER–11 SEPTEMBER

On 8 September GHQ requested a short report from each Army commander, to include comments on German 'dispositions and probable intentions' on their fronts and recommendations for the future conduct of 'deliberate operations' by British forces.[68] The Army commanders' real choices were, in fact, rather more circumscribed than this might suggest. In negotiations with Foch, Haig had already virtually committed the British

Armies to breaking the Hindenburg Line (and any other German defences between them and it) as part of a general offensive by all the forces of the Allies and Associated Powers within the next few weeks.[69] What he really wanted to know from his Army commanders was how each of their forces could contribute to the achievement of that aim.

On 7 September, the day before questioning the Army commanders about future moves, GHQ had set in motion a fairly elaborate deception plan to convince the Germans that the next main British blow would fall between the River Scarpe and La Bassée Canal on the northern part of the First Army front. (This indicates, of course, that such an attack had already been ruled out as a real option.) The Cavalry Corps radio sets, then in the Fourth Army area, were to be transferred to First Army and to generate traffic such as to make the Germans believe that the Cavalry Corps was in position, ready to exploit a major breakthrough. A small number of tanks was to be sent to the First Army area to 'carry out training with troops in back areas and to make tracks as if a concentration of Tanks was taking place in the northern part of the First Army area'. Cavalry and tank officers were to carry out reconnaissance and there was to be a build-up of aircraft and anti-aircraft activity. Traffic to, and movement within, forward areas was to be increased and the number of casualty clearing stations expanded. An increase in the size of ammunition dumps was to be simulated and a rumour spread that the II American Corps was coming to the area.[70] While there is no evidence that these measures actually convinced the Germans that an attack between the Scarpe and La Bassée Canal was imminent, they may have contributed to the absolute befuddlement which generally characterised German military intelligence at this period of the war.[71]

In response to GHQ's enquiry of 8 September, Byng, Horne and Rawlinson were all fairly positive about tackling the formidable German fortifications facing them. Byng was the first to submit his views, reporting on 9 September. He now seemed in a much more confident and aggressive mood than in mid-August, when preparing for the Battle of Albert. He believed the morale of German troops was generally poor: 'many would surrender if they dared; many fight extremely badly'. The Germans were trying to buy time to rebuild their shattered forces and, opposite Third Army, Byng expected them to make their main stand on the Hindenburg Line. Byng, however, considered the Hindenburg Line a formidable obstacle, and was afraid of allowing the Germans to settle down behind it. If that happened the campaign might revert to trench warfare and it might be difficult to regain momentum. In order to avoid such a situation he wanted to break into the Hindenburg Line as quickly as possible.[72]

Both Horne and Rawlinson reported on 11 September. Horne felt that the 'true role' of the First Army was to co-operate with Third Army in a drive towards Cambrai. This would involve crossing the Canal du Nord, 'a difficult operation, but not an impossible one'.[73] Rawlinson pointed out that Fourth Army was presently held up well short of the Hindenburg Line proper. It faced a total of six defensive lines or positions. These were:

A) The Old British Reserve Line
B) The Old British Main Line
C) The Old British Outpost Line
D) The Advanced Hindenburg System
E) The Main Hindenburg System
F) The Reserve Hindenburg System.[74]

What Rawlinson referred to as the 'Main Hindenburg Position' had been constructed during the winter and spring of 1916–17. In the sector of the Hindenburg Line which Fourth Army now faced the German engineers had used the St Quentin Canal, a formidable obstacle in itself, as the basis of the defensive position. This, however, placed their defences in a valley overlooked by a ridge. In view of the growing power and efficiency of Allied artillery, they began to realise early in 1917 that this was somewhat dangerous. So they heavily fortified the ridge in front of the canal, creating what Rawlinson called the Advanced Hindenburg System. Later they added the Reserve Hindenburg System, which was still not complete. More recently still, the Germans had started to refortify the British defence lines which they had overrun in March 1918: lines A–C in Rawlinson's analysis. None of these were especially formidable and A, the Old British Reserve Line, had already been partially overrun by Fourth Army. A number of villages in the Old British Main Line, including Epéhy and Le Verguier, had, however, been turned into mini-fortresses. Tired and depleted as it was, Rawlinson considered that Fourth Army should attempt to close up the Advanced Hindenburg System, fairly quickly. Something of a pause would then be necessary before assaulting lines D and E.[75]

On Tuesday 10 September, the day before Horne and Rawlinson reported, and probably before he had read Byng's report, Haig was in London having an interview with Lord Milner, the Secretary of State for War. Haig had specially requested the meeting. His object, as he recorded in his diary, was to:

explain how greatly the situation in the field has changed to the advantage of the Allies . . . Within the last four weeks we had captured 77,000 prisoners and nearly six hundred guns. There has never been such a victory in the annals of Britain. German prisoners now taken will not obey their officers or NCOs . . . The discipline of the German army is quickly going. It seems to me to be the beginning of the end. From these and other facts I draw the conclusion that the enemy's troops will not await our attacks in even the strongest positions.

On the basis of this assessment he pleaded for the immediate release to him of all available manpower. Army units kept in Britain for civil defence should be brought to France without delay, he insisted. Men earmarked for the Royal Navy should be sent to the Army. The War Cabinet should not even worry too much about future munitions production. 'If we act with energy now', Haig claimed, 'a decision can be obtained *in the very near future*'.[76]

Haig believed that, as a result of this interview, Milner would do his best to supply him with the manpower he required. Milner, however, seems to have been more sceptical of Haig's arguments than he allowed Haig to see. On 23 September Milner allegedly told Henry Wilson that he thought Haig 'ridiculously optimistic and [was] afraid that he [might] embark on another Paschendaele [sic]'. If Haig wrecked his existing army there would be none to replace it.[77] The picture which Haig had presented to Milner on 10 September was, in fact, somewhat over drawn. By the time he presented it, German opposition was already stiffening considerably in front of the British Third and Fourth Armies.

THE BATTLES OF HAVRINCOURT AND EPÉHY: 12–18 SEPTEMBER

In accordance with the philosophy he had outlined to GHQ on 9 September, Byng decided to try to make a breach in the Hindenburg Line even before the IV and the V Corps, on his Army's southern wing, had fully closed up to that position. In an attack planned for Thursday 12 September, Byng intended to secure two spurs running roughly parallel to his front, the Havrincourt Spur to the north and the Trescault Spur to the south, the two separated by the valley of a stream known as the Grand Ravin, and to capture the village of Havrincourt. This would involve breaching at least the outer defences of the Hindenburg Line.[78]

The 62nd Division (VI Corps), the 37th Division and the New Zealand Division (both IV Corps) executed the attack at 05.20 on 12 September with fire support from a total of 18 brigades of field artillery and nine of heavy artillery. The 62nd Division took Havrincourt and the 37th Division took Trescault, but both had very hard fighting in the process. The New Zealand Division, on the right, met the most intense resistance of all and gained little ground that day. At about 18.30 that evening the 62nd Division was counter-attacked by German infantry, including elements of the fresh German 20th Division, supported by low-flying aircraft. The

62nd Division comprehensively smashed the counter-attack and held Havrincourt. However, the small dent which the 62nd Division had made in the outer defences of the Hindenburg Line had, however, no dramatic operational or strategic result. Over the next fortnight Third Army's progress was (except on the V Corps' front on 18 September) distinctly slow.[79]

In mid-September Fourth Army gained a new corps to help it close up to and attack the Hindenburg Line. On 11 September command of the 32nd Division, formerly the right-hand division of the Australian Corps, and the 6th Division, formerly in Army reserve, was taken over by Lieutenant-General Sir Walter Braithwaite's IX Corps. The 1st Division, which had been with the Canadian Corps, joined IX Corps over the next few days and the 46th Division joined on 19 September. The consciousness that his Army was being reinforced allowed Rawlinson and his staff to frame ambitious plans.[80]

On 12 September Rawlinson held an informal conference with his corps commanders at which he outlined his ideas for a very large-scale attack by Fourth Army, which was to be supported by Third Army and First French Army on its left and right flanks respectively. His corps commanders seem to have raised no objections to the scheme and it was incorporated in Army orders issued on 13 and 14 September. Z day was Wednesday 18 September. All three Fourth Army corps (the III, the Australian and the IX) would attack on a total frontage front of about 20,000 yards. The Old British Main Line and the Old British Outpost Line were the first and second objectives. The Advanced Hindenburg System was the 'line of exploitation' – to be seized if the other lines fell easily.[81]

Rawlinson had good reason for confidence in planning the attack of 18 September. Though Fourth Army had suffered heavy losses in recent weeks, it appears to have been greatly superior in manpower (as well as in fire-power and morale) to the German forces facing it. On 11 September Fourth Army's intelligence identified seven German divisions to its front (eight were in fact engaged on 18 September) and these were thought to have a rifle strength of only 12,000 between them. On 18 September Fourth Army was to attack with eight divisions: III Corps with four and the Australian Corps and IX Corps with two each. A recent estimate suggests that these were about 40,000 strong in total and that some 27,000 infantry made the initial assault. If these figures are correct, Fourth Army had a large manpower advantage on its front as a whole.[82]

German artillery strength in this battle is not known, but there can be no doubting that the British had a vast firepower advantage, probably even greater than their superiority in manpower. Fourth Army alone had a total of 1,488 guns and howitzers. Some 978 of these were field pieces, the other 510 were heavy. But all that firepower would, of course, have been of limited avail without effective target acquisition. Until 15 September the weather was unsuitable for aerial photography. On that day, however, the skies cleared and by 17 September the RAF had photographed the German side of the Fourth Army front to a depth of four miles. Such photographs, of particular importance to the gunners, were issued to every officer and NCO taking part in the attack.[83]

Fourth Army's fire-plan was similar, in broad outline, to that used on 8 August. In an effort to achieve surprise, a preliminary bombardment would be forgone. From Zero hour about three-quarters of the heavy guns would be used for counter-battery, while the other quarter bombarded identified German strong-points. A creeping barrage, fired by 750 18-pdr guns and 228 4.5-inch howitzers, was to cover the advance to the first objective. It would move in 100-yard lifts, the lifts being after three minutes in the earlier stages of the advance and four minutes in the later stages. Ten per cent of the shells used would be smoke. Just beyond the first objective, the 'creeper' would stop creeping for an hour and become a static, protective barrage. It would then move in four-minute lifts to the second objective. Fewer guns would be used in firing the barrage to the second objective, because some would be rushed forward so that they could support the infantry in the exploitation phase.[84]

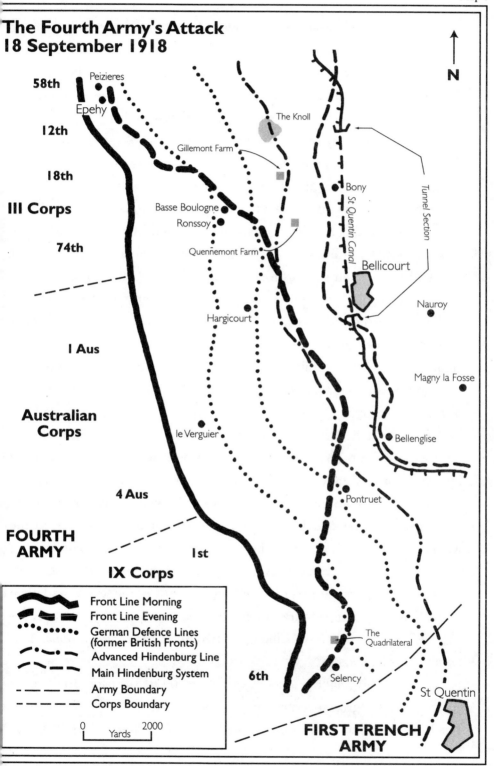

Map 8

The Fourth Army's Attack
18 September 1918

N

58th

Peizieres

Epehy

12th

The Knoll

18th

Gillemont Farm

III Corps

Bony

74th

Basse Boulogne

Ronssoy

St Quentin Canal

Tunnel Section

Quennemont Farm

Bellicourt

Hargicourt

Nauroy

I Aus

Magny la Fosse

Australian
Corps

le Verguier

Bellenglise

4 Aus

Pontruet

FOURTH
ARMY

IX Corps

1st

6th

The
Quadrilateral

Selency

St Quentin

FIRST FRENCH
ARMY

～～～	Front Line Morning
▬ ▬ ▬	Front Line Evening
••••••••	German Defence Lines (former British Fronts)
–·–·–·	Advanced Hindenburg Line
▬ ▬ ▬	Main Hindenburg System
— — —	Army Boundary
– – – –	Corps Boundary

0   2000
   Yards

Machine-gun barrages were employed by at least three of the four attacking corps (including Third Army's V Corps) as a supplement to the artillery. Tanks were in rather short supply at this stage in the campaign and there were only 20 available for this attack. All of these were allotted to Fourth Army – eight to the III Corps, eight to the Australian Corps and four to the IX Corps. They were such a scarce and valuable asset that Fourth Army decreed that they were not to be used beyond the first objective. (The Australians decided to supplement their real tanks with dummies which they intended to tow into German view during the attack for the dual purpose of demoralising the Germans and dissipating the fire of their anti-tank guns.) The RAF's III Brigade and V Brigade seem to have organised most of the usual forms of air support for Third and Fourth Army respectively, but bad weather on 18 September largely negated these arrangements.[85]

The attack began at 05.20. It was raining hard, misty and slippery underfoot. Though the rain stopped during the morning, it remained cloudy all day and visibility was poor. Contact patrols by aircraft saw little and senior commanders had very little idea what was going on most of the time. Despite this, Fourth Army's counter-battery appears to have been very effective. German artillery fire was not severe except on the far right, where the problem appears to have been weak support from the French. Initial resistance from German infantry and machine-gunners was intense. On the Australian front, though not elsewhere, this tended to collapse after the first couple of hours. The Australian Corps overran the whole of its first two objectives and took part of the Advanced Hindenburg System. The two other Fourth Army corps made shallower advances, capturing nearly all of their first objective line but little of the second and none of the Advanced Hindenburg System. On the left, Third Army's V Corps had a fairly good day, advancing up to two miles and taking a substantial number of prisoners.[86]

The relatively shallow advances achieved by III Corps and IX Corps compared to the greater success of the Australians need some explanation. The III Corps attacked the most strongly defended stretch of front. It was immediately ahead of the section of the Main Hindenburg System which the Germans considered the most vulnerable, where the St Quentin Canal ran through the Bellicourt tunnel. The Germans had therefore taken special care with its defence, turning the villages of Peizières, Epéhy, Basse Boulogne and Ronssoy into mini-fortresses and defending them with the Alpine Corps and the 2nd Guards Division, their two best divisions. The III Corps captured all the villages named above, but by the time it had done so its attack had lost momentum.[87] The main problems for the IX Corps, on the other hand, were enfilade fire from the right flank, where the support of the First French Army was relatively weak, and fire from mini-fortresses such as The Quadrilateral and Selency on the ridge ahead.[88]

These difficulties were external and largely beyond the control of the corps commanders. Time would reveal that there was nothing much wrong with the IX Corps or with Sir Walter Braithwaite's leadership of it. With the III Corps, however, it was different. Its divisions had been fighting continuously since 8 August and were very tired. (Both the attacking Australian divisions, by contrast, had recently been rested and were fairly fresh.) There were, moreover, definite question marks against Sir Richard Butler's fitness for corps command. He had only returned to duty on 12 September, having been forced, by exhaustion, to take leave in the middle of the Battle of Amiens. Rawlinson suspected, rightly or wrongly, that Butler was not really in control of his divisional commanders and that, as a result, the III Corps' planning for the attack of 18 September had become excessively complicated and confused.[89]

The BEF did not, in fact, do all the attacking on 18 September. During the afternoon the Germans mounted a number of attacks against the Third Army's VI and IV Corps in an effort to take the pressure off their forces further south. These efforts, however, cost the Germans very dear and availed them nothing. As Haig recorded in his diary on 19 September:

Our Third Army reports that the losses suffered by the enemy in his counter-attack yesterday afternoon against Trescault and

Havrincourt were the heaviest ever seen by our troops. Evidently the 6th (Brandenburg) and 20th Divisions had been called upon to sacrifice themselves to save the situation on the front of the Second Army (Marwitz) further south. These divisions belonging to the Seventeenth Army (von Below). After a bombardment by forty batteries (that is 160 guns or more) the two divisions advanced in great masses. The attack came against our 37th, 3rd and Guards Divisions . . . I am told whole platoons of the enemy infantry were simply mown down . . . The ground in front of our position is covered with German corpses. Our losses were very small.[90]

Despite some disappointments, the attack of 18 September (later designated the Battle of Epéhy) was a major victory. More than 9,000 Germans were taken prisoner: the V Corps capturing 1,848, the III Corps 2,300, the Australian Corps 4,243 and the IX Corps 559.[91] So dramatic was the success that Sir Henry Wilson felt the need to send Haig his congratulations, though he expressed these in the flippant and facetious tone ('Well done! You must be a famous general!') all too characteristic of him.[92] Von der Marwitz, commanding the German Second Army, had survived the 'black day' of 8 August, but was sacked after this further disaster.[93] One of the battle's most important effects was on Rawlinson. His personal morale hit new heights and he became supremely confident of Fourth Army's ability to break the Hindenburg Line.[94]

Map 9

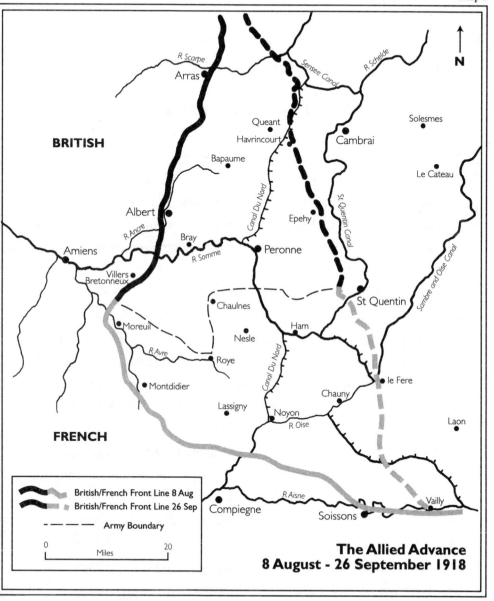

N

R Scarpe

Arras

Sensee Canal

R Schelde

BRITISH

Solesmes

Queant

Havrincourt

Cambrai

Bapaume

Le Cateau

Canal Du Nord

St Quentin Canal

Albert

Epehy

R Ancre

Bray

Amiens

R Somme

Peronne

Villers
Bretonneux

St Quentin

Chaulnes

Sambre and Oise Canal

Ham

Moreuil

Nesle

R Avre

Roye

Canal Du Nord

le Fere

Montdidier

Chauny

Laon

Lassigny

Noyon

FRENCH

R Oise

Vailly

R Aisne

Compiegne

Soissons

British/French Front Line 8 Aug

British/French Front Line 26 Sep

- - - - Army Boundary

0   20
                    Miles

**The Allied Advance
8 August - 26 September 1918**

7

THE GENERAL OFFENSIVE

PLANS FOR THE GENERAL OFFENSIVE (See Map 1)

By mid-September the efforts of the armies of the Allies on the Western Front were building to a climax. Foch and the commanders of the national contingents – Haig, Pétain, Pershing and Albert, King of the Belgians – all realised that to gain the best advantage from an already favourable military situation their armies must co-ordinate their efforts more closely. For the foreseeable future the German Army was likely to be able to contain the pressure of being attacked by one or two Allied contingents at a time. Certainly it would suffer attrition and would have to give ground, but it would be a long time before its reserves were consumed and it faced final collapse. What the Allied cause needed, therefore, was a 'general offensive' in which a high proportion of the forces of all the nationalities arrayed against the Germans on the Western Front would mount co-ordinated and sustained attacks.

By Sunday 11 August, the last day of the Battle of Amiens, Haig had conceived the possibility of bringing the war to an end that autumn. In this, he was ahead of Foch who, at that time, was still thinking of 1919 as the decisive year.[1] Foch, however, soon became a convert to Haig's point of view. From mid-August a scheme for a general offensive was gradually developed, Foch and Haig playing virtually equal parts in shaping it. In its final form the scheme was:

1) On 26 September the French Fourth and American First Armies would attack between the Meuse and Reims towards the town of

Mézières, some 50 miles distant, on a main lateral railway line vital to the Germans.

2) On 27 September the British First and Third Armies would attack simultaneously, capturing the heights of Bourlon Wood and crossing the Canal de l'Escaut (Schelde Canal) respectively.

3) On 28 September the Group of Armies in Flanders (GAF) comprising the Belgian Army, the British Second Army and some French divisions would mount an offensive in Flanders aimed initially at gaining a line stretching from the Ypres–Commines Canal to Clerken, ten miles north of Ypres.

4) On 29 September the British Fourth Army, supported by the French First Army on its right, would attack the Main Hindenburg System in its sector, crossing the St Quentin Canal. A preliminary bombardment for this assault would start on 27 September.[2]

Haig's concept was that, for maximum mutual support, all the Allied attacks of the general offensive should be converging.[3] Sound enough in theory, this concept, when accepted by Foch, had a major influence on the way the American Army was employed, and was to cause the Americans serious problems. In late summer 1918 most of the American Expeditionary Force was based at the southern end of the active part of the Western Front, around the St Mihiel Salient. This German-occupied salient projected like a huge thorn 16 miles deep into the Allied lines. By its interruption of the railway from Paris to Nancy it had made it difficult for the French to mount an offensive in Lorraine. Since July, the staff of the American commander-in-chief, General Pershing, had developed a plan first to pinch out the St Mihiel Salient and then to break through the still incomplete German Michel Position which ran across its base. Pushing more or less due north, the Americans would then take Mars la Tour.[4] Ultimately they hoped to take the heavily fortified city of Metz, to liberate the Briey iron region and perhaps threaten the Saar Basin. Their ideas for operations beyond Mars la Tour were grandiose and, for an inexperienced army, rather unrealistic. On 17 August, however, Foch approved the essentials of the American plan, giving a line just a little beyond Mars la Tour as the ultimate objective.[5] Haig's intervention upset this arrangement.

Haig was much annoyed by Pershing's withdrawal, during August, of three of the five American divisions which had been training with the British Armies.[6] The concept of the main American effort being towards Mars la Tour and Metz did not appeal to him because it meant that the American attack would be remote and somewhat divergent from those to be mounted by his own Armies. Haig had earlier expressed a suspicion about 'the French desire to keep the Americans as far away from the British as they can', so he may have questioned Foch's motives in endorsing this American proposal.[7] On 27 August Haig wrote to Foch urging him 'to put the Americans into the battle *at once* in order to enable an important advance to be made without delay *concentrically*, viz. against Cambrai against St Quentin, and against Mézières from the south.'[8] (See Map 1)

To have committed the Americans 'at once' to an attack in the direction of Mézières would have been quite impossible. No preparations had been made for such action. Foch, however, did accept Haig's scheme of concentric offensives and did decide to launch the main American effort on an axis towards Mézières. As Foch explained to a somewhat shaken Pershing, if they were to mount this effort by the end of September, it would be necessary for the Americans greatly to scale down their St Mihiel operation, preparations for which were already well advanced.[9] Foch later suggested that the St Mihiel operation might be dropped altogether. Pershing ultimately insisted on going ahead with the St Mihiel operation, but accepted that it would have to be in a reduced form, confined to the reduction of the salient. On condition that the Americans fight as an independent Army under his own command, he accepted that the main American attack should be alongside the French Fourth Army, the combined Franco-American effort being on an axis taking in Mézières and Sedan. The American sector in the general offensive would be between the western edge of the Argonne forest and the River Meuse.[10]

Though Pershing had agreed to Foch's scheme he was not altogether happy with it. In a letter he wrote to Foch on 31 August, he foresaw (all too accurately as it turned out) serious logistical problems: 'Since our arrival in France our plans have been based on the organisation of the American Army on the front St Mihiel–Belfort. All our hospitals, training areas and other installations are located with reference to this front, and a change of plans cannot easily be made.'[11] Pershing was not, of course, facilitating the logistics for the main offensive by his insistence on persevering with a version of the St Mihiel operation. When the Americans attacked the St Mihiel salient on 12 September, however, they caught the Germans withdrawing from it and had an easy but impressive victory. Within 30 hours the salient had ceased to exist and the Americans had taken more than 16,000 prisoners, although on a closer analysis even this rapid triumph showed some serious weaknesses of discipline and staff work in the American Army.[12] 'The Meuse–Argonne', as the larger American offensive would become known, was to be a much more complicated story and was to expose American weaknesses much more painfully.

The last part of the general offensive to be arranged was the Flanders operation. This was settled between Foch, the King of the Belgians and Haig by 9 September.[13] Oddly, Haig, who had been somewhat obsessed with the Flanders area earlier in the war, played a relatively small part in arranging this aspect of the general scheme. He accepted, however, that in the early stages of the Flanders operation, the British Second Army would operate as part of an Army Group (the 'Group of Armies in Flanders' or GAF) which would be commanded by the King of the Belgians and it would therefore no longer be under his own operational control. By the middle of September, all the British Army commanders knew in broad terms what their missions in the general offensive would be.[14] Orders issued on 22 September gave them the sequence of attacks,[15] although their actual dates were not fixed until 25 September.[16]

The British Armies in the centre of the active front, the Fifth, First, Third and Fourth, faced both the strongest fortifications and the least favourable numerical balance. In this 67-mile sector (roughly between Armentières in the north and St Quentin in the south), 52 infantry divisions (two of which were American), plus three cavalry divisions, faced 63 German divisions, of which 30 were in reserve.

In the north, the GAF, holding the 37-mile stretch of front between Armentières and the sea, had 12 Belgian and 10 British infantry divisions, and one Belgian cavalry division. It also had 6 French infantry and 3 cavalry divisions in reserve. This made a total of 28 infantry and 4 cavalry divisions, facing 15 German divisions, 5 of which were in reserve.

The French Fourth Army under General Gouraud had 27 infantry and 3 cavalry divisions and the American First Army under General Pershing had 15 American infantry divisions and one French cavalry division in a 65-mile sector from about 6 miles east of Reims to the Meuse below Verdun. In this sector a total of 42 infantry and 4 cavalry divisions faced 36 German infantry divisions. But this grossly understates the numerical advantage to the Allied side. In terms of rifle strength, American divisions were at least twice the size of an average British or French division. If American divisions are counted twice, then in this sector 57 infantry divisions on the Allied side faced 36 on the German side.

Even this understates the true situation. Practically all German infantry divisions at this period were very much under-strength so that, even in Haig's sector, where the Germans actually outnumbered the British in terms of divisions, the Germans were markedly inferior in rifle strength. The fact remains, however, that it was on the wings that the numerical balance most favoured the Allied cause. In the sector of Gouraud's and Pershing's armies it has been estimated that the Allies may have had a numerical advantage of six to one in riflemen.[17]

It is not clear to what extent Foch actually welcomed the very heavy weighting of the wings of his general offensive, leaving the centre numerically relatively weak. Given that the general pattern of the attacks was converging, it could, in theory, have been an advantage. It might have faced German forces in the centre with the threat of envelopment. Foch had, however, a rather limited degree of control over where his forces were concentrated and how exactly they were used. The Belgians could only be employed on, or very near to, their national territory and Pershing insisted on massing the great bulk of the American forces under his own command. During the emergency of the German spring offensives French divisions had sometimes been used in the British sector and vice-versa, but this sort of arrangement never worked smoothly. Given these problems, Foch had great difficulty getting any sort of concerted action at all. It is doubtful whether he counted on executing any particular scheme of manoeuvre. In all probability his only 'strategic' assumption was that if all these forces attacked at once the Germans were bound to cave in somewhere. In late August Haig thought that: 'Foch's strategy is *a simple straightforward advance by all the troops on the Western front and to keep the enemy on the move!*'[18] In September General Du Cane, Foch's principal British liaison officer, put the Generalissimo's programme just as simply: 'Everyone is to attack . . . as soon as they can, as strong as they can, for as long as they can.'[19]

Haig was keen that the British Armies should make a vigorous contribution to the general offensive, but was well aware that his forces would be attacking the Germans at their strongest point. He therefore hoped that the Franco-American offensive which was to be mounted on 26 September would draw off German reserves from his front before his own attacks went in.[20]

THE FRANCO-AMERICAN OFFENSIVE: 25–28 SEPTEMBER

At 23.00 on 25 September the preliminary bombardment commenced for the great Franco-American offensive between the rivers Suippe and Meuse. The infantry attack began the following morning, at 05.25 for the Americans, 05.30 for the French. It was mounted on a 44-mile front, evenly divided between the armies of the two nations: the French on the left, the Americans on the right, the western edge of the great Argonne forest forming the dividing line between them. The Germans had long expected some sort of attack in this vicinity and had received some information from French deserters to confirm their suspicions. But they do not seem to have detected the presence of American troops in the area until about three hours before the infantry attack commenced. The scale and violence of the offensive initially shook the Germans. Yet the advance achieved on the first day was not particularly spectacular, generally between two and three miles, rather less at the junction of the two armies, and from the beginning of the second day onwards American tactical and logistic inexperience became obvious to all.[21]

'On the 27th and 28th', said General Max von Gallwitz, commanding the German Army Group in this sector, 'we had no more worries'.[22] General Pershing's American First Army was unable to overcome German resistance to its front and had 'an unbelievable logistic snarl', the 'worst traffic jam of the war', in its rear. In the words of one historian it was 'as if someone had taken the Army's intestines out and dumped them all over the table'.[23] The Argonne–Meuse offensive, moreover, seems to have failed to draw off substantial forces from the central sector of the active front which Haig's Armies began to attack on 27 September.[24]

THE CANADIAN CORPS AND THE THIRD ARMY PLAN FOR THE BATTLE OF THE CANAL DU NORD

From 5 September to 27 September the front of the Canadian Corps, on First Army's right, faced elements of General von Below's German Seventeenth Army along the Canal du Nord. The Germans had broken all the bridges over the canal and, on most of the front which the Canadians initially faced, had flooded its banks. Without a very carefully prepared operation the canal was not passable in either direction by any substantial force. After their efforts in breaking the D–Q Line Currie's men gained some well-earned rest in these weeks. Unfortunately, as the Germans had good observation over their positions, the Canadians continued to suffer, on average, about 100 casualties a day.[25]

At a conference held at Third Army headquarters on 15 September Haig had explained that he wanted a joint First and Third Army operation towards Cambrai, towards the end of the month. First Army was to seize the commanding ground of Bourlon Wood and cover Third Army's left as it advanced towards Cambrai. As with virtually all his offensive missions during this campaign, Horne delegated the responsibility for both the planning and the execution of the First Army attack across the Canal du Nord on 27 September to Currie and the Canadian Corps.[26]

The outbreak of war in 1914 had halted work on the Canal du Nord, leaving different sections in different stages of construction. It presented a more serious obstacle to military movement in some places than in others. From Sains-lez-Marquion northwards across the Arras–Cambrai road there was a naturally swampy area which the Germans had flooded. An assault through this area would have been suicidal. Inevitably Currie decided to make the assault in the dry section further south. To make use of this he arranged a southward extension of the corps boundary by 2,600 yards.

Even attacking across a dry stretch of the canal would, however, present serious problems. The canal was about 40 yards wide and had a western bank about ten to twelve feet high. Fortunately, the eastern bank, the one which the Canadians would have to climb, was lower, only about four to five feet. But immediately behind it, covering it with machine guns was the German Canal du Nord Line. The trenches of this system were not particularly impressive and aerial reconnaissance suggested they would offer relatively little protection against bombardment, but the system was covered by dense belts of wire. About a mile east of the Canal du Nord Line was the Marquion Line, a similarly well-wired position. Between it and the high ground in and around Bourlon Wood, the Canadian Corps' principal objective for 27 September, the landscape was dotted with old dug-outs and shelters, all of which were potential machine-gun positions. To what extent Bourlon Wood itself was likely to be defended was not easy to tell from air photographs, the principal source of intelligence, as the foliage was still thick on the trees. In mounting its attack across the Canal du Nord and through the terrain behind it, the Canadian Corps knew it would be taking on seven and a half German infantry divisions which were already in the line and another four in reserve. Most of those in the line seem to have been depleted but two of the reserve divisions had been recently reinforced.[27]

In essence Currie's plan for tackling this lethal obstacle course was simple enough. The attack would be in two phases. The initial assault would be made, between Sains-lez-Marquion and the Corps' boundary with Third Army, by 1st Canadian Division on the left and 4th Canadian Division on the right. The 1st Division would attack with two brigades up, the 4th Division with only one, their frontages being 1,700 yards and 800 yards respectively. Currie designated three lines to be reached in this initial phase: the Red, Green and Blue Lines. The most distant, the Blue Line, lay a little beyond Bourlon Wood and the village of Bourlon, and sloped back in a north-north-easterly direction as far as the outskirts of the village of Sauchy Lestrée. Bourlon Wood itself was to be enveloped by the 4th Canadian Division, leaving its interior to be mopped up later. So that the same troops would not have to lead the attack all the way, there were to be leap-frogs at the Red and Green Lines.

The second phase of the attack would involve exploitation beyond the Blue Line, if possible as far as Cambrai to the east and the Canal de la Sensée in the north. This further advance would be carried out on a four-division frontage, the British 11th Division moving up on the left of the 1st Canadian Division, and the 3rd Canadian Division on the right of the 4th Canadian Division. The 2nd Canadian Division was to remain in Corps reserve. Each of the three Canadian Divisions actually taking part in the attack was to have a company of eight tanks from the 7th Battalion of the Tank Corps.[28]

The achievement of complete surprise by the Canadians was impossible. The Germans had fairly good observation of the Canadian Corps area from their positions behind the canal. On 23 September, Currie ordered all further movements east of a line through Neuve–Vitasse to be carried out at night. But so many men and so much material had to be assembled for the assault that preparations were bound to become fairly obvious to German aerial reconnaissance. If, however, the fact that an attack in this area was being prepared could not be concealed, its precise timing could. A programme of wire-cutting by the heavy artillery had started as far back as 18 September, but there was no intense bombardment immediately prior to the assault.

The Canadian infantry were to have the support of 22 brigades of field artillery and 9 brigades of heavy artillery. Of these, 10 brigades of field artillery and 2 brigades of heavy artillery were allotted to the 2 divisions leading the attack. A creeping barrage composed of 50 per cent shrapnel, 40 per cent HE and 10 per cent smoke was to be fired in support of the infantry. This was to halt for lengthy periods on both the Red and Green Lines. A machine-gun barrage was to supplement the creeper and some of the heavy artillery was to be used to fire a rolling barrage ahead of the latter. Because of the restricted initial frontage of the attack and the consequently cramped assembly area, much of the field artillery had to be positioned further back than normal. In the case of the 4th Canadian Division, which had to advance 4,000 yards to get to the Blue Line, the field artillery would have run out of range had it all remained in its starting positions. Four brigades were, therefore, to limber up and, at Zero, to follow the infantry as far as the canal. From there, they would fire the creeping barrage as far as the Green Line. Another four brigades would then be brought over the canal, two to fire the creeper up to the Blue Line and two to fire a standing barrage on the far side of Bourlon Wood. In order to get guns, ammunition and other supplies over the canal it was obviously imperative that the sappers should make arrangements for it to be promptly bridged.[29]

Byng's Third Army was also scheduled to attack on Friday 27 September. When Haig visited Third Army headquarters two days before the attack, however, he found Byng and his chief of staff, Major-General L.R. Vaughan (not for the first time in this campaign) far from eager. They suspected that the Germans had strong reserves on the Cambrai–St Quentin front and wanted Haig to wait several days before mounting the British offensives, apparently in the hope that the Franco-American efforts further south and east would draw some of these away.[30] Haig, who refused to reschedule the British offensives at this late stage, was not the only one to become aware of Byng's lack of confidence. The Third Army commander betrayed the same mood speaking to Currie. Byng had no criticism of Currie's plans, which he considered the best possible in the circumstances, but asked: 'Old man, do you think you can do it?'[31]

Undoubtedly the task facing Third Army, like that confronting the Canadian Corps, was extremely demanding. Third Army faced the right of the German Second Army and the left of the Seventeenth, their junction being near Havrincourt. The Germans occupied a maze of trenches comprising parts of the Main Hindenburg System and the Hindenburg Support System. Third Army, however, had the advantage over the Canadians in that, except for the XVII Corps and the left division of the VI Corps, it was already across the Canal du Nord, and that everywhere in its sector the canal was dry.

Byng's orders were issued on 20 September. The XVII, VI and IV Corps were to attack on 27 September. The V Corps, on the far right would not move until the following day. The attack was to be carried out in echelon from the left. Fergusson's XVII Corps would start the soonest and advance the furthest. Harper's IV Corps would start last and advance the shortest distance. The start time for the XVII Corps, as for the Canadians, was 05.20. It was to cross the Canal du Nord, keeping pace with the Canadian advance, and, if possible, to seize a bridgehead over the Schelde Canal. The VI Corps was to capture the Flesquières ridge and a spur running from the ridge in a northerly direction towards Graincourt and Anneux. The IV Corps was ordered to attack some hours later than the VI Corps (eventually the interval was fixed at 3 hours), to capture Beaucamp and Highland Ridge and to clear the Main Hindenburg System which ran almost at right angles to the IV Corps' front as far east as Couillet Valley. Like that of the

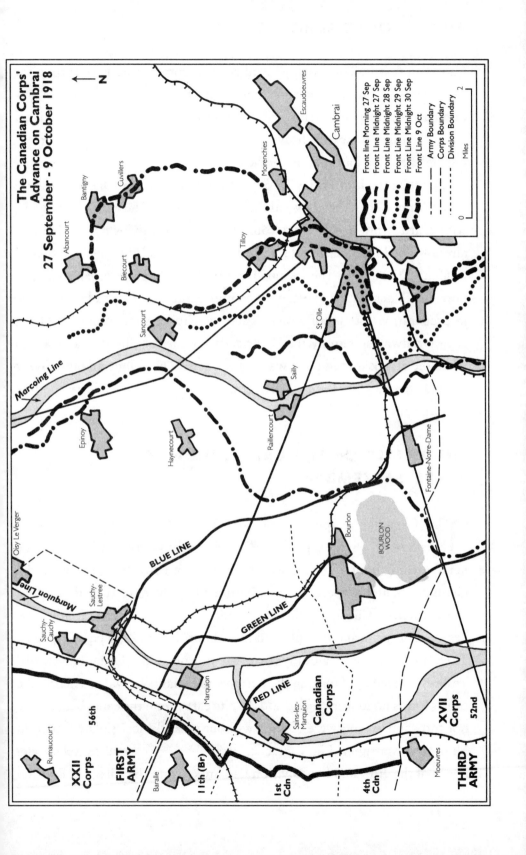

The Canadian Corps'
Advance on Cambrai
27 September - 9 October 1918

N →

Front line Morning 27 Sep
Front Line Midnight 27 Sep
Front Line Midnight 28 Sep
Front Line Midnight 29 Sep
Front Line Midnight 30 Sep
Front Line 9 Oct

Army Boundary
Corps Boundary
Division Boundary

0   2
|————————————|
        Miles

Escaudoeuvres

Cambrai

Morenchies

Cuvillers

Bantigny

Abancourt

Biecourt

Tilloy

St Olle

Sancourt

Marcoing Line

Sailly

Epinoy

Haynecourt

Raillencourt

Fontaine-Notre-Dame

Bourlon

BOURLON
WOOD

Oisy Le Verger

BLUE LINE

Marquion Line

Sauchy-
Lestree

Sauchy-
Cauchy

GREEN LINE

Rumaucourt

Marquion

Sains-lez-
Marquion

RED LINE

Canadian
Corps

XXII
Corps

56th

FIRST
ARMY

Baralle

11th (Br)

1st
Cdn

4th
Cdn

XVII
Corps

52nd

THIRD
ARMY

Moeuvres

Canadian Corps, Third Army's artillery had commenced wire-cutting for this operation on 18 September but would fire no intensive preliminary bombardment. Third Army would support its attacks with the usual counter-battery fire by the heavy artillery and with a combination of creeping and standing barrages by the field artillery.[32]

For the attack of Friday 27 September both the Canadian Corps and Third Army were to have a good deal of air support. The RAF's III Brigade, with Third Army, had 15 squadrons plus one flight, giving it a total of 261 aircraft. The I Brigade, with First Army, had 12 squadrons plus two flights, totalling 236 aircraft. The 13 squadrons of the IX Brigade were also in support. Much aerial reconnaissance and photography had already been done in preparation for the offensive. There was to be some bombing of the enemy railway system by the IX Brigade the night before the attack and when the attack started there was to be offensive patrolling and low-flying ground attack by fighters as well as contact patrolling and artillery spotting by corps aircraft.[33]

THE BATTLE OF THE CANAL DU NORD: 27-28 SEPTEMBER

The Canadian Corps gave the outstanding performance of Friday 27 September. On the night of 26/27 September Currie's men spent some nerve-racking hours. Their assembly area was grossly overcrowded and a German counter-preparation bombardment could have turned it into a charnel house. Currie and his staff had, however, achieved an adequate degree of surprise and the cold and rainy hours before Zero passed quietly. Then, at 05.20 on a gloomy, overcast morning, the Canadian Corps' artillery opened up. Hugging the barrage, the infantry advanced across the canal. It was no longer raining and despite earlier rain the canal banks were not too slippery and were tackled without great difficulty. The Canal du Nord and Marquion Lines were successfully stormed and by 09.45 elements of the 4th Canadian Division had broken into the village of Bourlon and others had moved on to envelop Bourlon Wood from the north. Some troops had reached the village of Fontaine Notre-Dame by 19.00 when the advance ceased. Owing to the relatively slow progress of Third Army's XVII Corps, the 4th Canadian Division's right flank was exposed to serious enfilade fire. The double envelopment of Bourlon Wood which Currie had planned could not proceed as scheduled. Nevertheless by nightfall the whole of the wood, which did in fact contain German posts, had been taken and the Blue Line reached along its entire length except for a short stretch on the extreme right.[34]

The 1st Canadian Division attack was even more successful. Having crossed the canal and overrun the Canal du Nord Defence Line, its 3rd Brigade turned sharp left and, pushing northward, cleared the villages of Sains lez Marquion and Marquion, rolling up the Marquion Line in the process. The British 11th Division was thus able to cross the canal unopposed around midday. By mid-afternoon the 1st Canadian Division seems to have reached all its Blue Line objectives. Taking its place on 1st Canadian Division's left, the 11th Division continued the advance north and north-east and had seized the villages of Epinoy and Oisy le Verger by dusk.

Perhaps surprisingly, the 16 obsolescent Mark IV tanks allotted to the two leading Canadian divisions were, in the majority of cases, able to negotiate the canal successfully under the cover of a smoke screen. They performed some useful work on the far side, helping to overcome wire and machine guns and making themselves especially useful in the clearance of Marquion. Five tanks, however, were knocked out by enemy fire and most of the others appear to have succumbed to mechanical difficulties by the end of the day.[35]

Third Army's progress on Friday 27 September would have been considered good if judged by standards less exacting than those of the formidable Canadian Corps. The leading division of Fergusson's XVII Corps, the 63rd (Royal Naval) Division, ultimately achieved an advance of some four miles, taking all its objectives including the villages of

Graincourt and Anneux, though it fell behind schedule in doing so. Owing to a communications failure, two brigades of the 57th Division failed to pass through the 63rd Division to continue the advance (though they did arrive in time to help beat off a counter-attack around the village of Anneux) and at nightfall the XVII Corps was lagging some 3,000 yards behind the Canadians.

Haldane's VI Corps, attacking with the Guards Division and the 62nd (West Riding) Division, took Flesquières and Riecourt. Some of the West Riding Division troops got as far as Marcoing though they were driven out again. The VI Corps' advance on this day kept parallel with, but did not exceed, that of XVII Corps on its left. The real failure for Third Army on 27 September was the attack of Harper's IV Corps. Byng's decision that it should begin its attack more than two and a half hours after the other corps was almost certainly a mistake. The Germans were fully alert and IV Corps met intense resistance from the outset. It achieved an advance of little more than a mile and failed to take the Highland Ridge.[36]

The fairly lavish air support provided by the RAF on Friday 27 September proved useful both to the Canadians and to Third Army. Corps aircraft were over the battlefield 20 minutes after Zero reporting on enemy batteries which were still active. Many calls for artillery fire made by air observers were promptly answered, and some German batteries were thus silenced and some concentrations of German infantry dispersed. The contact patrols helped keep corps staffs informed of the progress of attacks and in some cases they were able to do more. The pilot and observer of an RE8 of No. 13 Squadron, which was working with XVII Corps, noticed German infantry forming up for a counter-attack near the village of Anneux. The observer made a radio SOS call for artillery to disrupt this hostile concentration. The airmen were able to give warning to troops of the 63rd (Royal Naval) Division, using prearranged signal procedures – lighting wing tip flares and dropping a smoke bomb amongst the German troops. Forewarned, the ground troops defeated the counter-attack. Air activity was not quite one-sided. On one occasion leading troops of the

63rd Division were strafed by a large concentration of German fighters. But the RAF had most of the airspace for most of the day.[37]

Third Army and the Canadian Corps both renewed their attack on Saturday 28 September. The Canadians, after their spectacular advance on the Friday, had difficulty in maintaining momentum. They gained relatively little extra ground, though they did capture a section of the Marcoing Line and the villages of Sailly and Fontaine Notre Dame. For Third Army, however, 28 September was a day of steady gains. Noyelles, Marcoing and Gouzeaucourt were all taken. The VI Corps reached the Schelde along a fairly broad front. Small numbers of its troops managed to get across both the river itself and the Schelde Canal a short distance beyond it. British forces were now so close to Cambrai that it became practically useless as a railhead, hitherto its main function in the German war effort. By nightfall on that Saturday, Currie's and Byng's forces between them had, in two days, driven a wedge twelve miles wide and six miles deep into the German defences and had taken some 10,000 prisoners and 200 guns.[38]

SECOND ARMY AND THE OPENING OF THE FLANDERS OFFENSIVE (See Map 11)

On the morning of Saturday 28 September it was the turn of the GAF to join the general offensive. Numerically the balance of forces was extremely favourable and the Belgian and the British forces in Flanders were fresh. The region had seen heavy fighting in the spring but had been fairly quiet for several months. The British Second Army had followed up some German withdrawals and conducted a small, successful action to seize the Outtersteene Ridge on 18 August. Since then it had done very little fighting. Second Army's troops, their spirits raised by the Allied victories of the last couple of months, were, according to the 9th Division's historian, 'full of confidence' when they assembled on the night of 27/28 September. The Belgian Army had no experience of conducting a major

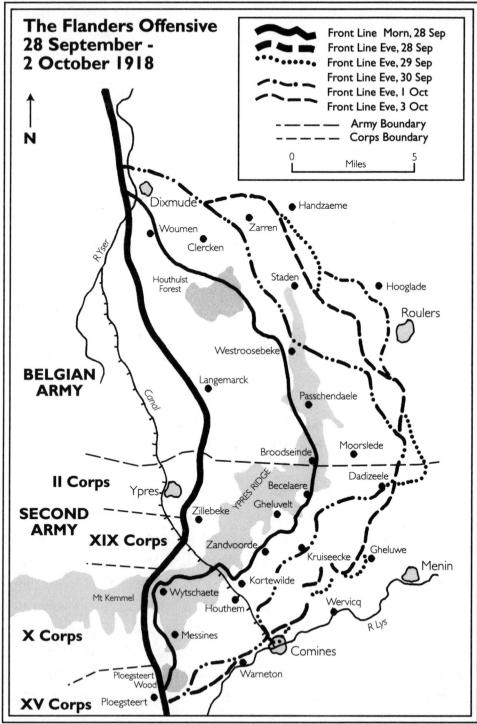

Map 11

offensive but its troops appear to have been confident and keen to play a part in the liberation of their own country.[39]

General Sir Herbert Plumer, Second Army's commander, came from an old-established Yorkshire family and had gone direct from Eton into the 65th Foot. His illustrious pre-1914 military career included war experience in the Sudan, Matabeleland and South Africa. He had spent most of this war in Flanders, having taken command of Second Army in May 1915. He had a very detailed knowledge of the ground and he and his Second Army staff had developed a high reputation for the thoroughness of their planning and the efficiency of their administration, a reputation sealed by his victory at Messines in June 1917.[40]

In September 1918 his Army was holding a 16-mile front. It ran from just north of the ruined city of Ypres to the River Lys, just west of Armentières, in the south. The front bulged to the west of the Wytschaete–Messines ridge, lost to the Germans in the spring, and ran through the middle of Ploegsteert Wood. Holding this front were four corps: from north to south the II, the XIX, the X and the XV Corps. The two northerly corps had three divisions each, the two southerly corps two each. Not lavishly equipped, Second Army had no tanks. There were 400 heavy guns and howitzers and 20 brigades of field artillery (about 480 field pieces), working out at only one field gun to 38 yards of front. Only the weakness of the German forces to Second Army's front made this seem adequate. The 16 squadrons of the RAF's II Brigade gave Second Army a very high degree of air superiority, though in the days immediately prior to the offensive, the Flanders weather somewhat reduced the advantage to be gained from this.[41]

The enemy which the British Second Army faced comprised five under-strength divisions of the German Fourth Army, only one of which was considered good. With inadequate forces to employ the defence-in-depth principles they had used with some effect in this area the previous year, the Germans had most of their troops well forward. As in 1917, the Germans made much use of pill-boxes. The greatest strengths of their positions, however, were the excellent observation they afforded over the whole Second Army area, and the difficult nature of the ground which an attacker would have to cross to reach them. On 28 September the ground was, after the recent rain, a slimy brown wilderness, full of shell craters and so heavily fought over in the recent past that it was virtually devoid of vegetation.[42]

Plumer issued his basic operations order on 19 September, after a briefing from GHQ three days previously. The GAF was to attack between Dixmude and St Eloi. Only the two northern Second Army corps – Lieutenant-General Sir Claud Jacob's II Corps and Lieutenant-General Sir Herbert Watts' XIX Corps – were to attack at Zero hour. The other two were to observe and take advantage of any opportunities. Jacob decided to attack with the 9th and the 29th Divisions, Watts with the 14th and the 35th. With the thoroughness customary in Second Army, Plumer's staff constructed a large-scale model of the positions to be attacked at his headquarters at Cassel. In the days preceding the attack, officers from each attacking division were brought to see it in order that they could better understand their own roles in the attack and how they might best contribute to the achievement of the overall aim.[43]

During the planning of the operation General Degoutte, the King of the Belgians' French chief of staff, tried, as Foch seems to have intended, to act as *de facto* Army Group commander. Given the Belgians' lack of experience in mounting offensive operations of this magnitude some such arrangement was probably necessary. Plumer and his staff seem, however, to have regarded Degoutte as officious and inefficient and to have thought that he did little to co-ordinate planning between themselves and the Belgians. This was a particular problem for the artillery. The British, making their usual efforts to achieve at least a modicum of surprise, wanted no preliminary bombardment. The Belgians, with their relatively inexperienced infantry, wanted an artillery overture of three hours' duration. At a conference on 24 September the British agreed that the Belgians should have the artillery preparation they wanted, and to provide the assistance in this of the heavy artillery of the British II Corps. No preliminary bombardment, however, was to be fired on the British front. From Zero, in addition to the usual creeping barrages fired by the field artillery, it was decided that the heavy artillery fire should fire a sort of rolling barrage which would keep ahead of the 'creeper' and move in somewhat bigger jumps. At the same time, the rest of the heavy artillery would be employed in the more traditional roles of counter-battery and bombardment of important localities.[44]

The Germans had been expecting an attack. They had fired a counter-preparation bombardment at dawn for several mornings prior to Z day and did so again on 28 September. The assembly of Second Army's troops was not much disrupted, however, and the attack was launched on schedule, at 05.20. It was still dark for the first half an hour or so and the use of a substantial amount of smoke in the barrage helped keep casualties down once dawn had broken. According to the 9th (Scottish) Division history, 'The whole operation went like clockwork . . . The resistance of the German infantry was feeble and their artillery practically negligible.'[45] The two northern corps took all their objectives and advanced beyond them. The X Corps joined the attack in the course of the morning and the 31st Division, the northernmost division of XV Corps, in mid-afternoon. The 31st Division ran into fairly serious resistance and took some of the heaviest casualties of the day. In general, however, the battle of 28 September was a major victory at very low cost. By evening, a greater advance, up to six miles in places, had been achieved in one day's fighting than had been gained in more than three months in 1917. Second Army claimed more than 2,000 prisoners and 'numerous' guns. The Belgians on the left had been equally successful. By the standards of previous campaigns in Flanders it was all quite remarkable.[46]

For the continuation of the Flanders push, however, the omens were not good. It had rained heavily for a few days immediately prior to the offensive, and after a few dry hours on the morning of 28 September the Flanders weather reverted to type with driving rain and fierce squalls. The

RAF flew anyway, attempting to offer all the usual forms of support, but losses to aircraft, especially to those engaged in ground attack, were high. Twenty-six machines were lost altogether, many of the losses probably not due to hostile fire.[47] If the weather were to remain so adverse the implications for air support, for the accuracy of the artillery and, above all, for logistics would obviously be serious.

THE MORAL EFFECT OF THE GENERAL OFFENSIVE

The formidable Allied blows in the west from 26–28 September seem to have stretched Ludendorff's nerves to breaking point. According to some reports, on the afternoon of Saturday 28 September, after hearing that the Bulgarians were seeking a separate peace, he had a form of fit or seizure. That evening he and Hindenburg agreed that Germany must immediately seek an armistice. They arranged an audience with the Kaiser at 10.00 the following morning to give him this grim advice.[48] A little over four hours before that fateful meeting the British Fourth Army added its formidable force to Foch's general offensive. Over the next ten days Rawlinson's Army would do more than any other to sustain the pressure on the Germans.

Map 12

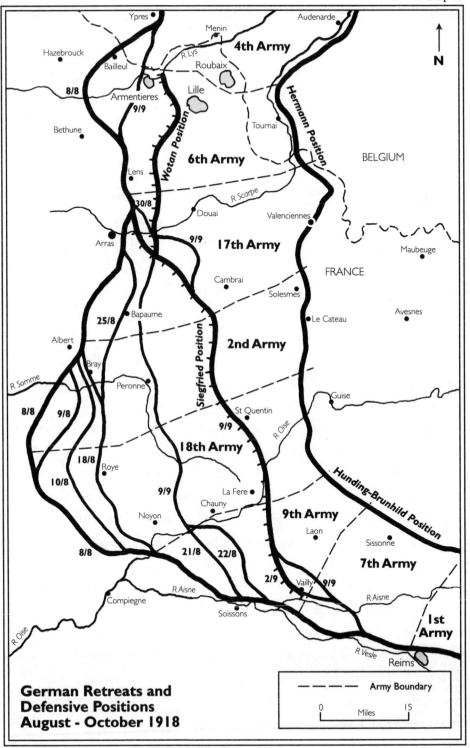

Ypres
Menin
Audenarde
4th Army
Hazebrouck
Bailleul
Roubaix
R Lys
8/8
Armentieres
Lille
9/9
Tournai
Bethune
Hermann Position
BELGIUM
Wotan Position
Lens
6th Army
30/8
R Scarpe
Douai
Valenciennes
Arras
9/9
17th Army
Maubeuge
Cambrai
FRANCE
Solesmes
Avesnes
Bapaume
Le Cateau
25/8
Albert
2nd Army
Siegfried Position
Bray
R Somme
Peronne
Guise
8/8
9/8
St Quentin
9/9
R Oise
18th Army
18/8
Roye
10/8
9/9
La Fere
Chauny
Noyon
9th Army
Hunding-Brunhild Position
Laon
Sissonne
8/8
21/8
22/8
7th Army
2/9
Vailly
9/9
R Aisne
R Aisne
Compiegne
Soissons
R Oise
1st Army
R Vesle
Reims

**German Retreats and
Defensive Positions
August - October 1918**

N

— — — Army Boundary

0   Miles   15

8

BREAKING THE
HINDENBURG LINE

RAWLINSON REPORTS

The Fourth Army attack towards what Rawlinson termed the Advanced Hindenburg System on 18 September had been an important victory. But triumph had been complete only in the central (Australian Corps) sector. On the left, III Corps' attack had achieved only a limited success. There, and in the IX Corps sector on the right, there was a great deal of ground which still had to be captured before Fourth Army would be in a good position to assault the Main Hindenburg System.[1]

If, however, Rawlinson had any doubt about his Army's capacity to storm that formidable position he gave no indication of it in his report to GHQ on 19 September. Sir Henry, indeed, exuded optimism. He declared himself highly satisfied with the results of the previous day's operation. He now had most of the ground he needed overlooking the main position and he was confident that his forces could 'secure the remaining observation required within the next 48–72 hours'. He regarded it as a proven fact that the morale of the German troops facing Fourth Army was 'steadily deteriorating'. German troops, according to some captured officers, now refused to face the Australians and the moral effect of tanks appeared greater than ever. The German artillery response had been somewhat weak, and according to prisoners, the Germans were now seriously short of guns. Rawlinson concluded that 'an attack on the main Hindenburg system with a view to piercing it on a considerable front between Vendhuile and St. Quentin is an operation which, under present circumstances, has every prospect of success'. Indeed, Rawlinson submitted, with this report, an outline scheme for such an attack.[2]

Haig was naturally delighted with reports of another Fourth Army success and welcomed Rawlinson's apparent eagerness to assault the Main Hindenburg System.[3] Since 8 August the BEF had made most of the running in the Allied offensives and Rawlinson's had been its most consistently aggressive and successful army. Both Rawlinson and Haig seem to have been convinced that, in the great military drama which the Allied high command intended to stage at the end of the month, Fourth Army would again play a leading role.[4]

FOURTH ARMY OPERATIONS: 19–24 SEPTEMBER 1918 (See Map 13)

But in his report to Haig on 19 September Rawlinson had considerably underestimated the difficulty of gaining the rest of the ground needed for an attack on the Main Hindenburg System. Piecemeal attacks mounted by both the III Corps and the IX Corps forces over the next couple of days generally resulted in bloody frustration. More concerted efforts mounted by the III Corps on 21 and 22 September were only a little more successful and left its troops utterly exhausted. Positions on the ridge-line such as Quennemont Farm, Gillemont Farm, Tombois Farm and the Dados Loop, which Fourth Army's planners considered it vital to hold before attacking across the St Quentin Canal, were still in German hands when the American II Corps relieved the III Corps in this sector on 24 September.[5]

General Sir Walter Braithwaite, the IX Corps commander, decided on a pause in major operations after 19 September in order to rest his troops. When, after meticulous planning, IX Corps renewed the attack on 24 September, it achieved a high degree of success, advancing between 600 and 2,000 yards on a front of about four and a half miles and capturing about 1,500 prisoners.[6] By the evening of the following day the IX Corps had captured virtually the whole of the Advanced Hindenburg System in its sector.[7]

PLANNING THE BIG ATTACK

The Australian Corps had been crucial to practically all the successes which had so boosted Rawlinson's reputation since April. When contemplating the assault on the Main Hindenburg System in mid-September, Rawlinson appears to have assumed that it would again be his principal instrument of victory. For that reason, and because of the special trust placed in his ability and judgement, Sir John Monash was given a major role in planning the operation.[8] Indeed, the first draft of the Fourth Army plan for this great assault, submitted to Fourth Army HQ on 18 September, was written entirely by the Australian Corps commander and his staff.[9]

One of Monash's problems in planning this operation was that much of his corps was not going to be available for it. The 1st and 4th Australian Divisions were very tired and due to be withdrawn for a rest as soon as they had fulfilled their role in the battle for the Advanced Hindenburg System. Monash was in need of two strong divisions to replace them. Rawlinson had suggested the last two American divisions left serving with the BEF, the 27th American Division and the 30th American Division, which together formed the II American Corps. Monash seems to have been delighted at the prospect. He had commanded American troops at Hamel on 4 July and Americans and Australians had also fought side-by-side north of the Somme during the Battle of Amiens. American troops were, on average, of better physique than their British counterparts and their general demeanour and attitude – 'bold, free and aggressive' as the Australian official history puts it – had much in common with that of the Australians. American divisions were also, as we have noted, exceptionally large, about double the strength of British divisions. They had 12 large infantry battalions, three times as many machine-gun companies as their British equivalents and twice as many engineers.[10] But the Americans also had distinct weaknesses. The most important was inexperience. They were largely untried troops under equally untested officers. They were also virtually devoid of artillery and their signals organisation was incomplete. In order to help offset these American deficiencies Rawlinson decided, with the consent of its commander, General G.W. Read, that II American Corps should, for operational purposes, be temporarily amalgamated with the Australian Corps and should work under the direction of Monash and his staff. Monash created a special team of officers drawn from all arms to familiarise the Americans with Australian Corps methods.[11]

But what was the nature of the military problem which Monash was planning to tackle? British military intelligence believed (correctly as it turned out) that seven German divisions held the Main Hindenburg System immediately to Fourth Army's front, with another three in reserve and others capable of reaching the battlefield in two or three days. Most of these divisions were far below full strength, with some of them very depleted indeed. One of the reserve divisions had only three battalions instead of nine and battalions in some divisions were down to little more than 100 men. But the German defenders had the advantage of exceptionally powerful fortifications.[12]

The Main Hindenburg System had been constructed during the Battle of the Somme in the latter part of 1916, and during the winter and early spring following that great struggle. It was essentially a fortified canal line. In the southern part of the Fourth Army front the St Quentin Canal ran through open country. The bed of the canal was 35 feet wide and was full of mud and water to a depth of about six feet. The canal banks were up to 50 feet high and very steep and faced with brick up to a height of 10 feet. The canal was thus a tank-proof obstacle – something probably not considered very important when the Hindenburg System was first constructed but of considerable significance by September 1918. To many observers the defences in this sector might have seemed infantry-proof as well. West of the canal there was a system of heavily-wired trenches equipped with numerous dug-outs and communication trenches. Behind that there were formidable wire entanglements on the inside slopes of the western bank of the canal, these being covered by machine guns in concrete emplacements on the eastern bank. On the eastern bank, behind the concrete emplacements, was another system of well-wired trenches.[13]

On the northern half of the Fourth Army front the nature of the obstacle was very different. The canal there ran into the 6,000 yard Bellicourt tunnel, constructed in the days of Napoleon I and then considered something of an engineering marvel. From a military point of view, the tunnel could be considered a ready-made and exceptionally broad bridge. Potentially it was the Achilles heel of the whole system. Needless to say, the Germans themselves had recognised this. In the tunnel sector they had drastically altered their scheme of defence, placing the main defences in front of, not behind, the canal. Here the defences, consisting of two or three strong lines of trenches, each protected by several thick belts of wire, bulged out 400 to 1,200 yards west of the canal. In addition to these main defences many additional trenches had been dug to counteract local weaknesses and to take advantage of good fields of fire. The villages of Bellenglise, Bellicourt and Bony had also been heavily fortified. The tunnel itself was being used as a sort of underground, shell-proof barracks, most of the German troops within it being accommodated on barges.

On the whole of the Fourth Army front, including both the tunnel sector and the southern sector, where the canal ran through open country, there was a further system of trenches behind the Main Hindenburg System. It was known to the British as the Hindenburg Support Line or Le Catelet–Nauroy Line. Its wiring was not complete and if the Main System were to be penetrated on any considerable front, it could not offer much of an obstacle. About 5,000 to 6,000 yards to the east of the Hindenburg Support System there was another trench system, the Masnières–Beaurevoir–Fonsomme Line or Hindenburg Reserve System (often referred to simply as the Beaurevoir Line), but that was too far back to play any part in the battle for the Main Hindenburg System itself. Beyond that, the Germans had no properly prepared systems of fortifications. Once Fourth Army had broken the Beaurevoir Line it would be in open country.[14]

In preparing schemes to assault the Main Hindenburg System, Fourth Army had one quite extraordinary advantage. On 8 August, during the Battle of Amiens, armoured cars of 17th Battalion Tank Corps had overrun a German corps headquarters in the village of Framerville.[15] There they had captured extremely detailed plans of all the defences of the Hindenburg System between the Oise and Bellicourt and a memorandum describing the system and the methods which the Germans anticipated using for its defence. In addition to showing the positions of the trenches and belts of wire, this document gave the position of all gun batteries and artillery observation posts, dug-outs, bunkers and machine-gun emplacements and the locations of ammunition and supply dumps, railheads, billets and camps in the German rear.

In addition to a certain pride in their own ingenuity, industry and thoroughness, the captured memorandum appeared to indicate that the Germans had some grave doubts about the system they had constructed. They had been attracted by the idea of using the canal line as the basis of their defence, but that had meant siting the main position in a valley. If the attacker gained the high ground in front of it he was likely to be able to suppress the defender's artillery prior to an assault upon it. Given that the Main Hindenburg System had very little depth, the attacker's artillery would be able to dominate it during an assault and it would be difficult for the Germans to move supporting troops and reserves around without incurring terrible casualties. In order to make such movements easier and less costly, the Germans had constructed a system of tunnels running from front to rear, but the positions of these, including exact locations of entrances and exits, were revealed in the captured documents. Instead of being aids to German freedom of movement, therefore, the tunnels could be turned into traps.

As Archibald Montgomery admitted in his account: 'It has fallen to the lot of few commanders to be provided with such detailed information as to the nature of the enemy's defences.'[16] Yet even with such excellent intelligence the Fourth Army planners would have dreaded to tackle fortifications like these had the German Army still been on the peak of its form. It was only the perceived decline in German fighting power which enabled Fourth Army to contemplate tackling the position with something approaching confidence.

Indeed, even though possessed of such complete information on the German defences, and taking into consideration the decline in German fighting spirit, Monash's verdict seems to have been that the southern sector, where the canal ran through open country, was practically impregnable. He focused all his thoughts on the tunnel sector. His plan was, in essence, simple enough. The operation was to be divided into two phases. The initial assault, under the cover of a creeping barrage laid down by 17 field artillery brigades, would be carried out by the Americans, the 27th Division attacking on the left and the 30th Division on the right. They would have the support of 60 tanks. Starting from the Advanced Hindenburg System they were intended to storm the trenches of the Main Hindenburg System, go over the tunnel mound and seize Le Catelet (Hindenburg Support) Line. This would involve an advance of 4,400 yards. Then the 3rd and 5th Australian Divisions, assisted by another 30 tanks, would carry out an 'exploitation' beyond the range of the barrage, seizing the Beaurevoir Line and the village of Beaurevoir. Elements of both the III and the IX Corps would then move into the gap created by the American breakthrough and, pushing outwards, roll up the inner flanks of the Main Hindenburg System. This would help the rest of those corps get across the canal, thereby greatly expanding the bridgehead.[17]

When he drafted the plan Monash assumed that Fourth Army would, by the time of the assault, hold the whole of the Advanced Hindenburg System in its sector. This assumption was to prove invalid. But even had it been justified by events, Monash would still have been demanding an outstanding performance of the two inexperienced American divisions. These would be required to advance 4,400 yards through some of the most formidable defences ever encountered on the Western Front – more than Monash had ever asked of the most battle-tested Australian divisions. But perhaps the most serious weakness of Monash's plan was that the frontage of attack which he was proposing, a mere 6,000 yards, was perilously narrow. A high proportion of the troops involved might be subjected to enfilade fire from Germans on the flanks who were not being directly assaulted themselves. Monash was, of course, counting on subjecting the Germans to a very intense preliminary bombardment, using all of Fourth Army's heavy artillery, and providing intense barrage and counter-battery fire in support of the assault itself. Nevertheless, careful analysis of this plan inevitably raises questions about Monash's reputation as a great master of the set-piece attack in positional warfare.[18]

Monash submitted an outline of this plan to Rawlinson on 18 September and, at a Fourth Army conference held the following day, Monash's scheme for an attack by the combined American–Australian corps was, with some modifications, accepted. The most significant change in the plan for Monash's own corps was Rawlinson's decision to make the attack by the Australians on the Beaurevoir Line, contingent on complete success in rupturing the Main Hindenburg System and the Hindenburg Support (Le Catelet) Line. Rawlinson seems to have thought that Monash was being over-ambitious in expecting to penetrate the Main Hindenburg System, Le Catelet (Support) Line and the Beaurevoir (Reserve) Line all in one day, the Beaurevoir Line without even the support of a creeping barrage.[19]

But Rawlinson's biggest departure from Monash's concept was his acceptance of an apparently unsolicited plan which had been submitted by the IX Corps commander, Lieutenant-General Sir Walter Braithwaite. Braithwaite and his staff believed that, using life-belts, light, portable boats, ropes and ladders, they could get a single division, the 46th (North Midland) Division, across the canal south of the tunnel. Some of the crossings would take place in the Bellenglise Salient, an area of the German defensive system very vulnerable to converging fire by Fourth Army's artillery. Another IX Corps division, the 32nd, would then pass through the 46th, while the two remaining divisions, the 1st and the 6th, formed a southward-facing flank, west of the canal. Once the 32nd Division had secured the tunnel at Le Tronquoy (a tunnel similar to, though a good deal smaller than, that at Bellicourt) the 1st and 6th Divisions would cross the canal by means of it, to be followed by elements of the French First Army.[20]

Monash was vehemently opposed to the inclusion of the IX Corps scheme in the final Fourth Army plan of attack and seems to have had some difficulty in accepting the need to defer to his Army commander's views.[21] Rawlinson, however, backed his own judgement and incorporated the IX Corps' scheme into the orders which Fourth Army issued on 22 September.[22] Rawlinson's decision to broaden the assault on the Main Hindenburg System, not staking all on an attack across the Bellicourt tunnel, was to prove judicious. It illustrated the benefits of his greater experience at the higher levels of command (won at the cost of many lives) when compared with Monash. But Rawlinson himself did not address the most fundamental weakness in Monash's scheme for the attack of his combined American–Australian corps. In the plans endorsed by Rawlinson at the Fourth Army conference of 19 September, untried American divisions who had (to mention just one aspect of their status as *ingénues*) no previous experience of working with a creeping barrage, were going to be asked to carry out tasks which veterans would have considered daunting.

In the final version of the Fourth Army plan the III Corps was not to assault the Main Hindenburg System itself, but was to secure the left flank of the Australian-American Corps by taking the high ground south-west of Vendhuile and, when the Americans had crossed over the tunnel, by clearing Vendhuile and the area west of the canal in that area. GHQ ordered the VI and V Corps of Third Army, immediately to Fourth Army's north, to co-operate by attacking between Vendhuile and Marcoing, and arranged with Foch that the French First Army was to attack on a 6-mile front immediately to Fourth Army's south.[23]

When he drafted his version of the plan Monash had not known how much armour would be available to Fourth Army though he had considered this an important factor. GHQ made a generous allocation: the III, IV and V Tank Brigades and the 17th Armoured Car Battalion. Fourth Army allocated IV Tank Brigade to the Americans and the III Tank Brigade to IX Corps. The V Tank Brigade was attached to the Australians, renewing a partnership first developed in the preparations for Hamel. Some 34 Mark V tanks were to support the attack of the 27th American Division, 33 that of the 30th American Division. Comparable numbers would support the Australians as they leapfrogged the American Divisions. The 17th Armoured Car Battalion, as on 8 August, was to seek opportunities to pass through the Australians in order to wreak havoc in the German rear. The canal banks were too precipitous to allow tanks to cross except in the Bellicourt tunnel sector and therefore tanks assigned to help the IX Corps on 29 September would cross there and join the IX Corps troops on the far side. Sixteen Mark V tanks were to assist the 46th Division and eight Mark Vs and nine Whippets were to assist the 32nd Division. A total of 181 tanks were to see action in Fourth Army's attack on 29 September. In order to cross the broad, deep trenches of the Main Hindenburg System some tanks were fitted with 'cribs' – very strong hexagonal frames manufactured in the Tank Corps' Central Workshops. A crib could be automatically released from the front of a tank into a trench, blocking the trench and providing a robust structure over which the tank which dropped it, and others following, could drive.[24]

A good deal of cavalry was also made available for this operation though most of it arrived at the eleventh hour. When Fourth Army began planning this operation its staff knew that it would have the 5th Cavalry Brigade from the 2nd Cavalry Division. This brigade was to be attached to the Australian Corps. If the Australians were to be successful in achieving a breakthrough, it was to move into German rear areas, cause as much chaos and confusion as possible and endeavour to cut rail communications in the vicinity of Bohain and Bussigny. It would co-operate in these endeavours with the armoured cars attached to the Australians. But Haig had still not given up on the idea of a more substantial body of horsemen erupting into the German rear. There being no prospect of this on the First or Third

Army fronts in the foreseeable future, on the evening of 28 September he had deployed the Cavalry Corps, now consisting of 1st and 3rd Cavalry Divisions, in Fourth Army's rear. These formations, which were to remain under the operational control of GHQ rather than Fourth Army, were set extremely ambitious goals:

(a) To advance in the general direction of Le Cateau, securing the railway junctions at that place and at Busigny.

(b) To operate against the flank and rear of the enemy opposite the British Third and First Armies.

(c) To cut German communications around Valenciennes.[25]

During the assault on the Main Hindenburg System Rawlinson's ground forces were, of course, intended to enjoy a great deal of air support from the RAF's V Brigade, an integral part of Fourth Army. For this operation V Brigade had nine fighter squadrons (SE5as and Camels), one fighter reconnaissance squadron (Bristol Fighters), one day bomber and one night bomber squadron and five corps squadrons, a total of 337 aircraft. The V Brigade planned to help Fourth Army in all the usual ways, but on the morning of Sunday 29 September the weather would render the plans of Brigadier Charlton and his staff largely unworkable.[26]

FINAL PREPARATIONS

In order to be able to put his plans into effect towards the end of the month Rawlinson issued orders on 20 September for the reorganisation of the Fourth Army front. The main intention was to shift the front of the Australian–American Corps slightly northward so that it faced the Bellicourt tunnel squarely. The physical movements to implement the reorganisation were to commence on the night of 21 September and were intended to be complete by 25 September.[27] In the event, the reorganisation could not be completed in quite the time-scale and in quite the way that

Rawlinson intended. Owing to III Corps' limited success in operations from 18 September onwards, part of the ridge overlooking the Bellicourt tunnel, which Rawlinson had intended the American divisions to occupy, was still in German hands. Rawlinson was aware that some of the III Corps' divisions were extremely tired and he was very far from happy with the performance of its commander, Lieutenant-General Sir Richard Butler. Suffering from influenza and, perhaps from nervous exhaustion, Butler had been compelled to take leave in the middle of the Battle of Amiens and the performance of the III Corps since his return to duty on 12 September[28] had not been such as to occasion any surge of confidence in his fitness for this level of command.

On 22 September, after hearing Rawlinson's criticisms of Butler, Haig decided that the III Corps as a whole should be relieved. He decided to send Rawlinson Lieutenant-General Sir Thomas Morland's XIII Corps with three fresh divisions (the 25th, the 50th and the 66th Divisions) from GHQ reserve.[29] Haig apparently intended that Rawlinson use XIII Corps to secure the ridge line. But Rawlinson, while gratefully accepting Morland's formation as reinforcement, considered that he had no time to integrate it into his immediate plans. He had already set in motion a reorganisation of the Fourth Army front. To give counter-orders would cause disruption and result in the attack being delayed,[30] something which would have been unacceptable to Haig. Rawlinson thus concluded that he was going to have to use the American divisions in preliminary operations in order to secure their intended start line for the big attack on the Main Hindenburg System.[31]

The tasks assigned by Monash and Rawlinson to the American divisions in the assault on the Main Hindenburg System were very demanding, even on the assumptions that all their troops would be fresh for the big assault and that they would be in complete possession of that portion of the Advanced Hindenburg System immediately in front of the tunnel defences. In the case of the 27th American Division in the northern sector of Monash's front neither of these assumptions were to prove valid. The

30th American Division did improve its position by minor attacks on the night of 26 September and was in possession of practically all of its intended start line by the morning of 29 September. But an attack mounted by the 27th American Division at 05.30 on 27 September to secure a line Gillemont Farm–Quennemont Farm met strenuous resistance from the German 54th Division and failed almost completely.[32]

It would perhaps have been better had the 27th American Division's attack been stopped dead. In fact, there were reports that some parties of Americans had gained their objectives and were now isolated and pinned down. This presented a problem for the assault on the Main Hindenburg System now scheduled for 29 September. If the supporting barrage were to commence immediately ahead of the start line for the 27th Division attack, it would sweep through the positions of any Americans pinned down within German lines and was likely to cause casualties amongst them.[33] This was considered unacceptable by the Americans themselves and Rawlinson thus decided to commence the barrage about 1,000 yards to the east of the start line.[34] But, leaving sentiment aside, it would have been much better (as Rawlinson must have realised from experience) to have risked causing some casualties by what the Americans today call 'friendly fire', than to expose attacking troops to much greater danger by depriving them of a creeping barrage during a major assault.

Meanwhile, at 22.30 on 26 September, Fourth Army began a preliminary artillery bombardment of the Main Hindenburg System. It was intended to disrupt the Germans' defensive system, suppress their artillery and lower their morale. Forty-four brigades of field artillery, 21 brigades of heavy artillery and four long-range siege batteries were employed – a total of 1,044 field guns and howitzers and 593 heavy pieces. The heavy guns were mainly massed around Hargicourt and Lempire, with another big concentration at Le Verguir. The first phase of the bombardment, which lasted until 06.00 on 27 September, consisted of the firing of concentrations of 'BB' or mustard gas shells, which the British were using for the first time, against targets including headquarters and groups of batteries. At

06.00 on 27 September the main bombardment of high explosive shell began. As a finishing touch, just before Zero on 29 September there was to be an especially intensive shelling of telephone exchanges to cause German communications to fail during the attack.

Despite occupying a ridge overlooking the German positions (at least on the right of the front) and despite having very detailed plans of the German defences, Fourth Army's artillery was not without difficulties in the conduct of this bombardment. Rain, cloud and general atmospheric murk made it impossible to locate enemy batteries accurately either by direct observation or by aerial photography. Though Fourth Army had a fairly good idea of initial German gun positions from the captured document, the Germans appear to have been moving at least some of their batteries around.[35] Another difficulty was ammunition supply. The British, by this stage in the war, were producing shell in practically inexhaustible amounts. But, on this occasion, it proved impossible to maintain a smooth flow to the guns. Fourth Army's artillery was dependent on the newly opened railway line to Templeux-le-Guerard and, although about 15 ammunition trains a day were arriving, they were tending to run late. Getting ammunition forward from the railhead to the troops was also difficult. Ammunition lorries were frequently delayed on roads choked by the movements of troops and other supplies and batteries were sometimes obliged to interrupt their fire-programmes for want of ammunition. The Australian official historian went so far as to call the three-day bombardment 'desultory'[36] though Fourth Army's gunners fired about three-quarters of a million shells during its course, including 32,000 of the new mustard gas shells.[37]

The preliminary bombardment achieved differing degrees of success in different parts of the front. In some sectors, especially in parts of the Bellenglise Salient, it shredded virtually all the German wire. In others, lanes were cleared. At some points on the 46th Division's front the sides of the canal were battered down, forming ramps of debris which rendered access to and from the water much easier. Fourth Army's gunners were able to give the least help in the sector which 27th American Division was facing. They had not been allowed to bombard the German positions along the ridge in front of that division in case they hit the scattered groups of Americans thought to have been pinned down there since the failed attack of 27 September. The result of the counter-battery effort was generally disappointing and especially so in 27th American Division's attack sector where, the ridge still being in German hands, Fourth Army's artillery observation was least satisfactory. In most sectors of the front, however, while the bombardment appears to have killed few Germans, it did much to depress their fighting spirit. Intense shelling of the entrances to and exits from the tunnels and dug-outs of the Main Hindenburg System isolated their occupants and deprived them of rations, demoralising them so completely that, in many cases, they were to emerge only to surrender.[38]

While the bombardment was in progress a lot of work was being done to improve the communications in Fourth Army's rear. We have already seen that logistical problems were to some extent impeding the bombardment of the Main Hindenburg System and there was every reason to expect that these would get worse the further the advance continued if nothing were done about them at this stage. In each divisional sector roads were rapidly being constructed, infantry as well as pioneers being used as unskilled labour for the engineers in some cases. Traffic control was taken in hand by the military police. To make movement smoother some roads were allotted to infantry, some to artillery and some to tanks. Efforts were also in progress to extend the railway system and preparations were made to repair bridges over the canal at Vendhuile and Bellenglise which the III and the IX Corps respectively were intending to capture.[39]

THE GREAT ASSAULT

The early morning of 29 September offered almost perfect conditions for the attack. It was no longer raining hard, though there was some drizzle. The surface of the ground was somewhat slippery after recent

Map 13

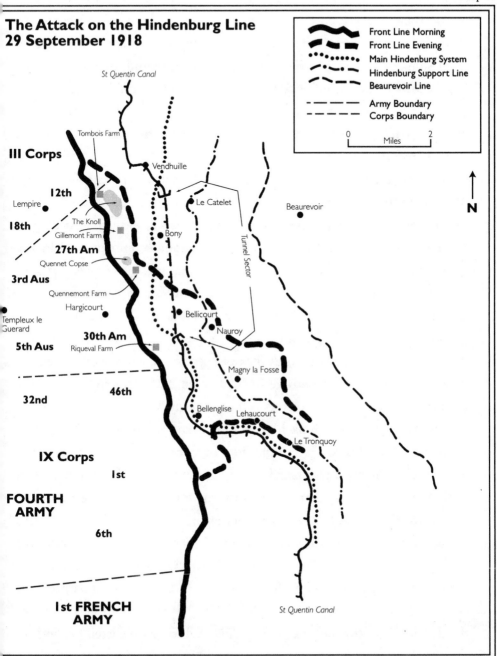

The Attack on the Hindenburg Line
29 September 1918

Legend:
- Front Line Morning
- Front Line Evening
- Main Hindenburg System
- Hindenburg Support Line
- Beaurevoir Line
- Army Boundary
- Corps Boundary

0 — Miles — 2

N

St Quentin Canal

Tombois Farm

III Corps

Vendhuille

12th

Lempire

Le Catelet

Beaurevoir

18th

The Knoll

Gillemont Farm

Bony

27th Am

Quennet Copse

Tunnel Sector

3rd Aus

Quennemont Farm

Hargicourt

Bellicourt

Templeux le
Guerard

Nauroy

30th Am

5th Aus

Riqueval Farm

Magny la Fosse

46th

Bellenglise

Lehaucourt

32nd

Le Tronquoy

IX Corps

1st

**FOURTH
ARMY**

6th

St Quentin Canal

**1st FRENCH
ARMY**

rains but reasonably firm underneath, offering good going for the tanks. Most crucially there was a thick ground fog similar to that which had shrouded Fourth Army's movements on 8 August. Together with the artificial smoke employed in the barrage, the mist would, as on 8 August, significantly reduce casualties from enemy fire. But it would also, again like 8 August, make it practically impossible for the RAF to offer close air support or artillery spotting or even to monitor the movements of Fourth Army's troops in the first few hours of the attack.[40]

By Zero at 05.50, the infantry was all formed up on its start lines. Some of it was in front-line trenches, some in shell holes and sunken roads ahead of the front line – the precise positions having been selected according to the lie of the land and the wishes of divisional commanders. In the American sector, where tanks were to lead the attack, they moved forward from their start lines shortly before 05.50 in order to pass through the infantry at Zero. The din of the preliminary bombardment did not altogether drown out the noise of the tank engines and these blended with the drone of aircraft. Tremendous as the noise level was before Zero, however, it became worse as the barrage opened some 200 yards in front of the infantry, giving the signal for the assault to begin.[41]

On the left wing of Monash's corps the 27th American Division had an unenviable task. The section of the ridge in front of the Main Hindenburg System which formed its first objective, had not, as we have noted, been subjected to the preliminary bombardment for fear of hitting parties of American troops thought to be still holding out within the German fortifications after the division's attack on 27 September. The formidable strong-points, including Quennemont Farm, Gillemont Farm and The Knoll, which had for so long frustrated the III Corps' had thus been left completely unmolested for a couple of days. To make matters still worse the division had, for the same reason, decided to deprive itself of the support of a creeping barrage for the first 1,000 yards of its advance. This inexperienced formation, therefore, found itself advancing into a hail of German fire and suffered very heavy losses from the outset.[42] By shifting positions on the night of 28 September many of the German batteries in this sector had avoided the particularly intense final stage of the preliminary bombardment and they now reacted vigorously to the American assault. In the absence of a creeping barrage 27th American Division was especially reliant upon the help of its 34 tanks. But German guns scored direct hits on eleven of these and seven became stuck in trenches or shell holes.[43]

The 3rd Australian Division was meant to exploit the success of the 27th American. But the Americans had barely dented the German defences on the ridge line though, under the cover of the mist, some groups had passed over it and had begun attacking the Main Hindenburg System further back. When infantry of the 3rd Australian Division attempted to pass through the 27th American Division in the latter part of the morning it ran into intense fire. The tanks supporting the Australians, like those which had led the American advance, were unable to help very much, many being knocked out by German artillery. In the early afternoon Australian infantry, greatly mixed up with the Americans, struggled grimly with the German strong-points on the ridge. Neither Monash who, in accordance with his normal practice, had his corps headquarters well to the rear, nor Major-General Gellibrand, commanding 3rd Australian Division, had any real idea of what was going on. Believing the Americans to have been much more successful than was actually the case Monash ordered the 3rd Australian Division to make a renewed effort, to commence at 15.00, to break through in this sector. The renewed all-out assault, unsupported by artillery, resulted in further heavy casualties for relatively little gain.[44] The situation when darkness fell was that Monash's corps, after bitter struggles in which it sustained some 5,000 casualties, had gained possession of Gillemont Farm, Quennemont Farm and the western slopes of The Knoll. It thus held virtually all of the positions on the ridge which had constituted the Advanced Hindenburg System in this sector. The Main Hindenburg System on the northern half of Monash's front was, however, virtually untouched.[45]

Further south, Monash's corps had done very much better. The 30th American Division held the ridge overlooking the Main Hindenburg System in its sector during the days of the preliminary bombardment. The bombardment had thus been fairly effective and had shredded much of the German wire. In even more critical contrast with the 27th American Division to the north, the 30th American Division's infantry enjoyed the support of a creeping barrage throughout its advance. Despite considerable enfilade fire from Quennemont Farm the Americans successfully overran the German trenches west of the tunnel mound and the tunnel mound itself. By noon, the Americans had taken Bellicourt, the Germans there being so stunned by the intensity of the bombardment that they offered little resistance. At the same time, some groups were pressing on towards the defended village of Nauroy in the Le Catelet or Hindenburg Support Line. The 30th American Division performed with zeal and valour that day. But, owing to their inexperience, its men had not taken sufficient care to secure the positions they had overrun.

In late morning, when the 5th Australian Division began to try to pass through the 30th American, it encountered intense machine-gun fire in some places from posts which the Americans had failed to clear. The Australians had to expend time, effort and lives neutralising these. By 12.20 Nauroy had, nevertheless, fallen to Australian and American troops, but 5th Australian Division made little further progress on this day. On its right flank it was under considerable pressure from counter-attacks mounted by German reserves until about 15.00, when the successful advance of the IX Corps eased the situation. On its left flank the division was still taking fire from German positions on the ridge until mid-afternoon, and by then most of its supporting tanks had been knocked out.[46]

The attack of Monash's corps on 29 September was far from being a complete failure. The American troops had performed creditably and 30th American Division had, by any standards, achieved a great deal. But the breach of the Main Hindenburg System in the Bellicourt tunnel sector was on a narrow front and distinctly precarious. It almost goes without saying that conditions were not right for exploitation by armoured cars or cavalry. It was fortunate that victory further south was more clear cut.

The artillery support for IX Corps' assault crossing was lavish. According to the 46th Division historian, on one 500 yard stretch of front there were 54 18-pdr field guns firing two rounds per minute and 18 4.5-inch field howitzers firing one round per minute. Thus during every minute of the eight hours that 46th Division was in action 126 shells were falling on the 500 yard frontage, immediately ahead of the advancing infantry. Not surprisingly the infantry reported the creeping barrage one of the best they had ever seen. Though the Germans undoubtedly expected an all-out attack on the Main Hindenburg System on this date, reckoning the open canal impregnable, they seem to have assumed it would be concentrated on the tunnel sector. Thus the 46th Division seems to have been favoured by a considerable degree of surprise as well as a massive amount of firepower.[47]

Together with the fog, these advantages made it possible for the 137th Brigade, which led the assault, to gain the line of the canal with modest casualties, overrunning the German trenches west of the canal and killing or capturing their inhabitants. The damage done by the preliminary bombardment to the west bank of the canal made access to the water (or to the canal bed) relatively easy. On the northern part of the 137th Brigade's front the water was still quite deep. There, officers of 1/5th South Staffords and 1/6th North Staffords took the lead in swimming across with ropes, the ropes being then used to assist the passage of light portable boats and men in life-belts or on planks. In a few places bridges had been imperfectly demolished and it was possible to get across on those. Near Riqueval Farm a daring *coup de main* by a company of 1/6th North Staffords and detachment of sappers seized intact a bridge which the Germans had prepared for demolition. Further south the 1/6th South Staffords, crossing immediately north-west of Bellenglise, found the canal almost dry. By 08.20 almost all of the 137th Brigade and leading battalions of the 138th and 139th Brigades had crossed the canal. Casualties were still remarkably light.[48]

At that point the creeping barrage stopped creeping and remained stationary for the next three hours. Behind this protective barrage the 46th Division consolidated its gains and a brigade leap-frog was carried out, the 138th and the 139th Brigades passing through the 137th. As the barrage lifted, at 11.20, these brigades advanced to seize the trenches of the Main Hindenburg System on the east bank of the canal. By this stage the mist had largely cleared and German fire, from both infantry and artillery weapons, was becoming very much more effective. The 138th Brigade, on the left, took heavy fire from German positions in the Advanced Hindenburg System, on the west bank of the canal, where the Americans and Australians were still in some difficulties. Nevertheless the whole of the Main Hindenburg System in its sector was in the hands of the 46th Division by 15.00. The 32nd Division then passed through to continue the advance.[49]

The IX Corps was considerably assisted in the course of the day by the tanks allotted to it. Sixteen tanks of the 9th Battalion, which, as planned, had crossed the canal at that part of the tunnel sector now occupied by 30th American Division, played a substantial role in the capture of German positions near the village of Magny-la-Fosse[50] shortly after 13.00. Late in the afternoon the 5th and 6th Battalions of the Tank Corps assisted the 32nd Division to widen the breach in a southerly direction.[51]

By nightfall the German defences on the IX Corps' front had been penetrated to a depth of 6,000 yards. Both the Main Hindenburg System and the Hindenburg Support System had been ruptured and over 5,100 prisoners and 90 guns captured.[52] Though resistance had stiffened during the course of the day, the IX Corps' operation had been a great triumph. The victory had been largely achieved by a single division, the 46th (North Midland) Division, which had taken 4,200 prisoners and 70 guns at the cost of less than 800 total casualties.[53] It was, perhaps, the most extraordinary achievement of any BEF division on a single day. The 46th Division was an ordinary Territorial Force division, in no sense an elite or glamorous formation. Its success on this day seems, in part, to have been owing to a young and dynamic commander. Major-General Gerald Boyd had been a captain in 1914. He was one of the few British general officers to have served in the ranks, from which he had been commissioned during the South African War.[54]

On the flanks of the main attack by Monash's and Braithwaite's corps relatively little happened on 29 September. The III Corps gave some assistance to the Australians and Americans but gained only a little ground. No direct help came from the Third Army. The attack of the French First Army was half-hearted and nowhere did it achieve a crossing.[55]

RAWLINSON'S REACTION

Considered objectively Fourth Army's action of 29 September 1918 may be regarded as one of the most impressive feats of arms in British military history. But Rawlinson's reaction was largely one of disappointment. He had expected a greater victory than his Army actually achieved,[56] and even on this day of triumph he was unable to avoid displaying some weakness of character. When he failed to gain the expected breakthrough in the tunnel sector, instead of accepting it stoically, he reacted with a degree of petulance, blaming the green American troops whom he and Monash had sent to do veterans' work. Someone at GHQ made the following note of a telephone message received from Rawlinson that afternoon:

> It appears that the American troops of the 27th Division did not mop up and passed over the German defences . . . The Americans are so disorganised and short of officers and ignorant of what to do that Sir Henry Rawlinson considers it would be necessary to withdraw them from the battle later on and substitute the XIII Corps. He did not think this was a matter for immediate action today but it would be certainly necessary at an early date.[57]

The same tone is echoed in Rawlinson's diary entry for 29 September, 'Americans did not mop up . . . We just missed a big thing by employing Americans.'[58]

ANALYSIS

Rawlinson undoubtedly deserves some credit for the victory of 29 September, but it is worthy of note that the plans of attack implemented that day were basically made at corps level. The successful implementation of the IX Corps plan owed a good deal to careful military calculation, to the sort of imagination and foresight best exemplified in IX Corps' use of the life-belts from Channel steamers, and to the sophisticated technology and tactics which the BEF had developed by late 1918. But the BEF's technical mastery of the battlefield was by no means complete. The moral element in war, stressed by practically all contemporaries, continued to be of vital importance. So did the ineradicable element of chance, most obviously manifested, during this operation, in the impact of the weather.

The BEF at this period generally excelled at counter-battery work. Largely because of the bad weather, Fourth Army's artillery was not, however, at its best in this respect in this particular operation. German artillery fire caused serious casualties to the 27th American Division and even in the IX Corps' sector it was not altogether suppressed. Quite a heavy counter-barrage came down on the 46th Division's trenches five minutes after the assault started, fortunately too late to do much harm.[59] As well as adversely influencing its counter-battery programme the weather also had positive effects on Fourth Army's operations. Of 'decisive' importance in reducing the effectiveness of German artillery and machine guns was the exceptionally thick and persistent fog.[60] This, while thickened by artificial smoke, was largely natural.

Morale was even more crucial. Its importance was most clearly manifested in the courage and initiative of the 46th Division troops compared with the inertia of the Germans they faced, an inertia which affected even troops well protected in the concrete mini-fortresses which lined the canal's eastern bank. Most of these were quite undamaged by the preliminary bombardment and their inhabitants physically unhurt. Admittedly, German machine-gunners would have been able to see little in the fog and smoke, but had they even kept their guns firing on 'fixed lines' it is difficult to see how the British could have got over the canal with such slight loss. It was the universal verdict of contemporaries that the German Army of 29 September 1916 had not the mettle of that of 1 July 1916. While praising the planning of the attack and especially the artillery support provided for it, the 46th Division historian, writing when the memory of these events was still fresh, characterised the formation's action on 29 September as 'like the Battle of Inkerman . . . essentially a soldier's battle'.[61] Continuing his theme of the moral element in war the same historian asserted:

Nothing is more significant . . . than the fact that as one strolls along the banks of the St. Quentin Canal one can see emplacement after emplacement, immensely strong, well-sited and undamaged by our artillery fire. Yet the occupants of these fortresses have long ago gone either to swell the death-roll of Germany, or to add to the number of German prisoners who are working behind our lines.[62]

It is certainly true that the BEF had made considerable technical and tactical advances since 1 July 1916. Many of these, including the creeping barrage, the tanks, the 106 graze fuse and smoke shell for field artillery were exploited in Fourth Army's attack on the Main Hindenburg System. But despite these improvements in technology and tactics, Sir Douglas Haig, himself far from modest about the fighting efficiency which the BEF had attained by 1918, did not believe that it could have cracked these fortifications had they been defended by the German Army at its best.[63] The acquisition of some new technology and new tactics clearly did not mean, in his view, that the BEF now had an invincible 'weapons system'.[64]

THE RESULT

On Sunday 29 September the Fourth Army had driven a wedge into the German defences between 5,000 and 6,000 yards deep on a front of 10,000 yards and had taken a total of about 5,300 prisoners.[65] It was clear to both sides that the Germans, with their diminished numbers, morale and fighting efficiency, would never be able to plug this gap. Once the Germans had been driven from the Main Hindenburg System it was also increasingly obvious that they could hold no position on the Western Front for very long. There were still six weeks of very large-scale and very high-intensity fighting ahead – the bloodiest in history up to this point. But in a rational mind, there could be no doubt that Germany had now lost the war. The German Army continued to fight not for victory but only to avoid the more extreme forms of humiliation which Germany's enemies might impose upon her.

9

THE END IN SIGHT

CRISIS IN GERMANY

Foch's general offensive, when combined with the collapse of Bulgaria, had an early and dramatic effect on the German high command and on high politics in Germany. When Hindenburg and Ludendorff met the Kaiser at the Hotel Britannique in Spa at 10.00 on Sunday 29 September they told him that Germany must immediately seek armistice terms which would allow the army to retreat to the frontiers to regroup. There was little logic in this. If the German Army's position in the field was desperate why should the Allies let it off the hook? If not, then why the need for an immediate cease-fire? The Kaiser, however, accepted the military advice he was given. Apparently intending to pre-empt revolution from below by a more controlled revolution from above (which might preserve the monarchy) he also decided to dismiss his current Chancellor, Count von Hertling, and to appoint a broadly-based government including the Social Democrats. On 3 October Prince Max of Baden, politically a moderate conservative, was sworn in as Chancellor. The following day the German government, at Ludendorff's insistence, and rather against Prince Max's own wishes, asked President Woodrow Wilson of the United States for an armistice.[1]

FOCH'S OFFENSIVE SLOWS

On the battlefields of the Western Front, however, events were moving at a slower pace. Indeed, after causing Ludendorff a crisis of nerves on 28 September, most of Foch's general offensive appeared to have ground to a halt by the end of the month. The German Army, though battered, did not immediately collapse and, in the short term, Ludendorff's personal morale revived.[2]

The American First Army in the Argonne–Meuse sector was in a grotesque state of disorder. Its logistics had collapsed and, despite its very large numerical superiority over the Germans in front of it, one of its formations, General Traub's 35th Division, actually broke and fled when Pershing tried to renew the attack on 29 September. On that date, according to a German official war diarist, 'For a while the entire American front between the Aire and the left wing of the [German Third] Army was moving back. Concentrated artillery fire struck enemy masses moving to the rear with an annihilating effect.' The Americans had to halt their part of the general offensive for the time being, and it was not clear when it might be renewed.[3]

The Flanders push had also stalled. The Belgian/British effort had started very briskly on 28 September and had continued to make fairly good progress the following day. But rain, the normal ally of the Germans in Flanders, had come to their aid within the first few hours. By 30 September, according to Second Army's own account, over a large part of the area conquered since the start of the offensive, 'every vestige of roads had disappeared'. The ground 'churned up by shell-fire and drenched by heavy rain, had become an all but impassable slough'. Second Army could have more or less coped with these difficulties, or so it later claimed, but the Belgian Army, 'with whose rate of advance it was necessary . . . to stay in close unison', could not. While the GAF's progress was being impeded by the weather the Germans brought up reserves and their resistance stiffened. There was to be very little further progress in Flanders until 14 October.[4]

Thus, to Foch's intense irritation,[5] both wings of his general offensive appeared paralysed by the beginning of October. The only hope of sustaining pressure on the Germans in the short term lay in the centre, where the balance of forces, considered in numerical terms, favoured the Allies least. But even in the centre progress was not rapid or general. The British First and Third Armies had, indeed, practically ground to a halt before the city of Cambrai.

The Canadian Corps, First Army's spearhead, had achieved remarkable success on Friday 27 September, the first day of the Battle of the Canal du Nord, but after that progress slowed drastically. The fighting on 29 September was especially grim. The Canadians suffered 2,089 casualties for little gain of ground. On each day up to Tuesday 1 October Currie continued to mount violent attacks, apparently convinced that, if he paused, the Germans would regroup and counter-attack. It seems possible that Currie would have gained at least equal results at lower cost had he adopted a somewhat more deliberate approach, pausing for a day or so to bring up artillery, and to restore communications, between major attacks. The Canadian Corps gained only about a mile at the point of furthest advance on 1 October, though this included some significant ground east of Tilloy, which gave observation over the valley of the Schelde and the city of Cambrai. Currie's troops took 1,300 prisoners, but they themselves sustained heavy losses – about 1,000 in 1st Canadian Division alone. On the afternoon of 1 October Horne who had, since 27 September, effectively delegated command of First Army's offensive almost entirely to Currie and his staff, at last intervened. He ordered Currie to halt his attacks, 'to maintain and consolidate positions gained by today's fighting and to reorganise in depth'.[6] As it turned out, the Canadian Corps (and First Army as a whole) was to remain largely quiescent for more than a week.

By the beginning of October, Byng's Third Army, too, had to a considerable degree lost momentum. It straddled the Schelde Canal with the XVII and the VI Corps, on the Army's left, across that obstacle, while the IV and the V Corps, on the right, were still stuck on the west bank. Over the next few days Third Army expanded its bridgehead somewhat but was not able to get over the canal on this whole front until 5 October.[7]

FOURTH ARMY: FROM THE HINDENBURG LINE THROUGH THE BEAUREVOIR LINE

In early October, therefore, the maintenance of the momentum of Foch's 'general offensive' depended very largely on the British Fourth Army. Rawlinson had been somewhat disappointed with his Army's progress on Sunday 29 September. His forces had ruptured the Main Hindenburg Position and penetrated a substantial section of the Hindenburg Support Line. But the breakthrough was not as clean as he had hoped. He was impatient to finish the job and to proceed to break the Beaurevoir Line, the last prepared defence line the Germans had in front of Fourth Army, a couple of miles further east.[8]

In Fourth Army on 30 September communications were, as usual on Z + 1 of a Western Front offensive, in disarray. Fourth Army's gunners were, in many cases, unclear as to the position of its infantry units in relation to those of the Germans. This was a particular problem on the front of Monash's Australian–American Corps where some pockets of American troops, finding themselves well ahead of the general line which the attack had reached the previous day, had been pinned down and cut off. High winds made flying dangerous and thick cloud and heavy rain severely limited aerial observation – these factors further reducing the effectiveness of artillery support. The difficulties of Rawlinson's forces, however, paled into insignificance besides those confronting the outnumbered, battered and demoralised Germans and Fourth Army continued to make good progress in generally somewhat scrappy and unco-ordinated fighting.[9]

The IX Corps, in particular, did, according to Rawlinson, 'exceedingly well'.[10] At 08.00 on 30 September, 1st Division, still operating west of the canal, put in a formal assault under the cover of a creeping barrage and took the whole of the Thorigny ridge that morning. During the afternoon it linked up with the 32nd Division at the Le Tronquoy tunnel. The 32nd Division gained ground east of the canal and, by the end of the day, was approaching the village of Joncourt. German troops apparently massing for

Map 14

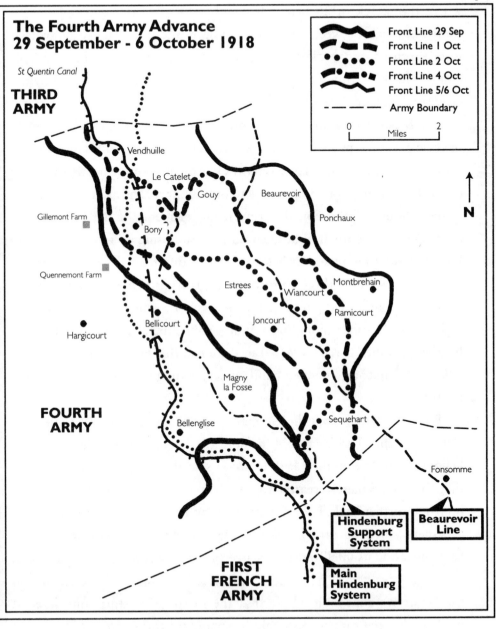

**The Fourth Army Advance
29 September - 6 October 1918**

〰〰	Front Line 29 Sep
- - -	Front Line 1 Oct
•••••	Front Line 2 Oct
▬ ▬ ▬	Front Line 4 Oct
〰〰	Front Line 5/6 Oct
— · —	Army Boundary

0   Miles   2

St Quentin Canal

THIRD ARMY

Vendhuille

Le Catelet

Gouy

Beaurevoir

Gillemont Farm

Bony

Ponchaux

N

Quennemont Farm

Estrees

Wiancourt

Montbrehain

Bellicourt

Joncourt

Ramicourt

Hargicourt

Magny la Fosse

FOURTH ARMY

Bellenglise

Sequehart

Fonsomme

Hindenburg Support System

Beaurevoir Line

FIRST FRENCH ARMY

Main Hindenburg System

a counter-attack east of that village were dispersed by artillery. Monash's corps also made considerable progress. The situation north of Bellicourt, where the attack of 29 September had largely failed, improved significantly. The spur between Bellicourt and Bony and the village of Bony itself were captured and pockets of Americans in this vicinity who had 'gallantly held out through the night, although practically surrounded by the Germans' were rescued.[11]

On Tuesday 1 October, for the third day running, the IX Corps made the best progress, penetrating the Beaurevoir Line between Wiancourt and Sequehart. On the same day, Monash's Corps secured the northern end of the Bellicourt tunnel and the Hindenburg Support Line as far north as Le Catelet. South of the Fourth Army front, elements of the French First Army entered the town of St Quentin, at last closing up to the canal line. Fourth Army took prisoners belonging to 11 different divisions, its intelligence officers taking this as 'proof of the great disorganisation existing in the enemy's lines'. Despite this, the Germans became quite active on the night of 1/2 October, mounting a number of counter-attacks to restore the Beaurevoir Line. These increased in vigour in the daylight hours, and the village of Sequehart changed hands twice, ending the day under German control.[12]

Prisoners taken from the German 241st Division since 29 September stated that they had been told 'to hold the Beaurevoir Line at all costs'. Fellow captives from the 119th Division said the same thing, but thought that they were merely rearguards while another defensive position was prepared further back. Fourth Army had, by 2 October, taken over 10,000 prisoners since its attack on the Main Hindenburg Position on 29 September and its intelligence indicated that, of the seven German divisions facing it, only one was reasonably fresh. The Germans were so stretched on the Western Front as a whole that the intelligence staff considered it unlikely that reinforcements could be spared for this sector.[13]

Yet it had become apparent that Fourth Army was not going to break the Beaurevoir Line without a full-scale assault. This was duly delivered at

06.05 on the fine morning of 3 October by, from left to right, the 50th Division of XIII Corps, the 2nd Australian Division and the 32nd, the 46th and the 1st Divisions of the IX Corps. These divisions were supported by 400 field artillery pieces, the heavy artillery of three corps and some 38 heavy and 16 Whippet tanks. An advance of 2,000 yards was achieved on a front of more than 10,000 yards and some 4,000 prisoners were taken. 'Useful day', Rawlinson commented.[14] But the villages of Beaurevoir and Montbrehain, though captured, were retaken by counter-attacks towards the end of the day and it was to take approximately another 72 hours' fighting before the Battle of the Beaurevoir Line could finally be considered over.[15]

At 06.10 on 4 October, in a dense fog which lasted nearly all morning, the XIII Corps mounted a hurriedly prepared attack with the 50th and the 25th Divisions. The 50th Division attempted to take Beaurevoir by envelopment and the 25th Division the high ground north of Gouy and Le Catelet. Only limited gains were made. The following morning, the 25th Division and the 2nd Australian Division mounted co-ordinated attacks focused on the villages of Beaurevoir and Montbrehain respectively. The Australians took Montbrehain after some hard fighting. The 25th Division initially failed. It renewed the assault in the afternoon with greater success, but the village of Beaurevoir was not finally cleared until the evening of 6 October, during which time the Germans counter-attacked on several occasions.[16]

Saturday 5 October 1918 was, nevertheless, a momentous day. Fourth Army had broken the last prepared defence line in its path and, in the words of its historian, had 'reached open country which . . . bore few traces of the ravages of war'.[17] That night most of the Australian Corps, which had played such a critical part in Fourth Army's victories up to this point in the campaign, was withdrawn for a well-deserved rest in Army reserve, west of Amiens.[18] While Australian artillery remained to serve the American II Corps, Monash's magnificent infantry had (though this was not known at the time) fought its last battle.[19]

HAIG'S STRATEGIC APPRECIATION:
1–6 OCTOBER

Haig was disappointed and rather annoyed at the poor quality of the support Rawlinson was getting from General Debeney's First French Army on his right flank. He was also well aware of the difficulties of the Belgians and the Americans. On 1 October he commented:

> *Reports from Americans (west of Meuse) and from Belgian Hqrs. state that their roads and communications are so blocked that the offensive has had to stop and cannot be recommenced for four or five days. What very valuable days are being lost! All this is the result of inexperience and ignorance on the part of the Belgian and American staffs of the needs of a modern attacking force.*[20]

When the Americans tried to renew their offensive on 4 October they had no greater success. Haig noted:

> *F[och]'s staff are terribly disappointed with the result of the American attacks . . . west of the Meuse. The enemy is in no strength on their front, but the Americans cannot advance because their supply arrangements have broken down. The divisions in the front line are really starving and have had to be relieved in order to be brought where the food is! There are many fine divisions available for action, and these cannot be used owing to the incapacity of the American Hqrs and Army staffs . . . but P[ershing] won't allow any of his divisions to be transferred to another sector, where their presence would at once produce decisive results . . . Reports from Flanders show that the Belgians have suffered heavily – 10,000 [casualties] since September 28th – and further operations will be delayed for six days.*[21]

As October drew on, Haig became increasingly convinced that only the British Armies were fighting effectively. Yet in the first half of the month, despite some disillusionment with his allies, he was intensely optimistic. Byng and Rawlinson told him on 1 October that the Germans had suffered so much that it was merely a question of keeping up the pressure to ensure that they broke completely. A German withdrawal of from 2,000–5,000 yards from a salient south of Armentières on 5 October gave more encouragement, as did Fourth Army's success against the Beaurevoir Line. The news was better still on Sunday 6 October, when it became known that the Germans had applied for an armistice. That Sunday Haig told Foch that, with three fresh American divisions, he could reach Valenciennes in 48 hours.[22]

THE BATTLE OF CAMBRAI

By that time preparations were well advanced for a major Allied attack south of Cambrai. On the night of 4 October Haig had told Lieutenant-General Sir Herbert Lawrence, the Chief of the General Staff at GHQ, to draw up plans for a broad front attack to be mounted on or about 7 October. Ideally, Haig wanted a combined and simultaneous attack by the British First, Third and Fourth Armies and the French First Army.[23] Eventually a joint Third and Fourth Army attack was arranged, to which the French First Army was intended to offer some support. The withdrawal, on 5 October, of German troops facing the right of the British Third Army from the Schelde Canal to the Beaurevoir Line, some three miles to the east, somewhat upset initial planning. On Sunday 6 October the decision was made, apparently at Rawlinson's instigation, to put Z day back to 8 October 'to give', according to Rawlinson's diary, 'Bingo [Sir Julian Byng] and my gunners more time'. That same Sunday Rawlinson's personal morale was boosted by news from further afield: 'Boche wireless says they have applied to Wilson for armistice to discuss terms . . . This is true. The end is not far off.'[24]

Effective co-operation between Third and Fourth Armies was not easy to arrange. Fourth Army's front had advanced further east than Third Army's; and whereas Fourth Army had already battered its way through the Beaurevoir Line, the V Corps, on Third Army's southern wing, still faced that obstacle. In order to avoid exposing Fourth Army to flanking fire Rawlinson and Byng considered it important that Third and Fourth Army should keep abreast of one another on 8 October. The result was that the big attack was to have three start times. Shute's V Corps was to mount a preliminary operation at 01.00 to seize the Beaurevoir Line on its front. The rest of Third Army was to attack at 04.30 and Fourth Army and the First French Army would pitch in at 05.10.[25]

Shute's V Corps had a long day of somewhat fragmented fighting. The Beaurevoir Line in this sector had a great deal of wire, and this had not been adequately gapped by the artillery. In order to break into the German defences the infantry became heavily dependent on a relatively small number of tanks. These proved effective, however, and by dusk the V Corps had overrun the Beaurevoir Line, taken the villages of Villers Outreaux and Malincourt and had made an average advance of about 5,000 yards, capturing 873 prisoners in the process.[26]

The attack of Fergusson's XVII Corps, on Third Army's northern wing, immediately south of Cambrai, was conducted mainly by the 63rd (Royal Naval) Division, supported by nine brigades of field artillery, four of heavy artillery and five tanks. The 63rd Division formed up in the VI Corps' area in order to take the village of Niergnies, from the south-west, avoiding exposure to German fire from the Cambrai direction. By 08.00 Niergnies was in British hands but half an hour later the Royal Naval Division troops were hit by a German counter-attack led by four captured British tanks. The German tanks knocked out three of the four tanks still operating in support of the 63rd Division, heavily damaged the fourth and, with infantry support, retook Niergnies.[27] This was, however, a temporary set-back. After a brief bombardment the 63rd Division captured the village for the second time that day. By dusk, XVII Corps had taken more than 1,200 prisoners. The simultaneous attacks of Haldane's VI and Harper's IV Corps resulted in the capture of another 1,900 prisoners between them and achieved advances of up to 5,000 yards.[28]

Fourth Army attacked, as planned, at 05.10. Each corps, from left to right: the XIII, the II American and the IX advanced on a front of about 4,000 yards. The infantry followed a deep, dense creeping barrage which started 200 yards in front of the start line. Lifts of 100 yards were made at three-minute intervals until the twelfth lift and then at four-minute intervals. On their first objective the infantry were given a 30-minute protective barrage after which all barrage fire ceased, though some field artillery batteries limbered up and rushed forward to give a degree of fire support beyond that line. Meanwhile, the heavy artillery engaged in counter-battery fire and pounded German strong-points in the rear. Fourth Army used more shell in this attack than in any since 29 September. The field artillery fired 156,837 rounds of 18-pdr and 37,050 rounds of 4.5-inch howitzer ammunition. (The German artillery response, by contrast, was exceptionally weak, 'almost entirely absent' towards the end of the day.) In addition to all this fire support, Fourth Army's infantry had the assistance of 25 Mark V tanks and 28 Whippets and the Army's report attributed its success 'in no small degree to the efficiency of the Tank Corps', adding that the tanks performed 'exceedingly well' and 'on numerous occasions rendered invaluable service' to the attacking infantry. Despite weak support from the French First Army on the right, Fourth Army advanced about 6,000 yards along most of its front, took the villages of Sérain, Prémont and Méricourt and captured 4,000 prisoners and 40 guns. The prisoners came from 15 different divisions – a fact taken by the intelligence officers as further evidence of the administrative breakdown of the German Army.[29]

For the Germans Tuesday 8 October 1918 was a day of heavy defeat. They lost almost 8,000 men in prisoners alone. By evening, Cambrai was clearly untenable. That night the German high command ordered a retreat to a line on the map designated Hermann Position I. On the stretch of front facing the British Third and Fourth Armies, the line was drawn immediately behind the River Selle. By 05.00 on 9 October, across most of the fronts of the British First, Third and Fourth Armies and the French First Army, only weak rearguards faced the Allied forces. The remainder of the German Seventeenth, Second and Eighteenth Armies were in full retreat. At the same time, the German high command decided to break up General Boehn's Army Group which had comprised the Second and Eighteenth Armies. The German Second Army became part of the northernmost Army Group under Prince Rupprecht of Bavaria. The Eighteenth Army became part of the Army Group commanded by the German Crown Prince.[30]

THE GERMAN RETREAT TO THE SELLE

The 18th Reserve Division of the German Seventeenth Army, which had been holding the city of Cambrai, pulled out on the night of 8/9 October. Having already carried out a great deal of destruction, the Germans had apparently intended to set the whole city ablaze in their final withdrawal. But alert Canadian troops, moving in rapidly in the small hours of 9 October, put out some fires and prevented others being lit.[31]

The next morning, the German retreat was followed up with varying degrees of vigour by the British First, Third and Fourth Armies and by First French Army. Having broken the Beaurevoir Line on its front, Third Army was now in roughly the same position as the Fourth Army had been on the evening of 5 October in that the country ahead was 'untouched by war and there was no sign of trenches or wire'.[32] On 9 October the pursuing Allied forces met resistance only from rearguards consisting principally of machine guns and field artillery. The cavalry had its most exciting day since 8 August. The 6th Cavalry Brigade and the Canadian Cavalry Brigade, both of 3rd Cavalry Division, each made mounted charges near the village of Honnechy, taking, between them, 500 prisoners, 10 guns and about 150 machine guns, though at considerable cost to themselves. (The Cavalry Corps suffered 604 casualties to personnel that day and considerably heavier equine losses.) Cavalry patrols got as far as the outskirts of Le Cateau, a town of about 10,000 inhabitants on the River Selle.[33] By 11 October Fourth Army as a whole had closed up to the Selle, having advanced an average of 10½ miles on a 7½-mile front in the last four days. East of the river the Germans were digging in.[34]

The Canadian Corps' pursuit of elements of the German Seventeenth Army continued unchecked until 11 October. When Currie's forces tried to renew the advance at 09.00 that morning, however, they met stiff resistance. At 11.00 the Canadian Corps was hit by a determined German counter-attack. Employing five captured British tanks, this was aimed at the junction of its two leading divisions, the British 49th Division and the 2nd Canadian Division, near Avesnes le Sec. All the German tanks were destroyed or driven off by artillery and all the ground lost recovered by the end of the day.[35] Yet, from 11 October, in the face of this sort of intensified resistance, the First Army advance slowed considerably. Patrols of the 49th Division, by then transferred to the XXII Corps, managed to reach the left bank of the Selle at the village of Saulzoir on Sunday 13 October, but they were not able to stay there long. Byng's forces had reached the Selle at some points on the same date. The German defence behind the river was fairly solid, however, and the Third Army pursuit came to an end.[36]

In the pursuit to the Selle the RAF took advantage of some fine weather to harass the retreating Germans severely. German troops and transport were heavily bombed and strafed in the daylight hours and lines of communication in the rear bombed by night. The RAF's V Brigade, supporting Fourth Army, for example, flew 1,078 offensive sorties between 5 and 11 October and dropped 60 112-lb and 2,443 25-lb bombs. The V Brigade claimed eleven enemy aircraft for the loss of seven of its own and Fourth Army's ground troops noted with satisfaction that German air activity on its front was declining.[37] This was indeed the general pattern. For the RAF, August and September had been the war's bloodiest months, but October saw fewer casualties. In the air, as on the ground, the Germans were near breaking point. One of their most serious problems was a desperate shortage of aviation fuel. They assigned most of what they had to their most experienced and successful pilots. That meant, of course, that there was little available for training and that casualties amongst this elite could not be replaced. As autumn drew on, however, the aerial dimension of the war was tending to become somewhat less important. Visibility was often too poor for effective reconnaissance or artillery spotting.[38]

THE BATTLE OF COURTRAI: SECOND ARMY 14–19 OCTOBER

Though by 12 October the Allied offensive had slowed in the centre it was about to be renewed on the wings. The logistics of the GAF and the American First Army having been restored after their exertions in late September, both attacked vigorously on 14 October. In the American sector results were again disappointing and casualties excessive. The Flanders operation, on the other hand, was a major success.[39]

Zero hour for all contingents of the GAF was 05.35. It was a cold, dry morning with a heavy ground mist. Second Army, on the GAF's southern wing, did not enjoy particularly lavish artillery support and had no tanks. Nor, despite the fact that the GAF as a whole dispensed with a preliminary bombardment, did it achieve an appreciable measure of surprise. The Germans seem to have been alert and put down heavier than usual counter-preparation fire. The British barrage came down 200 yards in front of the start line three minutes before Zero. From Zero it moved forward at the rate of 100 yards every two minutes, with a pause of 15 minutes every 1,500 yards. This rapid rate, which according to the historian of the 36th (Ulster) Division, 'would have seemed incredible a year ago'[40] was a comment by the Second Army planners on the declining powers of the German Army. The comment proved valid. When the attack started, though there was heavy fire from machine-gunners in fortified villages, much of the German Fourth Army's infantry offered little opposition. By the end of the day the British Second Army had advanced about four miles on a broad front and claimed to have captured 131 officers, 3,542 other ranks and 50 guns. The GAF as a whole claimed 6,000 prisoners.[41]

Second Army attacked again on Tuesday 15 October with continuing support, on its left flank, from the Belgians, who had 'fought magnificently'[42] on the previous day. For Second Army, and the GAF as a whole, 15 October was another day of victory. The German Fourth Army began to pull back to the Lys that night.[43] On the morning of 16 October Plumer's forces began their pursuit. The 36th (Ulster) Division liberated Courtrai later the same day.[44] At 15.10 on 16 October, Ludendorff ordered his Northern Army Group under Prince Rupprecht to 'retire according to plan to the Hermann Position, running from Ghent, through Tournai and Condé, east of Le Cateau'.[45] German forces had anticipated the order. The idea behind it would be largely invalidated when Fourth Army, mounting an attack across the Selle, broke into the Hermann Position on the very next day.

On the evening of 18 October Second Army extended its left flank, relieving the Belgians as far north as the junction of the Lys and the Roulers Canal, and the French VII Corps entered the line, relieving the rest of the Belgian forces there. That night the 35th Division of the XIX Corps managed to cross the River Lys at a point between the villages of Bisseghem and Marcke[46] and the next evening II Corps' 36th Division, on Second Army's far left, established a bridgehead around the villages of Straate and Spriete in a daring operation commencing at 19.25.[47] By the evening of 20 October Second Army's XV Corps had established itself on the west bank of the River Schelde from Pecq to Lienfer.[48]

Owing, in the words of Second Army's own account, to 'weather conditions most adverse to work in the air', the RAF's II Brigade had been able to do little to support Plumer's Army. Even on the fine morning of Z day itself the RAF had been able to do little before 11.00, owing to the thick ground mist. From then on, however, Second Army judged its work to be 'of high value'. The 'Corps squadrons were assiduous in their efforts to locate hostile batteries and to contribute to the effective engagement of the same'. The Army Squadrons achieved air superiority, harassed the retreating enemy and performed valuable reconnaissance work which proved important to the logistics of Second Army's advance: 'Their photographs had exactly located all German railway lines so that, as the advance progressed it was possible to link up the railway systems of the Second Army with these at very short notice and with great rapidity.'[49]

FOCH, HAIG AND LAWRENCE: PLANS AND ASSESSMENTS 8–16 OCTOBER

In the eight days following the dramatic victory of the British Third and Fourth Armies on 8 October 1918 Haig's mood was one of enormous pride in his forces' achievements, combined with a high degree of confidence that conclusive victory lay immediately ahead.

At midday on Thursday 10 October Haig met Foch at Mouchy le Chatel to discuss future operations over lunch. According to his diary the British Commander-in-Chief found the French Marshal 'in very good spirits and very complimentary of what the British Army [had] done'. Haig proposed swinging his forces somewhat to the north, making his main effort between the Schelde and the Sambre, pinching out the German salient around Lille and thus 'joining hands with my Second Army and other Allied troops under the command of the King of the Belgians'. He did not want the right flank of the forces under his command to extend south of the Sambre. At this stage Foch would not sanction this change in the orientation of the British forces. He did propose, however, to address one of Haig's most serious complaints about the campaign so far – the lack of effective French support on the British right. Foch proposed to reinforce heavily Debeney's First Army, giving it 'all available reserves and resources in Tanks, guns etc.'.

After lunch Foch gave Haig an unsolicited paper he had prepared for the Supreme War Council on the subject of an armistice. Foch proposed that the Germans should be obliged to evacuate Belgium, France and

Alsace-Lorraine within fifteen days of the signature of the agreement, abandoning most forms of war material and leaving the railway system intact. He further proposed that they should hand over Germany west of the Rhine to Allied administration and allow the Allies three large bridge-heads east of that river. Haig commented that the only difference between Foch's conditions and a general unconditional surrender was 'that the German army is allowed to march back with its rifles and officers with their swords'. Foch, he noted, was 'evidently of the opinion that the enemy is so desirous of peace that he will agree to any terms of this nature that we impose'. It was an assessment from which Haig offered no dissent at this stage.

Not everyone was so sanguine. When Haig spoke to his chief of staff, Herbert Lawrence, that evening, Lawrence 'seemed in a pessimistic mood and foresaw many dangers ahead'. According to Haig's diary Lawrence said: '"the British Army is doing all the fighting, the French will do nothing, and the American Army is quite incapable of doing anything" and so on. If the enemy were to counter-attack us we should find ourselves in a difficult position!' Haig assured Lawrence that 'the enemy has not the means nor has the German High Command the will power, to launch an attack strong enough to affect even our front line troops. We have got the enemy down, in fact he is a beaten army, and my plan is to go on hitting him as hard as we possibly can until he begs for mercy.' Haig's diary entry continues: 'Lawrence has a cold and so is looking at things in a gloomy way to-night. I think the situation is highly satisfactory for us, and the results of our victories will be *very far reaching*. It may take a few days for the results to begin to show. The enemy is now in such a state that we can run all kinds of risks without any chance of his hitting back in any force.'[50]

Haig's optimism was confirmed on 11 October by reports that the Germans were preparing to abandon the Belgian coast and that they were already falling back on the British front between Lens and the River Sensée. On the same day he heard that the Germans were retreating on the French front, between the Ailette and the Aisne, and from Laon to the Meuse. The victorious attacks of the GAF including Plumer's Second Army on 14 and 15 October further reinforced Haig's sense that all was going well. This mood was, however, to change rather abruptly within a few days.[51]

THE BATTLE OF THE SELLE

The section of the River Selle which Fourth Army faced, from 11 October, was no great waterway but it was a serious obstacle to an infantry assault. Rawlinson did not think the German positions behind it could be rushed. He made some effort to turn them from the south, between the headwaters of the Selle and the Forest of Andigny, but IX Corps met determined opposition around Riquerval Wood. Rawlinson therefore decided to mount a deliberate attack. Surprise was hardly possible, so he intended to have a heavy preliminary bombardment to soften up the German positions. To bring up the necessary guns and ammunition he needed a logistical pause while the roads and the only main-line railway in Fourth Army's rear were repaired.[52] The damage to these arteries turned out to be worse than initially realised. The Germans had blown bridges and culverts, and left numerous delayed action mines, which made the tasks of the British sappers dangerous as well as difficult. Rawlinson was keen to attack the German positions in front of him at the earliest opportunity, but was eventually forced to conclude that this could not be before 17 October.[53] The Fourth Army advance was thus halted for six days. But it was not completely inactive in the interval. On 12 October the gunners began some wire-cutting and counter-battery fire and the bombardment of what appeared to be important defended localities. A more intense preliminary bombardment opened at 08.00 three days later by which time Budworth, Fourth Army's chief gunner, had available 33 field artillery brigades plus 20 brigades and 13 independent batteries of heavier pieces of artillery.[54]

Compared to the breaking of the Hindenburg Line, the task facing Fourth Army in mid-October must have looked easy. The German defences behind the River Selle seemed to consist mainly of recently dug and fairly

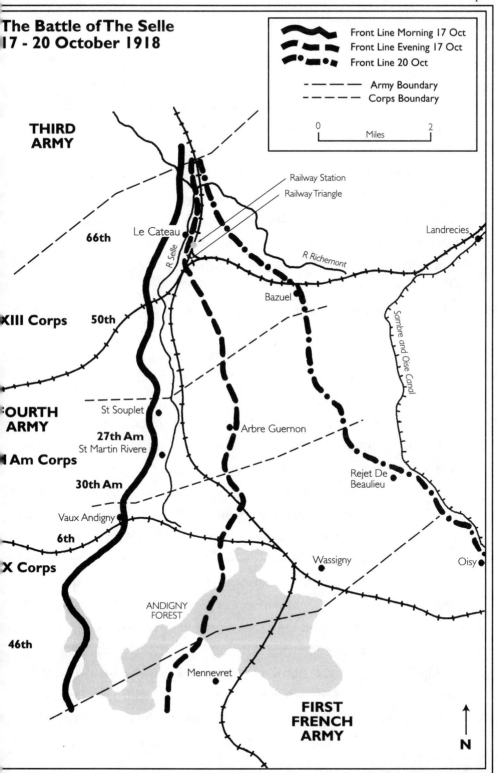

Map 15

The Battle of The Selle
17 - 20 October 1918

Front Line Morning 17 Oct
Front Line Evening 17 Oct
Front Line 20 Oct

Army Boundary
Corps Boundary

0   Miles   2

THIRD
ARMY

Railway Station
Railway Triangle

Landrecies

66th

Le Cateau

R Selle

R Richemont

XIII Corps   50th

Bazuel

Sambre and Oise Canal

FOURTH
ARMY

St Souplet

Arbre Guernon

27th Am
St Martin Rivere

Am Corps

30th Am

Rejet De
Beaulieu

Vaux Andigny

6th

X Corps

Wassigny

Oisy

ANDIGNY
FOREST

46th

Mennevret

FIRST
FRENCH
ARMY

N

shallow trenches. There were no great concrete blockhouses and bunkers. The river was only about some 4 or 5 feet deep at most and only about 15 feet wide at its broadest, though there were water meadows extending between 100 and 200 yards from either bank of the Selle in this sector. Admittedly, the Germans had dammed the river and, facing Morland's XIII Corps on Fourth Army's northern wing, the water was becoming broader and deeper. Even in the XIII Corps sector, however, the Selle did not constitute anything like as serious an obstacle as had the St Quentin Canal. The town of Le Cateau, through which the river ran, contained a number of easily defensible factory buildings and a good many solidly built houses with deep cellars, but the XIII Corps forces could largely by-pass the town itself in their initial attacks. In the American II Corps' sector, in Fourth Army's centre, the river was shallow enough to be forded. The IX Corps on Fourth Army's right wing was deployed south of the headwaters of the Selle and would thus have no assault crossing to perform, though its room for manoeuvre was somewhat constricted by the Forest of Andigny and some smaller woods in the area.[55]

Fourth Army's chances of success would, of course, depend even more on the strength and determination of the German forces it encountered than on the physical obstacles they had to defend. As far as Rawlinson and his staff knew, however, there was nothing much to worry about in that respect either. The best estimate available was that only four exhausted and two comparatively fresh German divisions lay immediately ahead, and that the only reserves the Germans would have available consisted of badly burnt-out divisions. Fourth Army headquarters thus faced the coming battle in a confident spirit, apparently expecting that its forces would push rapidly to the Sambre and Oise Canal some four to five miles to the east. The reality was to be somewhat different.[56]

The first day of the Battle of the Selle was to be the one occasion during the Hundred Days when British forces suffered from a serious intelligence failure. Air reconnaissance being restricted by the weather, and the river proving something of an obstacle to infantry patrolling, Fourth

Army's intelligence officers were unaware that the Germans had substantially reinforced this sector. Fourth Army actually faced five fresh and four fairly fresh German divisions with another division not far to the rear. It was patently obvious to the Germans that the Fourth Army intended to cross the Selle in force and the lengthy preliminary bombardment underlined this point. The German high command must have identified Fourth Army as posing the most serious threat of any Allied force in the immediate future and had concentrated against it the strongest and best forces available. It told these troops that Germany's chances of obtaining an armistice on reasonable terms depended on stopping 'the English' crossing the Selle.[57] Many were, indeed, to fight with desperate tenacity. Though Fourth Army still had, in all probability, a greater rifle strength and a much greater artillery strength than the Germans facing it, the first day of the Battle of the Selle was going to be a lot tougher than Rawlinson and his staff appear to have anticipated.

The divisions in the first wave of the Fourth Army attack were to be, from left to right: the 66th and the 50th (Morland's XIII Corps), the 27th American and the 30th American (Read's II American Corps), and the 6th and the 46th (Braithwaite's IX Corps). In IX Corps, the 1st Division was to pass through the 6th Division in the course of the day. Four battalions of tanks were available. The XIII Corps and the II American Corps were allocated one tank battalion each. The IX Corps which was south of the headwaters of the Selle, and thus in the best position to use tanks, was given two. Zero hour was to be 05.20 on Thursday 17 October. At that time, while the heavy artillery stepped up its counter-battery fire and bombardment of vital positions, the field gunners would commence the usual creeping barrages in support of the infantry advance.[58]

As it turned out, however, much depended that day on the morale, initiative and determination of Fourth Army's infantry. The tanks were too few in number to be a major factor (only 48 were actually engaged)[59] and the artillery, despite massive expenditure of shell, was not as effective as usual. The two days of intensive bombardment, 15 and 16 October, had been murky and wet. Low cloud and poor visibility gave the RAF little chance of helping the gunners and the effectiveness of the counter-battery fire, in particular, was much reduced. The thick ground mist which lasted for much of the morning on Thursday 17 October gave the RAF and Fourth Army's gunners similar problems. Severely depleted as it was by this stage in the campaign, German artillery was quite active in some sectors and remained so all day. A good deal of German wire was found intact and, in many places, German infantry and machine-gunners not only survived Fourth Army's preliminary bombardment and creeping barrages but did so in a condition to fight back hard.[60]

The XIII plan was for a double envelopment of Le Cateau, the 66th Division bridging the river north and the 50th Division south of the town, while the 25th Division remained in reserve. The 66th Division would devote a battalion and a half to clearing Le Cateau while the remainder of the attacking forces proceeded eastward. Because it was considered important to synchronise the envelopment, the 66th Division attack was timed to begin more than two hours after that of the 50th Division, which would have farther to go from its crossing points to accomplish its mission. Shielded by the mist and the barrage which contained a proportion of smoke shell, neither division encountered much opposition crossing the river. In the 50th Division sector, where the water was shallow, tanks were able to cross the river on 'cribs', the very strong hexagonal frames which had been used in crossing the trenches of the Main Hindenburg System. In the II American Corps sector, immediately to the south, both infantry and tanks were able to ford the river and, as with XIII Corps, casualties in making the crossing were light.[61]

The German main line of resistance across much of the front turned out to be the Le Cateau–Wassigny railway, part of which lay in a cutting. The South African Brigade, leading the 66th Division attack north of Le Cateau, encountered between four and six belts of wire, virtually untouched by the preliminary bombardment, in front of this obstacle, the sides of which were studded with machine-gun posts and rifle pits. The

South Africans also found, however, a shallow trench used by the Germans as a route from the railway cutting to an outpost and a path through the wire made for the use of German patrols. Supported by the fire of their Lewis gun sections, small groups of South African infantry fought their way along these avenues and into the cutting. Gradually they were reinforced until, by midday, the South Africans held most of the railway line in their sector of the front. They tried to push beyond the railway later in the morning but were forced back. The 50th Division, meanwhile, had encountered very intense fire from German troops in the railway triangle south-east of Le Cateau and from the station immediately south of the town. The division was repeatedly counter-attacked and the railway triangle was still in German hands at dusk.[62]

Once over the river the American infantry encountered heavy fire from the railway. Its advance slowed and it lost its barrage. The 27th American Division, on the II American Corps' left, had severe fighting and was held up for several hours. Having overcome the opposition along the railway, elements of this division were fighting for the village of Arbre Guernon when, at about 15.00, they were hit by a major German counter-attack. Delivered by the German 204th Division (a comparatively fresh formation), this struck the American left and the right of the British 50th Division. The Americans were driven back almost as far as the railway, but soon recovered and resumed their advance. By dusk they had taken Arbre Guernon and beaten off several attempts to oust them.[63]

The IX Corps attacked at 05.20, south of the headwaters of the Selle, supported by roughly twice as many tanks as either of the other two corps. It was advancing into fairly intricate terrain and initially it, too, met serious resistance. With the benefit of unusually effective support on its right flank by Debeney's reinforced First French Army, however, Braithwaite's corps ran true to form. It advanced to a depth of 4,500 yards, further than either of the other corps, defeated three German divisions and elements of three others and finished the day well-established on the crest of the watershed between the valleys of the Selle and the Sambre.[64]

By dusk, the crust of the German defence had been broken all along the front of the attack. Fourth Army had taken about 4,000 prisoners, and French First Army about 1,200. Le Cateau was in British hands. Except on the right, however, the extent of Fourth Army's advance was less than expected and the strength and ferocity of the resistance had been greater. Rawlinson recognised that the heavy losses to the II American Corps (which had received no casualty replacements since joining Fourth Army) meant that it was now practically finished as a fighting force, and that he would shortly have to send it to the rear.[65] Generally, however, Rawlinson appears to have taken the day's events in his stride. It was somewhat different with Haig. In his diary the Commander-in-Chief gave an accurate, balanced and reasonable account of Fourth Army's battle. But the advice he tendered to the War Cabinet a few days later showed that he had been profoundly influenced by the intensity of the resistance encountered.[66]

At 05.30 on the misty morning of Friday 18 October, Fourth Army resumed its attack. At the end of another hard day's fighting it had taken a further 1,600 prisoners. For the second day running, Debeney's First French Army offered Rawlinson's troops far more effective support on their right flank than they had become accustomed to expect. By the evening of Saturday 19 October, Fourth Army had made advances, since the start of the battle, of up to 9,000 yards on a front of seven miles and captured 5,139 prisoners. On the stretch of front between Tupigny and Rejet de Beaulieu the Fourth Army and French First Army between them had driven the Germans back across the Sambre and Oise Canal. Owing to the very heavy fire from the far side of the canal, Fourth Army did not yet occupy the west bank at any point, but the first phase of the Battle of the Selle was over.[67]

HAIG AND ARMISTICE TERMS

On Thursday 17 October Haig, based in his headquarters train in a siding at Bertincourt, had a busy day. In the morning he received reports of Fourth Army's battle on the Selle and of German withdrawals on other parts of the front. Later, Sir John Salmond came to brief him on the progress of the air war. During the afternoon he went out to tour the front, travelling, as was his wont, partly by car and partly on horseback. He spoke to Lieutenant-General Harper, the IV Corps' commander, a couple of divisional commanders and some French 'country folk'. At about 18.30 he returned to the train. There he received a message that the War Cabinet wanted to see him as soon as possible to get his advice on the armistice terms which might be offered to the Germans. Haig replied that he would set out for London next day and then went to dine with Geoffrey Dawson, the editor of *The Times*, his guest for the night. Before going to bed, Haig discussed with Herbert Lawrence the advice he should give to the government. Lawrence said that the terms demanded should not be too exacting as it was in British interests to end the war in 1918. He promised to put his views in writing and to give them to Haig the following morning.[68]

After spending much of the Friday travelling, Haig met Henry Wilson at the War Office soon after 10.00 on Saturday 19 October. Wilson, according to Haig's diary, gave the opinion that 'the Germans should be ordered to lay down their arms and retire east of the Rhine'. Haig stated that 'our attack on the 17th instant met with considerable opposition, and that the enemy was not ready for unconditional surrender. In that case there would be no armistice and the war would continue for at least another year!!' Wilson and Haig went together to 10 Downing Street where they met the Prime Minister, David Lloyd George, the Chancellor of the Exchequer, Andrew Bonar Law and the Secretary of State for War, Lord Milner. Lloyd George asked Haig directly for his views on the armistice terms which should be offered to the Germans. According to his diary Haig:

. . . *replied that they must greatly depend on the answers we gave to two questions:-*

1) *Is Germany now so beaten that she will accept whatever terms the Allies may offer, i.e. unconditional surrender?*

If he [she?] refuses to agree to our terms:

2) *Can the Allies continue to press the enemy sufficiently vigor-ously during the coming winter months as to cause him to withdraw so quickly that he cannot destroy the railways, roads etc.?*

The answer to both questions is in the negative. The German Army is capable of retiring to its own frontier, and holding the line if there should be any attempt to touch the honour *of the German people and make them fight with the courage of despair.*

The situation of the Allied Armies is as follows:-

French Army: *Worn out and has not really been fighting latterly. It has been freely said that the 'war is over and we don't want to lose our lives now that peace is in sight'.*

American Army: *Is not yet organised: it is ill equipped, half trained, with insufficient supply services. Experienced officers and NCOs are lacking.*

British Army: *Was never more efficient than it is to-day, but it has fought hard and it lacks reinforcements. With diminishing effectives moral is bound to suffer.*

The French and American Armies are not capable of making a seri-ous offensive now. *The British alone might bring the enemy to his knees. But why expend more British lives and for what?*

Haig went on to advise that the German Army would be able to destroy the railways and other communications as it fell back during the winter months. This would greatly delay an Allied advance if the war dragged on into 1919. During the winter the Germans would also have the chance to absorb their 1920 class conscripts. Haig therefore proposed that the only armistice terms which should be insisted upon were immediate German evacuation of Belgium, occupied France and Alsace-Lorraine, the return of all Belgian and French citizens forcibly evacuated from their homes and the return of rolling stock. He did not recommend that the German Army be obliged to abandon its artillery or any of its machine guns. Indeed, he appears to have been prepared to contemplate a compromise peace which would allow the Germans to keep at least some of their conquests in eastern Europe. Balfour objected 'to deserting the Poles and the people of Eastern Europe', but Lloyd George 'gave the opinion that we cannot expect the British to go on sacrificing their lives for the Poles'. Haig was asked to stay in London until the following Monday when there was to be a formal meeting of the War Cabinet.[69] Haig attended and repeated his advice.[70]

Haig had obviously undergone a drastic change of mind since 10 October when he had told Lawrence: 'We have got the enemy down, in fact he is a beaten army and my plan is to go on hitting him as hard as we possibly can until he begs for mercy.'[71] Haig's explanation for his cautious mood on 19 October, as given to Henry Wilson, and as recorded in his diary, was the intensity of German resistance on the first day of the Battle of the Selle, two days previously. Yet the battle of 17 October, though somewhat more costly than had been anticipated, was a victorious one. Why did it influence Haig's state of mind so much?

Haig had enough self-awareness to know that he was an optimist by nature. He referred to himself as such in his diary.[72] He probably realised that an excess of this quality had got him into trouble earlier in the war. Nevertheless, in the first half of October 1918, buoyed up by good news and by the high morale of his Army commanders, he was confident enough to dismiss Herbert Lawrence's anxieties. As he absorbed the news of Fourth Army's unexpectedly hard fight on 17 October, however, his confidence began to melt. He started to have serious doubts about his own judgement and took counsel of Lawrence's fears. Thus, having been in the grip of excessive optimism for most of his time as Commander-in-Chief, on the very cusp of final victory Haig became a pessimist.

10

FIGHTING TO A FINISH

THE GRAND STRATEGIC POSITION

The Western Front was not a world unto itself. News from the rear, from other fronts and even from enemy countries arrived there swiftly. In the BEF it was readily available to every private soldier and had a considerable influence on morale.[1] Contemporaries believed that the superior morale of the British over the German forces at this period was an important element in their operational success.[2]

By 20 October few German politicians or senior army officers doubted that Germany had lost the war. On the Western Front the dreary process of defeat and retreat continued and Germany's allies elsewhere had already begun to desert her. In Germany itself hunger was more acute than ever and industrial unrest out of control. Aided by malnutrition, the influenza pandemic was killing people in droves, debilitating most of the rest of the population and further driving down morale.[3] But face-to-face cease-fire talks had not yet opened and the terms (or lack of them) on which hostilities would be terminated were still undecided.

Negotiations, in the form of the passage of notes between the German Chancellor and the American President, had been in progress since 3 October. But President Woodrow Wilson's response to German initiatives had been increasingly tough, a fact which reflected the deterioration of the German military position and the consequent hardening of attitudes amongst most politicians in the Allied camp. Hindenburg and Ludendorff, having demanded an armistice at the end of September, and thereby having initiated the peace process, now wanted to distance themselves from the ignominy in which it seemed bound to conclude. The once-mighty duo seemed intent on making Germany's new broadly-based civilian government, as one minister put it, 'responsible for losing the already lost war'.[4] A third note from Wilson, received in Berlin on 23 October, effectively demanded that Germany convert itself into a parliamentary democracy before an armistice was granted. If the United States' government still had to deal with the 'military masters and monarchical autocrats of Germany', Wilson indicated, then 'it must demand not peace but surrender'. To this Hindenburg and Ludendorff reacted violently. On 24 October a note signed by them was telegraphed to the Armies at the front:

> *Wilson's answer is a demand for unconditional surrender. It is thus unacceptable to us soldiers. It proves that our enemies' desire for our destruction which let loose the war in 1914, still exists undiminished . . . Wilson's answer can thus be nothing to us . . . but a challenge to continue our resistance . . . when all our enemies know that no sacrifice will achieve the rupture of the German front, they will be ready for a peace which will make the future of our country safe for the great masses of our people.[5]*

This military pronouncement, made without consultation with the civil government, was seen by German ministers, and even by the Kaiser himself, as gross insubordination. During a heated interview with the Kaiser on 26 October, in which his monarch reprimanded him both for his unauthorised telegram to the troops and for his wildly fluctuating assessments of the military position, Ludendorff resigned. Hindenburg also offered to go but was ordered to remain. The famous Hindenburg–Ludendorff partnership dissolved in acrimony, Ludendorff accusing Hindenburg of betrayal.[6]

On 24 October, the same day on which Hindenburg's and Ludendorff's offending telegram was sent to the German Armies on the Western Front, the Allies launched a major offensive on the Italian front. Within a couple of days, Austrian forces there were in danger of total dissolution. Concurrent British offensives against the Turks in Palestine and Mesopotamia were making very good progress. The elimination of Bulgaria at the end of September was to be followed by a campaign on the Danube directed at the heart of the Habsburg empire. By 29 October the Austrian government had formally requested an armistice.[7] Meanwhile, the Kaiser, on Hindenburg's advice, appointed Ludendorff's old rival General Wilhelm Groener to replace him. Groener had to be summoned from the east where he had been attempting, rather unsuccessfully, to organise the Ukrainian economy for German exploitation. He had, of course, no solution to his country's military problems. Within days of arrival at his post he was demanding an armistice to save the army from collapse.[8]

SECOND ARMY: 20 OCTOBER–8 NOVEMBER

By nightfall on 20 October the XV Corps, on Second Army's southern wing, had closed up to the River Schelde but it would take the rest of Second Army until 30 October to reach that waterway. Plumer's other corps, from north to south the II Corps, the XIX Corps and the X Corps, all found the Germans holding a well-wired, though incomplete trench system which had been intended as an intermediate position between the more substantial defences behind the Lys and the Schelde. These defences could not be overcome easily and Second Army's progress slowed down.[9]

A number of factors slowed Second Army's advance. Plumer was receiving only weak support from the French Sixth Army at this period so that his left flank tended to become exposed. Until 24 October, moreover, most of his heavy guns and howitzers were stuck on the wrong side of the Lys, waiting for adequate bridges to be constructed. Wet weather and 'uniformly bad' visibility rendered RAF co-operation almost impossible, minimising the effectiveness of what artillery he had. The German Fourth Army took advantage of this. Compensating for the decline in the strength and quality of its infantry, it deployed a high proportion of its field artillery well forward, working in co-operation with well-concealed machine-guns, ably supported by 15cm howitzers further back.[10] In the last week of October, however, Plumer's heavy artillery caught up with the rest of the Army and, after 25 October, the skies began to clear. On 31 October Plumer mounted an attack (later designated the 'Action of Tieghem') with the 34th and 31st Divisions of the II Corps and the 35th Division of the XIX Corps. This action was completely successful and enabled Second Army as a whole to close up to the Schelde.[11]

At the beginning of November, therefore, the Second Army front rested on the River Schelde from the village of Eeuwhoek in the north to Pecq in the south, with a few posts beyond the river. There it stayed for eight days.[12] The only event of note which occurred to it in this time was that it was put back under GHQ's control. On 4 November, it ceased to be part of the Group of Armies Flanders under the command of the King of the Belgians, and returned to being a normal component of the BEF, a result achieved only after vigorous lobbying on Haig's part.[13]

FIFTH AND FIRST ARMIES: 20–24 OCTOBER

On 20 October Birdwood's Fifth Army and Horne's First were following up the German Sixth and Seventeenth Armies which were making a deliberate withdrawal from the Haute Deule Canal to what their high command had designated the 'Hermann Position II', behind the Schelde and in front of the little city of Valenciennes.[14] By 24 October most of Fifth Army's front rested on or near the Schelde, though there was a bulge in the centre of its front around Tournai and Antoing, both of which remained in German hands. Between then and 8 November Fifth Army was to do little except routine shelling and patrolling.[15] On 23 October Sir Aylmer Hunter-Weston's VIII Corps, on First Army's left, was making relatively slow progress through an area containing numerous woods. But Currie's Canadian Corps, in the centre, had closed up to flooded ground in front of a canalised stretch of the Schelde, immediately west of

Valenciennes. By the same date Sir Alexander Godley's XXII Corps, on the Army's right, had reached the little River Ecaillon, south and south-west of the city.[16]

THE LAST PHASE OF THE BATTLE OF THE SELLE: 20–24 OCTOBER

On 20 October the Fourth Army was approaching the Forest of Mormal on its left and the Sambre and Oise Canal on its right. General Read's II American Corps had distinguished itself in the opening phase of the Battle of the Selle, but, having received no casualty replacements since it joined Fourth Army, was now a spent force and had been pulled out of the line the previous night. The Australian Corps was still resting in Army reserve and Fourth Army was thus down to just two active corps, the XIII and the IX, both of which were of modest size. In GHQ's scheme of things, therefore, Fourth Army was henceforth to play a relatively minor role while First and Third Armies took a correspondingly larger share of the fighting.[17]

Although Byng's Third Army had some posts east of the Selle, up to 20 October most of it was still on the west bank. Facing Byng's troops, on a ridge just east of the Selle, were six divisions of the German Seventeenth Army, with another three in reserve. The Germans had established wire entanglements along the greater part of their front and showed no sign of retreating unless compelled to do so. On 17 October, therefore, Byng issued orders for a major attack intended to get Third Army across the Selle in strength and to drive the Germans off the ridge on the far side. Third Army arranged a joint attack with First Army, but by the time it was mounted the Germans on the First Army front were, largely in response to Second Army's success in Flanders, already in retreat.[18]

In planning the attack Third Army made every effort to achieve surprise. The corps were given freedom to organise wire-cutting fire as they thought necessary but there was to be no preliminary bombardment.

Taking advantage of a full moon, Byng decided to attack at night. Zero hour was 02.00 on 20 October. All four of Third Army's corps, the XVII, the VI, the IV and the V Corps, advanced under the cover of heavy barrages arranged by corps staffs to suit local conditions. All four crossed the river without difficulty. The two on the left met light resistance, though those on the right found the going somewhat bloodier and more strenuous. By dusk Third Army had taken most of its objectives and occupied the high ground east of the Selle. Its operations paused for two days while artillery was brought up. Then on 23 and 24 October Third Army and Fourth Army mounted concerted attacks. These were generally successful, though neither army quite reached the Forest of Mormal and, on Fourth Army's front, some points of importance west of the Sambre and Oise Canal remained in German hands. Minor operations continued, but between 24 October and 4 November neither Byng's nor Rawlinson's Army fought a major battle.[19]

Almost no-one has now heard of the Battle of the Selle. The Australians and Canadians, who have tended to commemorate their First World War endeavours rather more than the peoples of the British Isles, were but little involved. American historical attention has tended to focus on St Mihiel and the Argonne–Meuse offensive to the detriment of the II Corps' achievements. Perhaps because 1918 was so crowded with events, or perhaps because of the national tendency to focus on military disasters rather than triumphs, the Battle of the Selle seems never to have entered British national consciousness. Objectively, however, it must be regarded as one of the greatest military victories in the nation's history. A total of 1 New Zealand, 2 American and 23 British divisions had engaged 31 (numerically much weaker) German divisions. They had captured some 20,000 prisoners and 475 guns.[20]

Third Army's achievement in the latter half of the battle is particularly worthy of note, if only because of the greater contemporary publicity and subsequent historical attention given to Fourth Army. In the week ending at 18.00 hours on Friday 24 October, 189 German officers and 7,125 other ranks passed through Third Army's corps cages. Third Army's total casualties for this period were about the same as the number of prisoners it took but it recorded only 563 of its personnel as definitely killed and another 418 as missing.[21] It is obvious that behind these statistics lay great suffering and misery for many people on both sides. But it is equally apparent that the relative rate of attrition greatly favoured the Allies. In view of the further points that the Allies heavily outnumbered the Germans and that the latter had few reserves, it is also apparent that the Germans could not long have sustained fighting of such intensity at such a rate.

APPROACHING VALENCIENNES: FIRST ARMY 24–29 OCTOBER

The city of Valenciennes was the hub of communications in the area in which Horne's First Army now found itself and the focal point of the German defence. On the Army's left, Hunter-Weston's VIII Corps was struggling through heavily wooded terrain and had dropped behind the other two corps. Even when it had traversed this difficult country it would find itself on the bank of a defended canal. There was thus no immediate prospect of turning the city from the north. The Canadian Corps, in the Army's centre, had now closed up to the flooded area in front of the Schelde Canal. But, even for Currie's veterans, a frontal assault on Valenciennes, across many yards of boggy ground and then across the canal itself, would have been an extremely difficult undertaking. It would certainly have taken several days to prepare and probably could not have been implemented without very heavy casualties.[22]

The obvious thing to do in these circumstances was to swing south of the city. That gave the leading role to Sir Alec Godley's XXII Corps, which now faced the Ecaillon. A small river but quite a serious obstacle, it was about 25ft from bank to bank. The stream itself was about 15ft wide and the water was 4–5ft deep, fast-flowing and very muddy at the bottom. The banks were very steep and slippery and both had been wired. More wire

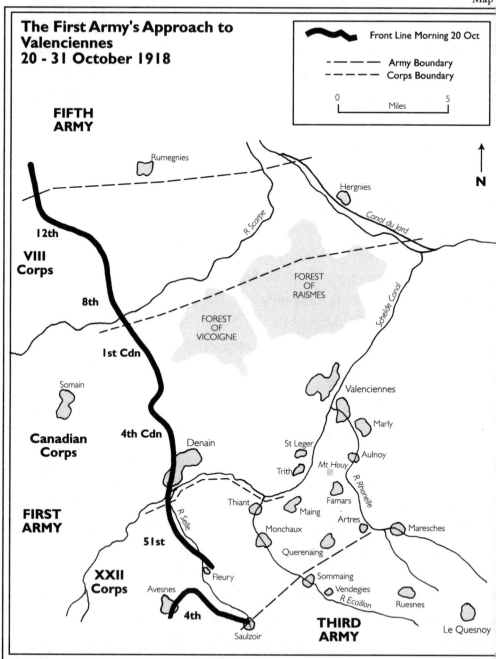

The First Army's Approach to Valenciennes
20 - 31 October 1918

Front Line Morning 20 Oct
Army Boundary
Corps Boundary

0   Miles   5

FIFTH ARMY

Rumegnies

Hergnies

Canal du Jard

N

R. Scarpe

12th

VIII Corps

8th

FOREST OF RAISMES

Schelde Canal

1st Cdn

FOREST OF VICOIGNE

Somain

Valenciennes

Marly

Canadian Corps

4th Cdn

Denain

St Leger

Aulnoy

Trith

Mt Houy

FIRST ARMY

Thiant

Famars

Maing

Artres

Maresches

R. Rhonelle

Monchaux

51st

R. Selle

Querenaing

XXII Corps

Fleury

Avesnes

Sommaing

Vendegies

Ruesnes

4th

R. Ecaillon

Saulzoir

THIRD ARMY

Le Quesnoy

criss-crossed the stream. German outposts were dug in on the right bank of the river, while half-way up the slope facing the river and commanding it at close rifle range, ran a series of short, disconnected trenches, each containing six to eight men and one or two machine guns. The Germans were alert and seemed disinclined to give up without a fight. Godley concluded that it was inadvisable to rush the position. He brought up his artillery and prepared a deliberate assault. From the morning of 22 October XXII Corps halted for two days.[23]

Then, in darkness, at 04.00 on Thursday 24 October, the XXII Corps attacked behind a heavy barrage, the 51st (Highland) Division on the left, the 4th Division on the right. The infantry had been equipped with footbridges to throw across the stream but the Ecaillon had been swollen by recent rains and in some cases the bridges turned out to be too short. This, however, did not check the assault. Around 50 per cent of the men waded or swam, while others crossed clinging to the strands of wire which the Germans had stretched across the stream. Owing to the cover of darkness and to the infantry's boldness and speed of movement, the 51st and 4th Divisions sustained relatively light casualties during the crossing.

Once over the stream, the infantry rapidly ascended the slope and overran the slit trenches on the far side, taking numerous prisoners in the process. The two attacking divisions then assaulted three consecutive lines of German trenches. By dusk they had taken about 1,150 prisoners and had reached a line from a point on the Schelde Canal opposite Trith down to the north-eastern edges of Sommaing and Vendegies. The same two divisions continued attacking over the next two days. By nightfall on 26 October the 51st Division was in possession of Famars. It had also reached a prominent hill called Mont Houy between Famars and Valenciennes, but a German counter-attack had thrown it back. The 4th Division had advanced as far as the River Rhonelle and secured a bridge near Artres. After three days continuously in action, however, both divisions were inevitably very tired.[24]

It must have been obvious to the Germans that First Army would try to take Valenciennes from the south. Of the five divisions which the German Seventeenth Army had in and around the city, three, the 6th, the 35th and the 214th Divisions, were standing guard between the southern suburbs and the village of Aulnoy, 2,500 yards to the south. Crucial to the German defence of Valenciennes was Mont Houy, rising some 150 feet above the Schelde Canal and dominating the southern approaches. This was the key to the city.[25] (See Map 17)

Haig was keen that Valenciennes should be taken quickly. The city, however, was crowded with civilians, including not only its normal inhabitants but masses of refugees driven out of their homes by earlier fighting. GHQ, presumably passing on the concerns of the French government, insisted that it should not be bombarded. On 27 October Horne held a conference with Currie and Godley at his advanced headquarters at Auberchicourt, a village 11 miles west of Valenciennes. He decided to mount an operation in three phases. The following morning, 28 October, the XXII Corps would strike north-east, taking Mont Houy and securing a line of departure from which the Canadians, a day or two later, would strike as far as the southern suburbs of Valenciennes. Finally, a day or so after that, the two corps would co-operate to secure the high ground east of the city, rendering the city itself untenable.[26]

On 27 October, Godley intended to bring up more artillery and ammunition, to improve the XXII Corps' communications and to make ready for the next day's attack. For the 51st Division, to which Godley gave the task of capturing Mont Houy, there was, however, to be little rest. The division was heavily shelled for much of the day, on some occasions with gas, and in the latter part of the morning it was obliged to fight off a determined counter-attack by the German 35th Division. Some German troops penetrated into the village of Famars but after furious street fighting the 4th Battalion of the Gordon Highlanders ejected them, taking 50 prisoners in the process.[27]

At 05.15 on Monday 28 October, the 4th Seaforth Highlanders, a battalion of the 51st Division advanced on Mont Houy, with the support of a barrage fired by four brigades of field artillery and one of heavy artillery, and of some machine-gun fire. By 08.00 it had overrun most of the German positions on the hill and pushed on to its final objective, a line between a point on the railway and the crossroads west of Aulnoy, about a mile further north. In the process it had taken about 190 prisoners. Casualties amongst the Seaforths had, however, been heavy. They found themselves too weak to hold the ground they had captured and seem to have received relatively little support from the rest of the Highland Division. As the day went on, the Germans gradually forced them back, retaking the northern slopes and summit of the hill, though leaving the Seaforths still clinging to the southern slopes at dusk. First Army had intended that the 51st Division should be relieved on the evening of 28 October. German counter-attacks during the afternoon and on the following morning, however, confused the situation. Currie was reluctant to send Canadian troops forward to the hill until the position had stabilised. The Highland Division was not relieved until the evening of the 29 October. On the left its troops were replaced by those of the 10th Canadian Infantry Brigade (4th Canadian Division), on the right by those of the 49th Division.[28]

The XXII Corps' generally fine performance in the advance to Valenciennes reflects well on Godley. His decision to have the 51st Division assault Mont Houy, with relatively modest fire support, on 28 October is, however, open to criticism. It must have been obvious that the Highland Division was extremely tired. The XXII Corps still had the fresh 49th Division in reserve. If Godley felt he could not rely on that division, it would surely have been better to have suggested to Horne that he wait a day or two while the 51st Division rested, and while he concentrated more firepower in support of the attack, perhaps by borrowing from the Canadian Corps. Alternatively Godley might have suggested that the whole task of taking Mont Houy be transferred to the Canadian Corps, saving the 51st Division from having to make a second attempt on that position.

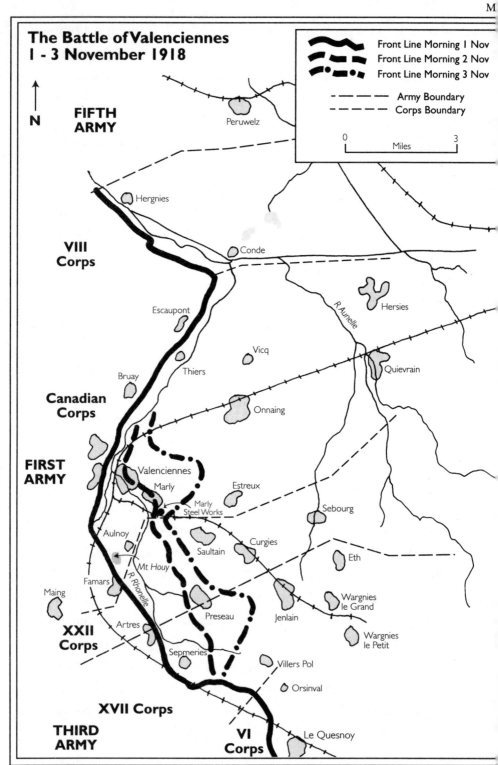

The Battle of Valenciennes
1 - 3 November 1918

N

FIFTH
ARMY

Peruwelz

	Front Line Morning 1 Nov
	Front Line Morning 2 Nov
	Front Line Morning 3 Nov
	Army Boundary
	Corps Boundary

0   Miles   3

Hergnies

VIII
Corps

Conde

Escaupont

Hersies

R Aunelle

Vicq

Bruay

Thiers

Quievrain

Canadian
Corps

Onnaing

FIRST
ARMY

Valenciennes

Marly

Estreux

Marly
Steel Works

Sebourg

Aulnoy

Mt Houy

R Rhonelle

Saultain

Curgies

Eth

Famars

Maing

Preseau

Jenlain

Wargnies
le Grand

XXII
Corps

Artres

Wargnies
le Petit

Sepmeries

Villers Pol

XVII Corps

Orsinval

THIRD
ARMY

VI
Corps

Le Quesnoy

THE PLANNING AND CONDUCT OF THE BATTLE
OF VALENCIENNES: 29 OCTOBER–2 NOVEMBER

The 51st Division had met such determined opposition on Mont Houy that First Army put back the next stage of its efforts to take Valenciennes until 1 November. Horne and his staff decided that both the Canadian Corps and XXII Corps should attack at 05.15 on that date in conjunction with the XVII Corps of Third Army immediately to First Army's right. The objective was a line running from the Schelde down the railway to Marly steelworks (but not including the steelworks itself) and from there to the eastern edge of the village of Préseau.[29]

As usual, Horne gave the Canadian Corps the most crucial role – to capture the vital Mont Houy position and push on into the southern suburbs of Valenciennes. The approach of Currie and the Canadian Corps to this operation affords the best example of a major trend at work in offensive operations by the British Armies in the second half of the war – the substitution of firepower for manpower to the greatest possible extent. The Canadian Corps was astride the Schelde and it was possible to bring converging fire onto the troublesome hill. Eight field artillery and six heavy artillery brigades were to be used in support of an attack by one infantry brigade, the 10th Canadian, the attack of which was initially to be made on a front of 2,500 yards. The fire-plan for the attack was worked out by Brigadier-General A.G.L. McNaughton, the talented and thorough artillery chief of the Canadian Corps.

Of the field artillery brigades, five were sited south of the Schelde, in the area around Maing, in order to fire a creeping barrage frontally. Another was sited on the left bank in Trith St Léger to add oblique fire to the barrage. The remaining two were placed at La Sentinelle, west of the Cambrai–Valenciennes road and were employed to deepen the barrage by enfilade fire. The creeping barrage itself was composed entirely of 18-pdr shrapnel, moving at a rate of 100 yards in four minutes in the early part of the attack, later slowing to 100 yards in five minutes. Three 4.5-inch howitzer batteries were used to lay a smoke screen to cover the attack from German positions to the west. Others were used to bombard groups of machine-gun nests, jumping from one group to another in advance of the barrage. The heavy artillery brigades were mostly sited on the left bank of the Schelde Canal so as to bring oblique, enfilade and even reverse fire onto the area of attack.

As well as for counter-battery and interdiction fire, the heavy artillery was to be used to demolish all buildings in the vicinity of Mont Houy which were suspected of containing German machine-gun posts. (The fate of any civilians who happened to remain in residence would have been pitiable.) A large number of 6-inch and 8-inch howitzers was to form a special sort of creeping barrage which would move along the rows of the houses in the valleys of the Schelde and the Rhonelle, demolishing them as it went. Barrage fire of this sort started only at Zero. But, as there was now no chance of a major surprise, the heavy artillery did a good deal of preparatory work from 31 October.[30]

At 05.15 on 1 November the First Army and the 61st Division of XVII Corps (Third Army) mounted an attack towards Valenciennes from the south. On the left was the 10th Canadian Infantry Brigade. Supported by a stupendous weight of fire, the Canadian infantry, attacking from the direction of Famars, met only limited opposition. The attack swept over Mont Houy and the open ground to the north of it. German troops of the 35th and 214th Divisions, stupefied by the barrage, surrendered in large numbers. By 07.00 the Canadians had taken Aulnoy and captured the bridge over the Rhonelle there intact. The Marly steelworks was heavily defended and fire from it eventually halted progress on the right. Further west, however, patrols were able to push across the railway into Marly and the southern outskirts of the city of Valenciennes itself.

According to their official history, the Canadians took some 1,800 prisoners on 1 November and counted more than 800 German dead on their part of the battlefield. The 10th Canadian Brigade reported 501 casualties after the action of 1 November of which only about 80 were killed. As the official account puts it: 'Careful co-ordination in employing a tremendous weight of artillery in . . . close support of minimum numbers of infantry had achieved victory at very low cost'. It is probable that in the whole course of the war no other attack by a single infantry brigade ever received such massive fire support. The Canadian Corps' artillery fired 2,419 tons of shell between noon on 31 October and noon on 2 November, more than both sides expended in the entire Boer War of 1899–1902.[31]

The attack towards Valenciennes on 1 November was an outstanding Canadian achievement. It was not quite unblemished. The 10th Canadian Infantry Brigade, though confident of victory, was in an ugly mood that day. Currie confided to his diary that:

'I know that it was not the intention of our fellows to take many Germans prisoner as, since they have lived amongst and talked to the French people here, they have become more bitter than ever against the Boche.'

The Germans surrendered so readily and in such numbers that the Canadians could not face the prospect of shooting or bayoneting them all, yet they seem to have taken fewer prisoner and killed more than was in strict accordance with the laws of war. This sort of behaviour in battle, even by troops of the most civilised nations, is all too common. So is the connivance at it by senior officers which Currie's diary implies. It is much to the credit of the Canadian official history that, though no details are given, this unpleasant aspect of the truth about a great national achievement is not altogether suppressed.[32]

On the Canadian right, the 49th and 4th Divisions (XXII Corps) also attacked on 1 November, supported on their right by the 61st Division of Third Army's XVII Corps. The XXII Corps' divisions crossed the Rhonelle without much difficulty, gaining high ground north-west and south of Presau. Leading troops of the 4th Division penetrated into Présau but were ejected by a German counter-attack at about 09.30. Despite this local reverse the XXII Corps' action gave effective support to the

Canadians and brought the total of prisoners taken by First Army that day to about 2,750. The 61st Division of Third Army took a further 761 prisoners.[33]

On 1 November First Army had fought its last real battle. On the morning of 2 November the Germans began evacuating Valenciennes and pulling back from the Schelde. From that time onwards First Army's operations took the form of a pursuit. Initially this was quite slow. The country over which First Army was advancing was broken by many steep valleys and was thickly wooded in some places. After the victory of the Third and Fourth Armies on the Sambre on 4 November the tempo increased.[34]

PREPARING FOR THE BATTLE OF THE SAMBRE

On 29 October GHQ ordered First, Third and Fourth Armies to make a concerted attack in the direction Mauberge–Avesnes, while the French First Army was (in a supporting operation which Haig had arranged with Foch) to attack towards La Capelle. This operation was clearly intended as a grand slam, a blow which would, at the very least, send the German Army reeling and would perhaps knock it out. Haig, however, wanted to capture Valenciennes first, and Z day for the grand slam was eventually fixed at 4 November.[35]

In the meantime, news of momentous events elsewhere reached the Western Front. The Turks established an armistice with the Allies on 31 October and the Austrians followed suit on 3 November.[36] The news from other sectors of the Western Front itself was also good. On 1 November, as First Army finally broke the German defence around Valenciennes, the French and Americans renewed their offensive in the Argonne–Meuse sector, this time with real success. They overwhelmed the German forces facing them and began to move quite rapidly in the direction of Sedan, the American V Corps advancing five miles on 1 November alone. Morale in the British Armies, already high, was further raised by these events.[37]

In the event, Horne's First Army did not carry out a concerted attack on 4 November. The Germans on the southern part of its front were already in retreat. But what was the nature of the task facing the Third and Fourth Armies? The ground over which they were to attack varied considerably. The northern half of Third Army – the XVII and VI Corps – faced open country. Though this contained a scattering of villages and an occasional steep-sided little valley, it presented no great difficulty to an attacker. The southern half – IV and V Corps – faced more serious obstacles. The New Zealand Division occupying the northern half of the IV Corps' front, near the centre of Third Army, faced the small fortress town of Le Quesnoy which had been fortified in the style of the celebrated late seventeenth century military architect, Vauban. Some three to four miles on the German side of the IV Corps' front lay the Forest of Mormal. Further south, facing the V Corps, on the far right of Third Army, the forest was much closer to the front line, in places only about half a mile away. For the troops in these corps, the task would be to fight through a number of small villages and hamlets, orchards and hedgerows west of the forest and then through the forest itself.[38] (See Map 18)

The same would be true of two of the divisions of Sir Thomas Morland's XIII Corps on the left of Fourth Army. The country around Hecq, Preux au Bois, Rosimbois, Happegarbes and Les Etoquies was especially intricate. These settlements were enclosed by thick hedges which drastically reduced visibility and were likely to make it difficult for the infantry to maintain direction in an advance. The southern end of the XIII Corps' sector faced towards an acute bend in the canal and the little town of Landrecies. Further south still, on the far right of the British attack sector, Braithwaite's IX Corps faced the Sambre and Oise Canal along its entire front. In front of the canal the Germans still held the villages of Ors and Catillon and the ground around them and so over the northern part of its front it would be necessary for IX Corps to fight its way to the canal as well as to cross it.[39]

The antique fortifications of Le Quesnoy might have caused problems to anyone stupid enough to have launched a frontal infantry assault upon them. But no-one intended to do so. The forest and the canal were, therefore, the most serious physical obstacles and it is necessary to look at these in a little more detail. Though many of the trees of the Forest of Mormal had been felled for firewood in the course of the war, some dense groves were still standing and there was a good deal of thick undergrowth. A number of steep-banked streams ran through the forest, offering further obstacles to a rapid advance. But, on the positive side, the forest contained quite a number of paths, including at least one fairly broad avenue which ran roughly west–east. The Sambre and Oise Canal was about 75 feet wide from bank to bank and about 35–40 feet wide at water level, except at the locks, where it was about 17 feet across. The water was of an average depth of 7 feet and the bottom was muddy. The canal, therefore, was the greatest obstacle facing the BEF's operations on 4 November.[40]

But what forces defended these obstacles? In early November, 14 German divisions, mostly belonging to the German Second Army, were identified on the front of Byng's Third Army, which itself consisted of 15 divisions. Rawlinson's Fourth Army, which had five divisions in the front line (and nine in total) faced eight and a half divisions belonging to the German Second and Eighteenth Armies, the boundary between which ran just south of Catillon. Each of these German armies had four reserve divisions near this boundary. On the Fourth Army front, therefore (as the British official history points out with evident pride) nine British divisions were about to attack into a sector containing more than 16 German divisions. Most British divisions were well below establishment by this stage. In Third Army the average divisional strength was about 8,000 instead of 13,000. But the German divisions opposing them were clearly very much weaker still and may have had a rifle strength averaging 2,000 or even less. In artillery, too, the Germans were certainly markedly inferior, though precise figures are not known.[41]

Tank casualties had been so very high that there were few available to the British Armies in this battle. Third Army had only 13 Mark Vs and 12

Whippets for its four corps. Fourth Army was somewhat better provided, with 42 heavy tanks (Mark Vs and Mark V*s) and nine armoured cars for its two corps.[42] But this was obviously going to be primarily an artillery/infantry battle. Fourth Army employed over 1,000 artillery barrels in support of five attacking divisions, Third Army a still larger number in support of eight. While Third and Fourth Armies issued some general instructions and allocated tanks and extra artillery to the corps, the nature of the ground varied so greatly across the front of the attack that much of the detailed planning was left to the corps. In some cases, they in turn delegated much of it to divisions.[43]

In order to achieve some degree of surprise with regard to the precise timing of the attack, both Armies decided that the volume of fire in the days and hours before Zero was to remain normal 'i.e. there was to be neither an increase nor a diminution'.[44] As the volume of fire was already high the Germans were, in effect, to be subjected to a lengthy preliminary bombardment. As usual, great stress was placed on counter-battery. The generally murky autumn weather was tending to make aerial observation and photography difficult and in Fourth Army's artillery instructions there was a considerable emphasis on sound-ranging. In order to help the sound-ranging sections identify German battery positions unimpeded by extraneous noise, a number of half-hour 'silent intervals' were arranged in the British bombardment.[45]

A particular problem for the gunners on the Fourth Army front was that the country east of the Sambre and Oise Canal was crossed by a number of steep-sided valleys belonging to tributaries of the Sambre, running roughly at right angles to the axis of attack. Rawlinson's staff anticipated that the Germans would concentrate troops and guns in the relative shelter of these folds in the ground and it was considered to be 'of paramount importance' to bring cross-fire to bear on them. For this purpose, IX Corps, which was to attack in the canal sector, was ordered to site at least two of its heavy artillery brigades in the XIII Corps area, these brigades remaining under its own orders.[46]

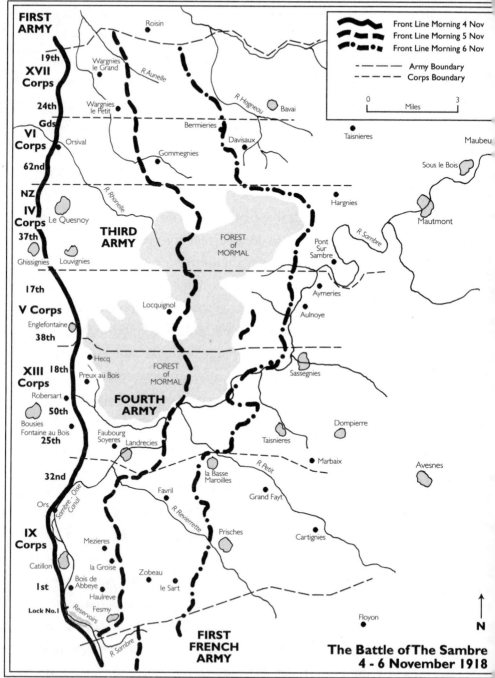

FIRST ARMY

19th

XVII Corps

24th

Gds

VI Corps

62nd

NZ

IV Corps

37th

17th

V Corps

38th

XIII Corps 18th

50th

25th

32nd

IX Corps

1st

Lock No.1

Roisin

Wargnies le Grand

R Aunelle

Wargnies le Petit

Bermieries

Gommegnies

R Hogneau

Bavai

Davisaux

Taisnieres

Maubeu

Sous le Bois

Orsival

R Rhonelle

Hargnies

Mautmont

Le Quesnoy

THIRD ARMY

FOREST of MORMAL

R Sambre

Pont Sur Sambre

Ghissignies

Louvignies

37th

Aymeries

Locquignol

Aulnoye

Englefontaine

Hecq

FOREST of MORMAL

Preux au Bois

Sassegnies

Robersart

FOURTH ARMY

Bousies

Fontaine au Bois

Dompierre

Faubourg Soyeres

Landrecies

Taisnieres

Marbaix

Avesnes

la Basse Maroilles

R Petit

Ors

Favril

R Revierrette

Grand Fayt

Sambre-Oise Canal

Mezieres

Prisches

Cartignies

Catillon

la Groise

Zobeau

Bois de Abbeye

le Sart

Haulreve

Fesmy

Reservoirs

Floyon

R Sambre

N

FIRST FRENCH ARMY

The Battle of The Sambre 4 - 6 November 1918

Front Line Morning 4 Nov
Front Line Morning 5 Nov
Front Line Morning 6 Nov

Army Boundary
Corps Boundary

0   3
Miles

The Armies recommended that those corps attacking into wooded country employ a system of 'block barrages', keeping some sections of wood or forest under constant bombardment for fixed periods while the infantry worked around them. Both Armies were intending a rapid and fairly deep advance, moving well beyond the range of the creeping barrages which would support the initial assault. Fourth Army reminded its corps of the importance 'of pushing forward units of artillery and trench mortars in close support of the infantry'.[47] The corps probably needed no reminders and in some cases intended to bring enough artillery forward to continue the barrage to their final objectives.

THE BATTLE OF THE SAMBRE: 4 NOVEMBER

The changeable autumn weather had significant influences, both positive and negative, on British operations in the Battle of the Sambre. In the days preceding the attack murky atmospheric conditions handicapped the British counter-battery effort. On the morning of 4 November German artillery was quite active, some BEF brigades being heavily shelled in their forming-up positions.[48] But a thick ground mist, which lasted up to 09.00, gave the attacking infantry a certain amount of cover and tended to reduce casualties from machine-gun and rifle fire. After this misty start, moreover, the weather on the Third and Fourth Army fronts turned out cloudy but fine, the RAF was very active[49] and German artillery was progressively suppressed, partly by counter-battery fire and partly by the infantry advance.[50]

Zero for Third Army was 05.30 (though only the IV Corps plus one VI Corps division actually attacked at that time). Fergusson's XVII Corps, which had been attacking for the last three days in support of First Army, had already taken about half the objectives it had been given by Third Army for 4 November. It therefore attacked at 06.00, half an hour after the central section of Third Army. It employed the 19th and the 24th Divisions, supported by ten field artillery and five heavy artillery brigades. The

Germans in this sector had no continuous lines of trenches or belts of wire. They relied on scattered rifle and machine-gun pits, laid out in considerable depth, and on fortified villages. The strength of the resistance they offered was variable. Germans defending the village of Eth proved stubborn. But in the open country between the defended villages even the normally dedicated German machine-gunners in many cases abandoned their weapons and fled. By dusk XVII Corps had taken all its objectives for the day, having made an advance of between three and four miles.[51]

Haldane's VI Corps attacked with the Guards Division and the 62nd Division, supported by nine brigades of field and five of heavy artillery. The Guards Division attacked at 06.00, in time with XVII Corps, the 62nd Division half an hour earlier, in time with IV Corps. The VI Corps' story on 4 November was in most ways similar to that of XVII Corps and the advance achieved about the same. But on approaching the Corps' objective, at about 11.00, troops of the two attacking divisions found large numbers of German troops and guns immediately in front of them, and decided to postpone any further advance until the following day, when more artillery could be brought up.[52]

The most remarkable feature of the fighting on the front of Harper's IV Corps – which attacked at 05.30 with the New Zealand Division and the 37th Division, supported by 12 field and five heavy artillery brigades – was the capture of Le Quesnoy. The town, in the New Zealand Division's attack sector, was enclosed within two concentric systems of fortification. Around the town itself there was a seven-sided bastion. Around this there was a continuous rampart of salients and re-entrants and there was a dry ditch (or 'covered way') between the two. Within the ditch there were a number of mounds of earth with trees growing on them. The IV Corps and New Zealand Division staffs had been unable to ascertain whether the place was garrisoned or not.

The plan for dealing with Le Quesnoy was fairly simple. First, a Royal Engineers' Special [Chemical Warfare] Company would use Livens Projectors to fire 300 cylinders of flaming oil onto the ramparts. The infantry would then advance to the town under the cover of a barrage. At that point the artillery would open fire on the ramparts, but cease firing on the western side after 15 minutes while patrols checked if the fortifications were still occupied. If so, they were to be placed under a two-hour smoke bombardment from 06.30 to 08.30. The infantry would then envelop them and most of the division would press on to deeper objectives.

The plan worked. The New Zealanders met fairly light opposition in front of Le Quesnoy. They took some rifle and machine-gun fire from the ramparts, but were able to sweep past the town on both sides. By early afternoon patrols had penetrated well into the Forest of Mormal (which in this sector was about four miles behind the German front) and found no sign of the enemy. The Corps' objective was reached with little difficulty. About 13.00, a prisoner was sent into Le Quesnoy to suggest surrender. This procedure was repeated on several occasions and a formal message to the garrison commander was dropped by aeroplane, all without apparent success. By 15.30, the German other ranks were prepared to surrender but the officers were still reluctant. No reply having been received from the garrison, the New Zealanders decided to seize the ramparts. From about 16.30 they bombarded them with trench mortars. Then, using a single ladder, a handful of officers and men of 4th New Zealand Rifle Battalion scaled the western side, the rest of the battalion quickly following when they knew the coast was clear. With the New Zealanders on the ramparts the Germans finally surrendered. By the end of the day the New Zealanders had taken some 2,450 prisoners and a great deal of artillery, the majority of both being from the Le Quesnoy garrison.[53]

The 37th Division encountered serious initial resistance on the railway east of Ghissignies and in the village of Louvignies. In the orchards surrounding the village fighting became hand-to-hand at some points. The assistance of half a dozen tanks proved valuable in overcoming resistance and ultimately the 37th had a very successful day. By 18.00, it had penetrated well into the Forest of Mormal, though not quite as far as the final corps objective, and had taken more than 1,000 prisoners, bringing the total for IV Corps to about 3,500.[54]

The 17th and 38th Divisions of Shute's V Corps, on the right wing of Third Army, and the 18th and 50th Divisions of Morland's XIII Corps, on the left wing of Fourth Army, had broadly similar tasks. Like the 37th Division, in Harper's IV Corps, they were to smash through an area of orchards, hedges and villages just west of the Forest of Mormal and then penetrate into the forest itself. The western edge of the forest was diagonal to the British front and to reach it the divisions on the left had further to go than those on the right. All four divisions attacked at 06.15. In all cases they encountered the most serious resistance before they reached the forest. In breaking through the hedgerows and dealing with resistance in the villages and orchards, tanks, when and where available, proved invaluable. In the forest itself resistance was much less than expected. The Germans presumably had too few troops of good quality by this stage in the war to organise a real defence in depth.[55]

The 17th Division on V Corps' left, had the hardest day. The 52nd Brigade, which led its attack, was shelled quite heavily in its forming-up position and then suffered heavy casualties in hedgerow fighting. Only one of the four tanks which the division had been allocated actually appeared and that was quickly knocked out. The 9th Battalion of the Duke of Wellington's Regiment, in the brigade's centre, suffered casualties to 13 officers and 226 other ranks out of totals of 15 and 583.[56] Such losses were, however, exceptional. The other three divisions attacking in this sector generally met rather less resistance or received better tank support. Even on the 17th Division's front German resistance collapsed in the second half of the morning. By dusk all of these divisions had penetrated well into the forest. The 18th and the 50th Divisions in XIII Corps each achieved advances of four miles in the course of the day.[57]

The mission of the 25th Division, on the XIII Corps' right, was to attack into the area of open country to the south of the forest, cross the Sambre and Oise Canal on either side of the village of Landrecies and clear the village itself. It had some stiff fighting, in which tanks gave useful assistance, in order to reach the canal. Having done so, some troops paddled across on rafts made of petrol tins fixed to a timber framework specially constructed by the divisional sappers. Others crossed by a number of small bridges which had been captured intact on both sides of Landrecies. The German troops in the town, apparently realising that they were in danger of being surrounded, began to abandon it around midday. By the end of the day, the 75th Brigade, which led the attack, had taken 838 prisoners and 27 guns.[58]

Braithwaite's IX Corps attacked at 05.45 with the 32nd and the 1st Division. Both divisions advanced behind heavy barrages and were covered by smoke screens provided by the 4-inch Stokes mortars of No. 1 Special [Chemical Warfare] Company Royal Engineers.[59]

The 32nd Division mounted its assault with two brigades plus attached engineers, one on either side of the village of Ors. The 96th Brigade, despite some extraordinary heroism by the sappers and infantry of the 2nd Manchesters and 16th Lancashire Fusiliers, failed to cross north of the village, being beaten back by intense artillery and machine-gun fire and suffering around 200 casualties. (Amongst these was the poet Wilfred Owen, a captain in the Manchesters, killed just a week before the end of the war.) The 14th Brigade was more successful south of Ors, getting across, shrouded by mist, on a pontoon bridge which the sappers had made with kerosene tins. Rather than having 96th Brigade persist in trying to cross north of Ors, in the face of heavy losses, 32nd Division's headquarters sent orders at 08.30 for the Manchesters and Fusiliers to use 14th Brigade's pontoon bridge south of the village. By the end of the day, the 32nd Division had secured a bridgehead, taken the village of Ors and captured 235 prisoners. But in the process it had sustained about 700 casualties, a good deal more than most other attacking divisions on this victorious day.[60]

The 1st Division, on the BEF's extreme right, generally had an easier and more successful time. The 3rd Brigade, on the left, rapidly took the village of Catillon with the aid of three tanks. Many of the German troops defending the place emerged from cellars in which they had sheltered from the barrage only to find their positions overrun and were thus compelled to surrender. Soon after 08.00, 3rd Brigade troops had crossed the canal on a civilian bridge still standing to the east of Catillon. The 1st Brigade, in 1st Division's centre, also had relatively little difficulty. The 1st Loyal North Lancashire and the 1st Cameron Highlanders, together with attached sappers, closed up to the canal behind the barrage while the morning mist was still thick, threw three footbridges over, and were across by 06.10, so fast that the German counter-barrage landed behind them.[61]

The 2nd Brigade, the most southerly brigade in the BEF, had a somewhat harder time. As officers and men of the 2nd Royal Sussex struggled across a small stream on their way to their designated crossing point at Lock No 1, they were hit by salvoes of German shells and came under intense machine-gun fire from the lock house, sustaining heavy casualties. 'So intense was the enemy's fire' states Fourth Army's historian, 'that it seemed impossible for any man to get to the lock and yet live.' The situation was saved by heroic action by individuals. Major Findlay of the 409th Field Company Royal Engineers, leading sappers and infantry alike by personal example, reached the lock and set up a bridge. Lieutenant-Colonel Dudley Johnson, commanding officer of the 2nd Royal Sussex, then played a vital role in bringing more of his men forward to the lock despite intense machine-gun fire from the lock house.[62] Once his men had partially suppressed the German fire with their Lewis guns and Lee Enfields, Johnson, personally led a party which dashed across the footbridge at about 06.10 and stormed the lock house. The fury with which the attack was pressed is indicated by a statement in a German unit history that most of the lock's defenders were shot dead with revolvers, only one man surviving, and he by feigning death.[63]

By dusk, with little support from the French First Army on its right flank, and at the cost of only 500 casualties, the 1st Division had advanced up to 4,000 yards beyond the canal, taken the villages of Catillon, Mézières, La Groise and Fesmy and captured about 1,700 German prisoners and 20 guns.[64]

The combined attack of Third and Fourth Armies on 4 November (with modest support from the French First Army) had indeed been a grand slam. About 10,000 prisoners were taken – 6,000 by Third Army and 4,000 by Fourth.[65] In many parts of the battlefield the Germans were in flight by the end of the day. In relation to the size of the battle and the scale of the achievement British casualties had been light.[66] The BEF had fought its last battle of the First World War.

THE FINAL ADVANCE: 5–11 NOVEMBER

When Third and Fourth Armies renewed their advance on the morning of Tuesday 5 November, they met only light resistance. Despite cloudy conditions, Germans troops, falling back under intense pressure on the ground, were much harassed from the air. Aircraft of the RAF's V Brigade engaged masses of transport and infantry fleeing down roads near the village of Maroilles and a single battalion of the 25th Division captured over 30 guns apparently abandoned in fear of air attack. By 6 November the Germans in front of Third and Fourth Armies were in full retreat.[67]

Over the next few days the main opposition on the front of Third and Fourth Armies came from rearguards mainly composed of field artillery and machine guns. The rearguards were sometimes stubborn, and 'severe' fighting for villages was reported on the Third Army front on the night of 7/8 November.[68] On the Fourth Army front, at 11.00 on 8 November, the German 9th Division even made a substantial counter-attack to regain the line of the Mauberge–Avesnes road as a rearguard position. But this forlorn endeavour was comprehensively smashed.[69] The following day, Saturday 9 November, the German retreat in front of the British First, Third and Fourth Armies accelerated markedly. The Germans were now fleeing so fast in this sector that contact with them was almost entirely lost. On the same day, the scope of the German retreat extended northward to the sea. The German Army was now in flight everywhere from the Belgian coast in the north to Sedan in the south.[70] (See Map 1)

Plumer's Second Army had for some time been preparing an assault crossing of the Schelde scheduled for the morning of 11 November. The German Fourth Army did not await the blow. Both it and the German Sixth Army to its south began their retreat from the Schelde on the night of 8/9 November. By dawn, they had virtually abandoned the east bank. Plumer's forces, realising a withdrawal was in progress, crossed the river the same night. Meeting only slight resistance, they advanced 22 miles in the last three days of the war, reaching the River Dendre. A bridge over that waterway at Lessines, wired for demolition with explosive charges, was captured by a charge of a squadron of the 7th Dragoon Guards just before 11.00.[71] Birdwood's Fifth Army, advancing on the right flank of Plumer's Second, had also crossed the River Dendre in its sector when the Armistice came into effect.[72] Canadian troops entered Mons at about 23.00 on 10 November and by dawn few Germans remained both alive and free in that town. First Army's war ended on a line just east of Mons, the place where the BEF had received its baptism of fire more than four years previously.[73]

In order to maintain some sort of contact with the fleeing Germans on their fronts, on Saturday 9 November both Byng and Rawlinson established Army advanced guards. When hostilities ceased Third Army's lead elements had reached the River Thure between Soire sur Sambre and Cousolre. Fourth Army's straddled the Franco-Belgian border, having reached the Thure south of Cousolre.[74]

THE ARMISTICE

General Groener arrived at Spa, to take over what had been Ludendorff's position in the German high command, on Wednesday 30 October. By that time a very serious mutiny had broken out in the

Navy at Kiel. On Tuesday 5 November, after spending a few days touring headquarters at the front, Groener told the Cabinet that the situation was extremely adverse but that there was still some time for negotiation before the Army finally collapsed. But on the following day, 6 November, apparently having received further bad news from the front and doubtless aware that armed naval mutineers were seizing control of several towns in northern Germany, he advised that in order to avoid complete military disintegration, an armistice was needed by Saturday 9 November at the latest. Monday 11 November would, he said, be too late.

A note received from President Wilson on the evening of Wednesday 6 November informed the German government that Foch had been authorised to meet its representatives with a view to arranging an armistice. Armistice commissioners left Germany the following day. On the morning of Friday 8 November, in a railway carriage in the Forest of Compiègne, Foch presented them with terms which were tantamount to unconditional surrender. These terms allowed the German Army to go home with its men carrying their rifles and the officers their swords, but compelled the abandonment of all the artillery and most of the machine-guns. The terms also gave the Allies bridgeheads over the Rhine and, less justifiably, maintained the blockade which was causing great suffering to the poorer part of the population of the German cities. Shocked but helpless, the commissioners referred the terms back to their government. The following day, Saturday 9 November, in order to placate the Berlin mob, the German Chancellor, Prince Max, without consulting the Kaiser, announced the latter's abdication. On the morning of Sunday 10 November the ex-Kaiser left Spa, where he had earlier taken refuge at the headquarters of his army, for exile in the Netherlands.

The Social Democratic government of Friederich Ebert, first Chancellor of the new German Republic, could see no choice but to sign the Armistice agreement, harsh as it was for Germany's civilians. The German high command seems, in general, to have been relieved that its troops were going to be allowed to depart with a modicum of dignity from the lands that they had violated. At 05.05 on Monday 11 November the Armistice was signed. At 11.00 it came into effect.[75]

In a message, announcing the Armistice, sent to the Armies that morning, GHQ insisted that no fraternisation with the enemy was to be permitted. German soldiers approaching the BEF's lines without prior permission were to be warned off, if necessary by fire. If they ignored the warnings they were to be shot.[76] At first, British and Dominion troops generally greeted the Armistice undemonstratively, going about routine duties, or, where possible, catching up on sleep. Celebrations that night were, in some cases, rather more vigorous, noisy and alcoholic.[77] The war, or at least the fighting of it, was over.

CONCLUSION

THE NATURE OF THE VICTORY

What sort of victory had the BEF helped to win? The fact that the Allies agreed to a cease-fire which allowed the German troops on the Western Front to march home in good order, the men with their rifles and the officers with their swords, has sometimes been taken to mean that military triumph was only partial. When the war ended the BEF had advanced, we are often reminded, only a little way past Mons where it had received its baptism of fire over four years previously. No-one denies that, by 11 November, the Allies had the Germans on the run. Some historians have suggested, however, that they were incapable of completing their victory. In fighting its way through the Hindenburg Line, the BEF, most battle-worthy of the Allied armies, had, in one version of this thesis, exhausted itself and no longer had the energy to close in for the kill.[1] In a slight variation on the same theme, other historians have indicated that, whatever their remaining combat power, logistical breakdown would have prevented the Allies from pursuing the retreating Germans to destruction.[2]

Was the BEF exhausted? Were the Allied armies as a whole exhausted? Did logistical difficulties make effective pursuit of the fleeing Germans impossible? Could the armies of the Allies have completed the destruction of German forces on the Western Front by the end of 1918 or by the end of the winter had they continued to resist? These questions are of some interest and attempts will be made to answer them below. But in the actual circumstances of November 1918 they were largely beside the point. Except for rear-guards, the German Armies on the Western Front had virtually ceased fighting by 5 November. By 9 November their retreat had become general from the North Sea to Sedan. By signing the Armistice on 11 November 1918 and by complying with most of its terms, the Germans left themselves quite incapable of further resistance. They had nothing but the tiniest of fig-leaves to cover what was, in effect, an unconditional surrender. Given that the Germans were prepared to concede the substance of total submission, few senior figures on the Allied side believed it worthwhile to expend lives to secure the form as well, though these included Pershing[3] and Mangin, the most aggressive of the French generals.[4] Forms and symbols are very important in human affairs. With the benefit of hindsight, and in view of the rise of Nazism, it might appear that Pershing and Mangin were right. Perhaps it would have been salutary for the German people to see their army utterly humiliated. In the actual circumstances of 11 November 1918, and without the benefit of such hindsight, the continuation of slaughter would have seemed an obscenity to most rational people.

Why did the Germans sign such an abject agreement? Obviously because they felt they had no choice. Germany had suffered a multi-faceted defeat in a multi-faceted war. The collapse of Germany's allies, partly owing to the German Army's inability to keep propping them up, was one aspect of this. Austria-Hungary's collapse was particularly serious as it exposed Germany's southern flank, though the danger there was long-term rather than immediate. Another aspect was the slow starvation torturing and the sickness ravaging the civilian population. The Armistice did not, however, remove the blockade. The German high command's acceptance of the Armistice, humiliating as it was, seems to have derived mainly from the belief that if the fighting went on much longer the German Army would disintegrate on the battlefield.[5] Such a disintegration would have been even more humiliating than the Armistice itself and would probably have ruined irretrievably the Army's social prestige and political influence. Although some German troops showed great gallantry and determination to the end, there can be little doubt that the high command was right to believe that collapse was imminent. Combat avoidance was widespread and many of those captured in the Battle of the Sambre made it clear that they were glad to be so. Even officers were captured drunk.[6]

THE ALLIES' FIGHTING POTENTIAL IN MID-NOVEMBER 1918

The general mood in the BEF during the last week of the war appears to have been one of great confidence. Though many officers and men were naturally very tired, there is little evidence of such a degree of collective exhaustion as would have prevented the BEF continuing its run of victories against a depleted and extremely demoralised opponent. Most of the French forces on the Western Front were certainly war-weary. Their performance during the Hundred Days had been patchy, often not very dynamic. In the last few days of the war, however, the French Armies sandwiched between the British and the Americans were moving rapidly, keeping pace with their allies. After more than a month of appalling frustration in the Argonne–Meuse sector the Americans had, on 1 November, finally broken the opposition in front of them and after that their progress accelerated dramatically. Unlike everyone else, they had virtually limitless fresh manpower and, given the condition of the German forces on the Western Front in November, their rather low levels of tactical skill hardly mattered any more. Any suggestion that the British, French and Americans collectively lacked the strength to complete the destruction of the German forces on the Western Front must be considered little short of ludicrous. How long this destruction would have taken would, however, have depended largely on logistics.

As far as the BEF was concerned, the situation at the time of the Armistice was that, after a period of exceptionally rapid advance, it had largely outrun its supplies. While using advanced guards of all arms to maintain contact with the fleeing Germans, it needed a logistical pause of several days before the pursuit could be resumed with any strength. The

Germans had, as usual, done a lot of destruction to roads and railways before their latest withdrawal and had left many delayed-action mines. But any idea that this would have prevented – rather than postponed – the destruction of the German forces facing the BEF seems far-fetched. Rawlinson's Army was in the most difficult logistical position of any of the British Armies but his assessment on 5 November was far from alarmist. On the first day of the Battle of the Sambre Fourth Army had captured

> *over 4,500 prisoners and 50 guns with the loss of 2,500 men. Such results are most satisfactory and, if necessary, we can go on doing this all winter, when the weather permits. But we cannot do it continuously, weather or no, till the railways are repaired. My army is now 30 miles in front of our railheads and the broken roads put a great strain upon the lorries. I can manage a further advance of ten miles, but after that we must call a halt for* a week or ten days.[7]
> [emphasis added]

Rawlinson believed that the Germans would be forced to conclude an armistice within that time, making the logistics of the situation an irrelevance. But, leaving that aside, all he was saying was that Fourth Army would need a short logistical pause. It had required a number of pauses during the Hundred Days, partly to allow the railheads to catch up and partly for rest and recuperation. There had been one such pause prior to the attack on the Main Hindenburg System in late September, another on the Selle between 11 and 17 October and yet another when facing the Sambre and Oise Canal from 25 October to 4 November. The BEF had efficient sappers and pioneers and, after a few days, the railways had always been repaired and sufficient ammunition had been delivered to permit some of the most colossal artillery bombardments in military history. The advance had always been resumed. While, on 11 November, the most forward troops were further beyond the railheads than ever before, they would also have required far less ammunition to keep the Germans on the move. The BEF's highly experienced Quartermaster General, Lieutenant-General T. E. Clarke, stated on 13 November that he would, if necessary, be capable of sustaining 40 divisions on the German frontier engaged in active warfare.[8] There can be no reasonable doubt that the rigours of a winter campaign, which the well-fed, well-equipped Allies were in a much better condition to endure, would have brought the total collapse of German forces in the west had they not effectively capitulated before then.

THE BEF'S CONTRIBUTION TO THE FINAL ALLIED OFFENSIVES

The virtually continuous run of Allied victories and pursuits from mid-July to mid-November 1918 was not initiated by the BEF. The credit for Second Battle of the Marne belongs primarily to the French Army and to American divisions under French command. But over this period as a whole the BEF's contribution was without doubt the predominant one. The generally accepted set of figures for captures of German personnel and guns between 18 July and 11 November is as follows:[9]

	PRISONERS	GUNS
British Armies	188,700	2,840
French Armies	139,000	1,880
American Armies	43,300	1,421
Belgian Armies	14,500	474

Because they render no account of captures made by American divisions serving in British and French Armies, these figures somewhat understate the American contribution and overstate that of the British and the French. American divisions played a substantial part in the Second Battle of the Marne and in the battles fought by the British Fourth Army from late September to mid-October. For the period from 8 August to 11

November, however, the British and Dominion contribution was proportionally still larger than these figures suggest and the French contribution smaller – the French Army's greatest contribution to the Allied effort in 1918 had been the Second Battle of the Marne. By the time of the Armistice the BEF was, in terms of numbers and also in terms of percentage of the front held, only the third largest of the armies under Foch's command. The French had about two and a half million men on the Western Front and the Americans nearly two million, as against about one and three quarters of a million in the BEF. The French held 55 per cent of the front (though quite a lot of their share was inactive) as against 21 per cent for the Americans and 18 per cent for the BEF.[10] There can, however, be very little doubt that on 11 November 1918 the British Armies represented by far the largest share of the combat power of the forces ranged against the Germans.

THE DOMINION CONTRIBUTION TO THE BEF

Just as the British Armies made a disproportionate contribution to the Allied offensives in the last four months, so the two Dominion corps played a disproportionate part in the victories won by the British Armies. During the Hundred Days the Australian Corps took 22,854 prisoners and the Canadian Corps 31,537[11] out of a total of some 186,500 taken by the BEF as a whole.[12] The above figures take no account of the efforts of the relatively unsung New Zealand Division, which fought splendidly through both the German spring offensives and the Hundred Days. They also ignore the smaller but still valuable contribution of the South African Brigade.

Some explanation of why the Dominion forces, and especially the two Dominion corps, were of such great importance to the British war effort during the Hundred Days has already been provided in Chapter Two. Divisions from the home islands had absorbed most of the shock of Ludendorff's offensives of the spring and had done most of the fighting necessary to bring them to a halt. They had taken very severe casualties in the process. In late summer 1918 a large proportion of the infantry of most British divisions consisted of very young and inexperienced conscripts. The morale of many of these divisions was uncertain and it was felt inadvisable to demand too much of them. At about the same time the two Dominion corps were reaching their peak as battle-hardened, cohesive, veteran formations. For approximately the first half of the Hundred Days, therefore, the BEF's reliance on these corps was exceptionally great.

The Canadian Corps, which had seen very little combat in 1918 prior to the Hundred Days, retained an extraordinary potency to the end of the campaign. The same was not, however, true of the Australian Corps. The Australians had done much more fighting in the spring and early summer than had the Canadians. From the start of the Battle of Amiens on 8 August to the Battle of Epéhy on 18 September their performance was, nevertheless, almost beyond praise. But after that, their heavy losses (impossible to replace because Australia did not have conscription), coupled with a general weariness, gradually overcame them. They played a relatively minor part in breaking the Main Hindenburg System, in late September, and their role in the Battle of the Beaurevoir Line, in the first few days of October, was their last, rather painful, gasp.[13] Australian infantry was withdrawn from operations on 5 October and by that time some quite serious cracks in morale had appeared. A relatively loose, informal sort of discipline had always characterised Australian formations. Under the extraordinary stress of the August and September fighting this, to some extent, gave way. During September there were a number of mutinies and quasi-mutinies, the most serious in the BEF at any point in the war. The occasions for these were various but the underlying cause seems to have been the understandable feeling that too much was being demanded of Australian troops.[14] To mention these incidents is not to denigrate the enormous Australian contribution to victory. It is merely to indicate that the Australian 'Digger' was no superman. Like the British 'Tommy' he was a normal human being who had a breaking point.

The withdrawal of the Australian Corps did not, of course, halt the run of success for Fourth Army or for the BEF as a whole. The major victories of the Battle of Cambrai on 8 October, the Battle of the Selle 17–24 October and the Battle of the Sambre on 4 and 5 November were all won without Australian infantry. They were accomplished predominantly by troops from the British home islands, though the New Zealand Division fought in all three battles and the II American Corps in the first two. The period of exceptionally heavy reliance on the Dominion corps in August and September 1918 was a phase through which the BEF passed. By October many British divisions, having recovered from earlier traumas, were performing very well, while German combat power had, of course, declined. The Mont Houy–Valenciennes episode might be used to argue a continuing dependence on Dominion troops. But it should be remembered that Mont Houy had been largely overrun (though not ultimately secured) by a single battalion of the 51st Division on 28 October with far less fire support than that used in the 10th Canadian Brigade's assault on 1 November. Though the Canadian Corps was still playing a leading role in First Army's operations, the period of dependency on Dominion troops in the BEF as a whole was arguably over by the beginning of October. Even in First Army, a good deal of the hardest fighting in the drive to the immediate vicinity of Valenciennes had been done by Godley's XXII Corps.

THE BEF'S FIGHTING METHODS

It was argued in Chapter Two that the BEF at the beginning of August 1918, though still battered and bruised from the German spring offensives, was a highly sophisticated army which had developed and adopted a broad range of operational methods and tactics. During the Hundred Days this repertoire was performed with impressive skill. While the BEF's attacks of August to November 1918 were, in some respects, less dramatic than the German offensives of the spring they were also more efficient. In war, the object is normally to cripple the enemy at a relatively modest cost to one's own side. In these terms the German offensives of March–July 1918, while gaining much ground, manifestly failed. In its offensives of August to November, the BEF, by contrast, consistently inflicted far heavier losses than it sustained. While taking approximately 186,000 prisoners, the BEF recorded fewer than 67,000 definite fatalities to its own personnel from August to November 1918, with approximately another 33,000 recorded as missing or prisoners.[15] It would be reasonable to suppose that, with its superior firepower, the BEF was inflicting at least as many fatal casualties as it was sustaining – and probably a good deal more. Thus, while these figures indicate colossal loss and suffering for the British and the peoples of the Dominions, as well as for the Germans, they also represent a very favourable rate of attrition for the Allied side in the war. This was achieved even though, in the Drocourt–Quéant Line and the Hindenburg Systems, the BEF had to tackle fortifications more formidable than any the Germans had faced earlier in the year. The BEF achieved, on the Fourth Army front, a maximum advance of more than 100 miles in the course of the campaign.

British offensives in the late summer and autumn of 1918 were generally conducted with greater caution than German offensives earlier in the year and, at least as far as the BEF's Armies and corps were concerned, with more limited objectives. This cautious style originated with neither Foch nor Haig. Both the British Commander-in-Chief and the French Marshal tried, at different times, to turn Fourth Army's offensive of 8 August into an unlimited drive deep into the German rear. Meeting resistance from corps and Army level, Haig eventually thought better of this. Encountering opposition from Haig, Foch did not press the point. Fourth Army headquarters had originally conceived the operation as a short, sharp, opportunistic blow and was very wary of its indefinite extension – a wariness born out of bitter experience. During the Hundred Days as a whole, the BEF, from Army level downwards, tended to favour battles with limited objectives. While British and Dominion infantry was not slavish in its reliance on creeping barrages, experience had made it reluctant to press far beyond the range at which some sort of effective artillery support could be offered unless the opposition proved exceptionally weak. It seems to have been widely understood in the BEF, at least from Army level downwards, that major attacks were at their most potent on Z day and that returns tended to diminish after that. There was also a general dislike of exposed flanks and salients, and hence of attempts to penetrate deeply on narrow fronts. The British official history appears to condemn such attitudes.[16] Though some commanders held them too rigidly, in the circumstances of the time they were pragmatic and sensible.

What emerged by process of interaction between Haig on the one hand and his Army and corps commanders on the other, was a tendency to widen offensive operations rather than to deepen them and to open a new attack on a parallel axis rather than to press any one attack too far. The Allies kept the Germans off balance during August and September by mounting successive blows at various points on the front. They were assisted in maintaining the initiative by their own growing numerical superiority, by the inadequacy of German intelligence and, as far as the BEF was concerned, by a range of techniques, including deception planning and the silent or disguised registration of artillery, which helped to achieve surprise. The opening of Foch's general offensive in late September did not change this pattern very much. The Germans did not immediately collapse under the general offensive's weight and no Allied army proved capable of mounting all-out attacks for more than a few consecutive days without exhausting itself. From late September it became more difficult for the Allies to achieve a high degree of surprise as the Germans were constantly expecting to be attacked. Surprise mattered less as the campaign progressed, however, as the Germans had progressively fewer reserves available.

The idea that Haig and GHQ, and the BEF's Army commanders and their staffs, were reluctant to exploit the full possibilities of the newer forms of military technology seems unsustainable.[17] The potency of all the new military technologies and techniques available was exaggerated by their most extreme advocates and the higher military authorities had to be wary of this sort of 'hype'. During the Hundred Days' campaign, however, the BEF seemed to have used all the technologies available to it to the limit of their potential. The Tank Corps was tested practically to destruction, suffering about 40 per cent casualties to its personnel in the course of the campaign.[18] Tanks were useful (within limits) and during the Hundred Days their services were in constant demand. Slow, sensitive to ground, toxic to their crews and vulnerable to all kinds of artillery, they offered no magic solutions to the BEF's problems. They were less flexible and far less important than infantry, artillery or aircraft. The fact that infantry and artillery continued to be the BEF's principal combat arms during the Hundred Days does not really mean that it was fighting in a 'traditional' style. Many of the technologies and tactics these arms employed in the Hundred Days had not been widely used before 1914 and some were, at that time, unheard of. The tactics the BEF employed were pragmatic and effective responses to the particular circumstances of the Western Front in this particular war.

One of the more interesting ideas recently presented about British fighting methods in the Hundred Days is the concept of the 'formula for success' or 'winning formula', put forward by the historians Robin Prior and Trevor Wilson in their account of Rawlinson's command. The winning formula, these historians have suggested, involved the employment of a particular combination of military instruments and tactics which they describe as a 'weapons system'. Prior and Wilson suggest that the formula was discovered at Hamel on 4 July and applied on 8 August and in subsequent battles.[19] While appealing, and not without merit, this concept should be treated with caution. It is quite true that Fourth Army's plan for the operation mounted on 8 August was essentially a scaled-up version of Hamel. The two attacks were mounted in roughly the same part of the front and under broadly similar conditions. Both were characterised by the achievement of a high degree of surprise against a distinctly somnolent enemy, by the forgoing of intensive preliminary bombardment, by massive (and extremely successful) suppressive counter-battery fire on the basis of excellent artillery intelligence, by well-laid-on creeping barrages, by the concentration of veteran troops against an enemy weak spot and by the concentrated use of tanks. Some of the methods the BEF used at Hamel and Amiens – creeping barrages, for example – were employed in all the major battles of the Hundred Days. Effective combinations of operational and tactical methods developed earlier in the war were crucial to the favourable rate of attrition which the BEF was able to inflict at this period. But somewhat different combinations had to be devised to meet rapidly changing circumstances. To think in terms of the constant application of a set formula would be to underestimate the dynamism and complexity of the campaign.

Some features of the attack of 8 August were never repeated, or at least never repeated to the same degree. Some were practically unrepeatable. Never again did the BEF secretly concentrate its two most powerful corps for an attack on an enemy weak spot. Never again was quite such a mass of tanks available for any one attack. Never was artillery intelligence quite so good and never was the counter-battery fire quite so effective. Very rarely did the BEF achieve anything like the same degree of surprise. An important feature of the Hamel/Amiens formula was that a preliminary bombardment was forgone. But in planning some of the subsequent set-piece battles, including that of the Main Hindenburg System on 29 September and the Selle on 17 October, commanders accepted that a very high degree of surprise was not achievable, and preliminary bombardments lasting for days were conducted. The notion of applying a 'winning formula' is, therefore, somewhat misleading.

The BEF 'weapons system' was a good deal more fallible than Prior and Wilson tend to suggest. The effectiveness of the BEF's artillery fire, especially in the counter-battery role, was heavily dependent on aerial observation and photography and hence on the weather. As late summer turned to autumn, the weather tended to deteriorate and so did the accuracy of British artillery. Though sound ranging could identify German battery positions when visibility was poor the Germans were able to respond to it by moving batteries frequently or by keeping them silent until a major attack started. Despite lengthy preliminary bombardments by the British Fourth Army, German artillery was active in some sectors during the attack on the Main Hindenburg System on 29 September and on the first day of the Battle of the Selle on 17 October. The portrayal of Fourth Army's attack of 17 October as just another overwhelming triumph for the BEF's weapons system seems particularly misleading.[20] On the fronts of the XIII Corps and the II American Corps, British artillery conspicuously failed to suppress German defences in the early stages of the attack, despite prodigious ammunition expenditure, and the Germans were able to deliver a serious counter-attack at the junction of these corps later in the day. More generally, while the Germans were unable to regain the initiative at the operational level at any point in the Hundred Days, they were able make some moderately effective responses to British tactics. On 31 October Haig noted that they had, for example, reacted to British counter-battery work by disposing their guns in great depth. While German artillery was still not especially effective,

> *the losses of our gunners are much greater than earlier in the year. This is due in great measure to the enemy placing his guns in small scattered groups. It is consequently difficult to find them, as time and good weather have been lacking for taking photographs; consequently our counter-battery work cannot be carried out very effectively.*[21]

British technical mastery of the battlefield was thus by no means complete.

The 'formula for success' idea is, in any case, really applicable only to the big set-piece assaults. Much of the Hundred Days' fighting was of the scrappier sort which occurred after the Z days of major attacks and which characterised the lengthy periods of pursuit. At such times counter-battery work was rarely so effective as in set-piece assaults and co-ordination between infantry and field artillery was inevitably much less refined. In this looser sort of fighting there was a greater premium on boldness and initiative at junior levels and on infantry skills, not that such things were unimportant even in the set-pieces. In terms of boldness and initiative the continuously increasing advantage in morale which the BEF enjoyed over the Germans was of great importance. While the Dominion divisions demonstrated these qualities most strikingly in August 1918, they were also very widely exhibited by British troops as the campaign progressed. The seizure of the Riqueval Bridge on the St Quentin Canal by the sappers and infantry of the 46th Division on 29 September, and the events leading to the taking of the lock house at Lock No 1 on the Sambre and Oise Canal by elements of 1st Division on 4 November, are just two of the most obvious examples of extreme daring. The BEF's tendency, common to both Dominion and British formations, to do much of its most serious fighting in the dark, is indicative of the high degree of trust that could be placed in the combat motivation and initiative of junior officers, NCOs and other ranks.

A factor of great importance, which naturally assisted the maintenance of the BEF's morale, was its numerical superiority. Though it is played down by the British official historians, and while it is difficult to be precise about its extent in each case, the BEF appears to have enjoyed a hefty numerical superiority in terms of both infantry and artillery in all the major battles of the Hundred Days. The British official historians seem to delight in offering instances of the BEF defeating larger numbers of divisions than it was itself employing[22] but, as Sir James Edmonds and his colleagues must have known perfectly well, counting divisions in this way was only likely to mislead the unwary reader. German divisions in the Hundred Days often had a rifle strength of 2,000 men or less, whereas, even as late as November, a British division might have four times that number.

HAIG'S ROLE

Haig played a crucial role in shaping the events of the Hundred Days. It is difficult to imagine the war coming to an end in 1918 without his influence. By 11 August he had conceived the possibility of terminating hostilities in 1918, being apparently the first senior figure on the Allied side to do so. Though Rawlinson showed much ambition in this campaign, Haig's drive and determination were crucial in overcoming the reluctance of Byng to mount major offensive operations in August and September and it is difficult to imagine Horne initiating serious action without pressure from above. It was very largely Haig's force of personality which set the BEF as a whole in motion. While Haig had a tendency to be rather over-optimistic, thinking a general enemy collapse imminent long before it really was, he did little harm by this. Army and corps commanders normally tempered Haig's ambition with a caution which had become habitual and which, without Haig, would probably have resulted in inertia. Haig's influence extended well beyond the BEF. As commander of the most powerful Allied contingent, he played a role almost equal to that of Foch in the direction of the campaign and in the planning of the general offensive of late September in particular.

By far the oddest aspect of Haig's performance in this campaign is the sudden loss of optimism after 17 October which led him to pour scorn (some of which was deserved, admittedly) on the efforts of his allies, to understate the German military weakness, to downplay by implication the magnitude of the victories his own forces had won, and, on this basis, to plead that the Allied governments offer the Germans remarkably lenient armistice terms. Foch appears to have read the situation better than Haig at this time[23] and, after 4 November, Haig seems gradually to have recognised the hopeless condition of the German Army.[24] His unwonted and unwarranted pessimism in late October had no discernible effect on the course of events, but it indicates a lack of the sureness of touch, of that capacity to read a complex military situation clearly, which is one of the hall-marks of the truly great commander. Yet Haig, though no military genius, conducted his last campaign, the greatest in British military history, with a combination of resolution and discretion which few of his contemporaries could have matched.

NOTES

INTRODUCTION

1 Actually 96 days but christened the 'Hundred Days' in books published immediately after the war presumably because of the historical resonance with the famous Hundred Days campaign of Napoleon in 1815 – another triumph for a British-led Army which was part of a coalition.

2 Haig's diary, 17 October 1918, PRO WO 256/37.

3 H. Essame, *The Battle For Europe 1918*, Batsford (1972).

4 R. Prior, and T. Wilson, *Command On The Western Front: The Military Career Of Sir Henry Rawlinson 1914–18*, Blackwell (1992).

5 P.H. Liddle, 'British Loyalties: The Evidence Of An Archive', p. 525 in H. Cecil, and P.H. Liddle, *Facing Armageddon: The First World War Experienced*, Pen and Sword (1996).

6 See for example R.E. Priestley, *Breaking The Hindenburg Line: The Story Of The 46th (North Midland) Division* , T. Fisher Unwin (1919), pp. 130–131, 157, 163.

7 Officer–man relations in the BEF are the subject of a forthcoming book *Officer– Man Relations In The British Army In The Era Of The Great War*, Macmillan, by my Sandhurst colleague, G.D. Sheffield.

8 Haig's diary, 1 October 1918, PRO WO 256/37.

CHAPTER 1 THE STRATEGIC BACKGROUND

1 S. Williamson, *Austria-Hungary and the Origins of the First World War*, St. Martin's Press (1991), pp. 103, 111.

2 F. Fellner, 'Austria-Hungary', pp. 9–25, and J. Rohl, 'Germany', pp. 27–46, esp. p. 39 in K. Wilson (ed.) *Decisions for War, 1914*, UCL Press (1995).

3 Rohl, op. cit., passim, esp. p. 45.

4 W. Goerlitz, *The German General Staff: Its History and Structure 1657–1945*, Hollis and Carter (1953), pp. 130–34.

5 H. Strachan, *European Armies and the Conduct of War*, Allen and Unwin (1983), pp. 130–33.

6 J. Gooch, *The Plans of War: The General Staff and British Military Strategy c. 1900–1916*, RKP (1974), 286–98.

7 C. Falls, *The First World War*, Longmans (1960), pp. 60–63.

8 P.G. Halpern, *A Naval History of World War I*, UCL Press (1994), pp. 1–20. C. Page,

'The British Experience of Enforcing Blockade', in H. Cecil and P. Liddell (eds), *Facing Armageddon: The First World War Experienced*, Pen and Sword (1996), pp. 134–6.

9   J.M. Bourne, *Britain and the Great War 1914–1918* (1989), pp. 177–98.

10 L. Moyer, *Victory Must Be Ours: Germany in the Great War 1914–1918*, Leo Cooper (1995), pp. 8–34.

11 On middle-class penetration into the German officer corps and the General Staff see, in particular, Goerlitz, op. cit., p. 96.

12 N. Stone, *The Eastern Front 1914–1917*, Hodder and Stoughton (1975), passim and Falls, op. cit., p. 271.

13 G. Wawro, 'Morale in the Austrian Army', Cecil and Liddell, op. cit., pp. 399–402.

14 Stone, op. cit., pp. 165–91.

15 Goerlitz, op. cit., pp. 176–7.

16 Falls, op. cit., 166.

17 Bourne, op. cit., pp. 214–19.

18 Falls, op. cit., p. 177.

19 Stone, op. cit., pp. 233–63.

20 Ibid., pp. 264–5.

21 Falls, op. cit., 251–2.

22 Ibid., pp. 259–63.

23 Halpern, op. cit., pp. 335–40.

24 Ibid., pp. 340–44 and 351–70.

25 L. Smith, 'The French High Command and the Mutinies of Spring 1917', in Cecil and Liddell, op. cit., pp. 79–83 and Falls, op. cit., pp. 260–63.

26 R. Prior and T. Wilson, *Passchendaele: The Untold Story*, Yale (1996), 1–53. Halpern, op. cit., p. 350.

27 Prior and Wilson, op. cit., 55–200.

28 A. Simpson, *The Evolution of Victory*, Tom Donovan (1995), pp. 93–114.

29 Stone, op. cit., p. 282.

30 R. Pipes, *A Concise History of the Russian Revolution*, Harvill (1995), pp. 56–149.

31 Falls, op. cit., pp. 289–91.

32 See notes on a GHQ conference of 4 Dec. 1917 in 'The Private Journal of Lt. Col. JFC Fuller . . . December 1917 to July 26 1918', Tank Museum, Bovington.

33 E. Ludendorff, *The Concise Ludendorff Memoirs*, Hutchinson (n.d.), pp. 233–6.

34 'German Methods in the Attack and Indications of An Offensive', Annex to Tank Corps Summary of Information, PRO WO 95/93.

35 On storm troops see B. Gudmundsson, *Stormtroop Tactics: Innovation in the German Army, 1914–1918*, Praeger (1989), passim and P. Griffith, *Forward Into Battle: Fighting Tactics from Waterloo to Vietnam*, Anthony Bird (1981), pp. 77–82 On British awareness of German storm troops see Haig's diary Tuesday 4 Dec. 1917 in R. Blake (ed.), *The Private Papers of Douglas Haig 1914–1919*, Eyre and Spottiswoode (1952), p. 270. On British knowledge of the time and place of the initial German offensive see 'Record of a Conference of Army Commanders held at DOULLENS on Saturday 2 March 1918', PRO WO 158/864.

36   Falls, op. cit., pp. 314–15 and J. Terraine, *To Win a War: 1918 the Year of Victory*, Sidgwick and Jackson (1978), pp. 47–51.

37   Haig's diary, 2 March 1918, PRO WO 256/28.

38   Falls, op. cit., p. 315.

39   Ibid., pp. 317–18.

40   Ibid., p. 319.

41   Ibid., pp. 321–7.

42   Ibid., pp. 327–9.

43   Ibid., pp. 331–3.

44   M. Kitchen, *The Silent Dictatorship: The Politics of the German High Command under Hindenburg and Ludendorff*, Croom Helm (1976), 247–50.

45   L. Ayres, *The War with Germany: A Statistical Summary* (Washington Government Printing Office), p. 104.

46   'Statement regarding the present situation on the Western front as given at the Conference of Army Commanders held at HESDIN on Tuesday, 11 June 1918', PRO WO 158/311 and GHQ intelligence summaries for August 1918, PRO WO 157/34.

47   See GHQ summary of information for 26–27 April 1918, WO 157/30 and J. Edmonds, *Military Operations, France and Belgium, 1918, May–July*, Macmillan (1939), pp. 3–6.

48   J. Edmonds, *Military Operations, France and Belgium 1918, Vol. IV, 8 August–26 September*, Macmillan (1947), pp. 1–8 and DMO No. 130, 19 Aug. 1918, PRO WO 158/84.

49   The artillery figures for March 1918 are from W. Deist, 'The Military Collapse of the German Empire: The Reality behind the Stab-in-the-Back Myth', in *War in History*, 1996 3 (2), p. 190. Heavy German losses in guns are referred to in J. Edmonds, *Military Operations France and Belgium 1918, Volume IV, 8 August–26 September*, HMSO (1947), p. 8, fn. 1. Air figures are from an American estimate quoted in, J.H. Morrow, *The Great War in the Air: Military Aviation from 1909 to 1921*, Smithsonian Institution Press (1993), p. 345. The figures appear to be global rather than Western Front only, but the great mass of both sides' air power was on the Western Front. On the Fokker DVII, pp. 300–1.

50   H. Strachan, 'The Morale of the German Army, 1917–18', in Cecil and Liddell, op. cit., p. 390.

51   Strachan, 'Morale', p. 390.

52   Ibid., pp. 390–91.

53   Ibid., p. 391. Deist, op. cit., p. 201 and GHQ intelligence summary, 7/8 August 1918, PRO WO 157/34.

54   GHQ intelligence summary, 27/28 April 1918, PRO WO 157/30.

55   GHQ intelligence summary, 16/19 June, PRO WO 157/32. DMO No. 78, 1 July 1918, PRO WO 158/84.

56   GHQ intelligence summary, 10/11 August, PRO WO 157/34.

57   G. Wawro, op. cit., in Cecil and Liddell, op. cit., pp. 407–10.

58   Ibid., pp. 408–9 and Falls, op. cit., pp. 364–85.

59   Kitchen, op. cit., pp. 247–51.

CHAPTER 2   THE BRITISH EXPEDITIONARY FORCE AND THE ART OF WAR

1   A.F. Becke, *Order of Battle, Part 4: The Army Council, GHQs, Armies and Corps 1914–1918*, HMSO (1945), pp. 17, 133, 139, 145.

2   I.F.W. Beckett and K. Simpson, *A Nation in Arms: A Social History of the British Army in the First World War*, Manchester University Press (1985), passim.

3   S. Bidwell and D. Graham, *Fire-Power: British Army Weapons and Theories of War 1904–45*, Allen and Unwin (1982), pp. 145–6.

4   One area in which the British were world leaders was the development of armoured forces. See J.P. Harris, *Men, Ideas and Tanks; British Military Thought and Armoured Forces*, Manchester University Press (1995), pp. 4–194.

5   J. Edmonds and R. Maxwell-Hyslop, *Military Operations France and Belgium 1918, Vol. V*, HMSO (1947), p. 615, gives 61 divisions for the time of the Armistice. The same figure is given in Haig's diary for 27 August 1918, PRO WO 256/35 and for 21 October 1918, PRO WO 256/37. M. Farndale, *History of the Royal Regiment of Artillery: Western Front 1914–18*, Royal Artillery Institution (1986), pp. 386–95, lists 51 British divisions in France and Flanders at the Armistice, not including the ten Dominion divisions or the three cavalry divisions. For personnel in the BEF at the Armistice see, *Statistics of the Military Effort of the British Empire during the Great War 1914–1920*, HMSO (1922), pp. 624–5.

6   Edmonds and Maxwell-Hyslop, op. cit., p. 477.

7   P. Simkins, 'The Four Armies 1914–1918', p. 262, in I. Beckett and D. Chandler (eds) *The Oxford Illustrated History of the British Army*, Oxford University Press (1994).

8   P. Griffith, *Battle Tactics of the Western Front: The British Army's Art of Attack 1916–18*, Yale (1994), pp. 77–8, 95, 130.

9   M. Farndale, *History of the Royal Regiment of Artillery: Western Front 1914–18*, Royal Artillery Institution (1986), p. 449.

10 Ibid., p. 367.

11 Edmonds and Maxwell-Hyslop, op. cit., Appendix IV: 'Order of Battle of a Division', p. 624. Bidwell and Graham, op. cit., p. 123 and Griffith, op. cit., pp. 120–29.

12 Edmonds and Maxwell-Hyslop, op. cit., p. 624.

13 Amongst the small number of divisions belonging to none of these categories was the 63rd (Royal Naval) Division. See Becke, *Order of Battle*, p. i.

14 Simkins, 'Four Armies', pp. 241–59.

15 Possibly the 36th Division had the most particular identity of all, being derived from a Protestant paramilitary formed to resist the policy of the British government. C. Falls, *The History of the 36th (Ulster) Division*, Mc Caw, Stevenson and Orr (1922), passim.

16 R.E. Priestley, *Breaking the Hindenburg Line: The Story of the 46th (North Midland) Division*, Fisher Unwin (1919), passim.

17 Griffith, *Battle Tactics*, pp. 80–82.

18 Simkins, op. cit., passim.

19 Falls, op. cit., pp. 184–5.

20 Though there are many British regimental and divisional histories, and even a few brigade histories, there are no corps histories except for the two Dominion Corps (the

status of which increasingly approached that of national field armies), the Indian Corps, which did not serve on the Western Front in the Hundred Days, and the Tank Corps, which was really an administrative organisation rather than a formation in its own right. The absence of corps histories is remarked upon in Becke, op. cit., p. ii.

21 The Canadian Corps' breaking of the Drocourt–Quéant Line on 2 September 1918 is a good example. See S.B. Schreiber, *Shock Army of the British Empire: The Canadian Corps in the Last 100 Days of the Great War*, Praeger (1997), pp. 71–86.

22 Fourth Army's operations to capture Mont St. Quentin–Péronne, 29 August–2 September 1918, were conceived by Sir John Monash, commanding the Australian Corps, and executed very largely by his troops. P.A. Pedersen, *Monash as Military Commander*, Melbourne (1985), pp. 262–72.

23 Farndale, op. cit., pp. 355–7.

24 I owe this point to A. Simpson, author of *The Evolution of Victory: British Battles on the Western Front 1914–1918*, Tom Donovan (1995), currently working on a PhD on the corps level of command at University College London.

25 Edmonds and Maxwell-Hyslop, op. cit., p. 623.

26 Ibid., p. 619.

27 See, for example, Fourth Army's artillery instructions for the attack on the Main Hindenburg Position on 29 September 1918 'Instructions for Operations', Fourth Army No. 273 (G), section 4, PRO WO 158/242.

28 H.A. Jones, *The War in the Air: Appendices*, Clarendon Press (1937), Appendix XXIV, pp. 116–23.

29 Becke, op. cit., p. 71.

30 G. Powell, *Plumer: the Soldier's General*, Leo Cooper (1990), pp. 153–9 and passim. L. Wolff, *In Flanders Fields: Passchendaele 1917*, Penguin (1979), pp. 161–2.

31 F. Maurice, *The Life of Lord Rawlinson of Trent*, Cassell (1928), pp. xv–xvi and 227–50. R. Prior and T. Wilson, *Command on The Western Front: The Military Career of Sir Henry Rawlinson*, Blackwell (1992), pp. 289–90.

32 GSO, *GHQ (Montreuil-sur-Mer)*, Philip Allan (1920), pp. 1–34.

33 Ibid., pp. 35–42.

34 J. Terraine, *Douglas Haig: The Educated Soldier*, Hutchinson (1963), pp. 1–65.

35 Haig to Kiggell, 20 July 1911, Kiggell Papers, Liddell Hart Centre for Military Archives (LHCMA), King's College London.

36 Ibid. and Pedersen, op. cit., pp. 254–5.

37 Haig's diary, 11 June 1915, R. Blake (ed.) *The Private Papers of Douglas Haig*, Eyre and Spottiswoode (1952), p. 95. Haig's diary, 23 Sep. 1918, PRO WO 256/36.

38 J. Terraine, *Douglas Haig: The Educated Soldier*, Hutchinson (1963), pp. 45, 46, 50.

39 Haig to Kiggell, 25 May 1911, Kiggell Papers, LHCMA.

40 Harris, op. cit., pp. 54–74.

41 The adverse criticisms of Haig contained in this paragraph are derived mainly from T. Travers, *The Killing Ground: The British Army, the Western Front and the Emergence of Modern Warfare*, Unwin Hyman (1987), passim, but esp. pp. 85–127, and from Prior and Wilson, op. cit., passim.

42 Terraine, op. cit., 384–445.

43 Ibid., pp. 385–8.

44 Becke, op. cit., p. 12. Haig's diary, 29 Aug., 1918, PRO WO 256/35.

45 Becke , op. cit., p. 12. Terraine, op. cit., p. 388.

46 On 7 Aug. 1918 Adv. GHQ took up two trains with a total length of about half a mile. Haig's diary, PRO WO 256/34. See also entry for 17 Oct. 1918, PRO WO 256/37.

47 Note Haig's comments to Byng on the night of 21 Aug., Haig's diary, PRO WO 256/35.

48 For example to the Australian Corps on 11 Aug. 1918, PRO WO 256/34 and to Canadian sappers on 9 Oct. 1918, PRO WO 256/37.

49 Edmonds and Maxwell-Hyslop, op. cit., p. 624. S.B. Schreiber, *Shock Army of the British Empire: The Canadian Corps in the Last Hundred Days of the Great War*, Praeger (1997), 17–32.

50 Amongst many references to the excellent physique of Dominion troops see A. Montgomery, *The Story of the Fourth Army in the Battles of the Hundred Days: August 8th to November 11th 1918*, Hodder and Stoughton (1919), p. 101.

51 C. Bean, *The Official History of Australia in the War of 1914–18, Vol. VI*, Angus and Robertson (1942), pp. 1084–6.

52 The most systematic analysis of the contribution of British (as opposed to Dominion) divisions at this period of the war is P. Simkins, 'Co-Stars or Supporting Cast? British Divisions in the "Hundred Days", 1918', in P. Griffith, *British Fighting Methods in the Great War*, Frank Cass (1996), pp. 50–69. On British-born Australian troops see E.M. Andrews, *The Anzac Illusion*, Cambridge University Press (1993), p. 44.

53 The peculiar cohesiveness of the Canadian Corps is discussed in Schreiber, op. cit., pp. 18–20, the shifting of British divisions between corps in Simkins, 'Co-stars', p. 60.

54 For the experiences of one good British division during the spring and early summer see E. Wyrall, *The History of the 19th Division 1914–1918*, Edward Arnold, pp. 132–249. On the reconstitution of divisions see Simkins, 'Co-stars', pp. 55–6.

55 Haig to Robertson (CIGS) 23 Nov. 1917, BCII/44, Fuller Papers, LHCMA.

56 On an NCO's use of a revolver in the Hundred Days see V.C. citation for Sgt. Statton in Montgomery, op. cit., p. 296.

57 Prior and Wilson, op. cit., pp. 41–2.

58 Farndale, op. cit., p. 367. Griffith, *Battle Tactics*, pp. 115–16.

59 Griffith, *Battle Tactics*, pp. 103–34.

60 Ibid., pp. 112–14.

61 Prior and Wilson, op. cit., p. 325.

62 Griffith, *Battle Tactics*, pp. 120–29.

63 Ibid., pp. 129–34, quotation from p. 79.

64 Table adapted from Griffith, *Battle Tactics*, p. 115.

65 Griffith, *Battle Tactics*, p. 78.

66 Ibid., p. 95. On the important French influence on British infantry tactics in 1916 see Lea? to Montgomery, 28 Nov. 1916, and attached 'Notes on an exercise carried out near CHALONS in the 4th French Army to demonstrate the new training of Infantry Units introduced in 1916', MM48/10, Montgomery-Massingberd Papers, LHCMA.

67 Griffith, *Battle Tactics*, pp. 96–7.

68 Lieutenant-General Sir William Furse to CIGS, 17 Dec. 1917, BCII/42, Fuller Papers, LHCMA.

69 The classic example of the use of this approach was the attack by 10th Canadian Infantry Brigade on Mont Houy near Valenciennes on 1 Nov. 1918. See S. Schreiber, op. cit., pp. 121–5.

70 See notes on the 'Fighting order' employed at Amiens. Edmonds, op. cit., p. 18, fn. 3. On numbers of grenades to be carried see Haig's diary, 28 Sep. 1918, PRO 256/ 36.

71 Farndale, op. cit., pp. 342, 348–349, 350, 355–357, 364–366.

72 Griffith, *Battle Tactics*, pp. 139–40. R.J. Lewendon, 'The Cutting of Barbed Wire Entanglements by Artillery Fire in World War I', *Royal Artillery Journal*, Vol. CXII, No. 2 (Sep. 1985), pp. 115–16.

73 J. Ewing, *The History of the 9th (Scottish) Division 1914–1919*, John Murray (1921), p. 178. J. Bailey, 'British Artillery in the Great War', in Griffith (ed.), *British Fighting Methods*, p. 29.

74 A.F. Becke, 'The Coming of the Creeping Barrage', *Journal of the Royal Artillery*, Vol. 58, 1931–1932, pp. 19–42. Ewing, op. cit., p. 107. Bidwell and Graham, op. cit., pp. 83–5.

75 Griffith, *Battle Tactics*, pp. 141–7. Montgomery, op. cit., p. 269.

76 Farndale, op. cit., pp. 341–5 and Bragg, Dowson and Hemming, *Artillery Survey in the First World War* (Field Survey Association) 1971, passim. Bidwell and Graham, op. cit., pp. 101–7.

77 Bidwell and Graham, op. cit., pp. 8–13, 91–3.

78 Ibid., pp. 104–8.

79 Ibid., pp. 108–9. Prior and Wilson, op. cit., pp. 292–5.

80 Bragg, Dowson and Hemming, op. cit., pp. 22–30.

81 Ibid., pp. 30–40. Griffith, *Battle Tactics*, pp. 153–4.

82 Griffith, *Battle Tactics*, pp. 156–8. L. Wolff, *In Flanders Fields: Passchendaele 1917*, Penguin (1979), pp. 75–214.

83 'Report on the Action at Neuve Chapelle', 22 March 1915, PRO WO 158/17.

84 Farndale, op. cit., pp. 216–30. Harris, op. cit., pp. 104–26.

85 The phrase is, of course, borrowed from the title of one the most famous German war memoirs: E. Juenger, *The Storm of Steel*, Chatto and Windus (1929).

86 Farndale, op. cit., p. 221.

87 Griffith, *Battle Tactics*, pp. 150–51.

88 Farndale, op. cit., pp. 341–2. J. Terraine, *The Smoke and the Fire*, Sidgwick and Jackson (1980), p. 219.

89 Table borrowed (with kind permission) and slightly adjusted from Griffith, *Battle Tactics*, p. 136.

90 Harris, op. cit., pp. 4–158.

91 D. Fletcher, 'The Origins of Armour', in J.P. Harris and F.H. Toase (eds), *Armoured Warfare*, Batsford (1990), pp. 5–26.

92 Harris, *Men, Ideas and Tanks*, pp. 176 and 179.

93 Fletcher, op. cit., passim.

94 Harris, *Men, Ideas and Tanks*, pp. 159–89.

95 S.F. Wise, *Canadian Airmen and the First World War*, University of Toronto Press (1981), 570–76.

96 Griffith, *Battle Tactics*, pp. 155–8.

97 J.H. Morrow, *The Great War in the Air: Military Aviation from 1909 to 1921*,

Smithsonian Institution Press (1993), p. 345.

98 Wise, op. cit., pp. 516–17, 522, 565–7. H.A. Jones, *The War in the Air, Vol. VI,* Clarendon Press (1937), pp. 444–5.

99 Wise, op. cit., pp. 518–76. Morrow, op. cit., pp. 301–10.

100 Wise, op. cit., pp. 575–6. G. Neumann, *The German Air Force in the Great War,* Hodder and Stoughton (n.d.), pp. 204–8. Morrow, op. cit., pp. 315–18.

101 R. Barker, *The Royal Flying Corps in France: From Mons to the Somme,* Constable (1994), p. 80.

102 Morrow, op. cit., pp. 310–29.

103 H.A. Jones, *The War in the Air: Appendices,* Appendix XXIV, 'Order of Battle of the Royal Air Force, France on 8th August 1918', pp. 116–23.

104 Ibid., Appendix XLVI, p. 172.

105 Ibid., Appendix XXXV, p. 160.

106 Bidwell and Graham, op. cit.,pp. 32–3.

107 S. Badsey, 'Cavalry and the Development of Breakthrough Doctrine', in Griffith (ed.), *British Fighting Methods,* pp. 138–74. Farndale, op. cit., p. 388.

108 Badsey, op. cit., pp. 152–62.

109 L.B. Haber, *The Poisonous Cloud: Chemical Warfare in the First World War,* Clarendon Press (1986), pp. 227–30 and passim.

110 Ibid., pp. 219–23. Griffith, op. cit., p. 119.

111 Haber, op. cit., pp. 223–7.

112 Ibid., pp. 259–83.

113 M. Occleshaw, *Armour against Fate: British Military Intelligence in the First World War,* Columbus (1989), passim.

114 J. Ferris, *The British Army and Signals Intelligence during the First World War,* Army Records Society/Alan Sutton (1992), pp. 1–24, 171–94, 329–32.

115 Falls, op. cit., pp. 137–9.

116 A.M. Henniker, *Transportation on the Western Front 1914–1918,* HMSO (1937), pp. 264–507. Amongst the elements of the BEF which performed important logistical services were the sappers, who provided much of the technical expertise, pioneers units who did much of the donkey work, the Army Service Corps, which provided lorry drivers and, of great importance, the Corps of Military Police who were responsible for traffic control. On the last of these see G. Sheffield, 'The Operational Role of British Military Police on the Western Front 1914–18', in P. Griffith, *British Fighting Methods.*

117 Griffith, *Battle Tactics,* pp. 179–91. For just one attempt to analyse the lessons of recent operations see 'Artillery Lessons Drawn from the Battle of the Somme', n.d., MM48/12, Montgomery-Massingberd Papers, LHCMA. For suicidal crudity of some German infantry attacks in the Hundred Days see Haig's diary 19 Sep. 1918, PRO WO 256/36.

118 'Fourth Army – Summary of Operations from 29 June to 5 July, 1918', Fourth Army No. G.S. 10/9, PRO WO 158/244 and Prior and Wilson, op. cit., pp. 289–300.

CHAPTER 3 PREPARING TO STRIKE

1 A.F. Becke, *History of the Great War: Order of Battle, Part 4,* HMSO (1945), p. 105, 111, 119.

2   Rawlinson to Sir Henry Wilson, 3 April 1918, Rawlinson Papers, National Army Museum.

3   P.A. Pedersen, *Monash as Military Commander*, Melbourne University Press (1985), p. 215.

4   F. Maurice, *The Life of Lord Rawlinson of Trent*, Cassell (1928), pp. 1–80.

5   J. Edmonds, *Military Operations France and Belgium 1918, Vol. IV*, HMSO (1947), p. 20.

6   R. Prior and T. Wilson, *Command on the Western Front*, Blackwell (1992), pp. 1–275.

7   Maurice, op. cit., 216. Becke, op. cit., p. 99.

8   Montgomery, *The Story of the Fourth Army in the Battles of the Hundred Days, August 8th to November 11th, 1918*, Hodder and Stoughton (1919), p. 5.

9   Rawlinson's diary 25 April–5 July, Pedersen, op. cit., p. 223 and Montgomery, op. cit., p. 11.

10 Edmonds, op. cit., p. 3.

11 Rawlinson to GHQ, 17 July 1918, 220. (G) , paras. 2 and 3, PRO WO 158/241.

12 Ibid., paras. 10 and 11.

13 Ibid., paras. 11–16.

14 Major-General J.H. Davidson (GHQ) to Rawlinson, OAD.900 23 July 1918, PRO WO 158/241.

15 Edmonds, op. cit., pp. 1–2.

16 Rawlinson to GHQ, 220 (G), 17 July 1918, PRO WO 158/241.

17 GHQ to Fourth Army, OAD 900/2, 28 July 1918, PRO WO 158/241.

18 Edmonds, op. cit., pp. 3–4.

19 'Record of a conference at Fourth Army HQ on 5 August 1918', OAD 900/13 and Lawrence to Rawlinson, OAD 900/14, PRO WO 158/241.

20 Montgomery, op. cit., pp. 16–17.

21 Ibid., p. 18.

22 'General Instructions', Fourth Army No. 32 (G), 31 July 1918, para. 1, PRO WO 158/241.

23 Montgomery, op. cit., p. 20, n. 1.

24 'General Instructions', para. 3 (h), PRO WO 158/241.

25 Montgomery, op. cit., p. 20.

26 Edmonds, op. cit., p. 23.

27 H.A. Jones, *The War in the Air, Vol. VI*, Clarendon Press (1937), pp. 433–6 and Montgomery, op. cit. pp. 24–5.

28 B. Rawling, *Surviving Trench Warfare: Technology and the Canadian Corps, 1914–1918*, University of Toronto Press (1992), passim.

29 C.E.W. Bean, *Official History of Australia in the War of 1914–18, Vol. VI: The AIF in France 1918*, Angus and Robertson (1942), pp. 483–4.

30 Montgomery, op. cit., p. 19. GHQ to the Armies, the RAF and the Tank Corps, OAD 900/1, para. 2 (a), PRO WO 158/241.

31 Ibid., para. 2 (b), (c) and (d).

32 Montgomery, op. cit., p. 19 and 'Operations to disengage the AMIENS–BRETEUIL Railway', Annexure to OAD 900/1, para. 5 (a), (b) and (c), 27 July 1919, PRO WO 158/241.

33   Edmonds, op. cit., p. 22.
34   Montgomery, op. cit., pp. 12–13.
35   'Fourth Army Artillery in the Battle of Amiens, August 8th 1918', section 1, Budworth Papers, Royal Artillery Institution, Woolwich.
36   Edmonds, op. cit., p. 23.
37   Jones, op. cit., pp. 434–6.
38   Edmonds, op. cit., p. 24.
39   Montgomery, op. cit., pp. 13–14.
40   Ibid., pp. 14–15.
41   Ibid., p. 22.
42   'General Instructions', Fourth Army No. 32 (G), Section 3, PRO WO 158/241.
43   Ibid. and 'Fourth Army Artillery in the Battle of Amiens, 8th August 1918', Sections 3–6.
44   Narrative of RAF operations on the Western Front, PRO AIR 1/677/21/13/1887, 96–9. Jones, op. cit., pp. 433–6. J.C. Slessor, *Airpower and Armies*, Oxford University Press (1936), pp. 169–70. 'General Instructions', Section 12.
45   Montgomery, op cit., p. 23
46   Anglesey, *A History of the British Cavalry 1816–1919, Vol. 8*, Leo Cooper (1997), pp. 223–9. Montgomery, op. cit., pp. 23–4.
47   Montgomery, op. cit., p. 23.
48   Bean, op. cit., p. 510 and Montgomery, p. 26.
49   G.H.F. Nichols, *The 18th Division in the Great War*, Blackwood (1922), pp. 338–41 and Montgomery, op. cit., p. 27.
50   Montgomery, p. 28 and Jones, op. cit., p. 433.
51   'Operations of the 2nd Canadian Division 1918, Battle of Amiens', Section III, para. 1, Vol. 65, Fourth Army Papers, Imperial War Museum and Montgomery, op. cit., p. 29.

CHAPTER 4   THE BATTLE OF AMIENS

1   J. Monash, *The Australian Victories in France in 1918*, Angus and Robertson (1936), pp. 100–1.
2   Ibid., p. 101. 'Fourth Army Artillery in the Battle of Amiens', section 3: 'Barrage Fire and Bombardment', Budworth Papers, Royal Artillery Institution. The 58th Division's 'Narrative of Operations: Period 8th to 13th August 1918', pp. 2–4, Fourth Army Papers Vol. 63, Imperial War Museum(IWM).
3   The 58th Division's 'Narrative', p. 4 and Montgomery, *The Fourth Army in the Battles of the Hundred Days*, Hodder and Stoughton (1919), p. 32.
4   Montgomery, op. cit., pp. 40–41.
5   Ibid., p. 41 and Bean, op. cit., pp. 526–43.
6   Montgomery, op. cit., pp. 41–2. A.D. Ellis, *The Story of the Fifth Australian Division*, Hodder and Stoughton (n.d.), pp. 329–31. 'Report on Operations of 17th (Armoured Car) Tank Battalion, 8th August 1918', p. 1, Fourth Army Papers, Vol. 65, IWM.
7   Montgomery, op. cit., pp. 41–2. Ellis, op. cit., pp. 331–2.

8   'Report on Operations of 17th (Armoured Car) Tank Battalion', pp. 1–2. Ellis, op. cit., p. 335. Montgomery, op. cit. p. 42. Bean, op. cit., pp. 577–84.

9   Bean, op. cit., pp. 574–600. Ellis, op. cit., p. 334. Montgomery, op. cit., p. 43.

10 'Operations of 2nd Canadian Division', pp. 1–3. '3rd Canadian Division, Report on Operations between the Avre and the Somme between Aug. 8th and Aug. 16th, 1918', pp. 1–3, Vol. 65, Fourth Army Papers, IWM and Montgomery, op. cit., p. 33.

11 '2nd Canadian Division', p. 5. '3rd Canadian Division', p. 6. Montgomery, op. cit., p. 33.

12 '2nd Canadian Division', pp. 6–7. Montgomery, pp. 35–8.

13 '3rd Canadian Division', pp. 6–7. Montgomery, pp. 33–5.

14 '2nd Canadian Division', pp. 7 and 8. '4th Canadian Division', pp. 1–7. Montgomery, pp. 38–9.

15 'Report on Operations of III Corps from July 1918 to October 1st 1918', pp. 3–9 and the 58th Division's, 'Narrative of Operations: Period 8th to 13th August 1918', pp. 4–9, Vol. 63, Fourth Army Papers.

16 A.B. Scott and P. Middleton-Brumwell, *History of the 12th (Eastern) Division in the Great War*, Nisbet (1923), pp. 190–94.

17 A good, and relatively recent, example of this sort of thing is Brereton Greenhous, '"It Was Chiefly a Canadian Battle": The Decision at Amiens, 8–11 August 1918', *Canadian Defence Quarterly Review*, Autumn 1988, pp. 73–80.

18 R. Butler, 'Report on the Operations of III Corps from July 1918 to October 1st 1918', Vol. 63, Fourth Army Papers. Montgomery, op. cit., p. 49.

19 See R. Prior and T. Wilson, *Command on the Western Front: The Military Career of Sir Henry Rawlinson 1914–18*, Blackwell (1992), pp. 325–6.

20 Anglesey, *A History of the British Cavalry 1816–1919, Vol. 8*, Leo Cooper (1997), pp. 229–43 and Montgomery, op. cit., pp. 44–6.

21 Edmonds, *Military Operations France and Belgium 1918, Volume IV*, HMSO (1947), p. 571. Anglesey, op. cit., p. 246 and Ellis, op. cit., p. 335.

22 Anglesey, op. cit., pp. 233–7. Bean, op. cit., p. 576.

23 Anon., *The War History of the Sixth Tank Battalion* (privately printed) 1919, pp. 117–40 and Anglesey, op. cit., pp. 234–5.

24 Montgomery, op. cit., pp. 50–51.

25 H.A. Jones, *The War in the Air Vol. VI*, Clarendon Press (1937), pp. 434–6. See also detailed narrative of RAF activity on the Western Front in PRO AIR 1/677/21/13/1887, pp. 99–104.

26 PRO AIR 1/677/21/13/1887, pp. 118–21. Jones, op. cit., pp. 437–41.

27 PRO AIR 1/677/21/13/1887, pp. 121B–6. Jones, op. cit., pp. 441–6 and S.F. Wise, *Canadian Airmen in the First World War*, University of Toronto (1980), pp. 530–34.

28 PRO AIR 1/677/21/13/1/1887, pp. 127–8.

29 Ibid., p. 128.

30 P. Griffith, *Battle Tactics of the Western Front: The British Army's Art of Attack 1916–18*, Yale (1994), p. 157.

31 PRO AIR 1/677/21/13/1887, pp. 128–9. Jones, op. cit., pp. 45–6.

32 E. Ludendorff, *The Concise Ludendorff Memoirs 1914–1918*, Hutchinson (n.d.), p. 290.

33 These statistics are compiled from Montgomery, op. cit., pp. 30–51. Working out

numbers of prisoners captured on a particular day presents problems. The most authoritative count was that conducted at corps cages, but it did not include wounded prisoners being treated in aid posts and hospitals. The number of prisoners which had passed through Fourth Army's corps cages up to 06.00 on 9 August was 281 officers and 12,134 other ranks. But these figures include only 76 (presumably lightly) wounded. Fourth Army 'Summary of Information No. 234', PRO WO 157/197.

34 Edmonds, op. cit., pp. 84 and 88–9.

35 Compiled from Montgomery, op. cit., pp. 30–51.

36 Edmonds, op. cit., p. 85.

37 Ibid. op. cit., p. 162.

38 On the achievement of surprise see Haig diary, 8 Aug. 1918, PRO WO 256/34 and Fourth Army's 'Summary of Information', 8 Aug. 1918, PRO WO 157/197. On artillery see Prior and Wilson, op. cit., p. 315, 'Fourth Army Artillery in the Battle of Amiens August 8th 1918, esp. section 4, 'Counter-Battery', Budworth Papers and E.C. Anstey, Unpublished history of the Royal Artillery on the Western Front, p. 269, Royal Artillery Institution.

39 For Fourth Army's estimate of German divisional strengths as under 3,000 effectives see Montgomery, op. cit., p. 11. The estimate of the numerical balance is from Prior and Wilson, op. cit., p. 316.

40 Edmonds, op. cit., pp. 48–50, Bean. op. cit., pp. 535, 560. Montgomery, op. cit., pp. 286–7, 294 and 296.

41 Haig's diary, Thursday 8 Aug. 1918, PRO WO 256/34.

42 Advanced GHQ to Fourth Army, O.A.D. 900/20, 8 Aug. 1918, PRO WO 158/241.

43 Fourth Army Operations Order 20 (G.), 8 Aug. 1918, PRO 158/241.

44 Edmonds, op. cit., pp. 86–7.

45 Prior and Wilson, op. cit., pp. 138–53.

46 Tank Corps records of tanks engaged day by day during the Hundred Days, Vol. 65, Fourth Army Papers, IWM and Edmonds, pp. 93 and 116–17.

47 Montgomery, op. cit., p. 57. Edmonds, op. cit., pp. 116–18. M. Kitchen, *The Silent Dictatorship: The Politics of the German High Command under Hindenburg and Ludendorff 1916–1918*, Croom Helm (1976), p. 250.

48 AIR 1/677/21/13/187, pp. 129–38. Wise, op. cit., pp. 240–41.

49 Edmonds, op. cit., p. 114 and G.W.L. Nicholson, *Canadian Expeditionary Force 1914–1919*, Queen's Printer, Ottawa (1962), pp. 410–14.

50 '4th Canadian Division', pp. 8–9. Prior and Wilson, op. cit., p. 330. Edmonds, op. cit., pp. 93–5 and 103. Butler, 'Report of Operations of III Corps', 10–13.

51 Nicholson, op. cit., 414. Montgomery, op. cit., p. 57. Edmonds, op. cit., p. 114.

52 Fourth Army Operations Orders 20 (G) and 20/1(G), 9 Aug. 1918, and G. 847. 10 Aug. 1918, PRO WO 158/241. Tank Corps record of number of tanks engaged day by day in the Hundred Days, Vol. 65, Fourth Army Papers, IWM.

53 Edmonds, op. cit., pp. 119 and 139.

54 Rawlinson's diary, 10 Aug. 1918, National Army Museum.

55 Edmonds, op. cit., p. 133.

56 Haig diary Saturday 10 Aug. 1918, WO 256/34. Edmonds, op. cit., pp. 135–6.

57 GHQ to British Fourth and Third and French First Armies, OAD 900/22, para. 1, 10

Aug. 1918, PRO WO 158/241.

58 Ibid., para. 3.

59 Fourth Army Operations Order, 20/3. (G), 10 Aug. 1918, PRO WO 158/241.

60 Tank Corps records, Fourth Army Papers, Vol. 65, IWM.

61 Anstey, op. cit., p. 271 and Edmonds, op. cit. pp. 142–3.

62 Edmonds, op. cit., p. 143.

63 Haig diary, Sunday 11 August 1918, PRO WO 256/34.

64 Rawlinson diary, Sunday 11 Aug. 1918, NAM.

65 Haig diary, 11 Aug.

66 Rawlinson diary, 11 Aug. and Edmonds, op. cit., p. 153.

67 Fourth Army Operations Order, 20/6 (G), 12 Aug. 1918, PRO WO 158/241.

68 Edmonds, op. cit., pp. 154–5. German accounts admit to the loss of 400 guns on the first day. The figures of gun captures quoted in the British official history appear somewhat bizarre. Fourth Army is credited with capturing only 240 guns in the whole battle while the French, whose efforts are generally condemned by Edmonds as feeble, are credited with 259.

69 Kitchen, op. cit., pp. 247–52. Edmonds, op. cit., pp. 161–2.

CHAPTER 5   WIDENING THE OFFENSIVE

1 GHQ to Fourth Army, OAD. 900/23, 12 Aug. 1918, PRO WO 158/241.

2 Fourth Army Operations Order, 20/6. (G), 12 Aug. 1918, PRO WO 158/241.

3 A. Montgomery, *The Story of the Fourth Army in the Battles of the Hundred Days: August 8th to November 11th 1918*, Hodder and Stoughton (1919), p. 64.

4 Rawlinson diary, 13 Aug. 1918, National Army Museum.

5 G.W.L. Nicholson, *Canadian Expeditionary Force 1914–1919*, Queen's Printer, Ottawa (1962), pp. 379–82. S.B. Schreiber, *The Shock Army of the British Empire: The Canadian Corps in the Last 100 Days of the Great War*, Praeger (1997), pp. 17–32.

6 Rawlinson diary, 14 Aug. 1918.

7 Haig diary, 14 Aug. 1918, PRO WO 256/34.

8 J. Edmonds, *Military Operations France and Belgium 1918, Vol. IV*, HMSO (1947), p. 171.

9 GHQ to Byng, 13 Aug. 1918, PRO WO 158/311. Haig had outlined this scheme to Byng at a meeting the previous day, Haig's diary, Monday 12 Aug., PRO WO 256/34.

10 GHQ to Horne, 14 Aug. 1918, OAD 907/1, PRO WO 158/191.

11 J. Williams, *Byng of Vimy, General and Governor General*, University of Toronto Press (1983), p. 243.

12 Third Army to its corps, 10 Aug. 1918, PRO WO 95/372. Edmonds, op. cit., p. 168.

13 Third Army War Diary, PRO WO 95/372.

14 Adv. GHQ to Fourth Army, OAD 907/2, 15 Aug. 1918, PRO WO 158/311.

15 Williams, op. cit., pp. 1–239.

16 Ibid., p. 242, Edmonds, op. cit., pp. 181 and 183–4. Anstey, Draft History of the Royal Artillery on the Western Front, p. 271, Anstey Papers, Royal Artillery Institution.

17 Williams, op. cit., p. 243. Edmonds, op. cit., p. 181.

18 See for example GHQ letter OAD 907/4, 18 Aug. 1918, PRO WO 158/241. 'Notes for Operation GZ (Bucquoy–Moyenneville)', Third Army No. G.S. 73/5, 18 Aug. 1918, PRO WO 95/372.

19 GHQ to the Armies, the Tank Corps and the Cavalry Corps, OAD 907/4, 18 Aug. 1918, WO 158/241.

20 Third Army No. G.S. 73/11, 19 Aug. 1918, PRO WO 95/372.

21 Third Army No. G.S. 73/5, 18 Aug. 1918, PRO WO 95/372.

22 Third Army Artillery Instructions No. 39, 14 Oct., PRO WO 95/372. These instructions were issued before the German withdrawal from the Bucquoy–Hamel salient but their basic principles appear to have remained in force for 21 August.

23 Edmonds, p. 180 and Anstey, p. 271.

24 Anstey, op. cit., p. 271 and Third Army Artillery Instructions No. 39, PRO WO 95/372.

25 Third Army No. G.S. 73/1, 18 Aug. 1918 and Major-General Louis Vaughan (MGGS) to Haldane, Third Army No. G.S. 71/2, para. 3, 14 Aug. 1918, PRO WO 95/372.

26 'Previous Orders and Dispositions for the Army Offensive of the 21st August 1918', Third Army War Diary, Aug. 1918, and Third Army to Major-General R.L. Mullens, commanding 1st Cavalry Division, 18 Aug. 1918, PRO WO 95/372.

27 Third Army to Mullens, 18 Aug. 1918, PRO WO 95/372.

28 'Summary of Operations of Third Army from 21st August 1918 to 30th September 1918, Previous Orders and Dispositions', PRO WO 95/372.

29 Haig diary 19 Aug., PRO WO 256/35.

30 H.A. Jones, *The War in the Air, Vol. VI*, Clarendon Press (1937), pp. 470–71.

31 Ibid., pp. 471–2 and 'Summary of Operations by 3rd Brigade RAF from 21st August 1918 to 30th September 1918 (inclusive)', PRO WO 95/372.

32 Edmonds, op. cit., pp. 186, 188–9, Third Army War Diary, 21 August and Third Army 'Summary of Operations from 21st August 1918 to 30th September 1918', PRO WO 95/372.

33 Edmonds, op. cit., pp. 186–7 and 'Summary of Operations', p. 4 and Third Army War Diary, 21 Aug. PRO 95/372.

34 Edmonds, op. cit., pp. 188–92. Anstey, op. cit., p. 271, D. Jerrold, *The Royal Naval Division*, Hutchinson (n.d.), pp. 303–4. F.P. Gibbon, *The 42nd (East Lancashire) Division*, Country Life (1920), pp. 157–8.

35 Edmonds, op. cit., pp. 192–4.

36 'Summary of Operations', pp. 4–5 and Third Army War Diary, 21 Aug. 1918, PRO WO 95/372.

37 'Summary of Operations', p. 3.

38 Edmonds, op. cit., pp. 195–6, 204–5.

39 Appendix 2 to 'Summary of Operations', PRO 95/372. Haig diary, Wednesday 21 Aug. 1918, PRO WO 256/35.

40 Third Army No. G.S., 73/40, 21 Aug. 1918, PRO WO 95/372.

41 Haig diary, 21 Aug. 1918, PRO WO 256/35 and Edmonds, pp. 173–5 and 194.

42 Haig diary, 21 Aug. 1918, PRO WO 256/35.

43 Edmonds, op. cit., pp. 195–6, 204–6. 'Summary of Operations', pp. 5–6.

44 Montgomery, op. cit., pp. 64–6, 85.

45 Ibid., pp. 73–5.

46 Ibid., p. 74.

47 Ibid., pp. 74–7 and G.H.F. Nichols, *The 18th Division in the Great War*, Blackwood (1922), pp. 357–65.

48 Montgomery, op. cit., pp. 77–8.

49 Edmonds, op. cit., p. 220. Edmonds suggests that Byng replanned the Third Army attack on the *afternoon* of 22 August in response to a formal instruction from Haig but this does not accord with the sequence of orders issued by Third Army, the last of which was around midday. See n. 51, below.

50 Ibid. and Third Army No. G.S. 73/46, 22 Aug. 1918, PRO WO 95/372.

51 Handwritten note on 'C' Form (Messages and Signals) sent from Third Army at 11.45 and received at V Corps at 12.05, 22 Aug. 1918, modifying GS 73/46, PRO WO 95/372.

52 Montgomery, op. cit., pp. 78–9.

53 Narrative of RAF operations on the Western Front in AIR 1/677/21/13/1887, pp. 178–85 and Jones, op. cit., pp. 472–7.

54 'Summary of Operations', pp. 6–7, PRO WO 95/372. Edmonds, op. cit., p. 228.

55 'Summary of Operations', p. 7. Edmonds, op. cit., p. 221.

56 Edmonds, op. cit., pp. 222–8.

57 Third Army War Diary, 23 Aug., PRO WO 95/372. Edmonds, op. cit., pp. 225–7.

58 Anstey, op. cit., p. 273.

59 R. Butler, 'Report on Operations of III Corps from July 1918 to October 1st 1918', pp. 22–3, Vol. 63, Fourth Army Papers, Imperial War Museum. Nichols, op. cit., pp. 366–74. Edmonds, op. cit., p. 233.

60 Montgomery, op. cit., pp. 78–82.

61 Jones, op. cit., pp. 474–8. 'Summary of Operations by 3rd Brigade RAF', PRO WO 95/372.

62 Tank Corps record of operations in the Hundred Days, Vol. 65, Fourth Army Papers, IWM and V Tank Brigade, 'Supplementary Report', 1 Sep. 1918, answer to question 1 of a Tank Corps questionnaire, TCOIV/5, Fuller Papers, Liddell Hart Centre for Military Archives, King's College London.

63 Haig diary, Friday 23 Aug., PRO WO 256/35.

64 Appendix 2 to 'Summary of Operations of Third Army', PRO WO 95/372.

CHAPTER 6 THE ADVANCE TO THE HINDENBURG LINE

1 Haig to the Armies, 22 Aug. 1918, OAD 911, PRO WO 158/241.

2 Haig's diary, 23 Aug. 1918, PRO WO 256/35.

3 'Summary of Operations of Third Army from 21 August 1918 to 30 September 1918', PRO WO 95/372. Fourth Army, 'Summary of Information No. 240', para. 5, 24 Aug. 1918, PRO WO 157/197. Haig's diary 24 Aug., PRO WO 256/35.

4 Third Army Intelligence Summary, 27/28 August 1918, PRO WO 157/164.

5 GHQ offered some qualification almost immediately in a relatively cautious note by Lawrence: 'Offensive Action', OAD 912, 23 Aug. 1918, PRO WO 158/241.

6 Note the 18th Division's experience in the Trones Wood operation of 27 August.

G.H.F. Nichols, *The 18th Division in the Great War*, Blackwood (1922), pp. 375–83.

7   J.E. Edmonds, *Military Operations France and Belgium 1918, Vol. IV*, HMSO (1947), pp. 310–13.

8   'Summary of Operations of Third Army', PRO WO 95/372. Edmonds, op. cit., pp. 263–87.

9   Rawlinson's diary, 25 Aug. 1918, National Army Museum (NAM). Haig's diary, 25 Aug. 1918, PRO WO 256/35.

10   P.A. Pedersen, *Monash as Military Commander*, Melbourne University Press (1985), p. 262.

11   R. Prior and T. Wilson, *Command on the Western Front: The Military Career of Sir Henry Rawlinson 1914–18*, Blackwell (1992), pp. 341–2.

12   'Summary of Operations of Third Army', PRO WO 95/372. Edmonds, op. cit., pp. 338–45.

13   Prior and Wilson, op. cit., p. 342.

14   The Trones Wood action of 27 August is an example of the progressive delegation of control of a battle from Lieutenant-General to Lieutenant-Colonel within a few hours. Nichols, op. cit., pp. 375–83.

15   A. Montgomery, *The Fourth Army in the Battles of the Hundred Days: 8th August to November 11th 1918*, Hodder and Stoughton (1919), p. 87.

16   Prior and Wilson, op. cit., p. 345.

17   Nichols, op. cit., pp. 380–81, Montgomery, op. cit., pp. 85 and 104–5, Edmonds, op. cit., p. 251.

18   Edmonds, op. cit., p. 314. Montgomery, op. cit., p. 88.

19   'Annexe to Fourth Army Summary Dated 15 September: Captured Documents', PRO WO 157/198.

20   Lawrence to the Armies, 1 Sep. 1918, PRO WO 158/832. J.P. Harris, *Men, Ideas and Tanks: British military thought and armoured forces, 1903–1939*, Manchester University Press (1995), pp. 183–7.

21   'Summary of Operations of Third Army, Appendix 6, Operations by 3rd Bde RAF from 21st August to 30th September 1918', PRO WO 95/372. H.A. Jones, *The War in the Air, Vol. VI*, Oxford (1937), pp. 482–4.

22   GHQ to Horne, OAD 907/1, 14 Aug. 1918 and OAD 907/2, 16 Aug. 1918, PRO WO 158/191.

23   First Army to Adv. GHQ, 17 Aug. 1918, PRO WO 158/191.

24   GHQ to Horne, OAD 907/13, 24 Aug., PRO WO 158/191.

25   Haig's diary, 25 Aug. 1918, PRO WO 256/35.

26   G.W.L. Nicholson, *The Canadian Expeditionary Force 1914–1919*, Queen's Printer, Ottawa (1962), pp. 426–7.

27   On Horne see F. Maurice in the Dictionary of National Biography. For the deception plan see First Army C.S. 1331/1, PRO WO 158/191.

28   'First Army Weekly Summary of Operations: 23/8/18 to 30/8/18', PRO WO 95/21. Nicholson, op. cit., pp. 427–8.

29   Haig's diary, 26 Aug. 1918, PRO WO 236/35.

30   Nicholson, op. cit., pp. 428–9.

31 S.F. Wise, *Canadian Airmen in the First World War*, University of Toronto Press (1981), pp. 552–3.

32 Nicholson, op. cit., pp. 431–2.

33 Ibid., p. 432.

34 Edmonds, op. cit., pp. 356–7.

35 GHQ to First, Third and Fourth Armies, 29 Aug. 1918, OAD 907/16, PRO WO 158/241.

36 Fourth Army to its corps, 30 Aug. 1918, PRO WO 158/241.

37 Rawlinson's diary, 30 Aug., NAM.

38 Edmonds, op. cit., p. 357 and Montgomery, op. cit., pp. 97–8.

39 Montgomery, op. cit., pp. 98–9.

40 Ibid., pp. 99–100.

41 Montgomery, op. cit., pp. 101 and 103. Bean, *Official History of Australia in the Great War, Vol. VI*, Angus and Robertson (1942), p. 832.

42 Montgomery, op. cit., pp. 103–4.

43 Ibid., pp. 105–6.

44 A.D. Ellis, *The Story of the Fifth Australian Division*, Hodder and Stoughton (n.d.), pp. 349–50. Montgomery, op. cit., pp. 104–5.

45 Ibid., pp. 108 and 111.

46 Nicholson, op. cit., pp. 432–6.

47 Ibid., p. 434.

48 'Notes on Conference at Canadian Corps Headquarters, 29th August 1918', First Army G.S. 1376/30 and 'Notes on Conference . . . 30th August 1918', First Army G.S. 176/32, PRO WO 95/178.

49 Canadian Corps Operations Order No. 234, 31 Aug. 1918, PRO WO 95/ 179. Edmonds, op. cit., pp. 396–7.

50 Nicholson, op. cit., p. 435.

51 Edmonds, op. cit., pp. 397–8. S.B. Schreiber, *Shock Army of the British Empire: The Canadian Corps in the Last 100 Days of the Great War*, Praeger (1997), p. 80.

52 Jones, op. cit., pp. 494–5. Nicholson, op. cit., p. 435.

53 Wilson to Haig, 31 Aug. 1918, quoted in Edmonds, op. cit., p. 383.

54 Haig's diary, 1 Sep. 1918, PRO WO 256/36, quoted in Edmonds, op. cit., p. 383.

55 Haig's diary, 31 Aug. 1918, PRO WO 256/35.

56 Haig's diary, 1 Sep. 1918, PRO WO 256/36.

57 Edmonds, op. cit., p. 389.

58 Nicholson, op. cit., pp. 436–40.

59 S. Wise, *Canadian Airmen in the First World War*, University of Toronto Press (1980), pp. 554.

60 Nicholson, op. cit., p. 440.

61 'Summary of Operations of Third Army', PRO WO 95/372. C. Headlam, *History of the Guards Division in the Great War 1915–1918, Vol. 2*, John Murray (1924), pp. 146–8.

62 GHQ to the Armies, 3 Sep. 1918, OAD 915, PRO WO 158/191.

63 Nicholson, op. cit., p. 44. Montgomery, op. cit., pp. 119–20. 'Fourth Army Weekly Appreciation for Period from September 7th To 13th', and 'Weekly Appreciation from

September 14th to 20th', PRO WO 157/198.

64   H.A. Jones, *The War in the Air, Vol. VI*, Oxford (1937), p. 500.

65   Haig's diary, 3 Sep. 1918, PRO WO 256/36.

66   Edmonds, op. cit., pp. 467–8.

67   Annexe to Third Army Intelligence Summary No. 1153, 6 Sep. 1918, PRO WO 157/165. 'Fourth Army Weekly Appreciation for Period from September 7th to 13th', and 'Weekly Appreciation from September 14th to 20th', PRO WO 157/198.

68   GHQ to the Armies, 8 Sep. 1918, OAD 915/2, PRO WO 158/191.

69   Edmonds, op. cit., pp. 443–57.

70   GHQ to First Army, OAD 917, PRO WO 158/191.

71   J. Ferris (ed.), *The British Army and Signals Intelligence during the First World War*, Army Records Society/Alan Sutton (1992), p. 331.

72   Byng to GHQ, 9 Sep. 1918, PRO WO 158/311.

73   Horne to GHQ, 11 Sep. 1918, PRO WO 158/191.

74   Rawlinson to GHQ, 11 Sep. 1918, PRO WO 95/43.

75   Prior and Wilson, op. cit., pp. 346–8 and Rawlinson to GHQ, 11 Sep. 1918, PRO WO 95/43

76   Haig's diary, 10 Sep. 1918, PRO WO 256/36.

77   Haig's diary, 10 Sep. 1918, PRO WO 256/36 and Wilson's diary quoted in J. Terraine, *To Win a War: 1918, the Year of Victory*, Sidgwick and Jackson (1978), p. 151.

78   Edmonds, op. cit., p. 469.

79   Ibid., pp. 469–72 and E. Wyrall, *The History of the 62nd (West Riding) Division, Vol. II*, John Lane (n.d.), pp. 46–59.

80   'Offensive Operations Undertaken by IX Corps from 18th September 1918 to 11th November 1918', p. 1, Vol. 63, Fourth Army Papers, Imperial War Museum(IWM). Montgomery, op. cit., p. 119.

81   Edmonds, op. cit., p. 475. Fourth Army to its corps, 20/18 (G), 13 Sep. and 20/19 (G) 14 Sep. 1918, PRO WO 158/242. The account of the planning and execution of Fourth Army's attack of 18 September by the generally excellent historical partnership of Prior and Wilson (op. cit., pp. 351–7) seems, to the present writer, to be misleading in one important respect. Prior and Wilson present the aim of the operation as being the capture of the Advanced Hindenburg System. In reality, that position was merely the 'line of exploitation'. This leads them to present the III Corps attack as a near total failure (op. cit., p. 359) though it achieved a considerable degree of success in terms of the objectives actually set for it.

82   Information given here of German strength facing Fourth Army in mid-September is from Montgomery, op. cit., p. 121. Montgomery obviously believed Fourth Army to have had a hefty numerical superiority on its front up to and including 18 September. Estimates quoted of British attacking strength on 18 September are those of Prior and Wilson, op. cit., p. 352. These seem reasonable. But the present writer strongly doubts Prior's and Wilson's conclusion, apparently drawn from Edmonds, op. cit., p. 476, that Fourth Army had no significant numerical superiority in the attack of 18 September. Edmonds' statement of German divisions on his page 476 probably includes some facing Third Army. Fourth Army identified only eight divisions immediately facing itself on 18 September.

83 Edmonds, op. cit., p. 477. Montgomery, op. cit., p. 123.

84 Edmonds, op. cit., p. 477. Montgomery, op. cit., pp. 124–5.

85 Montgomery, op. cit., p. 125. Edmonds, op. cit., pp. 479 and 490. Jones, op. cit., pp. 505–6. Prior and Wilson, op. cit., pp. 353–7, indicate that no machine-gun barrages were fired in IX Corps, though this contradicts Montgomery, op. cit., p. 125, fn. 1.

86 Montgomery, op. cit., pp. 125–6. Edmonds, op. cit., pp. 476–94.

87 Montgomery, op. cit., p. 135.

88 'Offensive Operations Undertaken by IX Corps', pp. 5–7, Vol. 63, Fourth Army Papers, IWM.

89 Rawlinson's diary, 16 Sep. 1918. Prior and Wilson, op. cit., pp. 354 and 357.

90 Haig's diary, 19 Sep. 1918.

91 Edmonds, op. cit., pp. 489 and 494.

92 Wilson to Haig, 19 Sep. 1918, quoted in Terraine, op. cit., p. 150.

93 This fact is stated in Edmonds, op. cit., p. 496 though, in an unusual factual slip, the official history describes Marwitz as the Seventeenth Army commander, an error not made on other pages.

94 Rawlinson's diary 18 and 19 September and Rawlinson to GHQ, Fourth Army 270 (G), 19 Sep. 1918, PRO WO 158/242.

CHAPTER 7   THE GENERAL OFFENSIVE

1 Henry Wilson's diary, 11 Aug., quoted in B.H. Liddell Hart, *Foch, The Man of Orleans*, Eyre and Spottiswoode (1931), p. 354. Haig mentions his wish to 'get a decision this autumn' in his own diary on 21 Aug., PRO WO 256/35.

2 GHQ to Army commanders, OAD 926/4, 25 Sep. 1918, PRO WO 158/242.

3 Haig's diary, 27 Aug. 1918, PRO WO 256/35.

4 Liddell Hart, op. cit., pp. 355–6.

5 Ibid., p. 356.

6 Haig's diary, 12 Aug., 19 Aug., 25 Aug. 1918, PRO WO 256/34.

7 Ibid., 7 Aug. 1918, PRO WO 256/34.

8 Ibid., 27 Aug. 1918, PRO WO 256/35.

9 Haig's diary, 29 Aug., PRO WO 158/35. J. Pershing, *My Experiences in the World War*, Hodder and Stoughton (1931), pp. 568–78. Liddell Hart, op. cit., pp. 356–9.

10 Pershing, op. cit., pp. 577–8. The switching of the main American effort from the St Mihiel Salient–Mars La Tour–Metz area to the Argonne–Meuse sector still gives rise to some controversy in the United States. See J. Hallas, *Squandered Victory: The American First Army at St Mihiel*, Praeger (1997), passim.

11 Pershing to Foch, 31 Aug. 1918, quoted in Pershing, op. cit., pp. 572–3.

12 D. Smythe, *Pershing, General of the Armies*, Indiana University Press (1986), pp. 179–89. Pershing, op. cit., p. 591.

13 Haig's diary, 9 Sep. 1918, PRO WO 256/36.

14 See for example Rawlinson to GHQ, 19 Sep. 1918, PRO WO 158/242.

15 GHQ to Army commanders, 22 Sep., OAD 923, PRO WO 158/242.

16 GHQ to Army commanders, OAD 926/4, 25 Sep. 1918, PRO WO 158/242.

17 Liddell Hart, op. cit., pp. 364–6. A more recent work puts American numerical supe-

riority in infantry in the Meuse–Argonne at seven to one. S. Schreiber, *Shock Army of the British Empire: The Canadian Corps in the Last 100 Days of the Great War*, Praeger (1997), p. 107.

18   Haig's diary, 22 Aug. 1918, PRO WO 256/35.

19   Quoted in Liddell Hart, op. cit., p. 363.

20   Haig's diary, 21 Sep. 1918, PRO WO 256/36.

21   Smythe, op. cit., pp. 190–201. J. Edmonds and R. Maxwell-Hyslop, *Military Operations France and Belgium 1918, Vol. V*, HMSO (1947), pp. 9–10.

22   Smythe, op. cit., p. 197.

23   Ibid., pp. 199–200.

24   Liddell Hart, op. cit., p. 371.

25   Nicholson, *The Canadian Expeditionary Force 1914–1919*, Queen's Printer, Ottawa (1962), pp. 440–41.

26   Nicholson, op. cit., p. 442. Haig's diary, 15 Sep. 1918, PRO WO 256/36.

27   Nicholson, op. cit., pp. 442–3.

28   Ibid., pp. 443–4.

29   Ibid., p. 444 and Edmonds, op. cit., pp. 19–20.

30   Haig's diary, 25 Sep. 1918, PRO WO 256/36.

31   Nicholson, op. cit., p. 443, fn.

32   Edmonds and Maxwell-Hyslop, op. cit., pp. 30–32.

33   H.A. Jones, *The War in the Air, Vol. VI*, Oxford (1937), pp. 513–17.

34   Nicholson, op. cit., pp. 445–6.

35   Nicholson, op. cit., pp. 446–7. The account given here of the work of tanks in support of the Canadians is taken from Nicholson. Schreiber, op. cit., p. 103 casts some doubt on it.

36   Edmonds and Maxwell-Hyslop, op. cit., pp. 33–45. Headlam, *The Guards Division in the Great War 1915–1918, Vol. II*, John Murray (1924), pp. 166–79. D. Jerrold, *The Hawke Battalion*, Ernest Benn (1925), pp. 218–19. E. Wyrall, *The History of the 62nd (West Riding) Division, Vol. II*, John Lane (n.d.), pp. 73–83.

37   Jones, op. cit., pp. 518–21.

38   Edmonds and Maxwell-Hyslop, op. cit., p. 46. Jones, op. cit., pp. 521–3.

39   J. Edmonds, *Military Operations France and Belgium 1918, Vol. IV*, HMSO (1947), pp. 427–36. J. Ewing, *History of the 9th Scottish Division*, John Murray (1921), p. 338.

40   C. Harington, *Plumer of Messines*, John Murray (1935), passim.

41   'Second Army Operations from 28th September to 13th October 1918', sections 1 and 2, PRO WO 158/218. Edmonds, op. cit., pp. 60–63.

42   'Second Army Operations', section 4. Edmonds and Maxwell-Hyslop, op. cit., p. 64.

43   'Second Army Operations from 28th September to 13th October 1918', sections 1–4. Edmonds and Maxwell-Hyslop, op. cit., p. 64.

44   G. Powell, *Plumer, The Soldier's General*, Leo Cooper (1990), pp. 272–5. Edmonds and Maxwell-Hyslop, op. cit., p. 60. 'Second Army Operations'.

45   'Second Army Operations', Ewing, op. cit., pp. 339–41, H.M. Davson, *The History of the 35th Division in the Great War*, Sifton Praed (1936), pp. 257–60. S. Gillon, *The Story of the 29th Division: A Record of Gallant Deeds*, Nelson (1926), pp. 205–9.

46   'Second Army Operations', section 6.

47 'Second Army Operations', section 5. Jones, op. cit., pp. 532–3.

48 R. Asprey, *The German High Command*, Warner (1991), pp. 467–8. M. Kitchen, *The Silent Dictatorship*, Croom Helm (1976), pp. 254–6.

CHAPTER 8   BREAKING THE HINDENBURG LINE

1 For Rawlinson's initial analysis of the 'Advanced Hindenburg System' and the 'Main Hindenburg System' see Rawlinson to GHQ No. 265 (G), 11 Sep. 1918, PRO WO 95/438. For Fourth Army operations of 18 Sep. see A.A. Montgomery, *The Story of the Fourth Army in the Battles of the Hundred Days*, Hodder and Stoughton (1919), pp. 126–35.

2 Rawlinson to Haig, 19 Sep. 1918, PRO WO 158/242.

3 Haig's diary 18 and 19 Sep. 1918, PRO WO 256/35.

4 Ibid. and Rawlinson diary 18–28 Sep. 1918, Rawlinson Papers, National Army Museum(NAM).

5 Montgomery, op. cit., pp. 136–7.

6 Haig's diary, Tuesday 24 Sep. 1918, PRO WO 256/36.

7 'IX Corps Narrative of Operations', p. 11, Vol. 63, Fourth Army Papers, Imperial War Museum(IWM).

8 C.E.W. Bean, *The A.I.F. in France 1918*, Angus and Robertson (1942), pp. 941–3.

9 Monash to Fourth Army HQ, 18 Sep. 1918, Vol. 69, Fourth Army Papers, IWM.

10 Bean, op. cit., pp. 941–3.

11 Ibid. and Montgomery, op. cit., p. 151.

12 Edmonds, *Military Operations, France and Belgium 1918, Vol. V*, HMSO (1947), p. 97.

13 'IX Corps Narrative of Operations', p. 12, Vol. 63, Fourth Army Papers, IWM, and Montgomery, op. cit., pp. 147–9.

14 Montgomery, op. cit., pp. 148–9.

15 B.H. Liddell Hart, *The Tanks, Vol. I*, Cassell (1959), p. 183. Montgomery, op. cit.

16 Montgomery, op. cit., p. 149.

17 Monash to Fourth Army HQ, 18 Sep. 1918, Vol. 69, Fourth Army Papers.

18 Ibid. and R. Prior and Wilson, *Command on the Western Front: The Military Career of Sir Henry Rawlinson*, Blackwell (1992), pp. 360–62.

19 Monash to Fourth Army HQ, 18 Sep. 1918, Vol. 69, Fourth Army Papers, IWM, and Prior and Wilson, op. cit., pp. 360–62.

20 'IX Corps Narrative of Operations', pp. 11–18. Monash, op. cit., pp. 212–17.

21 P.A. Pedersen, *Monash as Military Commander*, Melbourne University Press (1985), p. 282.

22 Fourth Army Orders 20/23 (G), 22 Sep. 1918, PRO 158/242.

23 Montgomery, op. cit., p. 152.

24 Monash to Fourth Army HQ, 18 Sep. 1918, pp. 3 and 4, Vol. 69, Fourth Army Papers, IWM. 'Instructions for Operations', Fourth Army No. 273 (G) Section 5, PRO WO 158/242, Montgomery, op. cit., p. 155 and Tank Corps report in Vol. 65, Fourth Army Papers, IWM.

25 Montgomery, op. cit., pp. 156–7. GHQ to Fourth Army, OAD 928, 29 Sep. 1918, PRO WO 158/242.

26 H.A. Jones, *The War in the Air, Vol. VI*, Clarendon (1937), pp. 523–4.

27 Montgomery, op. cit., p. 138.

28 Montgomery, op. cit., p. 131.

29 Haig diary, 22 Sep. 1918, PRO WO 256/36.

30 Rawlinson to GHQ, 256/1 (G) 23 Sep. 1918, PRO WO 158/242.

31 Ibid., PRO WO 158/242.

32 Montgomery, op. cit., pp. 144–5.

33 Bean, op. cit., pp. 955–6.

34 Montgomery, op. cit., pp. 153–4.

35 Ibid., 154.

36 Bean, op. cit., p. 958.

37 Montgomery, op. cit., p. 154.

38 Ibid., p. 153–4.

39 Ibid., p. 150.

40 Ibid., p. 157 and Jones, op. cit., p. 526.

41 Montgomery, op. cit., p. 157.

42 Ibid., p. 163.

43 Ibid., p. 163.

44 Montgomery, op. cit., pp. 166–7 and Pedersen, op. cit., p. 289.

45 Edmonds, op. cit., pp. 108–9.

46 Montgomery, op. cit., pp. 162–6 and A.D. Ellis, *The Story of the Fifth Australian Division*, Hodder and Stoughton (n.d.), pp. 367–376.

47 R.E. Priestley, *Breaking the Hindenburg Line: The Story of the 46th North Midland Division*, Fisher Unwin (1919), p. 143. 'Account of the Part Taken by the 46th Division in the Battle of Bellenglise on the 29th September 1918', 46th Division G. 114/24, 7 Oct. 1918 and 'IX Corps Narrative of Operations', pp. 16–17, Vol. 63, Fourth Army Papers, IWM.

48 Priestley, op. cit., p. 58 and 'IX Corps Narrative of Operations', pp. 16–19. 'Account of the Part Taken by the 46th Division', passim.

49 'Account of Part Taken by the 46th Division', pp. 2 and 3.

50 Priestley, op. cit., p. 72.

51 Liddell Hart, op. cit., p. 190.

52 'IX Corps Narrative of Operations', p. 18.

53 'Account of the Part Taken by the 46th Division', p. 4. Priestley, op. cit., p. 78.

54 Edmonds, op. cit., p. 101.

55 Montgomery, op. cit., pp. 167–8.

56 Rawlinson's diary 29 Sep. 1918 and Montgomery, op. cit., p. 169.

57 'Telephone message from Sir Henry Rawlinson to General Davidson', 4.20 p.m., 29.9.18, PRO WO 158/242.

58 Rawlinson's diary, 29 Sep. 1918, NAM.

59 Priestley, op. cit., pp. 50, 51 and 75. Prior and Wilson, in their generally excellent account of Rawlinson's Western Front career, are incorrect where they state that: 'German artillery retaliation is not mentioned by any of the accounts, indicating that

the British counter-batteries had done their job'. Prior and Wilson, op. cit., p. 373. Priestley indicates that German artillery retaliation was 'comparatively small' but attributes this in large measure to the fog.

60   Priestley, op. cit., p. 76.

61   Ibid., p. 73.

62   Ibid., p. 78.

63   Haig reckoned that: 'Had the German army been in a good state of moral the position would have been impregnable.' Haig diary, Tuesday 15 Oct. 1918, PRO WO 256/37.

64   The notion that by August 1918 the BEF (or at least Fourth Army) had a 'weapons system' or 'winning formula', irresistible by even the best German troops, seems to be central to the analysis of Hundred Days' battles by the historians Robin Prior and Trevor Wilson. (See Prior and Wilson, op cit., pp. 320, 323, 379–80.) It is quite clear that very considerable advances in the art of war had been made in the BEF by late 1918. But the notion of a 'winning formula' is questionable. If there was a 'formula' the efficacy of one of its most crucial ingredients, counter-battery fire, still depended on a factor outside human control – the weather. Prior and Wilson give relatively little attention to this intractable and incalculable factor which much diminished the effectiveness of BEF artillery during the autumn of 1918. They also appear to wish to play down the importance of morale, a factor which contemporaries stressed but which cannot be quantified.

65   Montgomery, op. cit., pp. 168–9. All but about 200 of Fourth Army's prisoners on 29 September were taken by IX Corps, a fact which points up the relative failure of Monash's corps in the tunnel sector.

CHAPTER 9   THE END IN SIGHT

1   R. Asprey, *The German High Command at War*, Warner (1991), pp. 459–68. M. Kitchen, *The Silent Dictatorship: The Politics of the German High Command under Hindenburg and Ludendorff*, Croom Helm (1976), pp. 254–6.

2   Kitchen, op. cit., p. 261.

3   D. Smythe, *Pershing, General of the Armies*, Indiana University Press (1986), pp. 198–9.

4   'Second Army Operations from 28th September to 13th October, 1918', esp. sections 12 and 28, PRO WO 158/218.

5   B. Liddell Hart, *Foch, the Man of Orleans*, Eyre and Spottiswoode (1931), pp. 374–5.

6   G. Nicholson, *The Canadian Expeditionary Force*, Queen's Printer, Ottawa (1962), pp. 448–53.

7   Third Army's 'War Diary 1–5 October', PRO WO 95/374.

8   Rawlinson's diary, 29–30 September, National Army Museum, (NAM).

9   Fourth Army, 'Summary of Information, 1st October 1918', PRO WO 157/199.

10   Rawlinson's diary, 30 Sep. 1918, NAM.

11   Fourth Army's 'Summary of Information, 1st October 1918', p. 7, section 1, PRO WO 158/199.

12   Fourth Army's 'Summary of Information, 3rd October 1918', PRO WO 158/199.

13   Ibid.

14 Rawlinson's diary, 3 Oct. 1918, NAM.

15 A. Montgomery, *The Fourth Army in the Battles of the Hundred Days: August 8th to November 11th 1918*, Hodder and Stoughton (1919), pp. 183–91.

16 Ibid., pp. 184–9 and Fourth Army's, 'Summary of Operations, 5 October–11 October 1918', PRO WO 158/244.

17 Montgomery, op. cit., p. 192.

18 'Fourth Army Summary of Operations, 5 October to 11 October 1918', section 5, PRO WO 158/244.

19 C. Bean, *Official History of Australia in the War of 1914–18, Vol. VI*, Angus and Robertson (1942), pp. 1045–52.

20 Haig's diary, 1 Oct. 1918, PRO WO 256/37.

21 Ibid., 4 Oct. 1918.

22 Ibid., 1–6 Oct. 1918.

23 GHQ to Horne, Byng, Rawlinson and Kavanagh, 5 Oct. 1918, OAD 932, PRO WO 158/242.

24 Rawlinson's diary, 6 Oct. 1918, NAM.

25 J. Edmonds and R. Maxwell Hyslop, *Military Operations France and Belgium, Vol. V*, HMSO (1947), pp. 199–200.

26 Third Army's 'War Diary', 8 Oct. 1918, PRO WO 95/374. Edmonds and Maxwell-Hyslop, op. cit., pp. 200–3.

27 Third Army's 'War Diary'. Edmonds and Maxwell-Hyslop, op. cit., pp. 206–7. D. Jerrold, *The Royal Naval Division*, Hutchinson (n.d.), pp. 323–5.

28 Edmonds and Maxwell-Hyslop, op. cit., pp. 203–8.

29 All quotations from Fourth Army's 'Summary of Operations from 5th October to 11th October 1918', PRO WO 158/244. Statistics of ammunition expenditure are from Montgomery, op. cit., p. 330.

30 Fourth Army's 'Summary of Operations'. Edmonds and Maxwell-Hyslop, op. cit., pp. 210–12.

31 First Army operational narrative, 'From Cambrai and Douai to Valenciennes, Events October 9th', PRO WO 95/180. Nicholson, op. cit., pp. 457–8.

32 J. Williams, *Byng of Vimy: General and Governor General*, Leo Cooper (1983), p. 251.

33 J. Bickersteth, *History of the 6th Cavalry Brigade 1914–1919*, Baynard Press (n.d.), pp. 109–16. Anglesey, *A History of the British Cavalry, Vol. 8: The Western Front 1915–1918*, Leo Cooper (1997), p. 262–8.

34 Fourth Army's 'Summary of Operations from 5th October to 11th October 1918', PRO WO 158/244.

35 Nicholson, op. cit., p. 459.

36 'From Cambrai and Douai to Valenciennes', PRO WO 95/180.

37 Fourth Army's 'Summary of Operations from 5th October to 11th October 1918', PRO WO 158/244.

38 N. Franks, R. Guest and F. Bailey, *Bloody April and Black September*, Grub Street (1995), pp. 3 and 126–242. S. Wise, *Canadian Airmen and the First World War*, University of Toronto Press (1980), pp. 517 and 559–66.

39 'Report on Operations on the Second Army Front for the Week Ending Friday 18th

October 1918', PRO WO 158/128. Smythe, op. cit., pp. 212–16.

40   C. Falls, *The History of the 36th (Ulster) Division*, Mc Caw, Stephenson and Orr (1922), p. 273.

41   'Second Army Operations 14th October to 31st October 1918', PRO WO 158/218.

42   Falls, op. cit., p. 275.

43   'Report on Operations on the Second Army Front for the Week Ending Friday 18th October 1918', PRO WO 158/128.

44   Falls, op. cit., p. 277.

45   Edmonds and Maxwell-Hyslop, op. cit., pp. 293–4.

46   H. Davson, *History of the 35th Division in the Great War*, Sifton Praed (1936), p. 275.

47   Falls, op. cit., pp. 280–84.

48   'Second Army Operations 14th October to 31st October, 1918', PRO WO 158/218.

49   Ibid., section 31.

50   Haig's diary, 10 Oct. 1918, PRO 256/37.

51   Haig's diary, 11–15 Oct. 1918, PRO 256/37.

52   'Offensive Operations Undertaken by IX Corps from 18th September to 11th November 1918', pp. 26–27, Vol. 63, Fourth Army Papers, IWM. Rawlinson's diary, 10 and 11 Oct. 1918, NAM.

53   Montgomery, op. cit., pp. 203 and 207 and Rawlinson's diary, 13 Oct. 1918, NAM.

54   Montgomery, op. cit., 207.

55   'Offensive Operations Undertaken by IX Corps', pp. 26–7. Montgomery, op. cit., pp. 204–5.

56   Montgomery, op. cit., pp. 206–7.

57   Ibid., p. 225.

58   Ibid., p. 208.

59   Tank Corps record of actions 8 August–20 October, Vol. 65, Fourth Army Papers, Imperial War Museum (IWM).

60   Montgomery, op. cit., pp. 218–25. Jones, op. cit., 541. J. Buchan, *The South African Forces in France*, Nelson (n.d.), pp. 244–6.

61   'Operations of XIII Corps', pp. 19–21. Montgomery, op. cit., 216–25.

62   'Operations of XIII Corps', pp. 21–2. Buchan, op. cit., pp. 244–6. Montgomery, op. cit., pp. 219–26.

63   Montgomery, op. cit., pp. 216–17. 'Operations of XIII Corps', p. 21.

64   'Offensive Operations Undertaken by IX Corps from 18th September 1918 to 11th November 1918', pp. 27–9, Vol. 63, Fourth Army Papers, IWM. Montgomery, op. cit., pp. 209–16.

65   Rawlinson's diary 17 Oct. 1918.

66   Haig's diary 17–19 Oct. 1918, PRO 256/37.

67   'Summary of Operations on Fourth Army Front from 19th to 25th October, 1918', PRO WO 158/244. Montgomery, op. cit., p. 229.

68   Haig's diary, 17 Oct. 1918, PRO 256/37.

69   Ibid., 18–19 Oct. 1918.

70   Ibid., 21 Oct. 1918.

71   Ibid., 10 Oct. 1918.

72   Haig's diary, 8 Aug. 1918, PRO WO 256/34.

CHAPTER 10   FIGHTING TO A FINISH

1   R. Priestley, *Breaking the Hindenburg Line: The Story of the 46th (North Midland) Division*, T. Fisher Unwin (1919), pp. 158–9. C. Falls, *The History of the 36th (Ulster) Division*, Mc Caw Stevenson and Orr (1922), pp. 260–61.

2   There were Paris editions of some British newspapers including the *Daily Mail*. The *Mail* informed its readers of the German request for an Armistice on 7 October 1918. C.E.W. Bean *The Official History of Australia in the War, Vol. VI*, Angus and Robertson (1942), 1045. Priestley, op. cit., pp. 158–9.

3   L. Moyer, *Victory Must Be Ours: Germany in the Great War*, Leo Cooper (1995), pp. 273–92 and R. Asprey, *The German High Command at War: Hindenburg and Ludendorff and the First World War*, Warner (1994), p. 483.

4   Asprey, op. cit., p. 481.

5   Asprey, op. cit., p. 482. M. Balfour, *The Kaiser and His Times*, Cresset Press (1964), p. 399.

6   Balfour, op. cit., pp. 399–400. E. Ludendorff, *The Concise Ludendorff Memoirs*, Hutchinson (n.d.), p. 328. Asprey, op. cit., p. 484. M. Kitchen, *The Silent Dictatorship*, Croom Helm (1976), pp. 264–5.

7   C.R.M. Cruttwell, *A History of the Great War 1914–1918*, Clarendon Press (1934), pp. 562 and 604.

8   J. Wheeler-Bennett, *Hindenburg: The Wooden Titan*, Macmillan (1967), pp. 180–92. Kitchen, op. cit., pp. 266–7.

9   'Second Army Operations 14th October to 31st October 1918', PRO WO 158/218. Falls, op. cit., pp. 288–90.

10   'Second Army Operations 14th October to 31st October' and 'Report on Operations on the Second Army Front for the week ending 18.00 Friday 25th October', PRO WO 158/218.

11   'Report on Operations on the Second Army Front for the week ending 18.00 Friday 1st November, 1918' and 'Second Army Operations 14th October to 31st October, 1918', PRO WO 158/218 and H. Davson, *The History of the 35th Division in the Great War*, Sifton Praed (1926), pp. 284–8.

12   'Second Army Operations 1st to 11th November, 1918', PRO WO 158/218.

13   Ibid. and Haig's diary, 28 Oct. 1918, PRO WO 256/37.

14   J. Edmonds and R. Maxwell-Hyslop, *Military Operations France and Belgium, Vol. V*, HMSO (1947), pp. 343–9 and 416–23.

15   Ibid., pp. 404–24 and 538.

16   First Army, 'Narrative of Operations, Part V, From Cambrai and Douai to Valenciennes, Events October 23rd', PRO WO 95/180.

17   Rawlinson's diary, 19 Oct. 1918, National Army Museum. GHQ to the Armies, OAD 939, 17 Oct. 1918, PRO WO 158/242.

18   Third Army's 'Report on Operations for Week Ending 1800 hrs. October 24th 1918', PRO WO 95/374. Edmonds and Maxwell-Hyslop, op. cit., pp. 339 and 334–343.

19   'Report on Operations for week ending 1800 hrs. October 24th 1918', Third Army's 'War Diary', PRO WO 95/374, 'Narrative of Operations by Third Army', pp. 42–6, PRO WO 95/375 and A. Montgomery, *The Story of the Fourth Army in the Battles of*

the Hundred Days: August 8th to November 11th 1918, Hodder and Stoughton (1919), pp. 231–8.

20 Edmonds and Maxwell-Hyslop, op. cit., pp. 383–4.

21 'Report on Operations for week ending 1800 hrs. October 24th 1918', PRO WO 95/374.

22 First Army 'Narrative of Operations, Part V, From Cambrai and Douai to Valenciennes', pp. 53–5, PRO WO 95/180.

23 Ibid.

24 'Cambrai to Valenciennes', pp. 55–7, PRO WO 95/180. F.W. Bewsher, *The History of the 51st (Highland) Division*, Blackwood (1921), pp. 390–95.

25 G.W.L. Nicholson, *The Canadian Expeditionary Force 1914–1919*, Queen's Printer, Ottawa (1962), p. 471.

26 'Cambrai to Valenciennes', pp. 58–9, PRO WO 95/180.

27 Ibid., p. 59 and Besher, op. cit., pp. 399–400.

28 'Cambrai to Valenciennes', pp. 59–60 and Bewsher, op. cit., pp. 400–4. Nicholson, op. cit., p. 472. Edmonds and Maxwell-Hyslop, op. cit., pp. 316–17.

29 'Cambrai to Valenciennes', pp. 61–2. Nicholson, op. cit., pp. 472–3.

30 'Cambrai to Valenciennes', pp. 61–3 and S. Schreiber, *Shock Army of the British Empire: The Canadian Corps in the Last 100 Days of the Great War*, Praeger (1997), pp. 124–5. Schreiber suggests a somewhat greater care for the avoidance of civilian casualties in the making of the Canadian Corps fire-plan than does the First Army account compiled shortly after the event.

31 'Cambrai to Valenciennes', pp. 61–2, Nicholson, op. cit., p. 474.

32 Nicholson, op. cit., pp. 474–5.

33 'Cambrai to Valenciennes', pp. 61–2.

34 'Cambrai to Valenciennes', pp. 63–4.

35 Adv. GHQ to the Armies, OAD 948, 29 Oct. 1918 and Adv. GHQ to the Armies, OAD 948/1, PRO WO 158/311. Edmonds and Maxwell-Hyslop, op. cit., p. 463.

36 Montgomery, op. cit., p. 239.

37 D. Smythe, *Pershing: General of the Armies*, Indiana University Press (1986), pp. 223–37.

38 Edmonds and Maxwell-Hyslop, op. cit., pp. 463, 477–478.

39 'Operations of XIII Corps between 3rd October and 11th November 1918', pp. 30–31, Vol. 64 Fourth Army Papers, Imperial War Museum.

40 Ibid. and Edmonds and Maxwell-Hyslop, op. cit., pp. 463–4.

41 Edmonds and Maxwell-Hyslop, op. cit., p. 465.

42 Ibid., p. 477 and Montgomery, op. cit., p. 247.

43 Montgomery, op. cit., p. 246.

44 'Artillery Instructions', Fourth Army No. 20/49 (G), para. 5, 29 Oct. 1918, PRO WO 158/242.

45 Fourth Army No. 20/49 (G), paras. 3, 7 and 10, PRO WO 158/242.

46 Ibid., para. 2.

47 Ibid., para. 6.

48 A.H. Atteridge, *History of the 17th (Northern) Division*, Glasgow (1929), p. 456.

49 Jones, *The War in the Air, Vol. VI*, Oxford (1937), p. 550.

50   'Summary of Operations on the Fourth Army Front from 2nd To 8th November 1918', PRO WO 158/244.

51   Edmonds and Maxwell-Hyslop, op. cit., pp. 486–8. E. Wyrall, *The History of the 19th Division*, Edward Arnold (n.d.), pp. 222–7.

52   Edmonds and Maxwell-Hyslop, op. cit., pp. 484–6. C. Headlam, *The Guards Division in the Great War 1915–1918*, Vol. II, John Murray (1924), pp. 224–5. E. Wyrall, *The History of the 62nd West Riding Division*, Vol. II, John Lane (n.d.), pp. 128–35.

53   Edmonds and Maxwell-Hyslop, op. cit., pp. 480–83.

54   Ibid.

55   Ibid., pp. 479–81. 'Operations of XIII Corps between 3rd October and 11th November 1918', pp. 30–33.

56   Atteridge, op. cit., p. 457.

57   Ibid., pp. 458–61 and Edmonds and Maxwell-Hyslop, op. cit., pp. 473–6 and 479–80.

58   '25th Division Narrative of Operations 19th October to 8th November 1918', pp. 8–13, Vol. 64, Fourth Army Papers, Imperial War Museum. Montgomery, op. cit., pp. 252–3.

59   'Offensive Operations Undertaken by the IX Corps', pp. 33–4. Montgomery, op. cit., pp. 243–4.

60   Summary of Operations on Fourth Army Front from 2nd to 8th November 1918', PRO WO 158/244. Montgomery, op. cit., pp. 250–52.

61   Montgomery, op. cit., pp. 248–9.

62   Ibid., pp. 247–8.

63   Edmonds and Maxwell-Hyslop, op. cit., p. 468.

64   Montgomery, op. cit., p. 250.

65   'Summary of Operations on Fourth Army Operations on Fourth Army Front from 2nd to 8th November, 1918', Section 2 (ii), PRO WO 158/244. Edmonds and Maxwell-Hyslop, op. cit., pp. 477–88.

66   Fourth Army reported only 383 killed between 1 and 8 November 1918. 'Fourth Army Summary of Casualties reported between 18.00 Friday 1st November and 18.00 Friday 8th November, 1918', PRO WO 158/244.

67   'Summary of Operations on Fourth Army Front from 2nd to 8th November 1918', PRO WO 158/244. Third Army, 'War Diary', 6 Nov. 1918, PRO WO 95/375.

68   Third Army 'War Diary', PRO WO 95/375.

69   Montgomery, op. cit., pp. 259–60.

70   Edmonds and Maxwell-Hyslop, op. cit., pp. 518–51.

71   'Second Army Operations, 1st to 11th November', PRO WO 158/218.

72   Edmonds and Maxwell-Hyslop, op. cit., pp. 538–45 and 554–5.

73   Nicholson, op. cit., pp. 480–82.

74   Edmonds and Maxwell-Hyslop, op. cit., pp. 553–6.

75   Ibid., pp. 516–17 and 566–8. Cruttwell, op. cit., pp. 585–7. Kitchen, op. cit., p. 267.

76   GHQ to the Armies, OAD 953 and 953/1, 11 Nov. 1918, PRO WO 158/243.

77   Edmonds and Maxwell-Hyslop, op. cit., p. 558. Priestley, op. cit., pp. 170–71.

CONCLUSION

1 B. Pitt, *1918, The Last Act*, Cassell (1962) p. 253.

2 CRMF Cruttwell, *A History Of The Great War*, Paladin (1982), p. 597.

3 D. Smythe, *Pershing, General Of The Armies*, Indiana University Press (1986), pp. 220–221.

4 H. Essame, *The Battle For Europe, 1918*, Batsford (1972), pp. 204–205.

5 M. Kitchen, *The Silent Dictatorship*, Croom Helm (1976), p. 247–267.

6 Rawlinson papers quoted in F. Maurice, *The Life of General Lord Rawlinson of Trent*, Cassell (1928), pp. 247–248. Haig diary 5 November, PRO WO 256/37.

7 Rawlinson's papers quoted in Maurice, *op. cit.*, pp. 247–248.

8 Edmonds and Maxwell-Hyslop, *Military Operations France and Belgium, 1918, Vol. V*, HMSO (1947), p. 559.

9 *ibid*, p. 557.

10 L.P. Ayres, *The War With Germany: A Statistical Summary*, Government Printing Office, Washington (1919), pp. 140–141.

11 A. Montgomery, *The Story Of The Fourth Army In The Battles Of The Hundred Days: August 8 to November 11 1918*, Hodder and Stoughton (1919), p. 276, and S.B. Schreiber, *Shock Army Of The British Empire, The Canadian Corps In The Last 100 Days Of The Great War*, Praeger (1997), p. 132.

12 *Statistics Of The Military Effort Of The British Empire During The Great War 1914–1918*, HMSO (1922), pp. 269–271.

13 Pedersen, *op. cit.*, pp. 290–292.

14 On disciplinary problems in Australian formations in 1917 see A. Ekins, 'The Australians at Passchendaele', pp. 232 & 245, in P.H. Liddle, (ed.) *Passchendaele in Perspective: The Third Battle of Ypres*, Pen and Sword (1997). J.G. Fuller, *Troop Morale and Popular Culture In The British And Dominion Armies 1914–1918*, Clarendon Press (1990), pp. 24–25 & 50–52.

15 *Statistics Of The Military Effort*, pp. 269–271.

16 Edmonds and Maxwell-Hyslop, *op. cit.*, pp. 575–576.

17 This is argued by Professor Tim Travers in *How The War Was Won, Command and Technology in the British Army on the Western Front 1917–18*, Routledge (1992), *passim*.

18 Major-General Hugh Elles to GHQ, 29 October 1918, TCOIV/28, Fuller Papers, Liddell Hart Centre For Military Archives, King's College London.

19 R. Prior, and T. Wilson, *Command On The Western Front: The Military Career Of Sir Henry Rawlinson*, Blackwell (1992), pp. 289–308 & 308–391.

20 *ibid*, pp. 382–386.

21 Haig's diary 31 October 1918, PRO WO 236/37.

22 Edmonds and Maxwell-Hyslop, *op. cit.*, p. 465, f.n. 2.

23 Smythe, *op. cit.*, p. 220.

24 Haig's diary, 4–11 November, PRO WO 236/37.

BIBLIOGRAPHY

ARCHIVAL SOURCES

The Public Record Office Kew
AIR 1   Documents relating to the early history of British air power
WO 95   War diaries and narratives of operation
WO 157   Summaries of information, intelligence files
WO 158   Western Front operations
WO 256   Haig's diary

The Imperial War Museum
Fourth Army papers
Field Marshal Sir Henry Wilson papers
General Sir Henry Horne papers

The National Army Museum
General Sir Henry Rawlinson papers

The Liddell Hart Centre For Military Archives, King's College London
Major-General J.F.C. Fuller papers
Lieutenant-General Sir Launcelot Kiggell papers
Field Marshal Sir Archibald Montgomery-Massingberd papers

The Royal Artillery Institution, Woolwich
Brigadier E.C. Anstey papers
Brigadier-General C.E.D. Budworth papers

The Tank Museum, Bovington, Dorset
Major-General J.F.C. Fuller papers

PUBLISHED PRIMARY SOURCES

J. Ferris (ed.), *The British Army And Signals Intelligence During The First World War* (Alan Sutton / Army Records Society) 1992.
K. Jeffery, *The Military Correspondence Of Field Marshal Sir Henry Wilson 1918–22* (The Bodley Head/Army Records Society) 1985.

British Official Histories

A.F. Becke, *Order Of Battle, Part 4: The Army Council, GHQs, Armies and Corps 1914–18* (HMSO) 1945.

Sir J.E. Edmonds, *Military Operations France and Belgium 1918, Vol. IV* (HMSO) 1947.

Sir J.E. Edmonds and R. Maxwell-Hyslop, *Military Operations France and Belgium 1918, Vol. V* (HMSO) 1947.

A.M. Henniker, *Transportation On The Western Front* (HMSO) 1937.

H.A. Jones, *The War In The Air, Vol. VI* (Clarendon Press) 1937.

The War In The Air: Appendices (Clarendon Press) 1937.

Statistics Of The Military Effort Of The British Empire During The Great War: 1914–20 (HMSO) 1922.

Australian Official History

C.E.W. Bean, *The AIF In France May 1918 – The Armistice* (Angus and Robertson) 1942.

Canadian Official Histories

G.W.L. Nicholson, *Canadian Expeditionary Force 1914–19* (Queen's Printer, Ottawa) 1962.

S.F. Wise, *Canadian Airmen And The First World War* (University of Toronto Press) 1980.

Divisional Histories

H. Atteridge, *History Of The 17th (Northern) Division* (Glasgow University Press) 1929.

F.W. Bewsher, *The History of the 51st (Highland) Division 1914–18* (Blackwood) 1921.

J.O. Coop, *The Story of the 55th (West Lancashire) Division* (Liverpool Daily Post) 1919.

H.M. Davson, *History of the 35th Division In The Great War* (Sifton Praed) 1926.

A.D. Ellis, *The Story of the Fifth Australian Division* (Hodder and Stoughton) n.d.

J.Ewing, *The History of the 9th (Scottish) Division 1914–19* (John Murray) 1921.

C. Falls, *The History of the 36th (Ulster) Division* (McCaw, Stevenson and Orr) 1922.

F.P. Gibbon, *The 42nd (East Lancashire) Division 1914–18* (Country Life) 1920.

D. Gillon, *The Story of the 29th Division* (Thomas Nelson) 1925.

C. Headlam, *History of the Guards Division in the Great War, 1915–18, Vol. II* (John Murray) 1924.

V.E. Inglefield, *The History of the Twentieth (Light) Division* (Nisbet) 1921.

D. Jerrold, *The Royal Naval Division* (Hutchinson) n.d.

T.O. Marden, *A Short History of the Sixth Division: August 1914–March 1919* (Hugh Rees) 1920.

G.H.F. Nichols, *The 18th Division In The Great War* (Blackwood) 1922.

R.E. Priestley, *Breaking The Hindenburg Line: The Story of the 46th (North Midland) Division* (T. Fisher Unwin) 1919.

Sir A.B. Scott and P. Middleton Brumwell, *History of the 12th (Eastern) Division in The Great War, 1914–1918* (Nisbet and Co.) 1923.

J. Shakespear, *The 34th Division 1915–1919* (H.F. and B Witherby) 1921.

H. Stewart, *The New Zealand Division 1916–1919* (Whitcombe and Tombs Limited) 1921.

J. Stewart and J. Buchan, *The Fifteenth (Scottish) Division* (Blackwood) 1926.

D. Ward, *The 56th Division* (John Murray) 1921.

F.E. Whitton, *History of the 40th Division* (Gale and Polden) 1926.

E. Wyrall, *The History of the 62nd (West Riding) Division 1914–1919, Vol. II* (John Lane) n.d.

The History of the Second Division 1914–1918, Vol. II (Thomas Nelson) n.d.

The History of the 19th Division (Edward Arnold) n.d.

Army, Corps, Brigade, Regimental and Unit Histories

Addison *et al. History of the Corps of Royal Engineers, Vol. V* (Institution Of Royal Engineers) 1952.

Anon, *The War History of the Sixth Tank Battalion* (Privately Printed) 1919.

History of the 50th Infantry Brigade 1914–1919 (Privately Printed) 1919.

J.B. Bickersteth, *History of the 6th Cavalry Brigade 1914–1919* (Baynard Press) n.d.

J. Buchan, *The South African Forces in France* (Thomas Nelson) n.d.

C. Williams-Ellis and A. Williams-Ellis, *The Tank Corps* (Country Life) 1919.

Sir M. Farndale, *History of the Royal Regiment of Artillery: Western Front 1914–18* (Royal Artillery Institution) 1986.

D. Jerrold, *The Hawke Battalion* (Ernest Benn) 1925.

B.H. Liddell Hart, *The Tanks: The History of the Royal Tank Regiment and its Predecessors, Vol. I,* (Cassell) 1959.

Sir A.A. Montgomery, *The Story of the Fourth Army in the Battles of The Hundred Days August 8th to November 11th 1918* (Hodder and Stoughton) 1919.

G.D. Sheffield, *The Red Caps: A History of the Royal Military Police and its Antecedents from the Middle Ages to the Gulf War* (Brassey's) 1994.

Memoirs And Biographies Of Major Protagonists

M. Balfour, *The Kaiser And His Times* (The Cresset Press) 1964.

F. Foch, *The Memoirs of Marshal Foch* (Heinemann) 1931.

J.F.C. Fuller, *Memoirs of an Unconventional Soldier* (Ivor Nicholson and Watson) 1936.

Sir. C. Harington, *Plumer of Messines* (John Murray) 1935.

A.M.J. Hyatt, *General Sir Arthur Currie: A Military Biography* (University Of Toronto) 1987.

B.H. Liddell Hart, *Foch, The Man of Orleans* (Eyre and Spottiswoode) 1931.

E. Ludendorff, *The Concise Ludendorff Memoirs* (Hutchinson) n.d.

F. Maurice, *The Life of General Lord Rawlinson of Trent* (Cassell) 1928.

Sir J. Monash, *The Australian Victories in France in 1918* (Angus and Robertson) 1936.

R. Parkinson, *Tormented Warrior: Ludendorff and the Supreme Command* (Hodder and Stoughton) 1978.

G. Powell, *Plumer, The Soldier's General: A Biography of Field-Marshal Viscount Plumer of Messines* (Leo Cooper) 1990.

P.A. Pedersen, *Monash As Military Commander* (Melbourne) 1985.

J.J. Pershing, *My Experiences in The Great War* (Camelot Press) 1931.

D. Smythe, *Pershing, General of the Armies* (Indiana University Press) 1986.

J. Terraine, *Douglas Haig, The Educated Soldier* (Hutchinson) 1963.

J. Williams, *Byng of Vimy, Governor and Governor General* (Leo Cooper) 1992.

Other Books

E.M. Andrews, *The Anzac Illusion* (Cambridge University Press) 1993, p. 44.

Anglesey (Marquis of), *A History of the British Cavalry 1816–1919, Volume 8* (Leo Cooper) 1997.

R.D. Asprey, *The German High Command at War: Hindenburg and Ludendorff and The First World War* (Warner) 1994.

L.P. Ayres, *The War with Germany: A Statistical Summary* (Government Printing Office, Washington) 1919.

R. Barker, *The Royal Flying Corps in France: From Mons to the Somme* (Constable) 1994.

I.F.W. Beckett and K. Simpson, *A Nation in Arms: A Social Study of the British Army in the First World War* (Manchester University Press) 1985.

S. Bidwell and D. Graham, *Fire-Power: British Army Weapons and Theories of War 1904–1945* (George Allen and Unwin) 1982.

J.M. Bourne, *Britain and The Great War 1914–1918* (Edward Arnold) 1989.

Sir L. Bragg *et al.*, *Artillery Survey in The Great War* (Field Survey Association) 1971.

H. Cecil and P.H. Liddle, *Facing Armageddon: The First World War Experienced* (Leo Cooper) 1996.

D. Chandler and I. Beckett (eds.), *The Oxford Illustrated History of the British Army* (Oxford University Press) 1994.

W.D. Croft, *Three Years with the 9th (Scottish) Division* (John Murray) 1919.

C.R.M.F. Cruttwell, *A History Of The Great War 1914–1918* (Clarendon Press) 1934.

G.A.B. Dewar, *Sir Douglas Haig's Command 1915–1918* (Constable) 1922.

H. Essame, *The Battle for Europe 1918* (BT Batsford) 1972.

C. Falls, *The First World War* (Longmans) 1960.

N. Franks *et al.*, *Bloody April...Black September* (Grub Street) 1995.

J.G. Fuller, *Troop Morale and Popular Culture in the British and Dominion Armies 1914–1918* (Clarendon Press) 1990.

W. Goerlitz, *The German General Staff* (Hollis and Carter) 1953.

J. Gooch, *The Plans of War: The General Staff and British Military Strategy c. 1900–1916* (RKP) 1974.

'GSO', *G.H.Q. (Montreuil-Sur-Mer)* (Philip Allan) 1920.

P. Griffith, *Forward Into Battle: Fighting Tactics from Waterloo to Vietnam* (Antony Bird) 1981.
Battle Tactics of the Western Front: The British Army's Art of Attack 1916–18 (Yale) 1994.
(Ed.) *British Fighting Methods in the Great War* (Frank Cass) 1996.

B.I. Gudmundsson, *Stormtroop Tactics: Innovation in the German Army, 1914–1918* (Praeger) 1989.

L.F. Haber, *The Poisonous Cloud: Chemical Warfare in the First World War* (Clarendon Press) 1986.

J.H. Hallas, *Squandered Victory: The American First Army at St. Mihiel* (Praeger) 1995.

P.G. Halpern, *A Naval History of World War 1* (UCL Press) 1994.

J.P. Harris, *Men, Ideas and Tanks: British Military Thought and Armoured Forces, 1903–1939* (Manchester University Press) 1995.

G. Hartcup, *The War of Invention: Scientific Developments, 1914–18* (Brassey's) 1988.

I.V. Hogg and L.F. Thurston, *British Artillery Weapons and Ammunition 1914–1918* (Ian Allan) 1972.

E. Juenger, *The Storm of Steel* (Chatto and Windus) 1929.

M. Kitchen, *The Silent Dictatorship: The politics of the German High Command under Hindenburg and Ludendorff, 1916–1918* (Croom Helm) 1976.

P.H. Liddle, *Passchendaele in Perspective: The Third Battle of Ypres* (Leo Cooper) 1997.

R.H Lutz (Ed.) *The Causes of the German Collapse in 1918* (Stanford University Press) 1934.

Sir F. Maurice, *The Last Four Months: How the War Was Won* (Little, Brown and Company) 1919.

J.H. Morrow, *The Great War in the Air: Military Aviation from 1909 to 1921* (Smithsonian Institution Press) 1993.

L.V. Moyer, *Victory Must Be Ours: Germany in the Great War 1914–1918* (Leo Cooper) 1995.

G.P. Neumann, *The German Air Force in the Great War* (Hodder and Stoughton) n.d.

M. Occleshaw, *Armour against fate: British Military Intelligence in the First World War* (Columbus) 1989.

R. Pipes, *A Concise History of the Russian Revolution* (Harvill) 1995.

B. Pitt, *1918, The Last Act* (Cassell) 1962.

R. Prior and T. Wilson, *Command on the Western Front: the military career of Sir Henry Rawlinson 1914–18* (Blackwell) 1992.

Passchendaele: The Untold Story (Yale) 1996.

B. Rawling, *Surviving Trench Warfare: Technology and the Canadian Corps, 1914–1918* (University Of Toronto Press) 1992.

M. Samuels, *Doctrine and Dogma: German and British Infantry Tactics in the First World War* (Greenwood Press) 1992.

S.B. Schreiber, *Shock Army of the Empire: The Canadian Corps in the last 100 Days of the Great War* (Praeger) 1997.

A. Simpson, *The Evolution of Victory: British Battles on the Western Front 1914–1918* (Tom Donovan) 1995.

J.C. Slessor, *Air Power and Armies* (Oxford University Press) 1936.

N. Stone, *The Eastern Front 1914–1917* (Hodder and Stoughton) 1975.

H. Strachan, *European Armies and the Conduct of War* (Allen and Unwin) 1983

J. Terraine, *To win a war: 1918 the year of Victory* (Sidgwick and Jackson) 1978.

The Smoke and the Fire: Myths and Anti-Myths of War 1861–1945 (Sidgwick and Jackson) 1980.

White Heat: The New Warfare 1914–1918 (Sidgwick and Jackson) 1982.

T. Travers, *The Killing Ground: The British Army, The Western Front and the Emergence of Modern Warfare* (Unwin Hyman) 1987.

How the War was Won: Command and Technology in the British Army on The Western front 1917–1918 (Routledge) 1992.

S. Williamson, *Austria-Hungary and the origins of the First World War* (St. Martin's Press) 1991.

Wilson (Ed.) *Decision for War, 1914* (UCL Press) 1995.

Articles In Periodicals

A.F. Becke, 'The Coming Of The Creeping Barrage', *Journal of The Royal Artillery*, Vol. 58, 1931.

C.N.F. Broad, 'The Development Of Artillery Tactics 1914–18' (two parts) *The Canadian Defence Quarterly*, Vol. I, 1924.

I.M. Brown, 'Not Glamorous but Effective: The Canadian Corps And The Set-Piece Attack 1917–1918', *Journal of Military History*, Vol. 58, July 1994.

W. Deist, 'The Military Collapse Of The German Empire: The Reality Behind The Stab-in the-Back Myth', in *War in History*, Vol. 3 (2) 1996.

B. Greenhous, ' "...It Was Chiefly A Canadian Battle": The Decision At Amiens 8–11 August 1918', *Canadian Defence Quarterly*, Vol. 18, No. 2 (Autumn 1988).

R.J. Lewendon, 'The Cutting of Barbed Wire Entanglements by Artillery Fire in World War 1' *Journal of The Royal Artillery*, Vol. 112, No. 2, September 1985.

INDEX